WILD HEART
A Life

WILD HEART
A Life

Natalie Clifford Barney's Journey

from Victorian America

to Belle Époque Paris

SUZANNE RODRIGUEZ

An Imprint of HarperCollins*Publishers*

To my mother's love and laughter

"I want to be at once the bow, the arrow, and the target."

—*Natalie Clifford Barney*

Contents

ANCESTORS OF

Natalie Clifford Barney

Jeannette Poiret
Born: Unknown

Ennemond Meuillion
Born: 1737
Died: 1820

Ursula Meuillion
Born: 1784
Died: 1840

"Honest" Judge William Miller
Born: c. 1762
Died: 1845

Ellen Miller
Born: c. 1826
Died: 1908

Samuel Pike
Born: 1822
Died: 1872

Alice Pike
Born: 1857
Died: 1931

NATALIE CLIFFORD BARNEY
Born: 1876
Died: 1972

Laura Dreyfus Barney
Born: 1879
Died: 1974

Major J. Dudley Smith
Born: Unknown

Unknown

Nancy Potter
Born: 1784
Died: 1845

Julia Smith
Born: 1810
Died: 1887

Benjamin Barney
Born: 1780
Died: 1859

Eliam E. Barney
Born: 1807
Died: 1880

Albert Clifford Barney
Born: 1850
Died: 1902

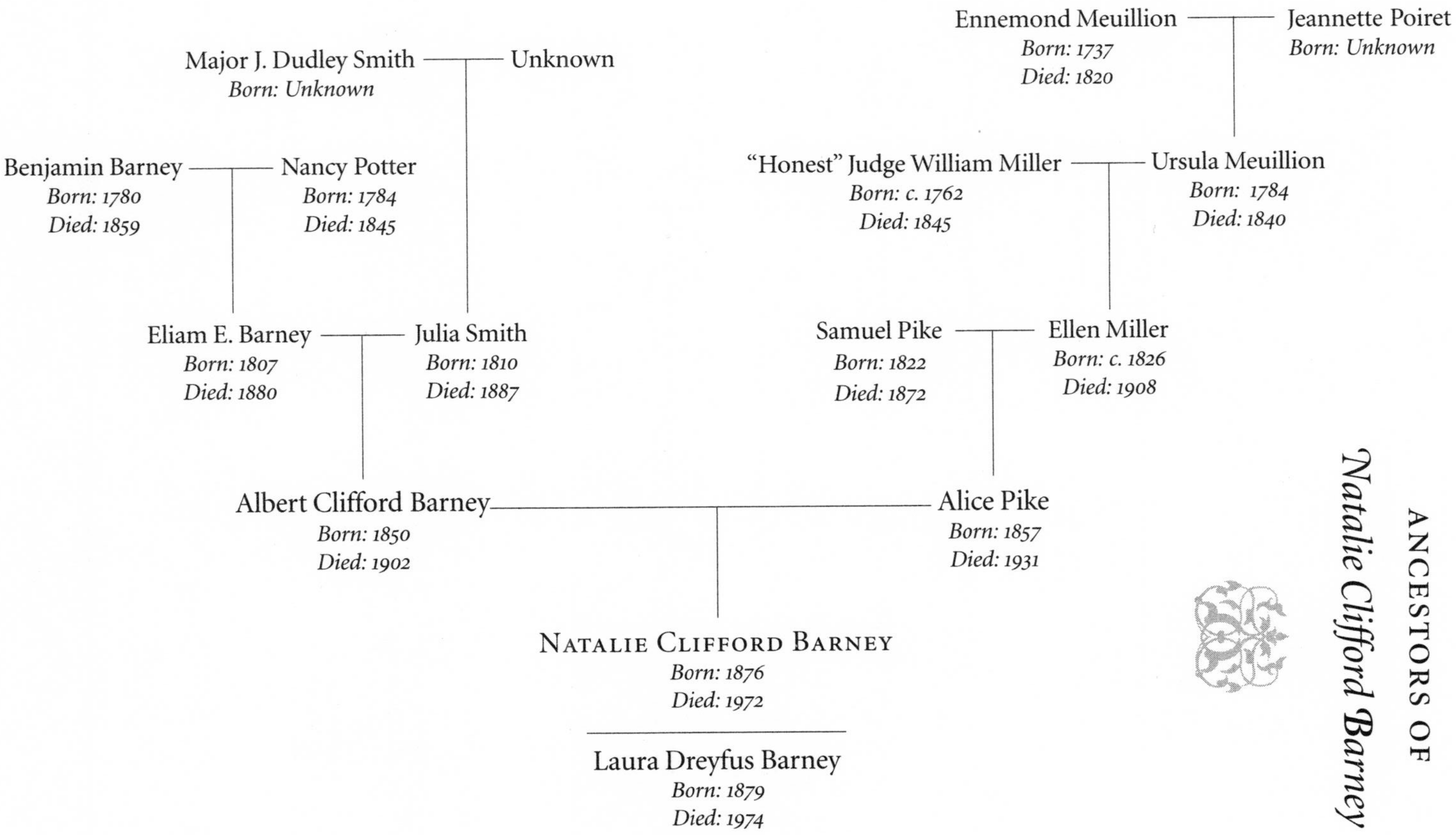

Preface

CHARISMATIC, BRILLIANT, AND WEALTHY, the American writer
Natalie Clifford Barney, who lived in Paris for most of her long life, is best
known for three things: her Left Bank literary salon; her books of *pensées,*
which are witty encapsulations of truth; and a liberated sexual life that she
refused to cloak, even in the midst of the Victorian era.

Natalie was born in 1876 to a wealthy Ohio couple. Her father was highly
conventional, but her mother, an accomplished painter, bordered on the
bohemian. When she was ten, her family moved to Washington, D.C. They
summered in Bar Harbor and traveled in Europe. From her late teens onward,
Natalie considered Paris her home.

As a young woman Natalie possessed long and billowing masses of blond
hair, a slender figure that she refused to corset, a grand intelligence, and
amused but icy blue eyes. She could ride a horse like nobody's business, spoke
a graceful and old-fashioned style of French, and was incapable of making a
commonplace statement. Needless to say, she was popular and heavily courted
by eligible young men. However, attracted to women since childhood, she had
no intention of ever getting married.

In 1899, in Paris, Natalie had a passionate affair with Liane de Pougy, perhaps the most famous of all Belle Époque courtesans. The next year Liane
transformed their love story into a best-selling novel that barely concealed
their identities, thereby launching Natalie's lifelong notoriety as a scandalous
high-society renegade.

Natalie's emancipated personal life was only one facet of a complex and brilliant character. In 1909 she moved to rue Jacob, an ancient street in the Latin Quarter, and instituted a weekly literary salon—often acknowledged as the most important of the twentieth century—that was to last for the next sixty years. During this time she welcomed into her elegant *pavillon* many of the greatest literary minds of the nineteenth and twentieth centuries. The nature of Barney's salon changed over the years. In her very young days—before coming to rue Jacob—she once hired Mata Hari to ride naked through her gardens on a white horse harnessed with turquoise cloisonné. Those were the days, too, when she held outdoor performances of racy playlets written by herself or friends like Colette and Pierre Louÿs. In her late eighties the salon was quite subdued; however, it remained intellectually vibrant, attracting younger writers such as Marguerite Yourcenar and Truman Capote.

Barney herself was a prolific writer. She produced twelve published books, and left behind scores of unpublished manuscripts and notebooks, and thousands of letters. She experimented with many genres, but her two favorite topics were love and the nature of womanhood. Her innate and unique brand of feminism colored everything she wrote.

A true rebel at a time when rebels weren't admired—particularly women—Natalie never felt the need to apologize for who she was. Such an attitude then required great courage, even in a wide-open city like Paris, but nothing about her life ever smacked of martyrdom or sacrifice. Quite the opposite. Natalie's world was vibrant and exciting, brimming with love, laughter, intellectual adventure, joy, and, of course, sorrow. Natalie's fascinating life and powerful personality destined her to be the thinly disguised heroine of half a dozen novels and a major entrant in scores of memoirs and biographies from the Belle Époque to the present day. To say that she lived fully seems somehow inadequate, as she herself admitted: "Having got more out of life, oh having got out of it perhaps more than it contained!"

MUCH OF THIS BIOGRAPHY is drawn from Natalie's unpublished works and thousands of her letters (as well as an equal number of letters to her from a variety of friends and lovers). Reading this material required visits to four major (and a half dozen minor) archival sources. The great bulk of Barney's papers are contained in the Bibliothèque Littéraire Jacques Doucet in Paris, where I made three substantial sojourns. A substantive but little-known treasure of papers about Natalie is contained in the Renée B. Lang Collection housed in the Special Collections of Memorial Library, the University of Wisconsin at Madison. The Smithsonian Institution Archives are home to the

Alice Pike Barney papers; aside from Alice's voluminous written works (including many plays coauthored with Natalie), this collection offers a wealth of photographs, correspondence, newspaper clippings, and other data (so much that it took two separate visits to scrutinize everything). More than six hundred letters exchanged between Natalie and Romaine Brooks can be found in McFarlin Library's Special Collections at the University of Tulsa. Other helpful archival sources included the Smithsonian Institution's Archives of American Art, which contains memoirs and other papers of Romaine Brooks; and the Other Minds Foundation, which holds papers of George Antheil.

Archival material has been richly supplemented by the published memoirs and other writings of Natalie's friends. Many of these books are rare in the United States, as they date to the early years of the last century and were published only in French. I am consequently grateful to the University of California at Berkeley for its astonishing collections, which contained almost every book I ever needed, as well as actual or microfilmed copies of relevant French periodic literature dating back to the nineteenth century.

Natalie and most of the people she knew were long gone by the time I began researching this book five years ago. Those who remained—particularly Jean Chalon, François Chapon, and Renée Lang—have been extraordinarily generous with memories, insight, documents, photographs, and, not least, time. Although quite different from one another, they were alike in their strong desire to keep Natalie's memory alive. Each offered me a different facet of their complex friend. As well—and this was a bit of magic—each allowed me to come into physical contact with the woman I was trying to understand. Jean Chalon served me tea in a violet-limned cup that once belong to Renée Vivien, then to Natalie. Each time I visited Renée Lang, she placed on the table beside us the small eighteenth-century marquetry box given by Remy de Gourmont to Natalie (and by Natalie to Lang). The always ebullient François Chapon put into my hands the turquoise cloisonné horse bridle used by Mata Hari at Natalie's garden party one day in 1905.

Somehow, somewhere along the line—probably that day I found myself arguing with her about something she'd done—Natalie Barney became my friend, too. I think she always will be.

WILD HEART
A Life

ONE

Beauty in the Blood . . .

All beauty comes from beautiful blood and a beautiful brain.
—*Walt Whitman*

"I told you once before that there were two times for making big money, one in the upbuilding of a country and the other in its destruction. Slow money on the upbuilding, fast money in the crack-up."

—*Rhett Butler to Scarlett O'Hara*

*D*OUBLE-BEING. *Dyad. Janus.* Natalie Clifford Barney was the essence of duality. No matter what one believed about her, the opposite might well be true. A self-described *debauchée*, she could be proper, even prim. Relishing her ability to shock, she was nonetheless imbued with formal, old-school manners. Far ahead of her time in the politics of personal freedom and feminism, she also harbored extremely conservative philosophies. She could be amazingly cruel and incredibly kind. She didn't always enjoy reading, yet ran the most important literary salon of the twentieth century. Possessed of little formal education, she was considered brilliant by many of the greatest minds in Europe. She celebrated the giving of love to others, but found it difficult to accept love for herself. Although she spent most of her life shining at the white-hot center of a crowd, she was often lonely. With her blond, angelic looks and scarlet blushes, she was the picture of innocence, and yet her private life caused such shock and scandal that some, including lovers and close friends, considered her a mixture of good and evil—and for a few she embodied the latter word in its entirety.

To begin to understand Natalie Barney we must first look to her family, an only-in-America mélange of Salem Puritans and agnostic Jews, adventurous paupers and careful millionaires, rugged pioneers and effete layabouts. It was a family in which polarities attracted. Like married unlike. In the end, they produced a charismatic dyad, a woman who was at once fire and ice. Natalie's beautiful blood was at war with itself.

From childhood Natalie loved all things French, and so we'll begin by exploring her mother's side—the French side—of the family.

In the Blood of the Mother

According to long-held family lore, Natalie's great-great-grandfather, Ennemond Meuillion, was a French aristocrat who fled the Revolution. In fact, he arrived in the New World nearly two decades earlier, coming to Louisiana "about 1770, soon after Spain took over the government of that vast territory."[1]

Enough facts exist about Meuillion to piece together a rough outline of his life. He was born in 1737 in the French province of Dauphiné, and the coat of arms on his personal seal indicates that, as his descendants believed, he was of noble birth.[2] Aside from the fact that he trained as a doctor, nothing is known of his early life until he journeyed to America in the 1760s. Crippling taxation had made life difficult in France, even for aristocrats, and young Meuillion might have decided to try his luck in a vibrant new land. The Louisiana Territory, heavily populated by Frenchmen, was a logical destination.

The French presence in Louisiana dated back to 1682 when the Sieur de La Salle claimed possession of the Mississippi River valley, naming the territory for Louis XIV. Over the ensuing decades French soldiers and trappers came to the region, staying on as small-scale planters and traders. Spaniards, too, settled in, emigrating from their own colony in Florida. Control of Louisiana would be tossed back and forth between these two European powers and Great Britain until, in 1803, the territory was purchased by the fledgling American nation.

Meuillion took up residence in one of the earliest French settlements on the Mississippi, Pointe Coupée, and married a widowed Frenchwoman with four children. When she died a short time later, he raised the children as his own. A few years on he married another widow with four children, Jeannette Poiret, daughter of the Chevalier de Brie. They had six children of their own, bringing their combined brood to a total of fourteen.

The Meuillions settled on the Red River near present-day Alexandria. The area, called El Rapido by the Spanish and Rapides by the French, was named for the nearby limestone rapids. A Spanish fort, the Post of El Rapido, fronted the river. Meuillion built a home nearby, cleared trees for a plantation, and prospered growing cotton.

When war broke out between Spain and Great Britain in 1779, Meuillion signed on as a sublieutenant in the service of Spanish general Bernardo de Gálvez, who aided the American cause. This wartime service qualified the doctor's descendants for membership in the Daughters and Sons of the American Revolution.

After the war Meuillion continued to grow cotton and doctor the community while serving under the Spaniards as commandant of Fort Rapides. He died in his plantation home in 1820 at eighty-three. In 1930 the Daughters of the American Revolution placed a marker on his grave to commemorate his role in the war, leading the *Louisiana Historical Review* to refer to him, half-jokingly, as "one of the most famous residents of the Rapides Cemetery."[3]

THE SECOND CHILD of Ennemond Meuillion and Jeannette Poiret, Ursula—Natalie's great-grandmother—was born in 1784. "Ursula Meuillion," her granddaughter Alice Pike Barney wrote more than a century later, "was exquisitely petite, delicate, and adorable. She refused to learn English, which meant that all those about her were forced to learn French."[4]

A favorite family legend told of the time that Ursula received a message from her husband: *"Lafayette vient! Préparez immediatement!"* Having no idea who Lafayette was but nonetheless terrified at the thought of his arrival, she urged the household into panic mode. Everyone scurried about, burying the silver, hiding the horses in the bayou, sending the chickens cackling. When everything was locked up, Ursula, the children, and the rest of the household fled deep into the woods. By the time her husband rode home with his illustrious guest, General Lafayette—American Revolutionary hero and friend of George Washington—they found not the hospitable welcome they expected, but a deserted house.

Ursula's husband and Natalie's great-grandfather, William Miller, was born in 1762 in Pennsylvania. At twenty he undertook a trading expedition to the West Indies, where he remained for a number of years before arriving in Louisiana in 1793. By the late 1790s he'd entered into a partnership with Alexander Fulton, whose brother Robert is credited with inventing the steamboat. Awarded exclusive rights by the Spanish government to trade with the Apalachee Indians, they set up a trading company, Miller & Fulton, across the river from Fort Rapides. Socializing or doing business at the Fort, Miller couldn't help but notice the commandant's pretty teenage daughter, Ursula. They married in 1802 and their first child, Louise, was born a year later. They would have eleven more children before producing Natalie's grandmother, Ellen, in 1826.

Miller and Fulton were wily traders, extending liberal credit to the Apalachees and encouraging them to run up huge bills. Unable to pay off their debts with furs and shell knives, the Indians were obliged to sign over large tracts of fertile bayou land. In one notable exchange the partners acquired 39,000 acres in "the most prosperous farming area of central Louisiana."[5] Selling the land at a hefty profit to new settlers, they grew rich. Fulton founded the city of Alexandria, Louisiana, while "Miller was recognized as one of the most prominent of the American citizens residing at the Post of Rapides."[6]

In 1800, anxious to staunch the financial hemorrhage caused by its American colony, Spain returned the Louisiana Territory to France, which soon sold it to the United States for $15 million. By now the territory had been passed around so often that its citizenry had a relaxed attitude about questions of nationality. During the French-Spanish exchange, William Miller, an American, served as the French representative from Rapides, while his French father-in-law, Ennemond Meuillion, represented the Spaniards. When France officially passed the territory to the United States, Miller again represented Rapides, this time as an American, while Meuillion stood in for the French. Most of their duties on each occasion had to do with handing off or receiving control of Fort Rapides on behalf of the represented nations.[7] Over time these duties became exaggerated within the family. Natalie would one day state (and believe) that Miller, "along with his French father-in-law, negotiated the treaty in which France ceded Louisiana to the United States."[8]

Miller earned praise for honesty and discretion in various governmental and community roles. Having proved himself "a citizen of talent and integrity,"[9] in 1805 he was appointed by Governor William Claiborne to be county judge, a position "whose jurisdiction seems to have been limited to the trial of small cases of a civil nature and misdemeanors."[10] In his two brief years as judge he earned such a reputation for fairness that the sobriquet "honest" was attached to his name. From then on he was known as "Honest Judge Miller."

In 1815, the Millers left Louisiana and headed north. Why they did so isn't known, but the reason must have been a compelling one to cause them to undertake the logistics of such a move in the days before train tracks, or even a network of decent dirt roads, crossed the land. The accompanying entourage was huge: fifteen children, the Millers' own and various nieces and nephews;

the same number of servants; and assorted friends and relatives. The journey began with the party working up the Mississippi in keelboats. They camped out at night, catching fish and shooting game for food. Each morning the judge held a roll call; even so, they twice left a child behind and had to travel back. Eventually the family settled in Cincinnati, Ohio, where the enterprising Miller prospered handsomely in real estate.

Ursula Meuillion Miller died in 1840 of yellow fever. Honest Judge Miller was struck down by cholera in May 1845. He lived just long enough to see his youngest daughter, Ellen, marry a poor but promising fellow named Sam Pike.

NATALIE'S GRANDFATHER, Samuel Napthali Pike, could easily have served as a real-life model for one of Horatio Alger's rags-to-riches tales. These stories, so popular in the latter half of the nineteenth century, always featured a poor youth who, by dint of hard work, honesty, and a little luck, wins fame and fortune. "Being born rich doesn't matter," Alger, a former minister, seemed to say. "Ability and merit do." That was certainly true of Pike. Born poor, he became exceedingly rich, thanks to a combination of personal ability, merit, and a friendly fate—or, as the title of an 1869 Alger novel put it, *Pluck and Luck.*

Born near Heidelberg in 1822, Pike was the first child of a German-Jewish father and a Dutch-Christian mother who married against the wishes of their parents. The couple came to America when Samuel was five years old, changing their surname, Hecht, to its English equivalent, Pike. Sam Pike often told his children that the only items of value his parents brought from Europe were two Dutch Renaissance paintings and a few pieces of family silver. A more precious birthright, he believed, was the deep love of art, music, and literature they nurtured in him. His daughter Alice, Natalie's mother, would be the only one of his four children to share that love.

The earliest details of Pike's life are fuzzy. He probably grew up in New York. At seventeen he left home to seek his fortune, and for the next five years tried his hand at whatever business seemed likely while seeking a good location to settle down. In Florida, he speculated in cotton and ran a dry-goods store, reputedly amassing more than $10,000, and then found further success as a wine merchant in Virginia. These early achievements were wiped out when he went flat bust in St. Louis. At this point, clutching a mixed scorecard of hits and misses, he decided to return to New York and lick his wounds.

In July 1844 he traveled via steamboat to Cincinnati, where he planned to connect with the New York stagecoach. Having inadvertently arrived on Independence Day, he was forced to delay his journey. Then, even more than now, the Fourth of July was a monumental American celebration. Everyone, including horse-handlers and coachmen, had the day off.

Making the best of his enforced stay, Pike walked high into the hills. From his aerie he could see that the town was securely nestled in a sunny basin bordered by thick forests and the busy Ohio River. He noted the cheerful red-and-white houses, colorful tile pathways, broad and well-planned streets, and lush gardens. "Cincinnati is a beautiful city; cheerful, thriving, and animated," Charles Dickens had observed two years earlier. "I have not often seen a place that commends itself so favourably and pleasantly to a stranger at the first glance."[11] Indeed, to Sam Pike, Cincinnati seemed like paradise.

Returning to the flatlands, he strolled about the busy waterfront, with its glistening warehouses and bustling factories. The "Queen City" had clearly prospered since its founding in 1788, helped significantly by the 1811 introduction of steam navigation on the river. With the railroad's recent arrival, the area seemed poised for major growth. Pike decided on the spot that his future lay here.

Any lingering doubts were erased shortly afterward, while Pike strolled on the main thoroughfare, home to Cincinnati's leading citizens and finest homes. Spying a lovely young woman sitting on a balcony, he stepped back for a better glimpse and promptly fell into an open coal pit. He lay there, stunned, gazing at the sky, until a few moments later the same young woman peered breathlessly over the pit's edge. Unmindful of coal soot, she reached a hand downward and helped him climb out. "I knew right then that Ellen was the girl I would marry," he often told his children, "and so I resolved to stay."[12] Within a year they had married.

That old saw about opposites attracting certainly holds true for Sam Pike and Ellen Miller. It's hard to imagine two people more dissimilar. Born to wealth, she gave little thought to money; born poor, his fierce ambition was to amass a fortune. She had always been pampered; he had known only hard work. She had little interest in socializing and wasn't much for conversation; he was notoriously quick-witted, charming, and convivial. She read voraciously but cultivated no talents; he was a musician, a published poet, a painter. She was a Catholic; he had no faith.

However, the two shared some essential characteristics. Both were modest and unassuming. He was a conservative dresser, eschewing the male fashion of oversized diamond rings for a single diamond stickpin; Ellen, too, showed little interest in jewelry or fancy clothes. They agreed on the value of compromise: the melding of their Catholic, Jewish, and Protestant backgrounds into Episcopalianism hints at it, and the usually peaceful resolution of marital conflicts, documented by Alice, confirms it. Sometimes their remedies seem a bit strange: since Sam loved to entertain and Ellen didn't, she usually stayed in her room reading French novels during his lively dinner parties. But by all indications the marriage was happy.

Sam's first Cincinnati business venture was another dry-goods store—a logical choice in the fast-growing port town. Unfortunately, the raging winter floods of 1847 destroyed most of his stock. He managed to carry what was left to the store's second floor, safely above the waters, but that very night river pirates sailed up, entered through the window, and stole his remaining goods. "He kept the news from everybody and with hard work soon made good his losses," wrote a Cincinnati historian. "The energy and business tact which so far he had displayed obtained him many friends who possessed ample means to assist him and he gained a large amount of credit."[13]

Pike's next endeavor was a grocery store equipped with a workshop to adjust the proof of alcoholic beverages. Soon Sam, a temperate drinker, was distilling and bottling Pike's Magnolia Whiskey. It found such a huge market that a contemporary chronicler called its success "unparalleled in the history of the trade . . . the favourite throughout the country."[14]

From this point on, Pike possessed the Midas touch. Almost everything in which he invested—land, hotels, office buildings, a trolley system—was hugely profitable. A friend from those days recalled Sam saying that, though he didn't understand why, when it came to making money "he couldn't help it." As the Pike fortune continued to grow, so did the family. Their first child, Lawrence, arrived in 1848, followed by Jeannette (Nettie), Hester (Hessie), and, in 1857, Alice.

SAM PIKE MIGHT BE just another rags-to-riches story were it not for an unusual decision he made in 1851. It all started innocently enough, with tickets to hear "the Swedish Nightingale," soprano Jenny Lind, during her celebrated American tour.

The diva's astonishing voice was at its peak. Possessed of a three-octave range and capable of sustaining a sixty-second note, she offered up endless cadenzas, chromatic runs, roulades, and super-fast trills that sounded like bird calls. She could even, by sending her elaborate vocalization echoing back and forth, ventriloquize her own voice. On top of everything she had the important ability, in the days before microphones, to project loud and clear into the farthest reaches of the balcony.

Lind's American tour was managed by P. T. Barnum, who brought to his task the brilliant promotional techniques he had honed for years with his "freak shows" and circus. Jenny Lind was famous in Europe, where young

Queen Victoria had recently attended all sixteen of her London concerts, but Barnum wasn't interested in gaining mere attention. He wanted, and created, something altogether new: frenzy. By the time the Swedish Nightingale stepped onto American soil, the nation's attention was completely riveted upon her. Newspaper gossip chronicled her every move. Unruly mobs showed up wherever she went. Seats for her performances sold at astronomical prices. Years later the term "Lindomania" was still used to describe a mass craze.

In Cincinnati, Sam Pike sat mesmerized at each of the coloratura's performances. As a musician, he was thrilled to the core by her voice. As a businessman, he studied the eager audience and took note of the dingy National Theater, an inadequate backdrop for a sopranic goddess. By the time Lind moved on to the next city, Sam had decided to build an opera house.

When Pike's Opera House was completed in 1859, it instantly became the most magnificent entertainment venue west of the Allegheny Mountains. Modeled on Milan's Teatro alla Scala, it was five stories high, seated three thousand, and had a beautiful gray sandstone façade adorned with allegorical statues of music and poetry, and murals painted by Italian artists. Such a showcase attracted the country's leading performers, transforming Cincinnati into the cultural mecca of the Midwest. A historian noted a century later that Pike's "opera house served as a symbol of the transition of Cincinnati from the raw, uncouth 'Porkopolis' to a center of mid-western culture."[15]

ELLEN PIKE SHOWED little interest in the Opera House, but then she showed little interest in much of anything except reading. "She was always the first one up," Alice later wrote, "dressed, and ready for the day's activity—first to see that the servants had their duties done, the meals ordered, and then she was ready for her novel-reading by nine in the morning. From this pattern she never varied."[16]

On rare occasions, when Sam insisted that Ellen emerge from her sanctum to act as his hostess, she did so with charm and grace. She was remarkably poised during the 1860 visit to Cincinnati by the nineteen-year-old Prince of Wales, who was honored at a grand ball in Pike's Opera House. Ellen led the *grande promenade* on the prince's arm, setting off to perfection tiered diamond-and-emerald earrings and a matching diamond pendant tiara, gifts from Sam to commemorate the occasion. Clad in a simple white taffeta gown, long tresses carefully arranged, lovely features framed by the priceless jewelry, she charmed the prince, "a remarkably handsome young man, with blue eyes and light hair, a most agreeable countenance, and a gracious manner."[17] When the ball ended, she returned to her novels, and never wore the jewelry again.

Of the children, only Alice shared Sam's love for the arts. They attended the theater arm in arm, and at home they performed for each other: he played the flute and recited poetry; she sang, danced, or played the piano. Bilingual from childhood, Alice enjoyed singing lively French ditties. She could mimic famous entertainers, many of whom she knew firsthand, since the era's greatest stars were wined and dined at the Pike table. Most of these celebrated guests are forgotten now: the high-spirited prima donna Parepa Rosa; the famous Italian ballerina Maria Taglioni; Irish dancer/adventurer Lola Montez. Still renowned is the great coloratura soprano Adelina Patti, of whom a Cincinnati newspaper critic noted: "We expected much and in all candor, we confess that the reality fulfilled the anticipation."[18]

As Alice grew up, taking on the role of her father's hostess, she became adroit at dealing with a wide variety of personalities, and developed the rare ability to accept people foibles and all. Natalie would eventually inherit her mother's nonjudgmental character and profound ability to make friends.

Like most girls of her class and time, Alice was educated at home by governesses, with occasional stints at boarding school. At six she spent a year in a convent school, where she so excelled in song, dance, and piano that she was constantly asked to perform for visitors. "That [I] could not learn the multiplication table or remember the alphabet," she admitted, "was a close guarded secret."[19] A few years later she attended Dayton's Cooper Female Academy, where E. E. Barney, the father of her future husband, had been headmaster.

During the Civil War, Sam Pike conceived the idea of building another opera house in New York City. As soon as the war ended, he moved his family to New York and hired famed architect Griffith Thomas to design a five-story opera house. It was a triumph of cast-iron framing, white Tuckahoe marble, sculpture, and Tiffany gaslights, all topped by a dormered mansard roof. (In 1960, *The New Yorker* would call it a "prime specimen of mid-nineteenth-century Italian Renaissance design" and "one of the most romantic buildings in town.")[20]

Pike's new opera house opened in January 1868 with Verdi's *Il Trovatore*. Newspapers the next day glowed with tributes, and the public agreed. People liked everything about Pike's new theater—except its location. At Eighth Avenue and Twenty-third Street, it was half a mile from the traditional theater district, a long way to go in a horse and buggy on a cold winter's night. Nearly two years after the new opera house opened, Pike sold the building to financial speculators James Fisk and Jay Gould.

Years of success hadn't dimmed Sam's ability to bounce back from adversity. Before long he started a new venture to drain New Jersey marshland. Some of the reclaimed land he intended to sell as railroad right-of-way; the rest would be transformed into low-cost immigrant housing. These plans were abruptly cut short on December 7, 1872. While lunching on oysters at Delmonico's, Sam Pike had a massive heart attack. He died later that day.

IN THE BLOOD OF THE FATHER

Another of Natalie's family legends held that the first Barney in America arrived on the *Mayflower* in 1620. That wasn't true, but it was close enough. A man named Jacob Barney, a native of Buckinghamshire, England, landed in Salem around 1630, probably on the ship *Lyon*. Bright, capable, and dignified, the dark-haired Barney had brown eyes, a glowing complexion, and stood slightly less than six feet. A staunch Puritan, he quickly emerged as a power in the budding Massachusetts Bay Colony. He was the official surveyor of roads and property boundaries, a church deacon, and active in government and judicial spheres. Jacob Barney was, in fact, a judge in one of America's most famous trials, that of the religious dissenter Roger Williams.

The line of descent from Jacob's parents to Natalie has been documented:

Natalie Clifford Barney, b. Oct. 31, 1876; daughter of
Albert Clifford Barney (1850–1902) and Alice Pike; son of
Eliam Eliakim Barney (1807–1880) and Julia Smith; son of
Benjamin Barney (1780–1859) and Nancy Potter; son of
Dr. Edward Barney (1749–1839) and Elizabeth Brown; son of
John Barney Jr. (1730–1807) and Rebecca Martin; son of
John Barney Sr. (1703–1757) and Hannah Clark; son of
Lt. Joseph Barney (1673–1731) and Constance Davis; son of
Jacob Barney Jr. (ca. 1630–1693) and Anne Witt; son of
Jacob Barney Sr. (1601–1673) and Anne; son of
Edward Barney (ca. 1570–1645) and Christian, of Buckinghamshire.[21]

The Barney name most likely originated in Norfolk County, England, in a town known as Berney, where the family was composed of prosperous landowners, yeomen, knights, sheriffs, baronets, and soldiers. A Barney probably fought at the Battle of Hastings in 1066, and, according to Natalie's amateur genealogist cousin, Colonel James Barney, she was distantly related to the Dukes of Norfolk.*

---

*Natalie took great pride in, and wrote about, her supposed kinship with a dashing early American naval hero, Commodore Joshua Barney. However, research by the Barney Family Historical Association indicates that the commodore and Natalie weren't related.

Natalie's Barney progenitors, beginning with the Puritan Judge Jacob, were rugged American pioneers who, generation after generation, hewed a rough existence from the wilderness. Her paternal great-grandparents, Benjamin and Nancy, were the last of this venturesome breed. After that, by the kind of magical alchemy that occurred so often in nineteenth-century America, the Barneys were transformed from pioneers into privileged.

SOMETIME IN 1806, Benjamin Barney, twenty-six, and his new wife, twenty-two-year-old Nancy Potter Barney, moved from Guilford, Vermont, where both had been born and raised, to the wilds of Jefferson County, New York. Benjamin's first wife had recently died, leaving him childless, and it's likely that he and Nancy wanted to make a fresh start. They may also have hoped to improve their lot by moving west, as the path to fortune, even at that early date, led inexorably westward.

The couple built a log cabin in Ellisburgh (now Henderson), first settled by Europeans in 1797. They set about laboriously carving a small farm from the heavy forest. Life was hard, and the land provided only a bare-bones existence. But like many early pioneers, the Barneys were educated, and their rough cabin was filled with books. Alexis de Tocqueville described in his journals just such a rustic forest cabin, containing "a Bible, the first six books of Milton, and two of Shakespear's plays . . . The master of this dwelling . . . belongs to that restless, calculating, and adventurous race of men who . . . endure the life of savages for a time in order to conquer and civilize the backwoods."

Benjamin helped found the Union Literary Society, a school in nearby Belleville, and saw service as a militia captain during the War of 1812. He and Nancy raised eleven children, christening them in the dammed-up stream outside their cabin. Their first child—Natalie's grandfather—was born in 1807. They named him Eliam Eliakim, but throughout his life he would be known as simply "E.E."

Pioneer life was ceaselessly hardscrabble, but there was always time in the Barney home for study, and at eighteen E.E. journeyed off to Schenectady's Union College "wearing a suit of clothes, which were spun, woven, dyed, and made up by his mother and sisters" from his father's Merino sheep.[22] To help pay his fees, he taught classes at night and discovered a sincere love of teaching. In 1831 he was recommended as one of seventy-six "young gentlemen, members of the Senior Class, as Candidates for the First degree in the Arts."[23] After graduation, he spent the next two years as principal of nearby Lowville Academy.

Hoping to improve his financial circumstances, E.E. moved to Ohio in

1833, accompanied on the two-week wagon trip by a few of his siblings. He found a temporary job teaching Greek and set about looking for a permanent position. His job-search method—in which he wrote to various Ohio postmasters and quizzed them about local teaching jobs—was straightforward, giving the hint of a no-nonsense businessman lying within. The only response he received was from the Dayton postmaster. It intrigued him enough to move to that town, where he was hired as principal of the Dayton Academy.

E. E. Barney was a popular teacher, strict but progressive. In one of his first acts as principal he dispensed with the ancient tradition of seating students together on long benches, giving them individual desks instead. "Mr. Barney was fifty years ahead of his time," enthused a fin-de-siècle journalist. "He made everything he taught so interesting one could not help learning."[24]

In October 1834, a few days before his twenty-seventh birthday, E.E. married Julia Smith of Galway, New York. Their first child, Eugene, was born in 1839. They would have four more children: Edward, Agnes, Albert, and Mary.

Barney loved teaching, but, then as now, it paid little. Lack of money was a constant problem, forcing the family to board students and endure ceaseless economies. E.E. wanted more for his family, a feeling that only increased with Eugene's birth. For the next dozen years his life was a constant push-pull between love of learning and loathing of want, something reflected in his erratic career path. He started his own school in a church basement, bought and ran a sawmill, and finally became principal of Dayton's newly built school for girls, the Cooper Female Academy. The school quickly earned a reputation as a center of high thinking, attracting wealthy daughters from all corners of Ohio "by reason of the strong personality, magnetism and culture of Mr. Barney."[25]

However, Barney was still plagued by money woes. He resigned his principalship in 1850 to go into business with Ebenezer Thresher, a fellow Baptist, and establish Dayton's first manufacturing facility. The town's tremendous water power and central location, they felt, made it a logical manufacturing site, and its population of ten thousand guaranteed a steady workforce. The only thing they were unsure about was what, exactly, they should produce. After considering a number of possibilities, they decided upon railroad cars.

IN 1850 the American railroad industry was still in its infancy. The horse-drawn Baltimore & Ohio had begun in 1827, but it wasn't until 1830 that a locomotive, the *Tom Thumb*, was successfully powered by steam. On its first journey, traveling along the just-completed thirteen-mile track from Baltimore to Endicott's Mills, the *Tom Thumb* achieved the amazing speed of eighteen miles per hour. Some aboard the small car that day pulled out notebooks and "wrote their names and some connected sentences, to prove that even at that great velocity it was possible to do so."[26] On the return trip the locomotive was overtaken by a horse.

Despite medical warnings about the dangers that excessive speed could wreak upon the human body, trains caught on, and by 1840 the United States possessed almost three thousand miles of short-distance track. This, however, was the merest prelude. Over the next decade, as the possibilities of expanded trade via rail became obvious, towns and cities across the country began slowly linking into a growing railroad network. Dayton was typical. Although it had no railroad in 1850, when Barney and Thresher planned their factory, the very next year it was connected by track to Springfield and those all-important points beyond. The entire nation would soon be united by rail, creating an explosive need for passenger and freight cars. The speed and power of that great steam-powered colossus, the railroad engine, would transform the United States, quickly making Barney and many others rich. Some railroad pioneers became so powerful that they took on the aura of royalty, giving rise to the term "railroad baron," still in common use today.

In many ways, the coming of the railroad in the nineteenth century can be compared to the rise of the Internet in our own day. The introduction of each innovation altered, in its own way, many aspects of social life and commerce. Even more important, each forced human beings to expand their perception of the physical world's limitations. Just as we marvel over the instantaneous speed with which a message can be sent from Albuquerque to Zanzibar, those in the mid-nineteenth century were astonished to travel quickly over long distances. "When I look back and remember how it used to be in my boyhood days," wrote a contemporary of Barney's, "when the time made by canal-boats and stages was considered *fast* . . . and stop to realize the life of today, with steam . . . It is impossible for the present generation to conceive of the wonder and amazement created by the sight of the first locomotive."[27]

And so it was that Messrs. Barney and Thresher established a manufacturing firm (after Thresher's interest was acquired by a gentleman with the wonderfully nineteenth-century name of Preserved Smith, the company became known as Barney & Smith). The cars produced were crude at first, but with constant technological and aesthetic innovation they quickly improved. By 1867 Barney & Smith was turning out twenty freight and two luxury passenger cars each month. That year *Railroad Record* referred to the company as "the best managed works in the West, if not the whole country." At its high point, the Barney & Smith Car Works employed more than one thousand and was Dayton's largest industry.

The passenger cars, known for their rich furnishings, artistically carved rare woods, art glass, and modern plumbing, were acknowledged as the best on rails. For many years the company produced cars for Pullman, justifiably famed for their luxurious elegance. According to an early historian, "the Barney and Smith . . . product is known all over the United States. North, south, east, west, the traveler occupies Barney and Smith cars."[28]

E. E. Barney, the poor lad who'd trudged off to college in a homespun suit, became enormously wealthy. Despite success, he remained modest and unassuming, a staunch Baptist with an unexpected sense of humor. He demanded honesty and hard work from his employees, and in return was generous, kind, and a reputedly soft touch. One of his eccentricities was in always wearing a high silk hat, even in the factory. The workers swore they could gauge his mood by the way it sat atop his head. If worn toward the back, they expected easy sailing; pulled down onto his forehead, "it was well to be on the lookout for breakers ahead."[29]

Like Natalie's other grandfather, E.E. used his newfound wealth and power to intelligently advance his other interests. A conservationist, he cultivated and wrote extensively about the commercial qualities of the catalpa, a fast-growing tree that he believed could solve the nation's growing hunger for wood. When he advertised free catalpa seed, hoping to increase the tree's popularity, he received responses from as far away as New Zealand, Japan, and England.

Among Barney's countless activities, he was vice president of the Second National Bank, a trustee of Denison University, a director of the Wisconsin Central Railroad, and a highly active member of the First Baptist Church. Loved and respected, when E. E. Barney died in 1880 at the age of seventy-three, more than two thousand mourners attended his funeral.

YOUNG BLOOD: ALICE

Samuel Pike's unexpected death in December 1872 stunned everyone he knew. It seemed impossible that such a brilliant, vigorous man should be cut down at a mere fifty years of age. For his family, who had "worshipped him for his wholehearted devotion and tenderness,"[30] the requisite year of mourning held no pretense. The five-story brownstone on Fifth Avenue, the scene of laughter and song during Sam Pike's life, fell silent.

Ellen took naturally to mourning, leaving the house only for a daily carriage ride and then retreating to her rooms. The three oldest children—Lawrence, Jeannette, and Hessie—were depressed and subdued for months, but it was sixteen-year-old Alice who took Sam's death the hardest. Her high spirits evaporated, replaced by constant sadness; she couldn't bear to sing, play the piano, or engage in any other activity she and her father had enjoyed together.

Eventually the children's grief subsided. The playboy Lawrence, who would never hold a job, returned to his social whirl. Jeannette resumed her rounds of parties and fashion fittings. The quiet Hessie brimmed with plans for her upcoming marriage, and Alice regained her upbeat nature. But Ellen retreated ever deeper into a private world in which "everything meant nothing to her, nothing meant anything and in this vacuum she hibernated."[31]

When the year's mourning ended, Ellen's daughters took her in hand. A big change was needed, they proclaimed, something along the lines of a Grand European Tour. A kind of finishing school for the rich, such tours were almost a social necessity. Ellen, though reluctant to abandon her comfortable routine, understood the benefits such a journey held for her children. Once in Europe, her daughters assured her, she could continue her quiet life, leaving her rooms only when required to act as chaperone. In the end she agreed to go, surprising everybody.

IN MARCH 1874 the Pikes sailed for Paris, putting up at the modish Hôtel Splendide. Hit hard by the city's magic, Alice was particularly intrigued by the bohemian artists in the Left Bank. To her young eyes they were the epitome of romance and glamour. Dressed head-to-toe in black, arguing intensely in forbidden cafés, they seemed to have stepped from the pages of Henri Murger's popular *Scènes de la vie de Bohème.* "Bohemia," declared one of Murger's artists, "has an inner language of its own, taken from studio talk. . . . 'Tis an intelligent argot, albeit unintelligible to those who have not the key to it."

Perhaps it was through her desire to understand this glamorous new argot that Alice discovered her own artistic leanings. Or maybe it was, as she wrote, merely the city's "heightening of color that exalted her. Color. It became a sudden world to her. The magic of the Louvre and the many galleries succeeded in increasing her desire for self-expression."[32] Alice began to sketch, pleased to discover that she not only enjoyed the creative process but had talent. These two simple facts would have great ramifications later.

Eventually the family traveled to London. Despite Alice's early dislike of that city's "maiden-lady" demeanor, she delighted in the social romp, pleased to find herself sought after. Small wonder. Not only was she pretty and petite, with a full mouth and large blue eyes, but she was also cheerful, amusing, and very rich. She'd been peppered by suitors throughout the trip, but had shown little interest. That changed instantly when she met the legendary explorer Henry Morton Stanley.

At that time Stanley was perhaps the most celebrated man in England, a result of having "found" the medical missionary and explorer Dr. David Livingstone in the depths of Africa. Livingstone, the first European to cross the Kalahari Desert and lay eyes on Victoria Falls, had set out in 1866 to find the source of the Nile. When nothing was heard from him after a few years, his whereabouts became a subject of international concern. Stanley, an Anglo-American orphan turned *New York Herald* reporter, embarked in 1870 on a dangerous journey to find him. Eight months later, on the shores of Lake Tanganyika, he supposedly greeted the ailing missionary with the now-legendary remark: "Dr. Livingstone, I presume?"

Stanley later searched for the source of the Nile on his own. On this and other expeditions he would survive cannibal attacks, follow the Congo River through Central Africa, and help form the Congo Free State under the despotic rule of Belgium's King Leopold II. He would be elected to Parliament in 1895 and knighted in 1899.

It was this man, then aged thirty-three, who met and fell obsessively in love with seventeen-year-old Alice Pike. Their recollections about the beginning of the romance differ. Stanley's journal entries reveal that his initial impressions of Alice were mixed; she wore too many diamonds and was "very ignorant of African geography, and I fear of everything else,"[33] he thought, but he admired her elegant figure and charm. Alice painted a romantic picture of instant love: "Stanley . . . suddenly appeared in the doorway. . . . The moment he entered, no one else existed. Alice looked up, their eyes met as he approached her. Neither one was conscious of the formalities they mechanically performed."[34]

If Alice's diamonds and lack of education caused hesitation on Stanley's part, it wasn't for long: within days he was considering marriage to his "Lady Alice." The inexperienced teenager was flattered. "Stanley, the man who had brought all London to his feet," she wrote. "He was an extraordinary looking man of about thirty some. There was not a man nor a woman in all London who did not know of Stanley, the Stanley. His name was on every tongue; it was his name that was spoken over the tea cups; it was his name that was mentioned at dinner; everyone everywhere heard it . . . Stanley was the 'LION OF LONDON.' "[35]

Ellen, disturbed by the explorer's aggressive pursuit of her daughter, reminded him of Alice's youth. In reply, he begged for Alice's hand. Ellen refused. Saying that it would be a tragedy to marry a "mere child" who might later have regrets, she insisted that he wait. He reluctantly agreed. Later that day Alice told Stanley that she loved him but, whereas he had seen and done everything, she was just starting out. "I want to do, to know, [to] just be myself," she said. "Then I, too, would be worthwhile."[36]

Grand Tour ended, the Pikes returned to New York City. Alice slipped into the active life of a wealthy and popular belle, replete with charity balls, singing lessons, fittings with the seamstress, and chaperoned parties at Delmonico's. She forgot all about Stanley.

He, on the other hand, retained his deep love. Within a month he arrived in New York to bathe in the aura of his "nymph-of-the-moon." As he was leaving for another African exploration, he pleaded that she wait for him. Reluctant at first, she eventually put her signature on a marriage pact, pledging to marry him upon his return. But his ship had scarcely sailed before Alice resumed the social whirl. She rarely read his letters, bundling them into packets for storage in a trunk. On the few occasions she wrote, she was chatty and impersonal. For all intents and purposes, Stanley had slipped completely from her mind.

Over the next two years, as he circumnavigated two great African lakes and sailed the entire length of the Congo, the great explorer's love remained steadfast. He carried Alice's oilskin-wrapped photo next to his heart. He painted the name *Lady Alice* on the prow of his boat. He christened a series of rapids the "Rapides Alice." He wrote to Alice every day, mailing letters en masse at every primitive outpost. His journals were filled with scenarios of a blissful future with Alice. It wasn't the thought of fame and fortune that kept Stanley going, but dreams of young Alice Pike.

Worried that her youngest daughter might marry the older, experienced Stanley—or, even worse, one of the rich New York playboys she frequented—Ellen packed her off for a long family visit in Dayton. Alice was delighted at the idea of staying with her adored Aunt Nett and favorite cousins. She wouldn't have been so keen to go, however, had she known that the visit was a scheme whipped up by her aunt and mother to unite her with a suitable husband. Aunt Nett, a leader of Dayton society, knew every eligible bachelor in town. She was determined to find one among them for her frisky niece.

And so, one spring day in 1875, Alice—a vision of youthful sophistication in a pricey Parisian frock—stepped lightly onto the station platform in Dayton. A small crowd awaited: Aunt Nett, Uncle Craighead, cousin Louise, and a group of old school friends (including Carrie Dudley, who, as Mrs. Leslie Ward, would be known as "the American Sarah Bernhardt" when she took to the stage). In their midst was a "very smart and handsome stranger . . . a rather short man in his late twenties, who was dressed with much taste and had about him a decided suave air of distinction."[37]

The man was Albert Clifford Barney. Aunt Nett introduced them with a reference to their mutual European travels, and the two young people exchanged friendly smiles. Albert escorted Alice to the waiting landau with cavalier assurance. Everyone piled in, the coachman cracked his whip, and away they went.

As they clip-clopped along, Aunt Nett pointed out the many changes in Dayton since her niece last visited: the elegant new hotel, the grand theater, the big department store. Alice nodded politely while discreetly observing Albert Barney. "He must be it," she thought, "the real reason I'm here."

And of course she was right.

YOUNG BLOOD: ALBERT

The mystery of Albert Barney can best be inferred from these lines of *Macbeth:* "If you can look into the seeds of time/And say which grain will grow and which will not/Speak . . ." Born to wealth, nurtured by Baptist work-ethic values, and gifted with exceptional intelligence, good looks, and charm, Albert might have attained anything. Instead, he lived a stunted life, plagued by alcoholism and beset by petty worries about appearance and social position. He was, in effect, the grain that would not, perhaps could not, grow.

Born in 1850, Albert was so bright and winning a child that, half a century later, Dayton teachers spoke "in terms of affectionate praise of his boyish powers and disposition."[38] His early academic excellence prompted E.E. to send him to New Hampshire's Phillips Exeter Academy, an exclusive preparatory school founded in 1781, where he excelled.

Entering Brown University at sixteen, Albert mingled with the East Coast scions of wealth. He embraced the leisured life of a rich playboy, developing a taste for alcohol and casual love affairs. Although shorter than average, he was extremely good-looking, with thick blond hair, a firm chin with a deep cleft, and full, sensuous lips. Throughout his life he was a meticulous dresser, even something of a dandy.

After his graduation, E.E. rewarded Albert with a yearlong European tour. Once abroad, his taste for dalliance ripened. He spent time in Paris, polishing his French in drawing rooms, but it was London, with the manly whiskey-and-cigars atmosphere of its elite private clubs, that earned his lifelong devotion.

In 1870 the magic abruptly ended. Albert returned to Dayton to begin his career at Barney & Smith, where E.E. expected his sons to learn the business from the ground up. That was fine with Albert's brothers, Eugene and Edward. Schooled in Ohio and by nature unassuming, they retained their father's simple values. Edward eventually left Dayton to pursue other endeavors.* Eugene thrived at the company, becoming president after his father's death.

---

*In 1878 Edward and his wife bought Virginia's Jamestown Island, then still in private hands. Ten years later they gave twenty-two acres, including the ruins of America's first Protestant church, to a preservation society. The Interior Department seized the rest of the island under eminent domain in the early 1930s, paying the Barneys $100 per acre.

Albert, however, yearned for the gentleman's life. The very idea of work was anathema to him, and the reality—his first assignment was in the noisy, smelly foundry—was worse. Day after day he breathed noxious gases from molten pig iron while learning the intricacies of wood patterns, hollow core casting, and iron wheels. To a fastidious snob like Albert, the foundry was far worse than anything Dante dreamed up for the circles of Hell. If he had to work, he thought, then it should be at something suitable to his Ivy League education and European refinement. Unfortunately, his father didn't agree. And so, for five years preceding his 1875 meeting with Alice Pike, Albert trudged dutifully through a career he loathed.

Away from work Albert luxuriated in a more appropriate role, that of the dashing man about town. Sharp-witted and wealthy, he was generally acknowledged as Dayton's most eligible bachelor. He was the target of marital hopes in the finest homes, but had so far disappointed the local belles by remaining firmly unattached.

It wasn't until Alice Pike stepped onto the railroad platform one spring day that Albert found a woman who matched his demanding qualifications. She wasn't just a wealthy, urbane young heiress; she was also vivacious, pretty, and, not least, her curvaceous and petite figure flattered his short stature. In sum, Alice Pike was good enough to marry.

MINGLED BLOOD: ALICE AND ALBERT

Within a week, Alice and Albert were a major item. "He simply and completely fell in love," Alice wrote, "and he knew how to show it." Lavish floral bouquets arrived every day, as did Albert, always with chocolates, books, or other gifts in hand. Soon there was no social occasion to which he didn't escort the diminutive visitor from New York City, including picnics, hayrides, dinners, and dances. By early summer the Dayton debutantes—or, as Alice called them, "the young lady contestants"—had dropped, one by one, from the struggle.

Alice, or so she would claim, remained blissfully unaware that Albert was courting her. It was probably true, at least on a conscious level. As she would do later in life, she showed an astounding capacity for packaging her feelings into discrete compartments. She wasn't in love with Albert, but, enjoying to the utmost his charming company, she dispensed with the reality of courtship by just not thinking about it. The desire for an intimate relationship was by her own admission not part of her makeup; she even suspected that she was incapable of feeling love. Unlike her friends, constantly chattering about romance and dreaming of the proverbial knight in shining armor, she didn't care about "all the customary sentimental rubbish."[39]

And so the unusual courtship continued. They often sat talking in the parlor while Alice sketched. They were doing so one summer evening when Albert suddenly proposed marriage. His uncharacteristically abstruse wording was so confusing—he said something about not having a silver platter and thus making his offering with two bare hands—that Alice later insisted she'd had no idea what he was talking about. That didn't stop her from politely responding, "And I may accept it with my own two bare hands."

She was startled by Albert's reaction. Suffused by an inexplicable joy, he jumped up, took her in his arms, and kissed her passionately. Then he broke away, shouting excitedly for Aunt Nett and Uncle Craighead to join them. They came running down the stairs, clutching their dressing gowns, followed by curious children and servants. When Albert announced that he and Alice were to marry, she interrupted him, stunned. "Why, Albert," she said. "You didn't say a thing about getting married!" Aunt Nett assured her that it was a foregone conclusion, and a happy one at that. Everyone joined in with exuberant kisses and congratulations, and Alice was too embarrassed to protest. By evening's end the engagement was a fait accompli.

Later, alone in her room, Alice considered calling off the marriage, but in the end decided to go through with it. While she didn't love Albert, she was certainly fond of him. Since she never expected to fall in love, and since she had to marry someone, "[I] thought it might just as well be he as another."[40]

She nursed a few doubts, though. Chief among them: Albert was "a bit of a snob and made too much ado about place and position. On the other hand, everyone lauded Albert to the skies, both men and women, young and old, for he was charming to everyone."[41] In the end she concluded that, with Albert, she had "done well enough." She experienced a few guilty thoughts about "dear, splendid Stanley . . . but [I] was too tired to think and turned over to sleep."[42]

In New York a week later, Ellen Pike received a letter from her sister spilling over with the good news. She read it, and, surprised, turned to her oldest daughter, Jeannette. "I can't imagine Alice loving anyone," she murmured. "She isn't the kind."

"I know," Nettie agreed.

ALICE WAS A FEW DAYS shy of her nineteenth birthday when she and Albert were married, before more than two hundred guests, in the Pike home on New York's Fifth Avenue. She was dazzling. Clad in yards of white point lace and an impressive array of diamonds, she exchanged vows with Albert beneath a bell composed of rare white flowers. A luxurious supper followed, and then the newlyweds slipped away to a long honeymoon in New Orleans and St. Augustine.

Six months later the young couple took up residence in Dayton and entered the routine of married life. They knew each other far better now. Each had discovered unexpected pleasure in the other, but also serious disappointment.

Alice now understood that, despite his charm and polish, Albert viewed the world through a narrow slit: there were a privileged few he wished to know and cultivate, but he had little interest in anyone else. His obsession with social position dominated their lives. By nature lighthearted, free-spirited, and a bit ditzy, Alice—whose favorite phrase was "live and let live"—already felt stifled and hemmed in.

Albert, for his part, worried constantly about his new wife. Seemingly unconcerned with propriety or what people thought, she'd say and do nearly anything, never considering how it might be interpreted. That she made a friend of everyone she came across was a saving grace, and her habit of sketching won compliments from people he respected. But more and more frequently he felt the need to control her excessive spirit.

One day soon after their return, Albert helped Alice unpack a trunk of belongings shipped from New York. Digging deep, past the gowns, hats, and toiletries, he unearthed a few packets of letters tied with heavy cord. Curious, he pulled a sheath of envelopes from the trunk. All bore exotic African stamps. The sender's name, written in a bold hand, was Henry Morton Stanley. Particularly upsetting was the fact that some postmarks were dated after their marriage.

Fearing that he'd been somehow betrayed and made a fool of, Albert demanded an explanation. Alice protested that the letters meant nothing, that she hadn't even read most of them—that her mother must have placed the recent letters in the trunk. But Albert's "jaw tightened and his eyes became hard. Those eyes had bothered her; they were set too near together, but the handsome head, fine features and delightful smile overcame this fault; but in terms of anger the small near-set eyes predominated."[43]

Cruel words were exchanged, followed by a long, dreadful silence. Albert regarded Alice with such icy contempt that she "was chilled from head to foot and felt a strange barrier between them."[44] Finally, he ordered her to burn all the letters, immediately, in his presence. She obeyed, throwing them, one by one, into the fire. When she was through, Albert kissed her hair. "You are a good wife," he said. He left the room, and with his fading footsteps died any last hope of love between them. Alice had been tried, judged, and condemned. She was not to be trusted. The sentence, she knew, would never be rescinded.

She wrote later that Albert's actions that day made perfect but unfortunate sense, "for Albert Clifford Barney, with all his charm of personality and nimbleness of mind and wit, had no pretense to breadth of soul. His ideas were often prejudices and very narrow."[45] She realized that she had made her life's biggest mistake by not marrying Stanley, who was in every way Albert's opposite. Her marriage, she saw now, would be unhappy at best.

And there was no turning back: she was stuck forever. Divorce, still the scourge of decent society, was out of the question. She and Albert would be united as man and wife until one of them died. To survive, she would have to find enough strength to live a successful charade. She must be a good and obedient helpmate, a worthy companion, a fine friend. She must run a model household, entertaining in a manner that properly reflected her husband's social station. She must do everything possible, anything at all, to present the illusion of perfection.

No, her heart would never be in this marriage, that was an indisputable fact. But it was something she could work around. She had to. Because, as it turned out, both she and her mother had been wrong: she *could* feel love, she knew that now. She was five months pregnant, and, quite simply, she loved the baby growing inside her. And no matter what it took, no matter the emotional cost, her child would be welcomed into a perfect world.

Child of Witches and Saints

1876–1890

Youth is not a question of years:
one is young or old from birth.
                    —*Natalie Barney*

From childhood's hour I have not been
As others were—I have not seen
As others saw . . .
                    —*Edgar Allan Poe*

ATALIE CLIFFORD BARNEY was born on October 31, 1876. As it turned out, that specific day of the year provided a perfect portal for the child's entry into life, symbolizing both the duality that would mark her nature and the wild essence of her heart.

Today we think of October's last day as simply Halloween, but to nineteenth-century Americans the date was so full of complexity and contradiction that it had two antithetical names: Holy Evening and Witches' Sabbath. One title was sacred, representing good; the other was profane and symbolized evil. Ironically, both names hailed from the same pagan source.

The date's sacred aspects emerged early in the seventh century, when Catholics began informally honoring saints at a yearly festival. When Pope

Gregory IV finally made the practice official in 835, his reasons were more political than spiritual. Church policy required that important festivals of conquered tribes be replaced with Christian celebrations on the same date, so Gregory decreed November 1, the start of the New Year for the Celts, as the day to honor saints. Called in early times Allhallows or Hallowmas, the name eventually evolved to All Saints Day. The preceding day, October 31, became known as All Hallow's Even or Holy Evening.

The more profane aspects of the day originated nearly two thousand years ago among ancient Druids, the Celtic priestly upper class. Druids worshiped nature and practiced magic. They believed that, on the last night of their year (our calendar's October 31), the Lord of the Dead ordered the unliving back to life. To ward off these spirits, Druids lit great fires and nurtured them until dawn. Down through the centuries the day evolved, transforming the dead into ghosts and adding various sorcerers and evil spirits, until it became known as the Witches' Sabbath. Every year on this night, it was said, witches, warlocks, ghosts, and other wicked creatures threw a raucous party. Through the night they leaped and frolicked before a huge bonfire while planning the coming year's mischief. When dawn arrived, bringing the holy day and all its saints to light, they fled.

Natalie, who thought of herself as a "double being," delighted in the fact that she had entered life through a kind of moral and spiritual warp, an alleyway papered on one side with the sacred and on the other with the profane. A devotee of astrology and numerology, she believed that her duality had its genesis in her birthdate. As an adult in Paris, she would form a club of friends born on the same day. They named themselves "The Scorpions," after their shared astrological symbol, and for decades celebrated October 31 as a group.

Natalie had the luck to be born into a large and wealthy family prepared to adore her in every way. Her grandparents lavishly bestowed money, gifts, and attention; family and friends marveled over her every gesture. Albert, overjoyed by the birth of his first child, bought Alice the purest diamond possible. "It was perfect," a family friend recalled. "You couldn't take your eyes off it."[1]

Natalie had some odd quirks. She disliked mother's milk, preferring a canned and condensed version flavored with chocolate. Even as a baby she showed little interest in dolls, and never would. She was a dreamy, thoughtful child, often so distracted that she didn't respond to questions or to the antics of other children. This caused her parents a good deal of worry. But her "absences," as they were called, became "rarer, disappearing completely when I gained further awareness and possession of myself . . . and I realized that I could do what I wanted to do, which was generally contrary to what was expected of me . . . such a disposition made me a difficult child, but since I seemed wise and quiet, I was left alone to develop according to my nature."[2]

DESPITE HER MOTHER'S INTENTIONS, the world that greeted Natalie was far from perfect. Unhappy with his work at the car factory and life in Dayton, Albert took to berating Alice, particularly on the subject of his self-styled nemesis, Stanley.

With the successful completion of his journey, Stanley was more famous than ever. He was constantly celebrated in the newspapers, a fact that infuriated Albert, capable as he was of "violent jealousy against a much better man."[3] His attitude wasn't helped by an article in the *New York Times* that discreetly linked Alice and Stanley for all the world to see: "It is said on excellent authority that Stanley will come to London in 1878. He would have returned to New York first, but that the lady to whom he was betrothed, tired of waiting for him, has lately married. I hope in reporting this I am not casting a reflection upon the constancy of a New York lady who is said to be as unassuming as she is good."[4]

Albert's jealousy might have evaporated had he realized that all the worldly acclaim meant little to his imagined rival. "What is the good of all this pomp and show?" Stanley bitterly demanded of a friend. "It only makes me more miserable and unhappy."[5] The lovelorn explorer hadn't learned of Alice's marriage until nearly two years after she rode off with Albert in a shower of rice. Arriving in Zanzibar at the end of his trek, he dashed eagerly to the home of the man holding his mail. Instead of the long-anticipated letters from Lady Alice, he found news clippings about her marriage and Natalie's birth ten months later. He was devastated.

A *New York Times* reporter described the ordinarily upbeat Stanley as being "sullen, morose, discontented and savage."[6] His publisher, Edward Marston, recalled that he was "very lonely and depressed" and "evidently suffering acutely from a bitter disappointment; what that was, I could well guess."[7] He could guess not because he was a mind reader, but because Stanley's great love for Alice was widely known; he had practically shouted her name from the rooftops of London and New York before disappearing into the jungle. When Alice married, many of his friends and admirers considered her action traitorous. Deep down, she agreed, and as the years passed she would often regret having tossed Stanley aside. Learning of his return from Africa, she sent a letter of apology and asked his forgiveness. He eventually sent her a copy of his book, *Through the Dark Continent*, with a warmly written inscription. His achievement, he admitted, "could never have been accomplished without you. Your image was always before me, Lady Alice."[8]

The story of Alice's "treachery" followed her for decades. In 1911, more than thirty-five years after the events, an article in a Chicago newspaper noted that Stanley's "hair turned snowy white in a single night" when he learned of Alice's marriage.[9]

A year after Natalie's birth, Ellen asked Albert to take over management of Samuel Pike's considerable estate. The job entailed a move to Cincinnati, three times the size and far more cosmopolitan than Dayton, which pleased Albert. The pay was handsome, and the work in keeping with his idea of a gentleman's occupation. He left immediately for Cincinnati, where he was later joined by Alice and the baby. They took a suite of rooms at the Pike-owned Burnet House, a luxurious hotel that had hosted Daniel Webster, Abraham Lincoln, the Prince of Wales, Horace Greeley, and Jenny Lind, and where Generals Grant and Sherman had brainstormed during the Civil War. The Barneys were living there in November 1879 when their second daughter and last child, Laura Alice, was born.

Albert and Alice were comfortably well off, but far from rich. That changed dramatically when, in December 1880, E.E. died. The bulk of his fortune went to his wife, Julia, but his five children inherited large sums and a share in the factory's profits. Albert's inheritance, combined with Alice's private income and his salary from the Pikes, transformed him into a man of relative wealth.

He and Alice wasted no time putting the money to use. They bought a house in Cincinnati's elite hillside suburb, Mount Auburn, with its beautiful forest and river views. According to Cincinnati society writers, they furnished it with taste and elegance. Albert bought expensive horses and a luxurious carriage, and Alice decked herself out in the finest clothes. As they became known for entertaining often and lavishly, "their home was the center of a most delightful hospitality."[10] The first in a long series of French and occasionally German governesses was hired to take charge of the children.

It was around now that Natalie began to see her parents as entities separate from herself. For years she would think of Albert as a handsome stranger, someone who came and went with regularity but who had little consequence in her world. Gradually she came to associate him with physical roughness. If she made a childlike dash for the street when they walked in town, he pulled her back with excessive force. When he hugged, he crushed her to his chest. His beard scratched. He hurt her without meaning to, and she didn't like it. Though he doted upon her, in some ways she feared him. "I chiefly remember him as one that hurt and never more than when he tried to be kind," she told

Laura six decades later. "Even when we were very young he always managed to hurt more than he helped."[11]

Conversely, she worshiped her mother, who "appeared more beautiful than anything in my dreams."[12] Her earliest memories involve a high-spirited Alice, scarcely out of her teens, singing operatic arias while accompanying herself at the piano. She also recalled that, after presenting her with a baby sister, Alice stopped singing. Alice may have experienced a prolonged depression following Laura's birth, as some of her own comments suggest. It's possible that Natalie's later horror of childbirth had its genesis here, with a young mother whose happy voice fell silent for years.

As a parent, Alice was loving but stingy with physical affection, hugging her children rarely. This lack of physical intimacy with the person she loved most had a bittersweet effect on Natalie. She often told of how, on nights when her parents went out, she would lie awake in her bed until hearing the rustle of her mother's dress in the hall. Once Alice and Albert were inside their bedroom, Natalie would tiptoe barefoot toward the ray of light spilling from beneath their door. Even on bitter winter nights, trembling from the cold, she wouldn't return to her room until the light had been extinguished. Natalie once said that she slept badly as a child because, loving her mother more than anything in the world, "I feared ceaselessly that she would have some kind of accident, and I couldn't sleep until I had ascertained her safe and sound return."[13]

In those pre-Freudian times such devotion would have been viewed as simply a daughter's deep love for her mother. Today, however, Natalie's thoughts and actions seem almost desperately insecure. Did she subconsciously fear abandonment? Did she interpret her mother's lack of affection as lack of love? Was hugging the door a substitute for her mother's hugs? Did she view her father as a rival, knowing that her mother's warmth was easily available to him, while she stood shivering outside that bedroom door?

We will never know. It wasn't Natalie's way to delve into such questions, or even to pose them. In retelling the bedroom-door story at eighty-four, she appeared oblivious to any deeper psychological meaning. For her the tale meant only that she had adored Alice. "The child who does not start life with a great love for her mother or father," she said, "has been deprived of one of the most absolute of human emotions."[14]

Like most wealthy women of that era, Alice saw her children infrequently, directing their care through instructions to nurses and governesses. Thanks to her laissez-faire attitude about discipline and rules, Natalie and Laura had unusual autonomy. "She never punished us," Natalie recalled. "We were not spanked, and the stick was spared in order, preferably, to spoil the child!"[15]

In the early 1880s, Auburn Avenue still had a countrified atmosphere that appealed to an adventurous girl like Natalie. "There were gypsy camps nearby," she recalled, "and we looked on [them] with envy."[16] From her hilltop she also spied on small encampments of Indians passing through the valley, imagining that their cooking fires were sending out smoke signals. She longed to travel with them. But home offered its own enticements, particularly the pets: a goat; a Mexican parakeet named Marisava who shared a cage peaceably with Jumbo the parrot; a collection of baby alligators brought back from a winter sojourn in Florida; and two dogs, a bulldog and a blenheim.

For Natalie, the most important pet was Tricksy. Albert had bought the Shetland pony and its violet-colored saddle from a traveling circus, instantly transforming his daughter into a "jeune Amazone." Natalie was attracted to everything about horses. She admired their shiny manes braided with colorful ribbons. She adored the "delicious" odor of the stables. She loved the way Tricksy licked the palm of her hand when lapping up the daily sugar ration, and she was fascinated by the soft spot between the pony's nostrils. She was given her first riding lessons by the Barneys' coachman, Preston, a Napoléon look-alike who taught her to trot and gallop in a circle traced on the stable's dusty floor. When she grew skilled enough, Albert allowed her to ride behind the "tea cart" when the family went driving. With Tricksy safely hitched to the rear, Natalie practiced her seat while becoming familiar with the gait of the two large horses pulling the cart. Soon she was allowed to rig Tricksy to a pony cart, take the reins, and trot around the neighborhood with Laura beside her.

Natalie was a naturally athletic child who took easily to sports of all kinds. When older she would excel at tennis, swimming, rowing, and fencing, but as a child on Mount Auburn she was drawn to simpler endeavors like climbing trees and running. It was a great source of pride to her that she always won the neighborhood footraces, even when competing against boys. In addition to physical prowess, Natalie was willful and strong-minded, forever egging on her playmates into adventures. Laura once stated that her sister was always the leader in childhood games.

Beginning in the early 1880s, the Barneys took summer seaside vacations at Atlantic resorts. When Natalie was about six or seven, Albert, deciding that the time had come for her to learn swimming, took her on his back and paddled about in the water. This worked fine until a powerful wave crashed into them, detaching Natalie's arms and sending her hurtling to the bottom. Albert quickly hauled her up. Stunned and scared, she retired to the warm sands, where Laura was hard at work constructing castles. When Natalie seized her pail, Laura hauled back and whacked her on the head with a small iron shovel. Blood gushed out, covering Natalie's face, and she was rushed to the doctor.

The stitches he administered left a small scar high on Natalie's forehead for the rest of her life.

M E A N W H I L E, trouble was brewing at home. Albert's initial satisfaction with Cincinnati had dimmed, and he was once again yearning for something he couldn't have, at least for the moment: the indulgent life of a gentleman at leisure. Rich, but not rich enough to support the lavish lifestyle he and Alice had adopted, he worried constantly about money.

Alice, by temperament a peacemaker, strove to placate him. Her desire for tranquillity meant that she had to obey his wishes and try to meet his exacting standards. "She had great patience with difficult characters," Natalie once observed, "ungenial though they proved to be, and I never saw her cross."[17]

Maybe so, but deep inside, Alice simmered. Her anger and bitterness toward her husband would eventually surface in her unpublished memoirs, written more than half a century later. Again and again, while allowing for Albert's charm and good looks, she is merciless in her depiction of him. At times—describing his foul temper, his problems with alcohol, his snobbery and posturing, his need to control—she can barely contain her contempt.

The one thing Alice refused to do was give up the tiny part of herself that yearned for creative expression. The things that made her feel happy and fulfilled—music, dance, art—didn't interest Albert, and he didn't want her interested in them, either. He wanted her to be no different from other wives in their social set. If those good women didn't spend their time with such foolery, neither would she.

Increasingly, Alice felt that she was masquerading as a happy player in Albert's "perfect" world, held constantly in check by his domineering nature and his growing concern that "his wife . . . moved in [her] proper setting and in a proper way and live smartly."[18] She would soon be emboldened to defy him, salvaging her artistic soul in the process. The impetus for doing so came from a most unusual quarter.

I N J A N U A R Y 1 8 8 2 a tall and massively built twenty-eight-year-old English poet stepped off the steamship *Arizona,* just docked in New York. Clad in a green fur-lined coat, yellow kid gloves, and a round sealskin cap, he glanced languidly at the crowd of reporters who stood breathlessly awaiting their first glance of the man reputed to be the real-life model for the simpering Bunthorne, a character in the wildly popular Gilbert and Sullivan operetta *Patience.*

The reporters were sorely disappointed. Although the poet's hair hung to his shoulders, at a burly six feet and two inches he didn't look anything like the slender, weak-kneed fop they'd expected. They'd been prepared for a delicate gent who caressed lilies. What they got was, as one reporter put it, "an athlete ... [who could] form a fist that would hit a hard knock." Or, as expressed in one of the countless verses about him that were soon to make the rounds, he had "Legs Apollo might have sighed for,/Or great Hercules have died for."

When he spoke, the newsmen hurtled from disappointment to confusion. It wasn't just the lazy-sounding, upper-class English drawl that baffled them, it was those incomprehensible pronouncements. He issued a stream of statements along the lines of "Man is hungry for beauty and must be filled," and "The secret of life is art." He tossed around phrases like "superlatively aesthetic" and "consummately soulful." At customs, asked by the inspector if he had anything to declare, he had turned to smile at the crowd of reporters and curious onlookers before answering. "Nothing," he announced. "Nothing but my genius."

Thus marked the start of Oscar Fingal O'Flahertie Wills Wilde's notorious American tour. Over the course of the next year he would traverse the country's length and breadth while lecturing on aesthetics. Though he was considered a poor speaker, certainly not the kind of windy orator Americans were fond of, his talks were usually packed. Admittedly the crowds came to bury, not to praise him, but quite often and usually in spite of themselves they went away pleased. Wilde was constantly in the headlines, usually portrayed as a kind of flower-toting namby-pamby. His exaggerated manner of speaking sparked massive fads, with seemingly half the nation exclaiming "How utterly utter!" or "Simply too-too!" In between lectures he was wined and dined by everyone from cowpokes to artistic and political luminaries.

In August of '82, Wilde came to lecture at New York's Long Beach Hotel, opened two years before on a Long Island barrier islet where once the Rockaway Indians had hunted, fished, and whaled. Although close to New York City, the hotel was situated on seven miles of pristine white-sand beachfront that was "equally agreeable for walking or driving." The elegant Queen Anne hotel boasted sixteen private cottages, bathing houses, picnic pavilions, horseback riding on the beach, private dining rooms, two elevators, and such niceties as a music gazebo, billiards room, and wine café. The hotel was popular among the wealthy, not least because the new railroad allowed "business men [to arrive] early after business hours in the evening and return to the city by swift early trains in the morning."[19]

Among the guests that summer were Albert and Alice Barney, accompanied by their two daughters, ages six and three, and a nurse. Albert spent his weekdays in the city conferring on business matters involving the Pike estate and relaxing at his club. On weekends he joined his family.

One day the knickers-clad Wilde was walking through the public rooms when a captivating little girl in a lace dress ran toward him. Hell-bent on escaping a pack of chasing boys, she moved so fast that her long golden hair streamed behind her. Sensing the child's distress, Wilde bent down and scooped her upward, rescuing her from, in her description, "my terrified course to his considerable height."[20] She always remembered that, despite his giant size, he was kind and gentle, placing her on his knee and sweeping her into a story. For the rest of her life Natalie thought of her encounter with Oscar Wilde as her mind's first great adventure.

Soon Alice appeared in search of her daughter and found her quietly listening to the poet's tale. She knew who Wilde was, of course: everybody did. He'd lectured in Cincinnati that year and been well received, thanks largely to his complimentary remarks about the city's artistic life. There were, admittedly, rumors about his depravity and the hopelessly mad members of the modern artistic cult to which he belonged, but in her typical live/let live fashion Alice wasn't terribly concerned with all that. Ever polite, she thanked him for his kindness to Natalie, gathered up her daughter, and disappeared.

The next day Wilde threw himself down on the beach, uninvited, beside Alice and the tiny Natalie, who was playing in the sand. "He was tall, broad of shoulder and of perfect physique," Alice wrote with honest admiration, "such as one generally associated with the ancient Greek youths, and in his bathing suit he showed to full advantage there on the white sands of Long Beach."[21]

The two near-strangers proceeded to have a conversation of startling intimacy, one which sent Alice ricocheting back and forth between hope and sadness. The free-spirited Wilde was accustomed to frank discourse. But Alice—familiar with the surface chitchat of polite society and married to a man with whom she couldn't really talk—wasn't. Wilde's probing questions and insightful comments rocked her to the roots.

After mocking the prudish swimming costumes of nearby women, with their long-sleeved tops, bloomers extending below the knee, skirts, shoes, and stockings, Wilde declared that it was imperative to follow natural impulses. "Expression is living," he said. "Suppression is dying, or worse." While Alice pondered his words, Wilde gently stroked Natalie's hair. Almost distractedly, he murmured: "You knew Stanley, didn't you, Madame Alice?" Unnerved, she admitted that, yes, she had known him well. Her manner was cold but her voice trembled: she hadn't mentioned Stanley's name aloud for more than six years, not since the ugly confrontation with Albert.

Wilde surprised her yet again by asking what interests her husband had. This brought Alice to a stop. What, after all, did interest Albert? She looked at Wilde, embarrassed, and then glanced at Natalie, "an angel of gold and ivory," and admitted the painful truth: Albert wasn't interested in much of anything, except . . .

"Natalie," she said, turning to Wilde. He looked at her so intently that she felt he was staring right through her.

"Then it is true," he said simply, and went on to say that he knew of and understood her love for Stanley, even if she couldn't admit it to herself. Alice was completely stunned, feeling that Wilde had "penetrated her most secret thoughts." She felt like crying. Unable to reply, desperate to change the subject, she looked blankly across the water and muttered, "Natalie . . . Mr. Barney is interested in Natalie!"

From there the conversation moved to safer subjects—Stanley's adventures, Wilde's observations about America—before veering back to dangerous ground. Wilde had heard that Alice was of an artistic nature, that she both "sang and drew." He glanced probingly at her. "Are you given a chance [to do so]?" he asked. She protested that she'd been too busy for art since Natalie's birth. And then, doubtless to divert Wilde's attention from the painful subject of her dead creative life, she told a lie.

"I was very ill," she said.

"And unhappy," he rejoined.

When Alice again cited the lack of time, Wilde cut to the heart of the matter. "Does Mr. Barney encourage you?" he asked bluntly.

"No," she replied bitterly. "Art means nothing to him."

"I see," he said gravely, and they fell into a companionable silence. Alice felt a profound bond of understanding and sympathy from the Englishman.

The rest of their time on the beach was uneventful. Alice watched contentedly while Wilde played with "the gold and white ball of fluff that was Natalie." He swung the child high in the air, making her happy laugh ring out. Before parting, Wilde asked Alice to meet him the next morning for a swim, daring her not to wear "that awful skirt, or those shoes or stockings!" She agreed, but only if they could do so very early, before Albert arrived from New York City.

Wilde knocked on her door at seven the next morning and a few minutes later they were marching to the water. The beach was empty at that hour, and Alice thrilled to the "fresh kiss of the morning wind on hair, face and limb." She drew back, afraid, from the unusually large waves, but was chastised by Wilde: "He who knows not daring knows not joy!" he said, laughing, and pulled her in.

In the water Alice broke her toe. Wilde carried her to her bedroom, summoned a doctor, and hovered—a purple silk dressing gown embroidered with white lilies stretched across his massive shoulders—while the doctor bandaged her up. Afterward he brought her breakfast on a tray and a huge assortment of roses. They talked until Wilde was forced to leave for the next segment of his lecture tour. His last words heading out the door were: "Joy is consummation and is its own ending . . . Adios, Madame Alice!" They would never see one another again.

In his wake Alice lay abed and contemplated her broken toe. How, she wondered, would she explain it to Albert? Bathing with a depraved, near-naked English poet at seven in the morning wouldn't sit well with him, but she'd think of something. Years later she summed up her Wildean adventure: "[I] had known daring and had gotten joy, plus a broken toe. It was worth it."

NATALIE FIRST VISITED Europe in 1883, when she was six years old. As an adult, most of her memories of the trip were vague, having to do with missing her pets, exploring the wonders of a Belgian zoo, and discovering "French baths" (bidets), which she used as swimming pools for her dolls. One incident, however, remained vivid: in Belgium, she and Laura were repelled and angered to see a woman and a dog harnessed to and pulling a cart weighed down with heavy milk tins, while a man ambled lazily alongside smoking a pipe. The girls were too young to grapple with ideas like feminism, but old enough to know injustice when they saw it. Years later, when Natalie said that she and Laura considered themselves feminists from that day on, she meant that the sight of that woman harnessed to the dogcart began to shape, and would forever color, their views on the role of women in the world.

The Barneys were accompanied on their European voyage by Alice's niece, a sweet-natured teenager named Berthe. Aboard ship and in crowded hotels, Natalie and her cousin shared a bed. Natalie developed a crush on the older girl, clinging to her throughout the night and refusing to leave her side during the day. Once, watching Berthe kiss a photograph of a boy back in Dayton, she felt strangely angry. Much later she realized that the kiss had provoked her first experience of jealousy.

The European trip, ostensibly arranged to find a boarding school for the girls, marked a turning point in the Barney marriage. Alice had taken Wilde's advice so much to heart that the phrase "Expression is living, suppression is dying" now characterized her outlook on life. Once abroad, the artist within her broke loose. She visited museums often, spending hours before the world's great paintings. She bought a sketchbook and, as on her first European trip, filled it with impressions of people and scenery. Now, however, she was no longer a teenager passing time; she was a woman in search of purpose.

Back home in Cincinnati, Alice signed up for a class in china painting. This art, which consisted of brushing elaborate nature scenes onto dinnerware, had grown increasingly popular with American women since the 1870s. A wealthy Cincinnati woman named Maria Longworth Nichols liked the art so much that she bought her own kiln and began experiments with glazes, colors, and clay mixtures. In 1880, she established Rookwood Pottery, one of the world's first industrial enterprises run by a woman. Today those early Rookwood pots are among the most collectible on the American scene.

Rookwood offered classes and the use of its kiln to local residents, and it was here that Alice came to learn china painting. She wasn't yet bold enough to take a class without Albert's approval, but he willingly gave permission. Since dishware painting was popular with other women in their set, he considered it harmless.

Harmless, indeed! Little did Albert realize that, with this simple step, Alice's path forever diverged from his. At Rookwood she met women who were serious about being artists. One in particular, Elizabeth Nourse, had recently graduated from Cincinnati's McMicken School of Design and actually made a living with her brush. She quickly spotted Alice's talent and encouraged her to draw, then to paint, and then to study painting in Paris. Eventually Alice's work would sell for handsome sums and win significant awards both in France and in the United States. Today many of her works reside at the Smithsonian American Art Museum in Washington, D.C.

But in 1883, twenty-six-year-old Alice Pike Barney, mother of two, was still struggling to find herself while coping with a difficult and demanding husband. And all the while she was being carefully observed by a tiny person of perception and intelligence: her daughter Natalie.

Just as her father's excessive drinking inspired Natalie's later temperance toward alcohol, surely his treatment of Alice affected her ideas about marriage, independence, and a woman's role. Natalie would one day write negatively, almost venomously, of marriage, and she formed her earliest views on the subject at home. Although she dated her feminism from that early sighting of a woman harnessed to a dogcart, her feminist views were nurtured and solidified within her own family—where Alice, burdened by Albert's tantrums and ultimatums, was symbolically harnessed to a cart of her own.

The truth about how often Albert berated Alice, and whether his abuse was solely verbal, is undocumented. Neither Alice nor her daughters left details, which is hardly surprising. Even today most women are loath to admit spousal abuse; in the Victorian era such behavior was often accepted as normal. Whether or not Albert was physically abusive, one thing is certain: his treatment of Alice enraged Natalie. She loved her father, but she would never forget or forgive his brutality. Writing him at the century's turn, she said:

You must understand how petty, how ugly our whole bringing up was. You showed me . . . all that marriage means—the jealousies, the scenes, the tyrannies . . . nothing was hidden from us. I was even made a witness when still a mere child of the atrocities and lamentable consequences an uncontrolled temper has when vented on even a good and surely kindly woman. I hope you will not make me repeat two fold the harm you have done me, by being . . . cruel toward my mother.—Seeing all this made me lose faith in you—respect for you. I no longer felt myself your daughter: is anyone fit to guide another who cannot even control his own passions?[22]

Although little could be done about Albert's venomous moods, their overall effect could be blunted. It's hard to know when, exactly, Alice hit on an effective modus operandi for dealing with his controlling ways, but by now she'd learned to remain calmly passive in the face of his complaints, agreeing with whatever he said. Then, once he was appeased and distracted, she turned around and continued doing whatever she'd been doing in the first place. Carving an artistic career in the face of her husband's resistance over the years practically demanded a gift for subterfuge. Observing her mother's machinations from an early age, Natalie, too, would become highly skilled at the art of hoodwinking Albert.

In middle childhood—at eight, nine, ten—Natalie's character began to sharpen enough so that it was possible to catch a glimpse of the woman she might become. She was a beautiful child with an extraordinary mass of long golden hair, delicate features, and large blue eyes. She was humorous, confident, and good-natured, and made friends easily. Her parents must have known they had a potential femme fatale on their hands. They were right, of course, though with a twist they could hardly have imagined.

Laura's character was also emerging as almost a polar opposite to that of her sister. Natalie liked to rebel; Laura was unquestionably obedient (Natalie once said that in childhood she played the devil to Laura's angel). Natalie was extremely charismatic, while Laura was shy, quiet, and serious-minded. Natalie was a natural athlete, and Laura wasn't. Natalie learned easily but rarely studied; Laura, who studied hard and learned more slowly, thought of Natalie as "the intelligent sister." Years later the journalist Janet Flanner summed up the two sisters in this way: "Natalie was not one for good works. She was one for bad works if they interested her. There was a reverse medal in the family; that was her sister, Mrs. Dreyfus—a very dull woman."[23]

On Mount Auburn, both sisters were learning French from their governess, Mélanie, who liked to seat them beneath the garden lime tree and read children's stories aloud from the *Bibliothèque rose*. She refused to translate, more or less forcing them to learn the language if they wanted to understand a tale. They were frequently joined in these readings by Violet and Mary Shiletto, the neighbors' daughters. Years later in Paris the Shiletto sisters would introduce Natalie to one of the legendary loves of her life.

Natalie loved the romantic French language, which she frequently heard at home; in fact, a few relatives on her mother's side spoke only French. The most interesting of these was Natalie's great-aunt Louise, the oldest child of William Miller and Ursula Meuillion, who had been born in 1803. Although long married to a descendant of Italy's Este family and living in Baltimore, Louise refused to speak English. Considered "a great hostess, schooled in European culture [who] took her pleasures seriously,"[24] she was reputed to keep the best table in Baltimore.

"She always arrived and departed in considerable style," her great-grandson recalled, "in a two horse carriage with a coachman and a footman. She was wildly extravagant."[25] She also loved theater and opera, drank bounteous amounts of champagne at lunch and dinner, and insisted on calling all her French maids Madeline. When she celebrated her 103rd birthday in 1906, newspapers nationwide marked the occasion. Louise was delighted by Natalie's schoolgirl French and her determination to become fluent. "You are someone after my own heart," this woman of strong and eccentric character assured the impressionable girl.

SOMETIME AROUND the age of ten Natalie had a sexual experience of some sort, most likely with a male cousin. Over the years she told various versions of the story. Most are harmless, echoing normal childish curiosity. One version, however, sounds a disturbing note.

The most commonly known version was told by Natalie, in her late eighties, to Jean Chalon, who included it in *Portrait of a Seductress*. In this tale, she is playing in a barn with a ten-year-old cousin who suddenly pulls out and displays his engorged penis. She refuses to touch his penis when asked, but finally agrees to tie it with a string and lead him about while he dances like a circus bear. He must have enjoyed it, she jokingly told Chalon, because afterward he was at her beck and call.

In the late 1940s, Natalie wrote *Mémoires secrets,** recollections of her life

---

*These memoirs had two alternate titles: *L'amant feminin* and *Nos secretes amours*. Natalie often recycled titles. She originally used *L'amant feminin* in the 1920s for an unpublished novel. *Nos secretes amours* would live again as the title for a posthumous collection of verse by poet Lucie Delarue-Mardrus, edited and published by NCB in 1951. To avoid confusion, I'll refer to Barney's memoirs only as *Mémoires secrets*.

from childhood through her affair with Pauline Tarn. These unpublished memoirs contain three separate tales of sexual encounters involving cousins. In one, Natalie and her female cousins are playing in the barn with a neighbor boy, Jessie, whose body fascinates them. They examine his penis, and one of the girls even sits atop him and jiggles about like a grown-up woman. Later, playing a game called "Bear," Natalie wants to attach Jessie to a leash around the neck and act as his trainer. However, since he is afraid of being strangled, she ties the leash to his "little sex" and makes him walk around on all fours. In another tale, when Natalie allows a young cousin to touch her budding breasts, he grows inflamed and murmurs, "Aphrodite, Aphrodite, don't tempt me!"[26]

The third and troubling version occurs early in *Mémoires secrets,* when Natalie is about ten years old. Her favorite boy cousin, wanting her to witness the astonishing manner in which his penis can grow, offers to let her touch it. Refusing "this honor," she runs away and hides in the photographic darkroom of another cousin, a handsome redhead of seventeen. This young fellow has been developing pictures, and while she studies them in the dim light, he stands behind her. "But why," she wrote with feigned naïveté, "did he seem to shudder while raising my dress and rummaging about with my underthings?" All the while he boasts of his adventures with the maid, who has a "well-feathered nest where he satisfies himself each night." Natalie, on the other hand, he describes as a deplumed little birdling. "A birdling," she recalled, "who escaped by quickly flying out the door."[27]

There seems no reason to doubt Natalie's story. While she had nothing against altering the truth when it suited her, she usually did so with the intent of putting herself in a more positive light. But here, in the tale of the older cousin, she had nothing to gain. She makes no attempt to shape the reader's perspective. She tells the story simply, without emphasis, and abruptly moves on.

In other tales involving cousins and sex, Natalie is the one in control, leading young boys by their cock or wielding her newly discovered powers as a temptress. Only in the darkroom is she forced to flee—by a cousin who is considerably older.

With so few facts available, it is useless to speculate on what actually may or may not have happened in that darkroom—let alone what effect the incident might have had on young Natalie. It's reasonable to assume, however, that, by finally recording the story in the pages of *Mémoires secrets,* she was attempting to come to psychological terms with, and close the door on, a disturbing memory.

IN 1887 three major events brought great changes to the Barneys. First, Julia Smith Barney died, leaving E.E.'s vast fortune to her children and transforming Albert, at long last, into a supremely wealthy man. Second, Natalie and Laura entered Les Ruches, a French boarding school the family had visited on their 1883 European trip. Third, Alice won Albert's permission to study painting in Paris.

Albert had two good reasons to agree to Alice's sojourn. First, Natalie and Laura, only ten and seven, had never before been away from home. Both parents felt comfortable with the idea that Les Ruches, located in Fontainebleau, was but a short train trip from their mother in Paris. The second reason was that, temporarily divested of his family, Albert would be able to enjoy a bachelor's freedom. "After ten years of marriage," Alice's biographer wrote, "the stage was being set for the establishment of a pattern based upon keeping up appearances. . . . [Albert] saw no reason why he could not abandon their marital farce and go to London. Let Alice amuse herself with putting brush to canvas."[28]

And so, in the summer of 1887, a few months before school would start, the Barneys came to France. Natalie had been too young on her first visit to appreciate Paris. Now, almost eleven, her lifelong love for the city was born.

Paris then was a relatively simple and quiet place, a city of horse-drawn cabs and lively river traffic: colorful barges, simple fishing skiffs, the large pleasure boats known as *bateaux-mouches*. A bridle path still ran along the Champs-Elysées, then a street of elegant private homes. Mornings saw the wealthy elite and the great courtesans riding in stately open carriages on the pathways of the Bois. Goats grazed and chickens pecked on the steep slopes of Montmartre, and looming over the city, visible from every corner, was the 984-foot iron tower being constructed by engineer Alexandre-Gustave Eiffel for the Paris Exposition of 1889.

In the late fall, arriving at Les Ruches for the start of school, Natalie and Laura were traumatized by the reality of leaving Mama and Papa to live with strangers. They cried; they sobbed; they created such a fuss that the Barneys decided to delay their enrollment. A few hours after arriving in Fontainebleau the entire family returned to Paris. Soon Albert traveled on to London, leaving the women on their own. It was the beginning of a pattern—Albert in London or America, his wife and daughters in Paris—that continued for years.

During this initial separation, Alice stayed busy with museums and art classes, leaving the girls in the care of a governess. They reunited with Albert for the Christmas holidays and traveled to the Côte d'Azur, where Natalie fell in love with the honey-perfumed scent of the Midi.

A new willfulness was emerging in Natalie. She disliked the new governess, Miss Bruce, and was forever urging Laura to escape her clutches. Once, taken ice skating, the sisters glided swiftly away, leaving the hapless woman unable to catch up (Miss Bruce was the first in a long, unhappy line of chaperones to meet a similar fate at Natalie's hands). When Alice learned that Miss Bruce was punishing her daughters by making them stand for hours in a corner, she fired her. Natalie considered this a victory, "but, fearful that she would just be replaced by another ogre, we declared ourselves ready to return to Les Ruches."[29] Thus, in late January or early February, the girls finally began school.

FONTAINEBLEAU'S LES RUCHES WAS Europe's most prestigious school for wealthy girls. As such, it appealed to Albert, who believed that only a European education would give his daughters the polish they needed to attract suitable husbands. A superb irony is at work here, because if Albert had paid less attention to the school's exclusivity and more to the ideas of founder Marie Souvestre, he wouldn't have let his girls anywhere near the place.*

Souvestre herself had recently left Les Ruches to establish another school, but her guiding principle remained firmly intact: to teach girls independent and logical thinking. Without such training, a more conventional Natalie might have emerged into adulthood to lead the life society expected of her, even if it meant suppressing her own desires. Instead of *l'Amazone*, we could have had *l'Anonyme*.

Souvestre was the daughter of French philosopher and playwright Émile Souvestre. Thanks to a childhood spent among liberal intellectuals, she grew into an original thinker and staunch feminist. For decades her principal aim as an educator was to nurture and develop independent women with sharp, analytical minds and strong character. Women, she believed, must learn to think for themselves.

The development of vigorous thought in others is a notable accomplishment in any age, but for a woman of the Victorian era to have produced scores of original thinkers, all of them adolescent and teenage girls, is remarkable. It was a time, after all, "when education was, in more mundane circles, considered dangerous to a woman's mental health, the pathway to madness and sterility. Independent and creative education for women was also thought to be dangerous to society. It would lead to votes for women, public activity, socialism, agnosticism, utopianism, opposition to war, the dissolution of empire. It was positively subversive. Marie Souvestre entertained it all. Her ideas were dangerous."[30]

---

*Ruches means "beehives" in French.

One of many pupils influenced by Souvestre was a painfully shy and gawky six-foot girl who ultimately became the most widely admired American woman of the twentieth century. In 1899, fifteen-year-old Eleanor Roosevelt came to England to board at Allenswood, Souvestre's school near Wimbledon. Eleanor soon became a favorite of the headmistress, who helped her gain confidence, poise, and maturity while encouraging the development of her keen intellect. Roosevelt wrote in her autobiography that Souvestre "exerted the greatest influence, after my father, on this period of my life."[31]

Les Ruches was strict and no-nonsense, with students subjected to an almost military discipline. French was the only language spoken, and those violating the French-only rule were expected to report themselves. The girls made their own beds, airing linens daily; a badly made bed earned a demerit. Closets and bureau drawers were inspected for neatness. Cold baths were taken nearly every morning in tin tubs. Two hours of daily outdoor exercise, with no excuses for bad weather, was mandatory, and skipping classes wasn't permitted. In a letter to her parents, Natalie mentioned that she had classes most days for six and a half hours, broken up by meals and exercise. Academic excellence was key to winning approval, and those who made the grade were praised and rewarded with special attention.

A girl named Dorothy Strachey (sister of writer Lytton Strachey) had attended the school a few years before Natalie. Decades later, when she was sixty-eight, Strachey published *Olivia*, a roman à clef about the sexual tension that ran rampant at Les Ruches (much of it involving passionate crushes on Souvestre, still in charge at the time).

According to Natalie, the feverish atmosphere of *Olivia* had disappeared by the time she arrived on the scene. Nonetheless, she added, there were, as at any boarding school, torrid affairs. She developed a crush on a beautiful older girl and took to climbing into her bed in the middle of night. They would hug and caress, causing the girl to refer to Natalie, in hushed giggles, as *mon petit mari* (my little husband). But, still young, Natalie was more intrigued by the year's great mystery: who had snuck up to a girl's bed in the wee hours to chop off her long, thick, chestnut-colored braid?

Despite the founder's radical feminist perspective, the curriculum at Les Ruches was quite traditional, so that parents analyzing the list of subjects found little if anything objectionable. As was considered fitting for girls, science was not on the agenda. Instead, history, poetry, literature, and languages were stressed.

Natalie's French was serviceable at that point, but gave no hint of her future fluent perfection. She earned a 3 in the language, the equivalent of a gentlewomanly C. Like all the girls, she wrote her parents dutifully each Sunday. She was expected to correspond in French, but usually offered feeble excuses for resorting to English. She enjoyed reading French literature, including La Fontaine's fables and the hymns of Victor Hugo. Her love of poetry began at Les Ruches: in one letter she tells her parents that her mind is so full of verse that it's affecting her concentration on other subjects.

The school's grading system ranged from a 5 for performance "without fault" to a 0. If her 1888 spring-term grades are a measure, Natalie was, depending on the subject, a middling-to-excellent scholar. Besides that mediocre 3 in French, she received a 2 in both orthography and history, a 4 in arithmetic, and a 5 in geography.[32] Her orthography, or spelling, improved greatly in the years ahead but was amusingly creative at the time: *gelly* (jelly), *meet* (meat), *panzys* (pansies), *jimnastic* (gymnastic), *valiable* (valuable).

Natalie also received training in the arts vital to the life of a proper lady: dancing, deportment, singing, calligraphy, drawing, and the ability to make a proper curtsy. Music was on the agenda, too. Considered an accomplished violinist in her twenties, Natalie began her musical studies here.

Plenty of time was made for little-girl activities. Natalie enjoyed climbing rocks and trees, and once made her way to the top of a nearby telegraph pole. She took up tennis and liked it so much that she played even in bad weather. One snowy day she talked a friend into a match inside a glassed-in passageway. Inevitably, a pane shattered, ending indoor tennis forever. Croquet and long walks were popular, as was gardening. Each girl received a small plot in which to grow whatever she liked; Natalie chose "panzys," radishes, and heliotropes. Obsessed with stamp collecting, she begged her parents to send stamps from their travels, marveled over a friend's stamps that were "thousands" of years old, and painstakingly arranged her own collection of more than seven hundred items.

The students enjoyed creating theatrical entertainments: circuses, musical concerts, chorales, and plays. Natalie once portrayed Sleeping Beauty. "I was in one of my white dresses on a sofa with gauze all around me," she related. "The prince . . . was kneeling down beside the sofa. She was dressed in red velvet pants all trimmed with gold braid and a white jacket trimmed with gold and a black velvet coat about like the one I run to the dining room in."[33] Natalie/Sleeping Beauty, upon being kissed by the Girl/Prince, awakened.

For Natalie, of course, the most important activity was horseback riding. Her letters from Fontainebleau are filled with chatter about horses. Presaging the future, there are constant appearances of the word *l'Amazone*. Depending on its context, the word can mean a horsewoman, a woman's riding habit or skirt, the act of riding sidesaddle, or a legendary female Greek warrior. *"J'aime beaucoup l'école d'amazone,"* she informed Albert in early 1888.[34] She rode every Thursday afternoon under the tutelage of her enthusiastic riding master, M. Lazare, and her equestrienne skill improved rapidly. She exchanged her pony for a gentle horse, and then moved to a "very lively horse."

Sometime during the school year Natalie menstruated for the first time, fainting at the sight of her own blood. She was brought to the private rooms of the school's director, who suggested that she stretch out on the chaise. The well-intentioned woman tried to calm Natalie by reading poetry aloud. Unfortunately, her choice of verse, André Chénier's "La Jeune Captive," was a disaster. One of the most beloved poems in French history, it was written while the imprisoned Chénier awaited trial for his criticism of the Revolution (he would be guillotined in 1794). The poem contains the tragic, frequent refrain, "I do not want to die yet!"

The terrified Natalie, convinced that the blood trickling from her body meant that her life was ebbing away, seized the refrain and repeated it again and again: "I do not want to die yet! I do not want to die yet!" In this traumatic way she entered womanhood.

Later, when her fear subsided, she recalled a comment her mother had made while Natalie studied an aquarium. Pointing out the curious red strings trailing behind certain fish, Alice murmured that something similar happened to girls around the age of twelve when they were ready to become women. "You must not be too surprised," she added. Natalie *had* been surprised—there was no doubt about that. It was one of the last times that anything of a sexual nature would catch her unawares.

WITH HER GIRLS tucked safely away at Les Ruches, Alice began carving out a place among the growing ranks of American artists in Paris. Most were men, but an increasing number of women had begun to appear. They came not only for the top-notch training obtainable in private ateliers and schools, but because Paris offered far more personal freedom than a woman could find at home.

Not that female art students of Alice's day were treated equally with men. They were not. To begin with, they weren't permitted entry to the most important place of artistic study in the world, the École des Beaux-Arts, which wouldn't open its doors to women until 1896. Denied that school's rigorous training and important contacts, women were forced to study elsewhere. A few private schools maintained separate studios for women, and many established artists accepted private students.

Once enrolled, women faced economic discrimination, paying twice as much tuition as men for half the instruction. According to art historian Lois

Marie Fink, the customary practice was to arrange "for instructors to visit the women's classes once a week, whereas in the men's studios they came twice weekly. Another difference was expressed in very tangible terms: money. Fees for women were exactly double those for men."[35]

But women persevered and many managed to succeed. Probably the greatest artistic success story among American women of Alice's time was Mary Cassatt (whose nephew would become Natalie's fiancé). Cassatt came to Paris in 1866, studied with Jean Gérôme, and was soon asked by Edgar Degas to exhibit with his Impressionist friends. Her subject matter (mothers and children) was dismissed by male critics, but she sold well. Today she is considered one of the major painters of the nineteenth century, and her works are essential to any serious collection of Impressionist art.

Some American women pursuing successful artistic careers in Paris in 1888 were, or would become, Alice's friends. Elizabeth Nourse, who first encouraged her to paint, was one of the first American women accepted into the Société National des Beaux Arts. New Englander Mary MacMonnies Low served as president of the American Woman's Art Association of Paris. And Lilla Cabot Perry, a Boston socialite who began painting in 1884 at the age of thirty-six, often worked beside her friend Claude Monet in Giverny.

Alice would have an impressive career, too, but in early 1888 she considered herself a beginner. Once the girls were in school she began classes with French painter Charles E. A. Carolus-Duran. Although largely forgotten today, he was then highly respected as a painter and teacher (his most famous pupil was John Singer Sargent). The fact that he "dressed like a comic opera idea of a bohemian artist"[36] appealed to Alice's innate sense of theater.

One weekend Alice took her daughters to meet Carolus-Duran at his studio, and he agreed to paint their portraits during the upcoming Easter vacation. Both girls posed in old-fashioned costumes. In *Mémoires secrets* Natalie said that she selected her costume in honor of Oscar Wilde's fairy tale *The Happy Prince*, but in *Souvenirs indiscrets* she claims the clothes were her mother's idea, chosen to keep the portraits from dating. The truth is probably somewhere in between, with Alice favoring historic dress and Natalie supplying a specific idea.

Costumes would play a big role in Natalie's life, something that can be attributed in large part to her mother. Alice's early years were spent behind the curtains of an opera house, thrilling to the spectacle of Roman soldiers, Greek maidens, Germanic goddesses, or whoever the night's performance demanded. Her daughters inherited her love of costume, along with a hand-colored tome, *Costumes Through the Ages,* that had once belonged to Sam Pike. They spent hours poring over it and both considered it their favorite childhood book.

For her Carolus-Duran portrait the dour Laura was portrayed against type as a sort of jovial Frans Hals *Bürgermeister* (never again, quipped Natalie, would her sister achieve such a cheerful expression). Natalie was very much in character in the luxurious garb of a Renaissance page. The painting shows the eleven-year-old quite at home in a handsome costume of thick velvet and rich brocade. Hands placed insouciantly on hips, short cape spread across her shoulders, long blond tresses escaping from a princely cap to tumble to her waist, she stares, at once somber and amused, at the world.

That summer Alice took the girls on a tour through Brittany, where she completed one of her first full-scale portraits, that of a peasant woman wearing the region's traditional white-winged headwear. Pleased with the painting, Carolus-Duran submitted it to the jury for the 1889 Paris Salon. It was accepted. Excited and happy, Alice signed on for a new series of lessons in October, when the girls returned to school.

Before she could begin, however, Albert arrived with surprising news: they were moving to Washington, D.C., and he needed Alice at home to supervise the packing and relocation. Her disappointment must have been great, but, as usual, she bowed compliantly to his wishes. Shoving her own desires to the back burner and leaving the girls at Les Ruches, she accompanied Albert back to Cincinnati.

WITH HIS MOTHER'S estate finally settled and distributed, Albert was now worth about $5 million ($90 million today). Given that he'd spent his entire life yearning for the money and freedom to live "properly," it's reasonable to assume that his choice of the nation's capital as a fit backdrop was carefully considered. He probably realized that New York society would not easily embrace the son of a midwestern industrialist. Washington's elite, on the other hand, composed of constantly changing politicians, the military, and old as well as nouveau money, would be receptive to a charming man of means and his handsome family. By moving to Washington and making a show of his wealth, Albert Barney could join the city's elite.

And make a show he did, not least by putting two lavish homes under simultaneous construction. The first was a town residence at 1626 Rhode Island Avenue, N.W., in the fashionable area off Scott Circle. With its music room, library, inner courtyard, and picture gallery, there was nothing modest about the huge Italian-style manor with its odd Gothic touches.

The second home was a twenty-six-room summer "cottage" in Bar Harbor, Maine. Called Ban-y-Bryn after a Welsh castle, it stood four stories high and had a spectacular ocean view. Alice had a studio in the round tower, complete with floor-to-ceiling windows and a fireplace. There were also five bedrooms and a nursery, various parlors, a large dining room, two covered verandas, a wine cellar, a servants' hall and bedrooms, a butler's pantry, various decks, and a loggia.[37] The front was graced with a beautiful, sweeping lawn; the rear faced a thick pine forest. Newspapers covered the home's debut in grand style. "A Palatial Residence: One of the Largest and Handsomest Cottages on the Island," one headline proclaimed. The general consensus: the Barney cottage, "in the matter of size and cost, will rank with the best houses at Bar Harbor."[38]

The Barneys had vacationed at Bar Harbor, located on Maine's Mount Desert Island, since the early 1880s. The island had attracted visitors beginning in the 1820s, when yachtsmen came to hike and hunt. By the 1870s wealthy summer visitors, tired of the crowded hotels, began to build summer homes known as cottages. At first simply designed, they soon became huge mansions with thirty or more rooms, and often included ballrooms, billiard parlors, and libraries. Surrounded by beautifully landscaped grounds and lush gardens, some even had private swimming pools, a great rarity at the time. By the time Ban-y-Bryn was built, "Bar Harbor was the place to be if you were a member of high society. It quickly rivaled Newport, Rhode Island in the caliber of its guests,"[39] who included Vanderbilts, Whitneys, and newspaper publisher Joseph Pulitzer. The island was particularly popular with socialites, diplomats, and high-level politicians from the nation's capital.

The resort's summer season was rife with teas, formal dances, coming-out parties, elaborate dinners, and sporting events. There were also plenty of activities for children, including picnics, beach parties, and hayrides. One newspaper reported on a summertime children's parade in which "the Misses Barney, who drove a tandem team, with mounted grooms, looked so pretty and sweet that they were applauded all along the line. Their trap was covered with wheat and poppies and . . . Miss [Natalie] Barney drove with her beautiful head uncovered, her flaxen hair, which falls below her waist, looking like gold in the sun."[40]

In short, Bar Harbor was summertime heaven for those with the connections and money to fit in. The wealthy and good-looking Barneys, with their charming manners, showplace homes, and lovely daughters (soon to be marriageable and highly dowered), entered this milieu with little fuss. But despite their surface acceptance and the social clout that Alice, especially, would come to wield, they would always be thought of as rich Ohio newcomers.

For their oldest daughter, however, it was another story. Until her tenth year, when she'd gone off to Europe and Les Ruches, all of Natalie's relatively inexpensive childhood wants—a pony or fairy-tale books in French—had been satisfied. When she returned to the States in the summer of 1889, she was twelve-and-a-half, hitting the age when her tastes could and would become expensive. With lucky timing, her parents had just became financially able to continue giving her everything she wanted, no matter the cost. Having always been given everything she'd ever wanted, her transition from moderate to extreme wealth was seamless. She thus approached this new, privileged world with a bedrock sense of entitlement.

And she fit the part. At Les Ruches she'd lived in close quarters with girls who possessed great wealth and highborn titles. Within these favored ranks the students had been democratized: they dressed alike, ate the same food, competed in the same games. Natalie left Les Ruches feeling that membership in this ruling class was her birthright. That she took her membership in this elite for granted may explain why she could so easily thumb her nose at it later.

NATALIE'S EARLIEST MEMORIES of Washington involved playtime with her sister and studies with their new German governess. Fräulein Nordheim had been their favorite instructor at Les Ruches, and they had begged their parents to hire her. Under the fräulein's watchful eye, the girls studied, took walks, and played in the magnolia-scented parks. On those happy days when the Italian organ grinder showed up, Natalie would stop whatever she was doing to watch his colorfully dressed monkey cavort to the toe-tapping hurdy-gurdy tunes.

Late one night, Natalie and Laura rose from their beds to investigate a strange noise. They found the sleepwalking governess clutching a pair of scissors, and watched, thrilled with horror, as she grabbed Albert's hat from the hallway rack and sliced it to pieces. The great Les Ruches mystery was finally solved: it had been Fräulein Nordheim who had sliced off their classmate's beautiful braid while she lay sleeping. Worried about employing a knife-wielding somnambulist, Alice and Albert fired the unfortunate young woman.

She was replaced by an Austrian whose constant tears over a broken engagement moved Natalie to offer solace and softly murmured words. Natalie had begun to see that she had a knack for comforting women, and was happy to practice her methods in Alice's studio. If a beautiful social belle grew stiff while posing, Natalie came to the rescue with a gentle massage. She grew so adept at the art of touch that she could reputedly soothe away her mother's bothersome headaches.

At a time when women painters weren't taken seriously, especially those who were wealthy socialites, Alice persisted in her work. It was in Washington that she first won esteem from critics and artists alike. Many who had scoffed at her efforts were silenced when, in 1891, she won an important commission to paint the State Department's official portrait of former secretary John C. Calhoun. The painting was eventually exhibited at the 1893 Chicago World's Columbian Exposition.

Alice's accomplishments are particularly remarkable if one considers that, to please Albert and maintain harmony at home, she was also a successful society matron. This role necessitated never-ending social calls and being either the hostess of or a guest at an endless round of teas, balls, and dinners. With extraordinary energy and unflagging high spirits, she did all of this and still managed to paint. Journalists adored her pluck. "Mrs. Barney is as clever as she is good looking," one reporter gushed. "She is an artist, not a dilettante, BUT A GENUINE WORKER, who loves her art and strives to do something worth while."[41]

Both Natalie and Laura were frequent subjects of Alice's paintings, which usually possessed straightforward titles: *Natalie at Seven, Natalie with Mandolin, Natalie with Flowing Hair; Laura Attentive, Laura in Arabian Costume.* The girls' posing styles were as different as their personalities: Laura could sit quietly for hours, absorbed in her thoughts; Natalie was always restless and impatient.

Observing their mother's determined struggle to succeed, both girls learned the value of perseverance. Laura would apply this quality selflessly during her life of public and spiritual service. Natalie incorporated it in a more personal way, learning never to be dissuaded from a goal by another's objections. As an adult, when friends or discarded lovers described her as "cold" or "without a heart," it was this quality of deeply bred and unswerving tenacity to which they referred.

But Natalie would also be known for other qualities, including an unusually open-minded tolerance about many things. All through her life, friends and acquaintances felt they could tell her anything, no matter how shocking, without being judged. This quality began to appear in early adolescence, as evidenced by a girlish sentiment she inscribed to Laura.

Autograph books were a rage among American girls in the late Victorian era. Often elaborately bound in expensive velvet, their pages limned with gold leaf, they were intended for inspiring messages from friends and relatives. Laura received such a book during the 1889 Christmas holidays. The first autograph within its red-velvet covers, dated January 3, 1890, is that of her older sister, who had recently turned thirteen. In a neat, schoolgirlish hand she wrote: *Give every man thine ear, but few thy voice: Take each man's censure, but reserve thy judgment.* [signed] *Natalie Barney.*

At first glance it seems an unusually wary sentiment for someone so young—especially Natalie, for whom caution would never be a byword. But a

closer look reveals something far more profound. Her words constitute a prag-
matic yet infinitely positive formula for dealing with people, one she would
successfully adhere to throughout life: *Listen to others. Keep your opinions, if
you have them, to yourself. Take an accurate measure of, but don't judge, those to
whom you speak.* We will see these three hallmark qualities of Natalie's repeatedly in the pages ahead.

Alice penned her philosophy in Laura's book, as well: *Nothing is sweeter
than love, nothing more courageous, . . . nothing finer nor better in heaven and
earth. Love one another.*

It's a lovely sentiment, one she doubtless believed. However, Alice was finding it increasingly difficult to hold to such a philosophy in light of Albert's
indiscreet love affairs and incessant drinking. With no need to work, his life
now centered around his many clubs. He belonged to at least one in each city
he visited regularly. In Washington he was a founder of the Chevy Chase Club
and a member of the Metropolitan, Washington Golf, and Alibi Clubs.

This last organization is particularly interesting. It was a very exclusive
men's party club whose limited membership of fifty came to drink, shoot pool,
play poker, and cook dinners for one another. Women were only allowed entry
once a year for a Thanksgiving tea. There were no phones, and any wife who
wanted to reach her husband on the premises could do so only by telegram. If
she was foolish enough to come in person, she would automatically be told by
the butler that her husband wasn't there whether he was or not. If she asked
the butler whether her husband had been in the club on a certain day and at a
certain time, he would automatically say yes. Hence the name, Alibi Club.

Albert had little need of alibis, however, since he'd dispensed with the need
for discretion. In various writings Natalie refers to her father's public exhibitions of marital infidelity, which she viewed as shameful humiliations for her
mother.

Despite his own amorous affairs, Albert frequently accused Alice of being
unfaithful (no evidence exists that Alice had an extramarital affair). Once,
drunk and raging with jealousy over an affair he imagined she was having with
an Irish painter, he ordered her to leave the house forever. When she refused,
he grabbed their frightened daughters and exclaimed, "Since maman won't
leave us, we'll leave her!"[42] He whisked them to the railroad station, hurried
them onto a train for Dayton, and continued drinking whiskey in their compartment. During the night he woke Natalie, drunkenly proposing that they
die together by jumping beneath the train's wheels. She tried without success
to reason with him, telling him that his suspicions about Alice were absurd.

Then she watched, horrified, as he headed toward her sleeping sister, who,
she knew, would do anything Albert asked. Jumping up, she slapped her hand

on the brake cord and warned Albert that unless he ended his crazy behavior, she wouldn't hesitate to stop the train and draw a crowd. Her hard, steady gaze caused him to waver. Collapsing into his berth, he took a last gulp of whiskey and fell into a "drunken stupor." By this time Laura was wide awake, and the sisters clung to each other, weeping. The next day a sober and chastened Albert cut the journey short, and they took the evening train back to Washington.

After this incident Albert promised, not for the first time, that Natalie would never again see him drunk. She didn't believe him. Only thirteen, she already viewed her father as a pathetic figure engaged in a game she didn't understand. "Perhaps he took pleasure from torturing my mother," she wrote.[43] Albert had long given Natalie an unhealthy idea of men in general, and of male duplicity specifically. Marriage, as she had come to view it, annihilated independence; it was stifling, restrictive, debilitating. Young as she was, she knew she wanted no part of it. Not ever.

Such an attitude was destined to bring Natalie into conflict with her father, whose greatest wish was that she marry well. He had no qualms about her ability to do so. Taking note of her effect on males, he anticipated a brilliant marriage. Although not conventionally beautiful, Natalie had a quality that dazzled others. It was probably the combination of her strong will and dynamic presence, her sharp intelligence and wit, her wide, unusually blue eyes, and that pre-Raphaelite mass of untamed blond hair.

Alice, who took pride in "directing [my children] in the fullest expression of their individual inclinations,"[44] may have had more flexible dreams for her daughter. But no elasticity on her part could have prepared her for, or allowed her to condone, a side of Natalie's nature that began to emerge at about this time.

THREE

Adolescent and Debutante

1891–1898

Gentlemen may prefer blondes—but who says that blondes prefer
gentlemen?
—*Mae West*

> Was she so chaste,
> (I see it, sharp, this vision,
> and each fleck on the horse's flanks
> of foam, and bridle and bit,
> silver, and the straps,
> wrought with their perfect art,
> and the sun,
> striking athwart the silver-work,
> and the neck, strained forward, ears alert,
> and the head of a girl
> flung back and her throat.)
> —*H.D.*

ONE SPRING DAY in her fifteenth year, Natalie Barney stepped onto
a wooden box, gracefully pulled her floor-length skirts to the side,
extended her free hand to a waiting groom, and allowed herself to be
helped atop her mount. There were few things the young woman liked so

much as riding, and she particularly enjoyed a springtime canter through the woodsy terrain of Washington, D.C.

On this day Natalie was accompanied by her close friend Helen Morton, whose father was the nation's vice president. Both girls were horse-mad. High on youth, freedom, and the sensation of power that comes from controlling a magnificent beast, they rode for hours that day through the city's blossom-filled woods. Long since graduated from her pony to a plump and capricious cob, Natalie had become a skilled and daring equestrienne. She would soon scandalize society and become the stuff of gossip columns by publicly riding astride. But, not yet old or bold enough to blatantly flout convention, she now sat easily in her sidesaddle.

There are many photographs of Natalie *en Amazone*—decked out in riding gear—so it's easy to imagine what she looked like that day. Let's say that she was clad in a fitted, long-sleeved, dark silk bombazine jacket nipped at the waist and flared at the hips; a matching ankle-length skirt; and high, laced leather boots. Completing this natty outfit would have been fine leather gloves, a knotted riding crop, and a fashionable ladies' bowler.

As the two girls cantered along on that long-ago spring day, exchanging adolescent secrets and gossip, they suddenly spied beautiful Mary Leiter in the distance. One of the first Gibson Girl models and the most popular belle in Washington, Leiter would soon marry British diplomat and future viceroy of India George Curzon. This day, accompanied by another young swain, she drove a smart phaeton harnessed to two of her father's prize-winning race-horses. As Natalie knew, Helen had a secret crush on Leiter.

Hoping to impress that young woman with their horsemanship, the teens urged their mounts into a gallop and raced wildly past the phaeton. The star-tled racehorses bolted, and by the time Leiter brought them to a halt she was furious. Her beau, Natalie remembered long afterward, had turned pale, prov-ing himself "unsportsmanlike." Leiter let loose with a piece of her mind, upbraiding the girls for their reckless behavior, and trotted off.

Dejected, Natalie and Helen later consoled themselves at the piano with their favorite songs. Singing was a popular activity with their circle of boys and girls, who also enjoyed playing tennis, riding to hounds, and dancing. The whole gang often met on Connecticut Avenue and walked to Raucher's for ice cream. Natalie liked flirting with boys, but, as she admitted to Helen that day, she, too, had a crush on a girl—a friend of her Bar Harbor vacations, "S.M. of Philadelphia." They hadn't seen each other since the previous summer, but Natalie hoped that frequent letters, filled with proclamations of her faithful adoration, had kept their strong feelings alive.

In Victorian days hugging, kissing, and effusive expressions of love between young girls were viewed as a normal stage of feminine development and a harmless way of dealing with adolescent emotions. Girls often discussed their "crushes" openly, which explains why Natalie's gushy Valentine's Day poem to S.M. that year had probably raised no eyebrows: "If you could only love me/What is there in this world that I/Could wish but to be near thee/Or exiled from thee—die!"[1]

But the words had serious intent. Natalie later claimed that, by age twelve, she not only knew what her sexual tastes were but was determined not to be diverted from them. Now, at fifteen, her sexual sap was bursting to be tapped. She may not have had a completely clear picture of what she wanted to do with S.M., but her speculation was rapidly coming into focus.

Natalie did know something of sexual pleasure. She probably first discovered her erotic zones while horseback riding, a not-uncommon occurrence among adolescent equestriennes. But the first sexual joy she wrote about involved her, Leda-like, with a swan. One day while bathing she discovered that, by shooting warm water between her legs from a swan-shaped spout, she could produce a "glorious" sensation. Experimenting with the water's force and direction, she learned to prolong and then multiply her pleasure. "I had become my own mistress-lover," she rejoiced.[2] But ultimately, she knew, sex had little to do with spouting swans or jaunts in the saddle, and everything to do with other girls. She hadn't had the chance to do anything about it, but circumstances would begin to change that summer.

PREPARATIONS FOR RESIDENCE at Ban-y-Bryn were so demanding that Natalie and Laura were sent off at the beginning of each summer to their grandmother Pike's home in New York City. This year, while the Barneys oversaw the packing of trunks, sent servants ahead to open the cottage, and shipped off carriages, horses, and dogs, their daughters lolled about the Pike mansion reading poetry and gorging on chocolate cake. One of the poets Natalie liked at this time was Thomas Moore, whose "Lalla Rookh" she cites as the kind of forbidden, passionate verse her grandmother unwittingly allowed them to enjoy. Moore's work seems tame today, but it's interesting to note that his poem "The Time I've Lost in Wooing," contains lines that would become firmly associated with Natalie: "My only books/Were woman's looks."

Natalie's Bar Harbor days were filled with tennis matches, horseback riding, mountain climbing, lakeside picnics, grilled lobster suppers, and occasional fishing trips into the open ocean. When the waters were calm, she rowed on Frenchman's Bay with her friends, and sometimes, on deserted beaches, they reverted to a favorite childhood pursuit of searching for buried pirate's treasure. On Sundays, Albert often rented a large buckboard and draft horses to take his family and the servants on a leisurely promenade around the island. And of course there was the constant round of balls, receptions, dinners, and other activities of the social season.

Men began to notice Natalie this summer, and, for the most part, she liked the attention. The fact that she was attracted sexually to women rather than men couldn't—and didn't—negate her upbringing. Raised by highly social parents and possessed of an enormous capacity for fun, she had developed into an outgoing person who loved parties, conversation, and gossip. Soon, old enough to attend balls, she would shine as a flirt and collector of hearts whose dance card was always filled.

One of the men who noticed Natalie that summer was a Belgian attaché whom she describes as having a taste for minors. He took to cornering her at social functions for conversations in French that became, on his part, sexually suggestive. He once showed her a photograph of the reigning Parisian courtesan, La Belle Otéro, with whom he claimed to have spent an unforgettable night. "Unforgettable," Natalie snorted in *Mémoires secrets,* "for him!"

Natalie preferred boys her own age. Her bedroom had a balcony from which she suspended a basket, woven of fragrant grasses by local Indians, to be used by her friends for leaving notes. She often hauled up lovelorn poetry from a boy in her group, and when she agreed to kiss him she found the experience pleasing. Another young man woke her late one night by climbing onto the balcony drunk. He was too woozy to climb back, so Natalie snuck him down the grand staircase and shooed him out the front door. When Albert learned of this caper he worried that his headstrong daughter might have compromised herself with a kiss. He moved her into Laura's room, which, perched on Ban-y-Bryn's high side, was unreachable by naught but a monkey. Natalie's humiliation was twofold: not only was she forced to bunk with her little sister, but the room adjoined that of their governess.

Natalie tried all summer to attract the attention of S.M. She rode by her cottage at every opportunity and sent her reams of poetry. Finally S.M. invited her on an early Sunday morning excursion. They met at dawn, drove a runabout to the pond, picked bunches of blooming goldenrod, and returned to S.M.'s Unitarian church in time to arrange flowers for that day's service. A morning of religious worship wasn't what Natalie—who had already decided that "love and friendship would be my only religion"—had in mind.[3] But, characteristically undiscouraged, she kept to the chase.

That summer a young Russian girl visiting Ban-y-Bryn developed a crush of her own on Natalie, staring at her with devotion and hanging on her every word. Natalie found her colorless, but that didn't prevent her from slipping into the girl's bed one night. Finding no resistance, she practiced with her fingers the soft caresses she had learned with the swan, "perhaps to succeed with her, as with myself, in obtaining those extreme sensations."[4] The girl remained so unresponsive that Natalie, discouraged, ceased her explorations.

Next day, to her surprise, the girl was even more adoring, "attached . . . to my neck and to my every step."[5] Her lovesick mooning attracted notice, particularly from the Belgian diplomat. Jealous, he accused Natalie of loving women, calling her a *"vicieuse"* (pervert) and another name so foul that she refused to spell it out. His words took Natalie aback. Until then she'd never questioned her desires, considering them perfectly natural. To learn that they were a vice and, in the bargain, to be called a horrible name were devastating. For a while she would have nothing to do with the man.

As for the Russian girl, Natalie was sick of her. Since she showed no signs of leaving Ban-y-Bryn, Natalie herself departed. She accepted an invitation to a house party at the mainland home of a family friend, a member of Congress, whose three sons were her buddies.

During this visit a young man with literary tastes, whom Natalie refers to as Alcée in her memoirs, introduced her to a book that changed her life.* Published in 1885, it pulled together fragments of works by an ancient Greek poet named Sappho, whose sensuous and often erotic verse is addressed to women. In words two-and-a-half millennia old, Natalie was stunned to learn "that the greatest poetess of ancient Greece shared my attraction" for women. For the first time she saw portrayed the same emotions of love and jealousy that she herself had felt. Perhaps she wasn't a pervert after all, she thought. Confidence renewed, she confessed to Alcée her attraction to women. Instead of showing disgust, as the Belgian had, he became the first of many to link Natalie with Sappho, penning a poem that began: "Come, let us stand together/Thou and I, my Sappho." And so, as the house party continued, Natalie lived "several idyllic weeks filled with music, poetry and fervent understanding."[6]

THIS IDYLL OF UNDERSTANDING ended abruptly when word arrived that Natalie must return to Bar Harbor: Laura had overturned the pony cart, damaging her leg, and was limping so badly that her parents wanted to consult specialists in New York City.

---

*Alcée was short for Alcaeus, an aristocratic male poet who lived on Lesbos at the same time as Sappho. Natalie's Alcée was really John Ellerton Lodge, son of then congressman (later senator) Henry Cabot Lodge. John grew up to become director of the Freer Gallery in Washington, D.C. Until his 1942 death, whenever Natalie came to town they retreated to his office and talked for hours.

Twelve-year-old Laura was put into traction and lay abed for months, enduring pain and tedium while trying to be stoic. Her anguish so distressed Natalie that the Barneys thought it best to enroll her in a Manhattan boarding school from which she could visit Laura no more than once a week.

Later in life, few people understood the relationship between Laura and Natalie, and many assumed a strong mutual dislike. It was no secret that Laura disapproved of Natalie's pleasure-loving ways, or that Natalie considered Laura a stick-in-the-mud. Natalie constantly upbraided Laura about her rudeness and lack of tact; Laura ceaselessly criticized Natalie's frivolity and lack of caution. They argued frequently, muttered about each other to friends, and occasionally avoided each other.

Yet beneath the bickering was a deep, unbreakable bond forged from their earliest years. Natalie loved Laura, confided in her about everything, and relied on her in countless ways. Laura, in turn, admired her big sister's outgoing personality and ability to attract others. She was also proud of Natalie's accomplishments as a writer and literary salonist, constantly scissoring articles about her from newspapers to paste into scrapbooks or mail to friends and relatives. Laura once described Natalie as "the greatest pleasure and the greatest trouble rolled into one person, but as pleasure is rarer than all things it is the only memory that remains."[7] The fact that Laura chose to be buried with Natalie rather than her own husband speaks profoundly of their sisterly union.

Natalie always suspected that their solidarity was based on the telepathy they had shared since childhood. They often played a game with friends wherein Laura would leave the room while Natalie and the others randomly chose a book and selected a page number. Laura would be called back, and Natalie, her back turned, silently communicated the answer. Time and again Laura walked directly to the chosen book and opened it to the exact page. When the sisters played this game during Laura's months in traction, one neuropath was so impressed that he wrote an article about their telepathic powers for a medical journal. At the insistence of their parents, Natalie and Laura remained anonymous. "We were nevertheless proud," wrote Natalie, "to learn that we figured in an article as the case of L. and N."[8]

That winter, as Laura endured agony, her sister also suffered. Natalie thought only of Laura throughout the endless winter, to the extent that she would later remember nothing about the boarding school, "or even if I was living in my own body."[9] She couldn't sit without stiffly extending her leg, sympathetically feeling Laura's pain. She, "who never moved without running," now walked slowly, refusing to run even in school games. As the months passed,

Laura grew gaunt and pale. The family spent a sad Christmas at her bedside, and it wasn't until spring that she improved enough to leave the hospital.

SUMMER ROLLED around again, bringing the Barneys back to Ban-y-Bryn. The 1893 season started unhappily for Natalie: learning that S.M. was getting married, she broke down sobbing. She was depressed for a while, but eventually turned her attentions to another young woman.

Evalina Palmer had grown up in New York City's Gramercy Park, and was, like Natalie, a child of wealth. She was not, as has so often been written, an heiress to the British Huntley-Palmer biscuit fortune; in fact, she had no connection to that family. Her true background is far more interesting, at least to Americans: she was the great-granddaughter of famed Connecticut sea captain and sealer Nathaniel Brown Palmer. In 1820, commanding a forty-one-foot sealing vessel named *Hero*, twenty-one-year-old Palmer became the first person in recorded history to lay eyes on Antarctica* (the Antarctic's Palmer Station is named after him). Back in New England he made a fortune designing and commanding clipper ships.

Eva Palmer was a fragile beauty with sea-green eyes and thick, ankle-length red hair. She looked, thought Natalie, like a medieval virgin. But behind her gentle demeanor lay a strong-minded girl with an unconventional, independent nature. Such traits were encouraged by her father, who had founded a well-known discussion and debating society, the Nineteenth Century Club, which attracted controversial speakers such as atheists, anarchists, and Hindu swamis.

The Palmers were not only wealthy, but talented and artsy. Mrs. Palmer, a pianist, led a small orchestra that played in society parlors. She passed her musical talents on to Eva's brother, Courtlandt Jr., who was a student of Paderewski and went on to a successful concert career. Another brother, Bob, who taught Eva to smoke cigarettes and play poker, became a cowboy out West and then a planter in South America. Sister May was a painter, and Eva's talents ranged from literature to dance. According to Eva's great-granddaughter, Gina Sikelianos, two of the children were homosexual.[10] Eva was bisexual.

The Palmers spent most summers at their Bar Harbor cottage, and it was here, one summer when they were young, that Eva and Natalie first met. As children, the two spent most of their time outdoors. Behind the Palmer home

---

*While most record books credit Palmer with having "discovered" Antarctica, Britain and Russia continue to offer up rival contenders. Both nations had ships in the area at the same time as the United States.

was a running stream called Duck Brook, where they enjoyed jumping from rock to rock while trying not to fall in. Together they climbed mountains, traversed footpaths blazed by island pioneers, rode horses, and played "Indians" on the hillsides. "Barely adolescent," Natalie recalled, "we spent entire days promenading beside the sea, atop the mountains, or in the thick woods." With their distinctive coloring they had always made a striking pair, and Courtlandt Jr. took pleasure in watching the play of their "long hair, red and blonde, unloosened, spread in the sun, or mingling with the sea breeze."[11]

The friendship had been interrupted for a few years. Natalie had been away at Les Ruches, and the summer after her return the Palmers were in Scotland, staying with their friend Andrew Carnegie at his castle. Now, reunited, they took up their acquaintance where it had stopped—and then some. Feelings of love hit them both. Neither one knew where they were headed, exactly, but they knew they were moving toward something important. Almost instinctively, they conspired to remove themselves from prying eyes as often as possible. After riding lessons they would leave the ring and ride deep into the woods. Resting their horses in a clearing, they took each other's hand innocently, but "like a promise."

Fulfillment of this promise came about, in an odd sort of way, through Alice. Increasingly spunky and willing to risk Albert's disapproval, she had become something of a Bar Harbor impresario, writing and producing amateur entertainments in which her friends, daughters, and others took roles. Usually held at the upscale Kebo Valley Club, these theatricals were noted for their elaborate costumes. Natalie had portrayed La Cigale in a flamboyant gypsy outfit, as well as a Spanish flamenco dancer with castanets and clicking shoes. Her most challenging role, the Virgin Mary, required the simplest costume.

Alice's biggest variety show yet was planned for that summer. Natalie would appear in a pantomime as "Fair Rosamond," while Laura planned to recite a passionate composition about social injustice. Natalie lent her precious Sappho book to Eva, who offered to recite one of its poems at the upcoming theatrical—in the original Greek. The suggestion delighted Alice, who was unaware of the poem's significance. Eva appeared on stage dressed *à la Greque,* feet encased in white sandals with straps crisscrossing her legs, a gold band encircling her forehead, red hair falling clear to her ankles. Standing beside several faux Greek columns and accompanied by a harpist, she recited Sappho's verse to an uncomprehending but enthusiastic audience. As the applause died away, Eva joined Natalie behind the scenes. They hugged each other and slipped away. The time had come.

"A liaison ensued," Natalie wrote, "where poetry, Plato's *Banquet,* and nudism, all had a part in our Arcadian life. . . . We knew the sensual delights of our nudity amidst the river sources and on the mossy underwood. So accustomed were we to our nudity in a state of nature that, if someone fully dressed had surprised us, they and not us would feel shame."[12] She wasn't exaggerating with the Platonic reference. Eva, who would eventually dedicate her life to reviving Greece's Delphic tradition, had already begun to study the classical writers. She and Natalie spent hours talking about Plato and other ancient philosophers.

But beyond such intellectual pursuits was the newfound joy of sex. By all indications their "liaison" was the first for each. Eva, Natalie would say, "inspired me and taught me about love. She . . . was the mother of my desires, the initiator of my first joys."[13] She also stated that she hadn't wanted to possess Eva "like a young man wants to possess a virgin," but—and this is important, because it later becomes a foundation in her elaborate theory of love—"to lead her toward herself through me."[14] Through the purifying experience of love and passion, Natalie believed, she could bring others to a higher, stronger, and more confident state of being.

Although Palmer was quiet and intellectual, she could be impulsive. One day, while brushing her long red hair, she suddenly snatched a pair of scissors and hacked off a thick lock. She held it out to Natalie, who accepted it with a confused mixture of delight and dismay—delight at the generous gift, dismay at the marring of Eva's beauty. Eva silenced Natalie's protests by confessing that cutting her hair was no sacrifice; rather, it was revenge for the way people seemed to admire her hair more than herself.

There was truth to her complaint. In memoirs of the time it seems almost obligatory to discuss Palmer's hair. "A miraculous redhead," marveled Colette, "with hair down to her feet." Wrote Pauline Tarn: "Her hair is like a glorious halo about her pale brow." Poet Lucie Delarue-Mardrus enthused over her "two enormous plaits of red hair wound around her head like laurels," and so taken by Eva's tresses was Liane de Pougy that she used her as the model for Yvée Lester, the heroine of her 1906 novel about a woman who was the "prisoner of her red hair." Perhaps Natalie summed up Eva's dilemma best in *Nouvelles pensées de l'Amazone*: "A redhead said to me: 'When one has red hair, one is all alone, like an island; no one dreams of landing!' "

It wasn't long before the new relationship attracted unwanted attention. The Belgian diplomat, still nurturing hopes for his own liaison with Natalie, informed her that tongues were wagging over her obvious preference for women. He begged her to come to her senses, or she would find herself condemned by society. Loving women, he warned was against nature. "Against nature?" she exclaimed. "Even when it's nature that has made us this way?"

Her tastes, he replied, were considered a shameful vice by honest people. "I'm as honest as any of them," Natalie said, "and I feel no shame."[15]

The Belgian persisted. People were distancing themselves and referring to her as a pervert, he said, but if she allowed him to show his love, he could ease her onto the correct path—one that would lead to happiness. He pulled her tightly against him. Astonished, she pushed him roughly away. He left with tears in his eyes, hurt and angry.

The diplomat was probably exaggerating the gossip about Natalie, hoping to use it toward his own ends. To most people, the sixteen-year-old girl was a prize: pretty, smart, funny, rich. She had a wide circle of friends her own age and was considered saucy and bright by adults. Few would have found anything odd in the fact that she and Eva had been inseparable that summer. If they disappeared into the woods all day, or locked themselves in a bedroom, what of it? Many other girls did the same thing. It was in the nature of teenage girls to stick together as if glued.

Still, some had definitely begun to notice Barney's "tastes," as they were called by the Belgian. In various writings Natalie has admitted that, in her innocence, she came right out and told close friends how much she loved women. She recalled being approached by May Palmer, who insisted that Natalie leave her "defenseless child of a sister" alone (and offered herself as a more challenging substitute). And, of course, a few observant individuals like the Belgian arrived at theories on their own. The word about Natalie was out there, but in a minor way. With summer's end approaching, the small amount of gossip in the pot remained at a bare simmer, tucked harmlessly away on a back burner.

Season's end also meant returning to studies. Natalie begged her parents to let her attend the same school as Eva, but arrangements had already been made elsewhere. She and Eva would board at separate pensions, seeing each other when they could and keeping their affection alive through correspondence.

SLOWLY BUT SURELY Natalie was emerging into full womanhood. In general, the transformation filled the Barneys with pride and pleasure. Their daughter was turning out to be exceptional, blessed with abundant athletic skill, intelligence, and charm. She laughed easily, was never mean-spirited or petty, and was widely considered a gifted conversationalist.

But one or two chinks had begun to appear in the armor of their pretty page. Albert in particular worried about her reckless and seemingly hell-bent nature, not to mention her lack of modesty and increasingly flagrant defiance.

For instance, while it was commendable to have a daughter who rode well, he thought, Natalie pushed it to extremes. At Bar Harbor she would harness a handsome pair to the two-seater and race it at top speed through the dusty streets. She'd stand up, leaning forward with the reins gathered in her left hand and a whip flicking in the other, urging the horses on to ever-greater speed. Passersby would stare open-mouthed as she passed, her long skirts and blond hair billowing wildly in the wind.

Even worse: she often galloped at a furious rate with a second steed on lead beside her. "Miss Nathalie Barney," wrote an admiring journalist, "has created quite a sensation in Bar Harbor this summer by making a rider and driver of herself, both at the same time. She is the first in Bar Harbor to do this novel feat. She sits with perfect ease upon the back of one horse and at the same time driving another ahead of her. Both her saddle horse and leader are spirited animals, but she has no fear nor uncertainty. There are very few so far who have the nerve and confidence to try this new fad, and as it takes an expert horsewoman, it will never become universal. However, it is a daring accomplishment and might be of service to her in the future should she ever find it necessary to make her own living, which she probably will not."[16]

All that was bad enough, but when Natalie took to riding astride she set off a profound controversy. So shocking was it considered for a woman to sit "pickaback" that a scandal-mongering tabloid, Town Topics, ran a sizzling article about the fact that she had done so. Albert, who had specifically forbidden her to ride in this manner, berated Alice for letting their daughter run wild; she replied that she saw no real harm in Natalie's riding style. "Good God, Alice," he barked. "You never do see harm. Will you never learn?"[17]

Natalie possessed other unconventional attitudes. She frequently went out without corsets, those close-fitting foundations with reinforced bone or metal stays that torturously shaped a woman's body. She hated petticoats, stiff underskirts that made natural movement difficult, nearly as much. Once, when Albert found a petticoat left in the carriage where Natalie had slipped it off en route to a party, he created a scene.

And her hair! It was true that Alice refused to let her wear it up, insisting that she was still too young, but it attracted no end of attention hanging loose. Young male admirers were already comparing it to moonlight, using words like "luminous" and "phosphorescent" to describe its captivating white-gold quality. There was something too undisciplined about that hair, Albert thought. Just like its owner.

Every day, it seemed, Natalie grew more disobedient and less willing to submit to her father's controlling hand. She argued, talked back, and was always ready with an insolent reply. As she herself informed her mother, "If a girl is apt to be foolish, no warning or forbidding will do any good, especially when she is obstinate and willful."[18]

On one occasion, as the family sat over dinner before going to the opera, father and daughter had sharp words. Suddenly, Natalie pushed back from the table, stood up, and announced that she was leaving. Thunderstruck, the family watched as she gathered her wrap, stormed through the front door, and hopped into the waiting carriage. Later, presumably calmer, she joined her family at the opera.

And then there was the White House caper. One Christmas the family received a luncheon invitation to the president's residence, a sure sign of capital-city acceptance that thrilled Albert to the core. Natalie was pleased, too, though her delight lay in the idea of breaking bread with the beautiful first lady, Libbie Cleveland.

At the lunch, Natalie, overcome by Mrs. Cleveland's charm, announced: "Ah! Madame President, if only you continue to preside over the White House with *anyone* who happens to be president!"[19] Albert was horrified, but Natalie, already aware of how beguiling boldness could be, won the reward she sought: Mrs. Cleveland singled her out for a smile.

His worries about Natalie aside, Albert loved his blond angel, had always doted on her, and always would. On occasion, he was surprisingly direct with his emotions. "I feel so much love for you," he once wrote Natalie. "Hourly, 120 times I am thinking of my first born and I love her 120 times that."[20] But increasingly she seemed to be slipping from his grasp, and he could no longer understand her. One can imagine him turning to Alice in despair, asking, as the parents of teenagers have always asked: "Where did we go wrong?"

Alice probably mouthed appropriate peacemaking replies, but she would have had little sympathy for Albert's complaints. She had always been an ally in Natalie's rebellion, at first unconsciously but then with increasing clarity. She allied herself to Laura, too. Although not a rebel, Laura had begun to develop unique spiritual and political philosophies that would eventually bring her into conflict with her father. Alice steadfastly supported both her girls. After years in a repressive marriage, she vicariously enjoyed, and on some level encouraged, their willful natures. In the years ahead, she only superficially cooperated with Albert's attempts to marry Natalie off. Instead, she smoothed the way for her to travel and live abroad. By keeping an ocean's distance between Albert and Natalie, she bought her oldest daughter a little time on that inevitable road to marriage.

THAT FALL, sixteen-year-old Natalie was packed off to New York City to finish her formal education at Miss Ely's, an exclusive boarding school. The grounds occupied an entire block at Riverside Drive and Eighty-sixth Street, where many elegant mansions had recently sprung up. Riverside Park was nearby, offering stunning views along the Hudson River and north up the New Jersey side to the Palisades.

Miss Ely's, with its four-story wood frame structure, Doric columns, and picket fence, looked more like a private residence than a school. The atmosphere stressed learning, however, and debates on current events were common. Soon after Natalie enrolled, the English suffragist Emmeline Pankhurst spoke at an assembly. She elicited a great deal of enthusiasm among the students, but less so with Natalie, who thought the time had come to talk "less of the wrongs done to women and more about their rights."[21]

By today's standards Natalie's education seems like a hit-or-miss mélange, but it was typical for wealthy girls of the day. Quite often the quality of a woman's learning depended on the worth or personality of her governess. Edith Wharton wrote regretfully of being tutored by a woman she liked and admired but who "never struck a spark from me . . . My childhood and youth were an intellectual desert."[22]

Such indifferent education amounted to intellectual suppression of women. Perhaps that was the point, since intelligence in a woman was often considered suspect. Mabel Dodge Luhan wrote of a female friend who excelled in Greek and Latin and studied advanced mathematics. Her father happily paid the bills because his daughter's "scholarly achievements . . . were protected by his own ignorance of her genius, which would have frightened him had he grasped it and would have led him to check her in activities not *comme il faut* for a *jeune fille du monde*."[23]

The boys Natalie knew had a far different experience. Sent at a young age to prep schools and expected to attend university, they had an opportunity to master a wide variety of subjects, including the sciences and mathematics. More important, they learned to sharpen their wits against, and form lifelong bonds with, an educated peer group.

Although it was unusual at that time for a woman to continue her education, it was certainly possible to do so. Women's colleges such as Wesleyan and Mount Holyoke had been around since before the Civil War, and, beginning with Vassar's founding in 1862, they became more common: Wellesley (1870), Smith (1871), Radcliffe (1879), Bryn Mawr (1880), and Barnard (1889). In the twenty-four years between Natalie's birth in 1876 and the turn of the century, the number of American women annually awarded bachelor's degrees more than doubled, from 2,094 to 5,237. Their numbers would double again by 1913.

It was largely daughters of the wealthy who entered these schools, and often, having received only a so-so education, they found the academic standards difficult. In fact, remedial courses were common. As Eva Palmer admitted, her desire to enter Bryn Mawr was considered "out of the question" by the college's president "because I had none of the requirements for the entrance examinations except a little French and less German."[24] Determined, Eva studied feverishly for six months and passed the exams.

As for Natalie, she simply never had the desire to attend college. To a woman who would model her existence on an epigram by Montaigne, "My art and profession is to live," college was a four-year delay in pursuing life. Studying what the world wanted her to study, and then forgetting it, "seemed less important than that evolution toward myself, under the direct tutelage of life. . . . What good to know what others know? . . . to learn the date of the Punique wars, the name of the Merovingien kings, the Roman caesars."[25] She questioned the validity of being forced to "learn a heap of useless things, when knowing how to read, write, feel and love seems to me sufficient."[26] In *The Color of His Soul,* a play she coauthored with Alice, Natalie wrote that it's "astonishing how college life un-individualizes one. It takes years to recover one's self."[27]

Instead of formal tutelage in a curriculum dictated by others, Natalie would go on to pursue an education of her own design. For years after completing her studies at Miss Ely's she engaged private tutors versed in the subjects she wished to master: French versification, Greek, violin. In a sense her entire life, with its pursuit of literature and littérateurs, can be seen as a ceaseless quest for self-education.

Natalie studied a reasonable amount at Miss Ely's, but still found time for the kind of hijinks that landed her in trouble. "You have probably heard of my 'disgrace'—as Papa calls it—so I will not bore you by repeating the sad story," she wrote Laura. "To think that I shall not be allowed to leave this school for four weeks will surely drive me to drink—(the only thing which remains since we are to be sent home if we smoke any more!). It really was gastley [sic] to get up there before the whole school; first for smoking—by the by I don't think Papa knows about this first offense so don't mention it to him—and then the very next day for going out without permission. These continual reports—lectures, and confessions are telling on me like the duce."[28]

Stuck at school, Natalie missed Eva terribly. Their correspondence was a poor substitute for being together, though Eva's letters filled her with joy. She also missed her family, a feeling made worse by her perception that they missed her not a whit. Letters from Albert enthused over the latest political bigwig or European royal to dine at their home. Alice's always-hurried notes tended to discuss whatever painting she was working on. Laura, happy in her Washington convent school, confided that she had decided to devote her life to noble causes.

When Natalie arrived home for Easter vacation, her feeling of alienation increased. It was as if the space she was supposed to occupy in the family had evaporated. No one paid the slightest attention to her, or so she felt. Alice socialized or worked at her easel with some society beauty poised before her. Albert spent most of the day at his clubs. Laura was preoccupied with her philosophical projects.

Natalie's spirits rallied when a lovely Washington visitor, whose beauty she equated to that of a wild rose, was brought to dine chez Barney. In those days of horse-drawn travel, guests routinely spent the night. When the number of guests exceeded the supply of bedrooms, younger people were expected to double up, which is how the Wild Rose came to sleep with Natalie, who forthrightly sought a kiss but was pushed firmly away. She continued her siege, at one point receiving a scratch on her arm from the woman's long and pointed nails (the defenses of a rose, Natalie thought). Finally, exhausted, she gave up.

In the ensuing calm the two stretched out on the bed and gradually fell into peaceful conversation. When Natalie next offered an embrace, the woman responded at first, but then changed her mind. She continued on this way, pushing and scratching while simultaneously moaning: "Don't stop! Don't stop!"[29]

"I obeyed," Natalie admitted, "and almost died between the contradiction of her fingernails and her voice. I possessed her painfully and deliciously."

Natalie's unhesitating seduction of this woman lacked suavity, but indicated that she had grown far bolder since the previous summer's sexual initiation in the arms of Eva. Her romantic technique would become much smoother, but she would never be one to shilly-shally around about what she wanted. In fact, one of the reasons she was so successful in her seductions was that she was straightforward. When interested, she made it obvious. Her sure and unswerving desire lit a flame of passion or simple curiosity within its target, so that even women who had never contemplated same-sex love found themselves willingly seduced.

Years later Natalie wrote to Eva of dining with two former lovers, both heterosexual women. "Nina [has] entirely forgotten that she was ever in love with me," she noted with amusement. "She, H[enriette Roggers], and I had supper together last night most peacefully and they both had a beautiful time saying they never could love women!" As the dinner conversation progressed, Nina and Henrietta explained away their affairs with Natalie by saying they had loved "a being, not a woman!"[30]

Aggressive techniques like Natalie's could backfire, too, and she endured her share of rejections. One of the earliest occurred during the same Easter vacation in which she seduced the Wild Rose. When she attempted to caress an English actress, a friend of her mother's, she was pushed brusquely away.

"Child, child!" the actress exclaimed. "What are we doing?" She then delivered a long lecture about how wrong it was to go against what was natural. Natalie smiled to herself. If there was one thing she was sure of, it was this: being unnatural felt good.[31]

ON JUNE 9, 1894, Natalie sailed aboard the German steamship *Elbe* for a European tour, a seven-country trip guided by her school's headmistress, Miss Ely. Also along were sisters Grace and Carol Lee and at least one other class-mate. After nearly three months of travel, the tour would end in Paris in late August. Natalie would then return to Germany to study for half a year. Albert planned to meet her in April and, after buying gowns for her upcoming debut, they would sail home together.

Only seventeen, Natalie was nervous and confused about the long separa-tion from her family. As departure grew closer, she couldn't decide from one day to the next whether she was being sent away or allowed to go. With a youthful lack of logic, she resolved the conflict by being angry at her mother for permitting the trip. At dockside, when Alice presented her with a diamond heart brooch, Natalie viewed it as an apology rather than a gift. She didn't understand how difficult this first major parting was for her mother, who still considered her a child. In fact, a great mother-daughter struggle had recently been waged over Alice's refusal to dress Natalie in long skirts like other girls her age. It was only just before sailing that she was given her first full-length dresses.

Despite her inner turmoil, Natalie didn't fail to notice a pretty, slightly older woman boarding the ship with a violin case: she was Leonora Howland, a concert violinist traveling to Europe on her honeymoon. The two struck up a conversation about music, and before long were comparing violins. Natalie's Steiner, good as it was, was no match for Howland's Stradivarius.

One night during the crossing, Natalie watched admiringly as Howland wielded her bow in a charity concert. Overcome by emotion, she left the salon, ran to the ship's prow, and stood beneath the starry sky in a state of exaltation. Later, finding Leonora alone in her stateroom, she spilled out her love in a rush of words. The worldly Howland smiled kindly. Natalie, she said, reminded her of Balzac's Seraphita Seraphitus, the celestial hermaphrodite whom men desire in vain and whose strange powers seduce women. "My husband thinks that you're a young woman like any other," Howland murmured, "which is how you appear. But if he saw you in this way, as I see you . . ."[32]

Aside from Leonora, little about the crossing excited Natalie. Like most girls her age, however, she noted even the most mundane events in her outsize diary/scrapbook, into which she also pasted postcards of the *Elbe,* a photograph of long-bearded Captain von Gössell, newspaper clippings, and the deck plan. She scribbled theatrical descriptions of passengers ("mysterious blonde, generally seasick," or "rosy cheeked maiden, silent and mournful"), and took careful note of daily menus. She wrote of fellow passenger Mr. Hagens, who, though meeting his fiancée at Bremen, flirted outrageously during the crossing: "I thought poor fiancée when witnessing the flirting, but when I saw [the fiancée at the dock] I thought poor Mr. Hagens."[33]

Before the Howlands debarked at Southampton, Leonora thrilled Natalie by signing her autograph book with the words "Yours lovingly." With a pang of guilt toward her mother, Natalie gave the violinist the diamond heart brooch. Since the Howlands were to settle in Paris, plans were made to meet there in late August.

Ely's group debarked at Bremen on June 19 and traveled to Berlin, where they spent the next few days exploring the city under their caretaker's haphazard guidance. "Miss Ely spends all her and our money on guide books," a bemused Natalie wrote Laura. "What information she gets from them I do not know for she seems as much in the dark after reading them as before."[34]

Nonetheless, the group stayed busy with edifying, often pleasurable, endeavors. Natalie's love of theater and music deepened. She sent home long musical critiques, filled her scrapbook with annotated programs, and collected photographs of her favorite musicians. She also enjoyed art museums, especially when accompanied by classmate Carol Lee. "Carol is very amusing," Natalie informed Laura. "She thinks she knows a lot about paintings. She stands off and squints at pictures by . . . Fra Lippo Lippi or Angelico and informs us that they are of the Impressionist school instead of relics of the 14th Century. She stands rooted to the spot, lost in admiration when she comes to pictures like the one we used to have of a lady holding a canary on her finger."[35]

From Berlin they traveled to Dresden, the ancient Saxon capital known for its baroque architecture and heavy population of artists and musicians. Natalie attended a Wagner opera and visited a "picture gallery," a beer garden, and a vault filled with jewels of the Saxon kings. Then it was on to Moscow. This blitzkrieg cultural grab would be the pattern as they toured Germany, Russia, Sweden, Norway, Austria, Poland, and Switzerland.

Along the way they had a few adventures. At the Russian border, caught in a welter of confusing passport problems, they watched helplessly as their train chugged away without them. A gentleman traveler, who later wrote Miss Ely asking for a photograph of Natalie, resolved their problems and they continued on. Leaving Russia, which had been hit by a cholera epidemic, they were unhappily quarantined for several days on a steamer outside Finland. In Norway, Natalie—decked out in a traditional costume of short skirt, apron, jacket, loose white blouse, and a "funny-looking" pointed hat—traversed the fjords in an open, fur-filled carriage decorated with twenty-four immense deer horns.

Arriving in Paris on August 25, Natalie thrilled to her first taste of the city without her parents. Perhaps she experienced the same excitement as Francisque Sarcey, another young visitor who returned to Paris at around that time:

> I was almost crazy with joy at breathing, during the drive, that perfume of Parisian life which arises so strongly from the asphalt of the boulevard and the macadam of its roadway. It was evening, the gas-jets (for electricity was yet unknown) spangled the darkness with yellow lights; the shops, all opened, shone brilliantly; the crowd was strolling up and down the wide sidewalks. . . . "Ah! how beautiful it is—the boulevard!" I exclaimed, and I breathed deep draughts of the air charged with joyous and spiritual electricity.[36]

During this short week of semi-independence Natalie realized for the first time just how much Paris meant to her. As a child she had come reluctantly to France, hating to leave her friends and pets. Now she viewed that earlier reluctance as a resistance to something preordained. Over the next few years her love of Paris would grow stronger until, finally, there would be little reason to return home.

On this visit Natalie may also have surmised for the first time that her love of women was considered more acceptable in France than at home. In fact, Paris at that time is sometimes referred to as "Paris-Lesbos." Along with the city's unofficial role as the world's capital of pleasure came a more or less accepting attitude toward decadence in its many forms. Discreet homosexuality, in particular, was almost a vogue. "When you first read Proust," notes Judith Thurman, "it seems implausible that nearly everyone in Paris society, male or female, had a secret gay life, but it turns out that Proust was exaggerating only slightly."[37] The key word, of course, is "secret." Even in Paris-Lesbos, a woman indulging in same-sex love operated with discretion if she wanted to remain respectable. Still, the city's partly open closet door offered more sexual freedom for women than anywhere else on the planet—one reason it attracted free-thinking foreign lesbians like Barney.

Natalie was constantly busy during this brief visit. She lunched and drove in the Bois with Leonora Howland. One lovely day, accompanied by Miss Ely and her schoolmates, she sailed to St. Cloud by *bateau-mouche* and returned that evening by train. There were trips to the theater, visits to museums, and after-dinner carriage rides. Once, riding through the Bois, she was stunned to see a woman balanced atop a bicycle while wearing a jersey and tights. The carriage driver shrugged his shoulders as if to say, "What's the world coming to?" Something about the biker's independent air must have struck a familiar chord with Natalie because that night she dreamed that her mother, dressed in plaid bike pants and completely oblivious to the shocked stares of passersby, was pedaling up Washington's Connecticut Avenue.

Natalie couldn't stand the thought of leaving Paris for Germany and cabled Albert begging to stay. His reply dashed her hopes: she could not be trusted on her own unless enrolled in a strict boarding school, and since such schools were closed until late fall, she must adhere to the original plans. "Papa and Mama do not seem to give me credit for more feelings or reason than a child of two," a dismayed Natalie wrote Laura. "Their letters hurt me very much, this breach of trust still more."[38]

After spending the month of September in Jena, a small village near the Thüringen forest, she took up residence in Dresden. The bustling, sophisticated city was a cultural mecca, just the kind of place she liked. Most mornings and afternoons revolved around lessons with a famed violinist, Herr Konzertmeister Petri. Natalie also studied German language and literature, took fencing classes, and read prolifically, or at least that's what she told her parents. According to letters home she was tackling Victor Hugo's *Les Miserables*, the novels of Bret Harte, Carlyle's *Essays*, Irving's *Life of George Washington*, Gibbon's *Decline and Fall of the Roman Empire*, Sir Edwin Arnold's *The Light of Asia*, Ruskin's *Sesame and Lilies*, and Hawthorne's *Marble Faun*. She failed to mention Balzac's *Seraphita Seraphitus*, which she had read with a distinct feeling of recognition for the double-being of its title character.

Opera played a significant cultural role in Dresden, where both Schumann and Wagner had composed major works. A few months earlier Natalie had attended her first Wagner festival in Bayreuth, where she was overwhelmed by performances of *Tannhäuser* and *Lohengrin*. In Dresden, sitting in inexpensive balcony seats at the majestic Semper, her love of Wagner deepened.

The ancient city had other diversions. Letters of introduction brought invitations to formal dinners and fancy dress balls. A slight acquaintance with the young princesses of the Saxon royal family took her to court functions, where she enjoyed the colorful uniforms, the splendid jeweled crowns, and the handsome cavalry officers who clicked their heels sharply before asking for a dance. One day Natalie and classmate Grace Lee had themselves professionally photographed in angel costumes. Natalie, who revealed a powerful set of wings and a good deal of décolletage, warned Laura not to show the photograph to their parents.

As April drew near, Natalie anticipated her father's arrival with mixed feelings. As always there would be his irascible temper and excessive drinking to deal with, not to mention his constant attempts to curtail her freedom. But now there were other, more philosophical reasons for dreading his presence. "Staying away this year has made me see [him] very clearly," she admitted to Alice shortly before his arrival. With the detachment that only distance can provide, she had reached devastating conclusions about her parents' marriage. She distilled her thoughts in a letter to Alice which, considering that it was written in 1894 by a woman not yet eighteen, is stunning in its depiction of feminist principles still being grappled with today:

> What have you gained by submitting all these 19 years? When you are in the right, stick up for your rights, you owe it to yourself as a woman—put here to better things and do good to those in your sphere by your good example. . . . It seems to me that those who dare to rebel in every age are those who make life possible—it is the rebels who extend the boundary of right, little by little—narrowing the confines of wrong and crowding it out of existence. So long as women like you will forgive anything, men will do anything—What better proof of this do you want than your own life! You have been wrong and weak to stand it all this time. . . . Don't be cowed by oaths or threats. No one needs to lead the life you lead—be strong and demand what is right, and your due whenever an occasion presents itself. Papa is like a spoilt child—and who has spoiled him—you partly. You owe it to him as well as yourself to show him that "women are no longer content to be part of the livestock about the place." They have acquired the right of reason—in matters concerning themselves in particular, and the welfare of the world at large. Public opinion is now composed of what <u>we</u> think—You remind me of what other women have done in all ages, and how patiently they have submitted. You see the same thing over and over again; but I have not seen any particular case where any great good has come from unjust submission. On the contrary . . . How is society, the world or humanity ever going to be improved if those who see things in the right light will not act? . . .
>
> But how are we ever going to improve things—surely not by acceptance and submission! Everything (society, politics) is in a groove and the longer it is left alone the deeper it becomes wedged in between conventionality and habit. It requires a few—many—strong people to pull together and lift it out of the mire into which it has fallen! . . . Well—well! You will think me a heretic, an anarchist or a crazy person if I continue in this tone much longer.[39]

Natalie resolved to choose a different path for herself starting now. "I intend to live up to my convictions and teach that spoilt child of a father of mine a lesson or two," she wrote her mother. "I think I shall be very polite and never answer him back, but have my own way when it's reasonable just the same. I wonder if that will work?"[40]

Of course it would work: Alice and Natalie, and to a lesser extent Laura, had long ago figured out how to have their own way no matter how much Albert objected. "Each one of us," Natalie coolly acknowledged, "did what we wanted."[41]

Natalie would always be quick to criticize her mother for what she viewed as weakness—kowtowing to Albert in particular—but she didn't seem to understand that, at her core, Alice possessed an innate and unshakable strength. Nor did she realize that from this tiny woman she had inherited her own daring, her willingness to stand against the crowd, her ability to be knocked down and stand right back up. In fact, Natalie's very Amazon-ness had been directly mainlined from her mother right in the womb.

In early April father and daughter met in Vienna and then traveled to Paris. Their time together was not a great success. They fought incessantly. Natalie hated everything about Albert's taste, from the clothes he forced her to buy, to his choice of theater and opera, to the rich, ultraconventional Americans with whom he preferred to socialize. He drank "not too much but too often,"[42] threw dinner parties she considered stiff and boring, and, as she'd feared, severely crimped her style.

At the opera one night they sat with friends of Albert's who talked throughout. Unable to hear the singing, Natalie recalled the pleasure of sitting in the "peasant gallery" in Dresden with people who sincerely loved music. Staring round at the Paris opera she saw nothing but bored-looking million-aires, including American heiress Anna Gould and the French husband she'd paid a $15 million dowry for, Count Boni de Castallane. "She is the most unwashed and dirty-looking creature I ever laid eyes on," Natalie hissed, "and he the most insipid. *Quel ménage.*"[43]

On June 1, Natalie and Albert sailed for New York.

AWAITING HER Bar Harbor debut, Natalie quickly determined that, while she had changed considerably during her time abroad, many of her childhood friends had not. Their lives seemed settled and they themselves prematurely aged, while her own great adventure in life had only just begun.

But new blood appeared. A handsome Italian visitor sent Natalie a long-stemmed American Beauty rose every day. One day he drew her away from their friends and into the trees to profess his love. Pulling her close, he grew so excited that he orgasmed and hastened back to his hotel to change his clothing. Another lovestruck fellow recited love poems that he claimed to have written himself, but which Natalie recognized as the work of Robert Herrick. He was dismayed when Natalie chimed in on the second verse.

Natalie took one suitor seriously, and in fact would come close to marrying him. In her writing she refers to him as "Will," but his real name was Robert Kelso Cassatt. He was the son of a wealthy Pittsburgh family connected to railroads, and the nephew of American Impressionist artist Mary Cassatt.* Natalie and Bob probably knew each other from earlier summers at Bar Harbor, where the Cassatts owned a cottage called "Four Acres." In the summer of 1895 they grew close.

Bob loved Natalie deeply, and was so insistent on marrying her that she told him point-blank that she preferred women and could only love him as a friend. Unfazed, he proposed the idea of a *mariage blanc,* a nonsexual marriage in which he would satisfy himself with other women, remaining free to love Natalie with his soul and protect her with his name.

Natalie suspected that even such a marriage would be too compromising of her independence. On the other hand, a *fiancé blanc* could come in handy, relieving the steady pressure from Albert to find a husband. Ensuring excellent matches for his daughters was one of Albert's chief goals in life; Robert Cassatt, with a politically powerful father worth an estimated $50 million, fit the bill. When Natalie and Bob became unofficially engaged around the time of her debut, Albert was ecstatic.

Natalie's Bar Harbor debut was the first private ball of the island's social season. More than five hundred people, "every one of social and diplomatic distinction summering at Bar Harbor,"[44] came to Ban-y-Bryn that night, their carriages ascending a steep pathway lit by hundreds of Japanese lanterns. Natalie dazzled in a white satin dress by Worth. The drawing room was crowded with dancers, conversations took place on the silk-draped balconies overlooking the ocean, and food was served in the Great Hall with its trailing pine boughs and silk-shaded candlelight.

The Washington debut took the guise of a late-afternoon tea. The house was lit by hundreds of candles, and great roaring fires filled the hearths. Natalie stood side by side with her parents in the music room to receive guests. She wore a gown of sheer white silk over white satin striped mull with a green satin collar and girdle, and carried a bouquet of lilies tied with a green ribbon. Tea was poured and presided over by Natalie's friend Miss Pauncefote, the British ambassador's daughter.

Both parties were liberally covered in the press, with particular attention

*Mary Cassatt painted a portrait of Bob with his father (her brother) in 1885. Entitled *Portrait of Alexander Cassatt and His Son Robert Kelso,* it's currently owned by the Philadelphia Museum of Art.

paid to Natalie's money, good looks, and wit. Wrote one reporter: "Miss Natalie Barney is as charming a debutante as one would want to see. Her golden hair, dark blue eyes and charming unaffected manner are among her many charms. [She has been] in Europe, adding the finishing touches to her education and preparing herself for the position in society which she is sure to occupy."

Perhaps the sharpest observation acknowledged Natalie's charismatic personality: "The Bar Harbor ingenue is a type duplicated at every turn. . . . Few [can be] distinguished from the others. These young girls all look alike, or rather they are so colorless as to be stamped with conventionality . . . and only serve to throw into relief young ladies with a cachet of their own, like . . . Miss Natalie Barnay [sic] . . . an acknowledged belle."[45]

The coming-out season ended with a glamorous cotillion at the Russian embassy and a hunt at Chevy Chase. Natalie was relieved when the whole thing was over. Planning for it, she had discovered, was a lot more fun than living through it. "We do not want the thing," she wrote Bob with a touch of disillusion, "but the idea of the thing."[46] She would bring that sentiment into most of her love affairs.

TO THE CASUAL OBSERVER, the young blond woman with a pink-and-white complexion probably didn't seem much different from other young women her age. Aside from a smattering of idle gossip, nothing indicated that she was at variance with society's norms. Recently turned nineteen, she had made her formal debut and was now expected to become a dutiful wife and a loving mother. Little else would ever be expected of her.

Nonetheless, thanks to a sharp mind, an energetic nature, and a strong competitive spirit, she had become fairly accomplished. At a time when women's sports were not encouraged, she was a superb equestrienne, an enthusiastic swimmer, a regular rower, and a good enough tennis player to have won at least one tournament prize. Fencing was in vogue, and, as the *Washington Post* reported, "the pretty Miss Barney [is] a fine fencer."[47]

She also played an excellent violin and was proficient on the mandolin and viola. With a flair for language, she was nearly bilingual in French, had a workable knowledge of German, and knew a bit of Greek. She had always loved reading poetry and found herself increasingly drawn to writing it.

Natalie loved fine clothing and would always dress in couturier designs. Photographs at this time show her in expensive suits and dresses. Many are simple and tailored, but a few are elaborately worked in the day's style with lace, embroidery, insets, high collars, peplums, pouffy sleeves and an occasional ruffle. Her hats and bonnets explode with feathers, bows, and lace. A magnificent painting by Alice, *Natalie in Fur Cape*, shows her face regally framed by a high-collared mink cape, her hair piled loosely atop her head and crowned by three long, insouciant black feathers. Her stance and expression can only be described as imperious.

Although Natalie didn't usually wear much jewelry—one or two rings, a delicate necklace, perhaps a bracelet or brooch—she possessed plenty of it, and much was valuable. En route to Bar Harbor that summer, she and her father took rooms at Boston's Hotel Touraine. While she was out one evening, two valuable rings, one a large emerald and the other set with two hundred small diamonds, were stolen from her suite. "Miss Barney's jewels attracted attention from the moment she arrived at the hotel," a reporter noted, tacitly blaming her for the theft. "She had a diamond necklace, a sunburst and finger rings."[48]

To most people, Natalie seemed pampered and carefree—but she was a good deal more complex than she appeared on the surface. Around the time of the debut Alice completed a pastel portrait entitled *Natalie with Flowing Hair*. The work seems to be honoring Natalie's cerebral side by showing her head detached from her body and floating in a surreal swirl of blond hair. Since nobody was paying the slightest attention to Natalie's intellect at the time, including Natalie herself, the portrait shows a great deal of prescience on Alice's part.

Even more interesting is the portrait's distinct air of sadness, the last thing one would expect to find in such a genial young woman. But then, who would know this subject's moods and nuances better than her own mother? Alice had sketched and painted Natalie hundreds of times from childhood on, and it's reasonable to assume that the portrait is an honest depiction of its subject in her late teens. The sadness seems underlined by a phrase scrawled in chalk at the portrait's bottom edge: *Sombre sans ennuis et triste sans détresse.* These same words form the opening line of a poem that Natalie wrote around this time. Entitled "About Myself," it's a work of profound disillusionment, doubly so considering her age. "My life grieves me and oppresses me," one despairing line reads. "What's wrong?" another anxiously asks, and then answers: "I don't know but I feel it deeply."

Few people would ever realize that Natalie's great capacity for joy resided side by side with a well-hidden strain of melancholy. Only those who knew her exceedingly well would be privy to her occasional bouts of sadness. Her admirers tended to see only the dazzling public persona, while her detractors were convinced that she had no feelings whatsoever. Yet, there it is: *somber without being bored and sad without distress.* With these plain and simple words Natalie admitted not only to an inner sadness but to her familiarity with and acceptance of it.

There is one last thing worth noting about Natalie at nineteen: she retained an endearing childhood quality, one that would grow increasingly incongruous in the years ahead. When surprised, embarrassed, or flustered, her face turned crimson. Many would remark upon this quality, but none so eloquently as a future lover: "[Natalie's] delicate complexion, her very feminine form, her hair like that of a blonde fairy, her Parisian elegance concealed for a moment the steely look of those eyes which saw everything and understood everything in a second. And, to better accentuate this false first impression, she could—and can do so to this day—blush like a shy novice."[49]

In July 1896 the Barney family spent a month at England's Brighton sea resort before traveling to Paris for an operation to improve Laura's limp. Later that fall Albert returned to Washington, leaving the women on their own. Their time passed peacefully. Alice returned to Carolus-Duran's studio. With his encouragement she submitted *Natalie in Fur Cape* for entry to the 1897 Salon. It was accepted and highlighted in the Salon's catalog. Laura, slowly recovering from her operation, stayed abed reading, and Natalie pursued her growing interest in writing French poetry. She experimented with free verse, but didn't like it nearly as much as the works of Symbolist poets such as Paul Verlaine, Charles Baudelaire, and Stéphane Mallarmé.

But as much as Natalie loved poetry, the studious life soon had her chafing at the bit. There was a less proper side of Paris, she knew, and she was curious to discover it. She finally got her chance when Alice and Laura returned home in April 1897, leaving her behind to fulfill a commitment to work at a charity bazaar. With the oblivious pension owner's daughter acting as chaperone, Natalie enjoyed another state of *demi-liberté*.

By now Natalie and Leonora Howland were old friends and saw each other regularly (the relationship was platonic). One day, distraught, the pregnant Howland despaired over social and family expectations that she give up her violin for the baby. She wondered idly how courtesans remained unburdened by children: did they possess some secret knowledge? Natalie, who had recently read an article against compulsory motherhood in a feminist journal, agreed that something was "flagrantly unjust" about Leonora's dilemma, "even antifeminist." She promised to discover the courtesanal method for warding off motherhood. The only person of her acquaintance who might know such secrets was her mother's favorite model, Carmen Rossi, to whom she sent a note requesting a meeting.

Rossi was a vibrant beauty with huge dark eyes, thick black hair, and a mouth that looked, Natalie thought, like a red carnation. She welcomed Natalie warmly, asked for the latest news about Alice, and then, without preamble, pulled the younger woman close. "I've always wanted to approach you in this way," she murmured, "but I didn't dare with your family around. Now, though, you're on your own. . . . If you like, pick me!"[50] And with that she offered Natalie the beautiful carnation of her lips.

In the bedroom, which Carmen shared each night with her quasi husband, Natalie had a sexual revelation. With the exception of Eva, who "bends to my least desire,"[51] her sexual experiences had so far been rushed and even childish. But now, with Carmen, Natalie understood the possibilities. "The young women with whom I'd been in love in the United States . . . hadn't been true mistresses like Carmen," she admitted.[52] The next day Carmen sent her a carnation bouquet and a note pledging a lifetime of love. Natalie trembled with desire.

Carmen Rossi was a simple, earthy soul who loved sex and made no bones about it, and she helped transform Natalie from a groping schoolgirl into an exquisite lover. In later years Natalie's lovers would write of her "famous hands," her tongue, her bravado, her tenderness—and all of it started with Carmen. Rossi also kicked off Barney's lifelong desire to write of love through poetry. Left gasping by their lovemaking, Natalie realized that only art could perpetuate the beauty they experienced together, and "it was thus necessary for me to become a poet of love." How, she wondered, had her favorite poets perfected their natural gifts, and how might she transform her gushing inspiration into something strong and durable? If she were to properly write of love's beauty, she decided, she must find a good teacher.

For a while Natalie was obsessed with Rossi. Most of their assignations took place during the day, when Carmen's lover was working. Once, when he was out of town, the two women went to the infamous dance hall Bal Bullier. With its "vast sea of heads, and a dazzling display of colors and lights and animation,"[53] Bullier was frequented by a democratic mixture that included shopgirls, courtesans, gangsters, cancan girls, and upper-crust slummers. With a friend of Carmen's they also attended the annual Neuilly Fair, with its wild-animal tamer, waffle-maker, and popular fart artist. Carmen and her friend gleefully took in the latter's performance while Natalie waited in the carriage.

They sometimes went to the Bois de Boulogne to watch the daily carriage procession of the city's wealthiest citizens, top socialites, and great beauties. "Many of these elegant persons knew one another," wrote a fin-de-siècle observer, "and a pretty part of the spectacle was the leisurely saluting from carriage to carriage, the women bowing beneath their parasols, their huge hats reaching a perilous angle like flower baskets about to spill, the men lifting their gleaming silk toppers with one yellow-gloved hand and adjusting their monocles with the other."[54] Natalie recalled it as a time when one had the leisure to exchange lingering looks and half-smiles in passing.

One morning Natalie was riding through the Bois in her parents' carriage, accompanied by a male friend, when she was startled by the sight of an angelically beautiful woman. Tall, thin, and wrapped in ermine, this angel rode slowly by in a luxurious carriage pulled by remarkably fine stallions. Entranced, Natalie asked her companion who the woman was. "Oh," came the dismissive reply. "Liane de Pougy—nothing but a courtesan."

The word *courtesan* meant nothing to Natalie, though she had the vague impression that the woman was in some kind of peril (she later wrote that young women of her generation were kept from knowledge of the demimonde). What she did know was that she'd never seen anyone so beautiful. She was particularly taken by de Pougy's androgynous slenderness, so at variance with the plump figures in vogue. She remained haunted by her brief sight of the courtesan, and continued trying to learn more about her.

NATALIE'S PARISIAN *demi-liberté* ended abruptly after the May 3 disaster at the Grand Bazar de la Charité. This event, cosponsored by the Catholic Church and the city's top families, had long been a fashionable, fun-filled way to raise money for orphans. During its annual run the Bazar drew thousands to its temporary wood-and-canvas structure. Booths were staffed by volunteers, mostly women with high French titles and a smattering of well-born foreigners like Natalie.

In 1897 the most talked-about attraction at the Bazar was the new *cinématographe* invented by brothers Louis and Auguste Lumière. The film program they'd designed was anticipated to be so popular that a turnstile had been erected to maintain orderly movement in and out of the projection room. At about four o'clock on opening day, problems with the ether lamp sent a flame shooting across the room. In seconds the canvas walls caught fire, and within minutes the entire Bazar, decorated with gauzy Turkish hangings and ribbons, was aflame. Many, including children, were trapped behind the projection room's turnstiles, unable to get out. Burning wood and canvas fell onto the crowd, catching clothing on fire, and the entire structure quickly collapsed. Fifteen hundred people panicked, crowding toward the Bazar's solitary exit. Those not consumed by flame were trampled to death in the rush to escape.

By the time the fire died out, 127 people lay dead, and even more were dying or seriously injured. The flames had blazed so furiously that many bodies simply burned to ash; others were so black and twisted they could be identified only by jewelry. Only five of the dead were men: perhaps the greatest scandal of the year was the cowardly behavior shown by Parisian dandies, who "ran like rats to save their well-tailored hides, beat their hysterical way to the exits, using their canes as cudgels, stepping over the bodies of the wretched women and children they had knocked down."[55]

Natalie was scheduled to work a booth at the Bazar, but not until the following weekend. She knew nothing about the fire; while it raged she had been in Carmen's arms. When she left Rossi's home in the late afternoon, she noticed a glow in the sky. The heavens, she mused romantically, were on fire to celebrate their love.

At home the next day her stunned parents opened the *New York Times* to this headline: FIRE HORROR IN PARIS: OVER 200 LIVES LOST IN A BAZAAR. "The dead were piled in heaps," the article stated, "especially near the exit, where the charred remains were five feet deep, arms, legs and skulls in a horrible confusion. In some cases only trunks remained with no vestige of clothing on any of the bodies."[56]

Frantic, they wired Natalie, but she didn't receive (or didn't bother to read) the telegram for days. It wasn't until the Barneys had imagined her death by fire a thousand times that she cabled a reply. Relieved but exasperated, they decided to bring her home. Albert sailed immediately to haul her back, and by early June Natalie was once again racing the two-seater along Bar Harbor's dusty roads. There and in Washington she successfully played the popular debutante. "No young woman of the gay* set at the capital is more admired than Miss Nathalie Barney," a columnist wrote around this time. "[She is] always in the latest Parisian style. Her features are pretty, her figure dainty. She is a girl who appears in fluff and frills, jewels, floating draperies, and who is picturesque in every costume she wears. . . . She rides and drives admirably, dances gracefully and is a witty conversationalist."[57]

Natalie would always have a gift for extracting pleasure from her circumstances, no matter what they were. Nonetheless, having tasted freedom's sinful fruit in Paris, she was bored with the old routine. She yearned for Europe, and was "eager to resume my exploration of other worlds and, particularly, to pursue the kind of adventures which excited me, in contrast to the rigid protocol of high society." But, as Albert made clear, she wouldn't be allowed to return unless she behaved herself.

---

*Amusing, isn't it? But in those days the word "gay" meant only: bright, lively, cheerful and/or given to social pleasure.

Reunited with Eva, Natalie was shocked to discover on her body a web of fine scars. Eva explained that she had been tempted by another woman but wanted to remain faithful to Natalie; the lacerations were her self-inflicted punishment, much as Christian martyrs beat themselves with thorns to drive away forbidden thoughts. "I possess too Christian a soul," she said.[58] Natalie softly kissed each of the scars. However, she neither understood nor respected Eva's punishment. She herself had no qualms about being unfaithful. In fact, she was coming around to the idea that infidelity was something to celebrate.

"To love," she would write, "it's necessary for me to love doubly, because it's not except by contrast that I can feel and make everybody else feel. I contrast the joy of one mistress with the sadness of another . . . between those two [beings] I can feel to the maximum and savor each feeling. Being fidel in my infidelity, it's next to one lover that I fully appreciate the worth of the other, and next to that other that I regret the one that I just left. Let me dare to proclaim: it's love that I love above everything else, love is the difficult god whom I adore through each of my lovers, a god whom I cannot attain except through them."[59]

NATALIE'S AMERICAN EXILE ended in the summer of 1898, when the Barneys departed for a long European sojourn. At Albert's insistence, they went directly to the fashionable French seaside resort of Étretat. Longing for Paris, Natalie was bored and unhappy with the conventional socialites who held sway in the casinos and on the tennis courts. She spent two restless months reading poetry, taking violin lessons, and swimming. She received weekly letters from Bob back in Pittsburgh, promising to join her in the spring. It wasn't until late fall that the family traveled to Paris. Albert quickly went on to London, leaving the women to rent a furnished apartment at Villa des Dames, a pension that catered to female artists.

This time Alice signed on for lessons at Carmen Rossi's new art school. It was backed by the American painter James Whistler, who came by now and then to critique the students' work. One day, glancing over Alice's shoulder, he chided her for being too clever. Then, pleased at her lack of offense, he asked to see more of her work. She invited him to call at Villa des Dames, and before long he was dropping by regularly for tea and conversation before the cozy fire. He even consented to pose for her. Natalie, who stayed in her room writing poetry and love letters during his visits, heard their serious conversation alternating with gales of laughter. In future years Alice credited Whistler with helping to develop her talent, and three decades later she wrote a play about him. The dialogue suffers from coyness, but the romantic innuendo is intriguing.

By now, Natalie had come fully into her own as a bold seductress. She rarely hesitated to proposition an attractive woman, even a complete stranger. She always expressed her desire forthrightly, making it clear that she offered not only physical but emotional transcendence. If she felt that the "no" greeting her proposal was in any way tentative, she pulled out all the stops. It wasn't unusual for her to call on a woman for weeks, showing off her many charms while gradually wearing down resistance. By her own admission she received rejections, but her percentage of conquests was high. In fact, it sometimes seemed as if conquest was all that mattered to her. She described herself in those days as a butterfly who, after sampling the scent of a particular blossom, fluttered rapidly to the next. "I enjoy them quickly," she wrote, "and [there is] usually no tomorrow."[60]

When Bob Cassatt joined Natalie in the spring, they went to see his aunt Mary, who had lived in Paris for years. In 1880, when he was seven, his family had come abroad to visit the famous painter, who had "discovered in her younger nephew Robbie an interest in art and had him painting beside her every day."[61] He had long ago given up artistic pursuits, however, and was now trying to follow in the footsteps of his successful father. Natalie's only recorded comment about the visit to Mary Cassatt, in the unpublished "Memoirs of a European American," was that "her scenes were too full of repressed motherhood."

Natalie's treatment of her fiancé, *blanc* or not, was shameless. Because her parents trusted Bob, she was allowed out in his company without a chaperone. After telling Alice that they were going to a gallery or the theater, Bob would escort her to a prearranged meeting place for one of her romantic trysts and return at a designated time to pick her up. Sometimes he simply waited outside in his carriage. He knew that sex with Natalie, even after marriage, could never be, and he'd promised not to expect anything but chaste, intellectual enjoyment. All he asked in return was that she keep a corner of her soul just for him. As long as she remained a butterfly, true to him in her way, their unusual arrangement managed to work. Each pursued women, often abetted or counseled by the other. Once, disguised with a curly black wig, Natalie accompanied him to two places in which decent women never set foot, Maxim's and the Folies Bergère, and helped him choose a prostitute from among the high-stepping kickers.

Perhaps their most unusual adventure involved Carmen, whom they invited to dine in a *cabinet particulier* at a restaurant called Larue's. These private dining rooms, equipped with soft couches, were designed for seduction. Unless invited inside, waiters left champagne and food on a table inside the door (they were prevented from observing the room's occupants by a strategically placed screen).

On this night, Carmen, after downing generous amounts of champagne, began to rain passionate, insistent kisses on Natalie. Feeling that things weren't about to stop there, Will (the pseudonym Natalie used for Bob) discreetly disappeared around the screen and firmly closed the door. Carmen and Natalie moved to the couch, aware only of each other, until:

> . . . our frolics and amorous sighs were interrupted by a big sob coming from behind the screen where Will had cagily remained . . . raised at the breast of Puritanism, he couldn't resist [watching us], and after driving Carmen home he despaired, "I didn't know how unbearable and how frightfully moving that would be. Ah! To see you give of yourself in this way, and so possessive of another, and all the while I was biting my fists watching . . . something that no man should have to contemplate."
> "I agree with you. So, then, why did you stay?"
> "I wanted to be a part of it."
> "Good! You were, weren't you? And it's me who must reproach you for your indiscretion, and for putting yourself in . . . this pitiful state."
> "Forgive me, but I love you, I love you so much."
> "So much, that at the first opportunity you find the life you have proposed we share to be unbearable!"[62]

As the conversation continued, Bob swore to Natalie that he could keep up his end of the bargain. It was obvious, however, that a *mariage blanc* would offer hardships for the young couple—far more for Messieur than for Madame.

After Bob returned to Pittsburgh, a friend of Albert's visited Paris and asked Natalie to show him the "bohemian nightlife." She took him to Bullier's, with its noisy, hectic atmosphere. As they tried to converse above the dance hall's boisterous crowd, a sudden hush filled the air. Glancing up, Natalie observed the entrance of three men, a handsome older woman of regal bearing, and an exquisitely beautiful younger woman. As more and more people caught sight of the young beauty, whistling and enthusiastic cheers filled the room. People rose to their feet, and a chant broke out: "The sultana of sex has returned! The sultana of sex has returned!" The beautiful creature smiled solemnly at the crowd, bending her head in acknowledgment.

Across the room, Natalie's companion asked the identity of the angelic-looking woman who was creating such a sensation. She scarcely heard him, so stunned was she by the woman's ethereal loveliness and queenly air of possession. She had seen this woman once before, and never forgotten her. She was the ermine-cloaked Aphrodite from the Bois de Boulogne—the courtesan Liane de Pougy. By now Natalie knew what the word *courtesan* meant. Undeterred, she resolved to become her lover.

FOUR

Natalie and the Courtesan

1899

At the head of all the beautiful courtesans who, along with the great Proustian women, made up the glory of Paris, Mlle. de Pougy triumphed . . . I'd never seen anyone so ideally beautiful . . . prodigiously thin, she had the air of a long hurt lily. She wasn't only ravishing, she was seraphic.

—*André Germain*

Liane de Pougy . . . was launched at the Folies-Bergère by Edward VII, then Prince of Wales, to whom, though he did not know her, she sent a note saying, "Sire: Tonight I make my debut. Deign to appear and applaud me and I am made." He did and she was. Shortly after this, men began dying for her. She made suicide fashionable.

—*Janet Flanner*

*I*MAGINE A TIME in which peace prevails, the economy is strong, and the arts thrive. Intellectual cultivation is encouraged, even celebrated. Books can't be written quickly enough, debates are passionate, scientific advances seem to occur daily. And, in a final touch of splendor, these dazzling times are wrapped in a madcap joie de vivre.

Such an era was France's Belle Époque, a period dating from about 1890 to the outbreak of the Great War in 1914. At least that's how we, looking back, like to imagine it. In reality, the Belle Époque produced the usual quotient of human misery and an outsized share of social upheaval, symbolized by the violent factionalism that rocked the country during the Dreyfus affair of the 1890s. And yet, despite the ugly realities, in many ways these years merit their nickname: *Belle Époque*—the Beautiful Era.

Paris, then the world's capital of culture, brimmed with theaters, galleries, cafés, music halls, bookstalls, and restaurants. The popular press came into being, feeding a hungry public with newspapers, journals, and topical chapbooks. Restless artists seized new ground. Impressionism, once shocking, had become old hat to painters such as Matisse, Picasso, or Toulouse-Lautrec. The ornamental, asymmetrical decorative style known as Art Nouveau was coming into its own. A young woman from California, Isadora Duncan, adopted the city and revolutionized the world of dance. Claude Debussy's exotic rhythms and innovative chord changes helped usher in the music of Erik Satie, Maurice Ravel, and Frederick Delius.

It was an age of cancan dancers and café concerts, of Sarah Bernhardt's dramatic excesses on the stage. Music halls abounded, among them the Jardin de Paris, the Parisiana, the Décadents, the Olympia. Everyone flocked to the Moulin Rouge to see Jane Avril dance her wild quadrille, or to Cabaret Mirliton, where the handsome Aristide Bruant—with his brown velvet trouser legs tucked into high boots, his blazing red shirt and black sombrero—was all the rage, singing sinister tunes of prostitutes and thieves. And people would go anywhere to hear the harsh-voiced, mournful, and intensely thin Yvette Guilbert sing of love.

It was a time when the literary salon still played an important role in cultivating great writers, when an overheard phrase from Anatole France or the Count de Montesquiou would make the rounds in literary cafés for weeks. The poet Arthur Rimbaud became celebrated for his brilliance, infamous for his decadence, and retired from writing, all by the age of nineteen. Marcel Proust, scribbling in a cork-lined room, produced the world's most notorious roman à clef.

Perhaps most important, it was an age of *le plaisir,* something few enjoyed more than the wealthy Parisian aristocracy. Most members of the privileged classes did not work, choosing to live instead a life of leisure, luxury, and frivolity. Lavish displays of wealth were admired. Extravagant costume balls, to which guests wore garments costly enough to feed a provincial family for a year, were common. Women dressed in elegant gowns from the House of Worth or sported the more daring and high-colored creations of Paul Poiret. Jewels dazzled. Gold gleamed. Furs warmed.

In the end, nothing symbolized the wild extravagance of the Belle Époque better than the courtesan—or, as she was also called, the Grande Horizontale, Demoiselle de Plaisir, Créature, or Cocotte. No mere prostitute, the courtesan was the direct descendant of the great royal mistresses of the past, when the love of a king translated into wealth and power. Diane de Poitiers played a role so prominent in the sixteenth-century reign of Henry II that she eclipsed his formidable wife, Catherine de Médicis. A century later the Marquise de Pompadour strongly influenced the political decisions of her lover, Louis XV, and lent powerful support to Encyclopedists such as Voltaire and Rousseau. For centuries courtiers and foreign ambassadors offered such powerful women lavish gifts of jewelry and money, hoping to gain their ear. Royal mistresses, in effect, ran a shadow court. And from the stratospheric heights of this demi-monde, this half-world, they reigned unofficially but supremely.

The Revolution of 1789 put an end to the royal mistress (and quite a bit else). It wasn't until Napoléon's fall in 1815, marking an end to generations of war, that she began to reemerge. Peace and a burgeoning economy, induced by the industrial revolution, replaced strife. A society that had once consisted of two classes—peasants and the aristocracy—had grown increasingly complex. A rising middle class accumulated wealth and power. New markets developed for clothing, homes, restaurants, travel, music, literature, theater, art . . . and pleasure.

Two decades or so into the nineteenth century the royal mistress was reborn as the courtesan. In a largely Catholic society, which demanded that its well-born daughters marry as virgins, the role of a courtesan was almost a necessity. Skilled lovers, courtesans kept husbands-to-be sexually satisfied. In addition, they cared for the needs of foreign visitors, husbands who strayed, and men who simply preferred their company to that of "proper" women.

Eventually courtesans, like their predecessors, developed power, though now it came from notoriety rather than through the channeled influence of a king or other prominent lover. Having a well-known courtesan as a mistress became such a great status symbol that men fought and schemed to be in the arms of the most desirable cocottes. Visiting dignitaries, including foreign kings and presidents, arranged to dine intimately with the demimonde's most celebrated members; in fact, the second floor of the Café Anglais contained a private dining room, lavishly decorated in white and gold and including a comfortable sofa, reserved for persons of royal rank. Duels were fought over courtesans. They were gifted with invaluable treasures, broke hearts, caused bankruptcies, and not infrequently precipitated the suicide of a rejected swain. The most sought-after women became wealthy, owning châteaux, fabulous horses, priceless jewelry.

A story that made the rounds tells of a French princess paying a call at the House of Worth. She sits in a room, waiting patiently to be helped, when suddenly the curtains part and a well-known courtesan enters. The princess turns her face away, horrified to be in the same room with such a woman. How, she wonders, can they allow such a creature into the establishment? Her world falls completely apart when the courtesan, a lavish spender, is helped first.

By the end of the century, the grand horizontals were in their full glory, so desired that they could choose those to whom they would condescend to sell their love. Admirers considered their work an art of the highest order, requiring beauty, skill, and charm. While some courtesans were vulgar, the best and most famous tended to be cultured and intelligent, capable of seducing not only a man's body, but his mind. Skillful conversationalists, they could make even a dullard feel like a masterful raconteur, and their dinner parties sparkled with brilliant talk. They enhanced their status as professional beauties by dominating women's fashion and by displaying their gowns, jewels, and immense hats at the theater or in daily carriage rides through the Bois de Boulogne.

"The courtesans of the epoch," wrote the Duchesse de Clermont-Tonnerre, "commonly called 'grues' or 'cocottes,' enjoyed a glory which has vanished. . . . When they passed by in their victorias, in showy dresses, their dyed, yellow hair under immense hats, in a physical exuberance often due to their country-origin, they had no great difficulty in fascinating the rutting males. It was the fashion among the young men to run themselves into debt for those 'creatures,' as the phrase then was."[1]

Aside from the direct transfer of sex for money, courtesans were yesterday's equivalent of today's superstar models and actresses. Like their modern counterparts, they transformed beauty into fame and riches. The Belle Époque's popular media devoted reams of print to their comings and goings (one profitable journal, *Gil Blas,* devoted itself to demimonde gossip). Photographs, postcards, and posters of the current stars were widely available for sale. Just as crowds gather now for the slightest glimpse of a movie star, so they gathered then in the Bois to watch the courtesans pass by in procession, their open victorias pulled by fabulous steeds, their lacy umbrellas unfurled to keep the sun from pale skin. The public knew the courtesans' names, gossiped about them like friends, and, of course, had particular favorites.

IN THE YEARS immediately before and after the century's turn there were perhaps forty courtesans in Paris who'd made it to the summit of their profession. They were widely known, their names were constantly heard, and their lives were breathlessly followed by shopgirls in the pages of *Gil Blas.* High above them, at the summit of success, riches, and notoriety, ruled three beauties known far and wide as "Les Grandes Trois." They were Emilienne d'Alençon, La Belle Otéro, and—the unquestioned queen—Mademoiselle Liane de Pougy.

Born in 1869 as Anne-Marie Chassaigne, de Pougy belonged to an old, royalist family who considered the yearly anniversary of Louis XVI's death by guillotine a day of mourning. Following a century-old family tradition, her father, Pierre, became a cavalry officer and was awarded the Legion of Honor. Though proud, the family was poor. Anne-Marie remembered her mother selling precious heirlooms to buy food, and she grew up dreaming of luxuries she could not have.

A good student, she received a convent education in Rennes. However, like most girls, she was expected to marry when her education ended, and at sixteen she was wed to a twenty-four-year-old naval officer named Armand Pourpe. On their wedding night he took her with such violence that, fifty years later, she still spoke of the experience with horror. They honeymooned in Paris, where they saw Sarah Bernhardt in *Tosca,* and returned to the provinces. Back home, Anne-Marie couldn't stop thinking of the luxury and beauty she'd seen in the city.

The initial lack of conjugal delicacy was the precursor to a brutal marriage. Jealous of Anne-Marie's beauty and alarmed by her independence, Armand tried ruling her through intimidation. In 1887, at eighteen, she gave birth to a son. She named him Marc and sometimes played with him as if he were a doll, but felt little maternal attachment. Soon a new assignment brought the couple to Marseilles, where Anne-Marie took a lover. Armand found them in bed, brandished a gun, and shot his wife in the lower back. Unharmed but for the scar that marred her perfect body, she ran away to Paris. Armand sent Marc to live with his parents in the Suez and sued for divorce, which was granted in 1890.

In Paris, Anne-Marie taught piano and gave English lessons. It's possible, even probable, that she also earned money as a street prostitute. Before too long, however, she'd changed her name, found her way onto the stage, and launched her career as a courtesan. The rest is Belle Époque history.

To say that Liane de Pougy was celebrated in her time is a marvel of understatement. The public referred to her as the Divine, the Queen of Love, the Pearl, the Sultana of Sex. Her beauty and intelligence were extolled from one end of Europe to the next. Her image on photographs, postcards, and posters guaranteed a sellout. An expensive toilet water by Delettrez was named for her and showed her picture on the label. Once, at the annual carnival in Nice, she was crowned *"Perle du carnaval,"* and then, tucked like a human pearl into a giant oyster shell, carried through the cheering crowds on the backs of French sailors.

She was a favorite topic of newspaper gossips, novelists, trendsetting journal writers, esteemed diarists, and others. The *Gil Blas* reporters doted on her to an almost ludicrous extent ("After a triumphant promenade of her beauty in England, where the Lords kneeled before her . . ."). In the acclaimed journal *La Revue Blanche,* writer Alfred Jarry claimed that she was the very incarnation of beauty. One of the snobby, diary-keeping Goncourt brothers wrote that she was the most beautiful woman of the entire nineteenth century. When she visited Italy the country's leading literary genius, Gabriele D'Annunzio, spread a gold cloth at her feet and sprinkled it with rose petals.

Liane's regal bearing and elegance were legendary. Once in the early 1890s, before her face was widely recognized, she attended the opera wearing a diamond tiara, a white gown covered with pearls, and an ermine coat. When she sat in her box, "as though at a signal, the whole house was on its feet and turned towards me, greeting me. Amused, I gave a gracious smile . . . The house applauded. I had no idea what it was all about." It was about this: the audience thought Liane was the queen of Sweden, who was expected at the opera that same night. Liane, her companion murmured, was "how people expect a Queen to look."[2]

Another time, informed that a rival courtesan intended to outshine her at a ball by wearing fabulously expensive jewelry, Liane retaliated with simplicity. She showed up clad in a severe white dress with a plunging neckline and carrying a single white rose. The only gem she wore was a diamond—very large—at her throat. Trailing close behind came her maid, dripping with layers of priceless bracelets, necklaces, brooches, and earrings.

There was far more to Mlle. de Pougy than a pleasing exterior. She played both piano and guitar quite well, spoke fluent English and Spanish, and rode horseback with panache. She was the eventual author of one play and seven potboiling novels (a few of which were best-sellers). Her daily diary jottings, fascinating for the matter-of-fact way they discuss both the dull and the dissolute, were published posthumously as *My Blue Notebooks.* Although she wasn't much of an actor, singer, or dancer, that didn't stop her from performing to sellout crowds at the Folies Bergère, the Olympia, the Théâtre Française in St. Petersburg, and other top venues. With characteristic frankness she admitted her lack of acting talent, and loved repeating the advice she once received from Sarah Bernhardt. "Display your beauty," the great actress advised her, "but once you are on the stage you had better keep your pretty mouth shut."[3]

As the century neared its turn, Liane de Pougy was unrivaled as a courtesan and free to pick and choose from the multitudes of titled, talented, and wealthy men who courted her. The fortunate few allowed the privilege of bedding her paid dearly. One young hopeful sent a dozen roses, in a solid silver vase, in a handsome carriage pulled by four exquisite horses in solid silver harness . . . all of it for Liane. On a voyage to Russia she was accompanied by her Parisian jeweler, who brought along his best stock; while there he sold it all (and it all ended up on Liane). Her favorite necklace, containing five rows of perfect, and perfectly valuable, natural pearls, was once stolen; a suitor went out and simply bought another. It's said that the librettist Henri Meilhac, who cowrote the book for *Carmen* and many other famous operas, paid 80,000 francs simply to gaze upon her naked body.

It was this woman who, one winter night in 1899, brought the crowd at the Bal Bullier to its feet. In return, the Sultana of Sex offered her sad, solemn smile, and took her seat. Bending her swanlike neck forward, she quietly conversed with friends. Across the room Natalie Barney sat stunned, gazing at the unapproachable goddess with longing.

That night Natalie dreamed about Liane. In the morning she awoke, chastising herself for having wasted so much time mooning from afar. Now, firmly determined to meet and woo the angelic-looking woman, she began laying plans. She neither worried about failure nor questioned her ability to seduce the greatest courtesan of the Belle Époque. From birth Natalie had been given or had seized almost everything she wanted; why should anyone, even Liane de Pougy, elude her grasp?

Typically, Natalie felt that a direct approach was best, but that timing was crucial. Gossip had it that Liane was currently in the thrall of a German "protector," and Natalie thought it wise to wait until he was out of the picture. In the interim, she would time her daily horseback rides to coincide with Liane's carriage procession through the Bois. When Liane began to appear unescorted, Natalie would know that the protector had returned home. Then—and only then—she would make her move.

LIANE DE POUGY was not the only thing on Natalie's mind. In fact, having discovered over the past year or so that she actually *possessed* a mind, Natalie was using it to the utmost. Disdainful of book learning, she had never excelled in classroom work, and until recently had thought of herself as someone with average intelligence. "In the old Bar Harbour days," she recalled, "the Hale boys used to allude to my mind as something that hardly belonged to me—and indeed I paid far less attention to it than to my long light hair."[4]

People had raved for years about Natalie's quick retorts and the way she could instantly sum up a complicated idea with a snappy epigram. She had slowly come to realize what others had long understood: such rare wit could only be produced by a mind of equally rare intelligence. Indeed, a year or two hence Natalie would hear herself described by Parisian intellectuals as "the rarest and most intelligent woman" of the time.

Since bidding good-bye to the boring make-work of governesses and finishing schools, Natalie's intellect had found a focus: poetry. She had always preferred verse over all other forms of literature, and for the last couple of years had poured her emotions into writing it. After a brief experiment with free-form verse, she had begun to pattern her poetics after Symbolists like Mallarmé and Verlaine. Eager to improve, she had lately toyed with the idea of taking on an instructor. "Me," she said, "who wanted to be a poet at all hours and above all a poet of life."[5]

Music was another of Natalie's major interests. She attended the opera often, and practiced her violin each day. Many people who knew her around the turn of the century remarked at how well she played. She also continued to study ancient Greek, albeit intermittently. In this endeavor she was encouraged by Eva, whose own interest in Greek language and culture was deeply serious. It wasn't simple whim that propelled these two young women in such studies. They were part of a societal trend that glorified the simplicity of the ancient past while viewing the industrialized present with disdain. A backlash against the increasing homogenization of the machine age, this trend ultimately resulted in movements like Dada and surrealism.

At the century's turn, however, protests against machines took prettier forms, including the graceful curvilinear shapes of Art Nouveau and the glorification of all things Greek. Ancient Greece, considered "purer" than the present, was wildly popular. People threw Greco-Roman costume parties, gave their children names like Helen and Homer, and devoured the myths in Frazer's *Golden Bough*, published in 1890. In some artistic circles, paganism— in the sense of honoring a pantheon of ancient deities—became fashionable, and people dallied in moon goddess cults and the like. Isadora Duncan, conquering Paris in her flowing Greek robes, epitomized the current ideal of freedom and beauty.

There were other reasons for Natalie to learn the ancient language. The knowledge of Greek or Latin was then the province of a mostly male intellectual aristocracy: those who could speak, read, and understand the idiom belonged; those who couldn't, didn't. So long as ancient languages were considered to be the realm of men, women were deprived of membership in a powerful elite. In learning Greek, women like Natalie and Eva not only obtained the credentials of entry, but announced their equality with men.

An even more compelling reason for Natalie's Greek studies was that she wanted to read Sappho—greatest of all Greek lyric poets and the earliest-known female writer in the West—in the original, perhaps completing her own translations. Although Sappho never explicitly referred to homosexual practices in her work, from ancient times onward she has been viewed as a lover of women. Natalie was not alone in her fascination with the poet. In fact, Sappho and her verse, much of which is erotic and directed to women, were experiencing a long-overdue and quite literal rebirth.

In the late nineteenth century, a wealth of papyri were discovered in the Nile Valley, some of them wrapped around corpses, stuffed inside sacred animals such as cats, or placed beside the dead as reading material in the next world. Papyri shreds were also found in ancient garbage dumps, where, covered by sand and protected by Egypt's dry climate, refuse had been preserved across the millennia. When archaeologists dug up the dried-out garbage in the 1890s, they found—amidst gnawed bones, broken pottery, and damaged trinkets—delicate bits of papyrus. Thus it was that fragmented works of the ancients, including Aristotle, Homer, Sappho, and Sophocles, were resurrected.

Sappho turned out to be amazingly popular in the modern age, exciting interest even among those who rarely cracked the pages of a book. Odd as it seems, in the midst of the prudish Victorian era—at a time when the queen herself dismissed the idea of love between women with the words *"That* does not exist!"*—the ancient lyricist fascinated the public. Perhaps the fact that a woman so liberated lived two thousand years ago titillated the repressed culture of the late nineteenth century. Nothing better sums up the sapphic fad of these years than an ironic fact gleefully revealed by Natalie in *Souvenirs indiscrets:* the ferry that transported her family and all of polite society between the mainland and Bar Harbor was named *Sappho.*

WHILE WAITING FOR the perfect moment to approach Liane, Natalie decided to pique the courtesan's curiosity by sending daily bouquets of long-stemmed flowers pinned with tantalizing notes such as "From a stranger—alas! And who doesn't want to be one any more." With the conscious intent of avoiding any possible scandal by remaining incognito, she signed herself Florence Temple-Bradford. For months after they met, Liane believed this to be Natalie's name.

Natalie also considered the all-important question of what to wear to their first encounter. The approach of Mardi Gras, traditionally a time of masquerade balls and fêtes, provided the perfect excuse to indulge her love of costumes, particularly her fondness for the attire of a Renaissance page or knight. A strong symbolism lies behind this predilection for knightly costumes. Natalie was immensely self-centered, but a part of her soul was nonetheless inhabited by, for lack of a better term, a knight—a dashing rescuer of damsels (and gentlemen!) in distress who never hesitated to wield a sword in the face of big and little dragons. Although entirely without religion, she nonetheless possessed a near-messianic belief in her ability to save or at least better another's life. She often spoke of dispensing her love to others as if it were a healing balm, or a pathway to a happier existence.

It should be noted that Natalie's knight operated only on a one-to-one basis. While she was capable of great affection for friends and lovers, she was indifferent to humanity en masse. The sufferings of a group or class meant nothing to her. "Perhaps she was not unfeeling after all," George Wickes noted, "but merely more honest than most in facing the fact that one can only love individuals, not abstractions. Hypocrisy had no part in her nature."[6]

At the well-known stage costumer, Landolf's, Natalie ordered a stunning page's outfit of snug, gray silk tights; a white linen shirt with billowing pleated sleeves; and a short green-brocade and lavender-blue velvet tunic embroidered in silver and pearls with a lily, Liane's emblem. On a conscious level she chose this costume because she intended to introduce herself as a "page of love," sent by Sappho to serve Liane. On another level, perhaps hidden from herself, the costume declared her knightly determination to rescue Liane from her courtesan's life. Natalie wanted not only to possess Liane, but to save her.

She didn't have to wait long. In early February, *Gil Blas* discussed Liane's breakup with the German baron. When Natalie next spotted the great beauty in the Bois, she rode in her carriage alone. The time had come. Natalie sent Liane a dozen of the year's first black iris, just shipped from the south, with the provocative note: "From a stranger . . . ?" Next morning, when Liane stepped from her carriage, a black iris was tucked at her waist. Natalie was thrilled. That very afternoon, when her mother was occupied with Whistler, she slipped into the page's outfit, covered the costume with a cloak, and took a carriage to Liane's residence.

What happened next was reported by Liane de Pougy herself in a tell-all saga, *Idylle saphique*. Reprinted nearly seventy times in its first year alone,[7] and the talk of Paris for months, it recounted every detail of her affair with Natalie (who read drafts and contributed a chapter). Published in 1901, *Idylle saphique* is a hothouse bouquet of a book overflowing with exclamation points, suggestive ellipses, and emotional excess. No roman à clef ever dressed its characters in more transparent disguises. Besides Natalie (known in the book as

Florence Temple-Bradford, Flossie, Moon-Beam, or Flaxen Flower) and Liane (Annhine de Lys, Nhine, Nhinon), other recognizable figures included Liane's best friend and sister courtesan, Valtesse de la Bigne (Altesse), Bob Cassatt (Will), and Eva Palmer, whose real first name is used.

On the opening page, Annhine de Lys, disillusioned with the glamorous but empty sterility of her life—dress fittings, horse races, voguish restaurants—complains to Altesse. "I'll tell you frankly," she says, "I'm suffering from this life." Tesse, a grand horizontal of the old school, offers little sympathy. "A courtesan must never cry," she proclaims, adding that Liane must "dedicate her life, and above all her youth, to laughter, joy, and pleasure."

Soon a caller is announced. According to the maid, she is a pretty young woman—blond, fresh-faced, and chicly clad in a couturier overcoat. In a note written on expensive pearl-gray paper, the caller begs in flowery words to be received. Liane decides to amuse herself. "You stretch out on my chaise lounge," she urges Altesse. "Snuggle into the cushions and under the ermine covers . . . and pretend you're me."

Florence Temple-Bradford is ushered into Annhine's gold-and-white boudoir, where the two practical jokers, one lying provocatively on the Louis XV chaise and the other hidden in a corner, are treated to the sight of a "ravishing young woman of twenty approaching with slow steps and lowered eyes. She carried in her arms a bouquet of pale chrysanthemums, gold lilies, and red roses." Flossie, trembling with emotion, falls worshipfully to her knees, seizes what she thinks is Nhinon's hand, and covers it with kisses. Blushing, she speaks softly of her love until, raising her eyes and finding not Annhine but Altesse, she breaks into sobs. Sorry for the hurt she's caused, Annhine jumps from her hiding place. Flossie, ecstatic, sweeps off her cloak to reveal her Renaissance costume, announces that she has been sent by Sappho, and falls to her knees at the courtesan's feet.

Nhine is delighted by the young woman's audacity. "How did you dare to come here like this?" she asks, running her fingers through the stranger's blond hair. "Weren't you afraid? Your family, your reputation, not to mention me—I might have received you quite badly . . . perhaps I don't share your tastes and your ideas."

"I'll convert you!" the confident Flossie replies, adding: "I'm not asking anything except to love . . . adore . . . admire. Nothing else, my Nhinon, than to be accepted as your Page, your fervent little Page of love."

With the eye of a professional beauty, Nhine takes stock of the young page and decides that she likes her beautiful blue eyes with their unusual violet tinge around the iris. Her ravishing hair is like a "moonbeam . . . I'll call you that: Moon-Beam!" Even Flossie's teeth come under scrutiny. "Very white," she murmurs approvingly, "very beautiful. They make me afraid. You have the mouth of a vicious infant, Moon-Beam. You have a vicious mouth . . . [your] lips are sensual, a little thick, [your] jaw is strong. . . ." She takes pleased note of Flossie's ready blush, and then returns to her eyes: "They're blue-green, and your pupil is enormous, almost intrusive." The young American, she decides, is beautiful—but, she adds, "not as beautiful as Altesse or me." Eventually, after winning permission to return, Flossie takes her leave.

The next morning Flossie watches breathlessly as Nhine, in her octagonal *salle de bain,* removes her lace underclothes, ascends a golden pedestal, and slowly lowers herself into the turquoise-and-crystal encrusted tub. At a gesture from Annhine, Flossie enthusiastically disrobes and joins her in the water, where she is permitted a few kisses and allowed to anoint Nhine with perfume. They kiss and fondle. Drinking tea in the nude, Nhine sips from her delicate Sèvres cup, bends forward, and fills Flossie's mouth with the warm, perfumed liquid. Flossie explodes with passion and throws herself at the courtesan, who moves away. "You're killing me," Flossie moans. "You're making me crazy." Such teasing goes on for a couple of days, but eventually Nhine cannot resist the American's golden charm. Pressing close to her, she murmurs: "Flossie, make me love you!" Needless to say, Flossie complies.

THERE WAS NOTHING new about sapphic literature in France, where the genre had made a steady appearance throughout the nineteenth century. Books like Adolphe Belot's *Mademoiselle Giraud ma femme* (1870) and Jane de la Vaudère's *Les demi-sexes* (1897) were trashy potboilers. Others have become classics: Théophile Gautier's *Mademoiselle de Maupin* (1835), Charles Baudelaire's *Flowers of Evil* (1857), Émile Zola's *Nana* (1880), Jean Lorrain's witty *Une femme par jour* (1896), and *Le journal d'une femme de chambre* (1900) by satiric novelist Octave Mirbeau.

Most such works, written by and intended for men, brazenly exploited their heroines' sexuality. After a reasonable amount of titillation for the reader, the women were usually punished for their perverted inclinations. In Belot's book, one woman drowns and her lover dies of meningitis. Vaudère condemned her female couple to perish in a symbolic blaze of hellish flames. Baudelaire wasn't so crude: he simply makes clear his dislike and disgust of Sappho and her "manlike" ways, accuses her of blasphemy and debauchery, and paints an altogether unpleasant portrait of life in her circle.

Liane de Pougy was much more democratic. *Idylle saphique* was intended to appeal to all readers, regardless of their sex, inclinations, or moral outlook. Her legion of fans was thrilled to learn more about her. Parisian insiders had fun deciphering allusions to real-life luminaries such as her former lover, Baron Maurice Rothschild, and her powerful enemy-turned-pal, writer Jean Lorrain. Just about everyone—gay or straight, man or woman—enjoyed reading the provocative sex scenes, which, though they always trailed off just short of indecency, offered glimpses of threeways, bordellos, and much more. And the moral prudes? They were rewarded with Annhine de Lys's eventual punishment for debauchery: death.

The demise of Liane's alter ego did not mean that she felt lesbianism should be punished. As she admitted later, a negative end for lesbian lovers "was necessary . . . in those days, in order to find a publisher who would consent to bring out a book on the subject."[8]

Liane's proclivities were no secret, and gossip sheets like *Gil Blas* had long made mention of her "petites amies." There is no denying that she loved women, and made love to them, for much of her life. Ironically, many of the grand horizontals were lesbians: the queens of love, when their duties were done, loved other queens. Zola acknowledged this in *Nana,* in which a courtesan so loved women that she picked up likely-looking prospects all over Paris, ravishing them in her carriage while being driven about. One of Liane's great passions was another famous Belle Époque courtesan, Emilienne Alençon, whose "tip-tilted nose you could eat . . . [and who] installed herself in my bed . . . to my great pleasure."[9]

EVEN THOUGH NATALIE contributed some of the writing in *Idylle saphique,* she would always have conflicted feelings about the book. Whenever she'd spot a copy in bookstores, she'd wince, and her longtime housekeeper claimed that Natalie asked her never to read it. Yet she continued giving away copies of the book into her eighties, saying, "There's our whole story. Minute by minute, or almost."[10]

Natalie felt that *Idylle saphique* created a flattering picture of Liane at her expense. While she admitted that most of the story was accurate, she disagreed with some portrayals. "Many truths suffered in [*Idylle saphique*]," she maintained. "Among others, that of the innocent courtesan swept away and seduced little by little by the vicious young foreigner." To the contrary, Natalie insisted, she had been in no hurry to initiate an all-consuming passion because "it would be losing her and losing myself as well. . . . I wanted to seduce not her body, already too monopolized, but her soul, which had been largely ignored."[11]

According to Natalie, that day she dressed as a page and went calling, she did not—as de Pougy related—spout frivolous words of worship. Instead, she argued strongly against Liane's life as a courtesan. "My life is freely chosen," de Pougy responded, "and what's more, it pleases me!"[12] She was so furious, says Barney, that Valtesse rose protectively to her feet. "When a Page becomes so brazen and impertinent," she announced, "it's time for her to take leave." Natalie did so.

Natalie wrote her own version of their story, *Lettres à une connue (Roman de notre temps)*. The handwritten manuscript dates from 1899 and remains unpublished, its pages now badly tattered. Here, Natalie is Fleur-de-Lis and Liane is Lilly. Fleur-de-Lis is far less worshipful of Lilly than Flossie is of Nhine. Lilly also shows a few minor flaws, which is never the case in Liane's book with Nhine. *Lettres à une connue* is just as wildly overwrought and cliché-laden as *Idylle saphique*. In later years Natalie described it, accurately, as naive, exaggerated, and clumsy.

However, the book has a few strong qualities. It's enthusiastic and written with an innocence that Natalie will never again exhibit on paper. It's also remarkable for its clear feminist vision and statements that sound like an early version of gay pride. It's here that Natalie first asks why, if no one blames albinos for their pink eyes, she is blamed for being a lesbian; such differences, she points out, are simply a matter of nature. She would use the same argument many times over the years.

No matter what Natalie's feelings were about *Idylle saphique*, there is no denying that its publication made her a person to know in Paris. Whereas before she was just another of the city's bright, wealthy, and pretty Americans, afterward she was "the" American—a bewitching, fascinating woman who had seduced the Queen of Love. Natalie's legend as a scandalous maverick began with Liane de Pougy, not least because of *Idylle saphique*. She knew this and, because she liked being infamous, she would always be grateful for the role the book had played in her life.

NATALIE WANTED TO believe that what Liane did with men, those acts arising from the professional demands of her "job," didn't take away from the purity of their own relationship. To that end, de Pougy vowed never to have another woman as a lover while they remained together. They pledged love by exchanging rings from Lalique's. Liane's had two intertwined gems meant to symbolize their linked lives. Natalie's deep blue enamel ring was incised by bats encircling heart-shaped moonstones; the inner engraving read: "I am so happy that you suffer from understanding and loving me."

The idea that love equaled suffering was one that Natalie would be forced to test frequently in their union, although not at first. For more than a month after they met, they were together whenever Natalie could come up with a halfway reasonable excuse to be away for a few hours. Alice, as usual, was preoccupied with her own life; between friends, social obligations, art classes, and visits from Whistler, she had little time or inclination for supervising her oldest daughter. On a loose rein, Natalie's liaisons with Liane were easy to arrange.

The two women spent many hours in Liane's elegant Louis XV boudoir. They also went to couturier fittings, rode horseback, took carriage rides, and attended the theater. Natalie, deliriously happy, thought their love would go on forever, but in late March their idyllic existence was placed on temporary hold. Liane had been summoned to Italy by another "protector." Without hesitation or apparent regret, she prepared for the journey. Natalie took the news badly, creating an angry, reproach-filled scene that did nothing to prevent Liane's departure.

Desperate to follow her lover, Natalie talked Alice into spending the Easter holidays in Rome. Once there, they called on the American ambassador's wife, whom they knew from home, and were consequently introduced into the social scene. One night at an embassy ball Natalie learned from a friend, the Marquis R.C., that she had just unknowingly danced with Liane's protector. When she asked why he wasn't in Lugano with Liane, she received shocking news: the protector and his wife were both having an affair with de Pougy, and it was the wife's turn to have the courtesan to herself. Tears sprang to Natalie's eyes over Liane's broken promise not to touch another woman. The marquis whispered, not unkindly: "You attach entirely too much importance to this."[13]

Natalie was in agony. It was one thing to detach herself from Liane's professional association with men, but another thing altogether to think of her being bought by a woman. She dashed off an irate diatribe to Liane about the ugliness of her profession. In reply Liane spoke without shame of her "honest commerce," and advised her Moon-Beam not to get so upset about her professional obligations.

Distraught, Natalie threw herself into socializing. Over the next couple of weeks she hunted in the countryside, went to a soirée at the palatial home of an American-born princess, and attended parties in every corner of Rome. Her Italian social whirl ended only when she and Alice departed for Monte Carlo to join Albert and Laura, just in from the States.

Natalie was shaken at the sight of her father, who looked extremely ill. His handsome face had become puffy and spotted, and his eyes seemed permanently bloodshot. He'd lost weight, was short of breath, and couldn't seem to shake a bothersome cold. He was drinking less, but his tolerance for liquor had plummeted so that now he became easily drunk.

Albert had brought a letter from Bob, which was frosty on the subject of Liane. He knew that kind of woman, he said, having frequented the demimonde since he came of age. He warned her to be on guard against the dangers of that world, most notably promiscuity and moral compromise.

Before leaving for Europe, Albert had discussed marital arrangements with Bob. As he reported now, Bob's father had indicated his own eagerness for the match by offering to forgo Natalie's considerable dowry (upon marriage, the money would instead be given to her). Listening to Albert making plans for her future, Natalie felt oddly chilled. How could she live in Pittsburgh, she wondered, with its propriety and prejudgments? It would be impossible. Their marriage would never work unless Bob agreed to live as they had discussed, following their own needs and desires. They would have to settle all this once and for all when he visited Paris soon.

With Albert planning to stay in Paris for a while, the Barneys rented a handsome home at 53, avenue Victor Hugo with stables and room enough for Alice to paint and entertain. They were settled by late May, in time for Bob's visit.

Natalie had looked forward to seeing him, but was dismayed at his negative opinion of Liane. Even after they met he didn't change his mind, continuing to dislike everything she stood for. However, he did help Natalie slip off for assignations, far more difficult to arrange now that Albert was on the scene. Natalie's contributory chapter in *Idylle saphique* relates an afternoon that she, Liane, and "Will" went to the theater to see Sarah Bernhardt as Hamlet (the play opened on May 20, 1899, and they attended one of the first performances). Will sits neglected in the orchestra while Flossie and Nhine secrete themselves in a latticed *baignoire*. Level with the orchestra, this private box was shielded from the audience's curious eyes by a wooden grille—a good thing, too, since Nhine and Flossie were quite indiscreet.

LIANE WAS OFTEN AWAY from Paris, but tried to be with Natalie whenever she could. These get-togethers usually involved labyrinthine planning, mostly through corresponding via a friend of Natalie's. The phrase "stolen moments of bliss" characterized their encounters, rushed but passionate. They might have seen each other more had Natalie been free to travel, but she couldn't leave Paris without a chaperone.

One day in early summer Natalie's go-between friend brought a letter from Liane telling of her upcoming visit to London to see an old patron. As it turned out, Leonora Howland—whose baby, now a happy toddler, could be left with a governess—would be in London at the same time for a series of private concerts. The Barneys had always considered the older, married woman a proper chaperone, and allowed Natalie to accompany her on the trip.

While the unsuspecting Howland was busy playing music in Belgrave Square mansions and country estates, Natalie and Liane met in unlikely locations: aboard a houseboat, in an auberge west of London at Maidenhead, and in a discreet hotel fronting the Thames. When the trip ended, Natalie was haunted by thoughts of Liane's "supple body, the ways she posed, the promises and projects, her bewitching words, her complaints, and even more eloquent, her silences. . . ."[14]

Later that summer came a far more daring escapade in Brittany. The Barneys planned a long vacation in the old fishing village of Dinard, which was fast becoming an upscale seaside resort with its beautiful sandy beaches, miles of seaside promenades, and profusion of flowers and palm trees. Natalie and Liane decided to have their own vacation in Dinard—without Alice or Albert knowing anything about it, of course. Natalie found a discreet Breton maid and assigned her the task of renting an out-of-the-way cottage for Liane, who would arrive the second week in September and stay until early October. The maid found a small villa in nearby Saint Enogat. Surrounded by a high wall covered with trellised plants, the place afforded privacy and wasn't far from the Barneys' lodgings.

The weeks before Liane's arrival stretched on endlessly, leaving Natalie impatient, anxious, and galloping her frustrations away on horseback. One day she traveled almost twenty miles, pausing at tiny villages along the way to drink fresh cider. Otherwise, she whiled away her time running with a young, "very turn of the century" crowd whose major occupations were sailing, tennis, and dancing. Natalie's interest was piqued by a vacationing Austrian princess. Nicknamed Baby, she lived in the town's most beautiful château, rarely went out in public, and did everything possible to avoid Dinard's gossipy society. Her aloofness made Natalie predisposed to like her, and, when they met a year or so later, they became good friends.

Contemplating the worldly gossips who populated the seaside resort, Natalie worried about whether she could really pull off secret visits to Liane's cottage. As luck had it, almost everybody cleared out in early September, and Liane managed to arrive by train and disappear into the cottage without being recognized.

Once she was tucked safely away, other problems arose. Natalie couldn't just disappear for hours without the Barneys knowing where she was, which meant concocting complicated schemes. During the daytime, when she and

Liane always stayed in the cottage, she would simply say that she was going out for a horseback ride or an afternoon of tennis. It was getting away at night that presented greater difficulties.

On one memorable occasion, Natalie told her parents that she was meeting a friend they knew, Martha. When Liane climbed into the carriage at a pre-arranged location, the family's coachman assumed her to be the expected Martha. He brought them, as asked, to a part of the waterfront not frequented by the trendy crowd, and promised to pick them up later. Once alone, they rented a rowboat. Beneath Natalie's cloak was a sailor costume, and that night she played the role of an old salt. She rowed the boat and sang popular American songs while Liane stretched out on a bed of flowers with her head thrown back. Tucked out of sight in a calm bay, Natalie let down the anchor and they stretched out together. The night sky was rich with stars; Natalie's soul was filled with joy. Years later she remembered feeling that it wasn't possible to survive such ecstasy.

Coming home on such blissful nights with Liane's kisses still fresh on her flesh and mind, Natalie found it difficult to disguise her elation around her parents. Being used to her high spirits, however, they never suspected anything. With the help of Laura, who knew all about Liane, Natalie was able to continue carrying out her schemes.

Happy though she was, Natalie could not keep their idyll going indefinitely. That was made painfully clear by the arrival of a letter from Valtesse de la Bigne. Liane ripped it open, obviously anxious to hear what was going on in the world she had left behind. Her eagerness caused Natalie's heart to drop.

In her youth Valtesse had been the lover of Napoléon III and had served as one of Zola's models for *Nana*. She once said to Liane: "I am a courtesan, and how I do enjoy my work!"[15] She took the profession seriously, and from the beginning had been appalled at the way Liane frittered away valuable time on Natalie. Now she wrote of a young, rich, and handsome man who wanted to meet Liane; she also lectured the younger courtesan sternly for neglecting her professional duties. She was staying too long with "that young one. Come on, that's not serious, is it? You can reward yourself with a caprice, but a caprice that lasts three weeks! Think of the future. Don't throw your youth away. Soon they'll be saying that you're no longer the premier courtesan in Paris . . . don't be ridiculous."[16]

The two lovers fell into their ongoing argument about Liane's profession. Natalie adamantly refused to believe that Liane enjoyed her role in the demi-monde, or that she could endure a life in which she served a man's desires instead of her own. Her recriminations on these and other points had been relentless from the beginning, and she had recently recruited Laura into a plan for "rescuing" Liane. Not only did Liane not want to be rescued, but she found it irritating to be hectored by two rich girls bent on reforming her.

Again and again, Natalie begged Liane to leave her old habits behind. Instead, Liane left Natalie behind, abruptly cutting short her stay and returning to Paris. After receiving a barrage of angry letters from Barney, Liane wrote: "You bore me by repeating all those sermons about my life! My life is probably less hypocritical, less false, and also less calculating . . . than yours. What I do, I do openly . . . everyone knows my aims . . . [and] I don't steal the good will of anyone." However, in one of those tantalizing reversals that kept Natalie intrigued, she admitted that, if she had money, "no man would ever touch me!"[17]

This left Natalie in despair, as she had taken pains to embrace Liane with a love that had a strong spiritual component. Now she needed to prove that she could also provide for Liane's material needs. For that, she needed a lot of money, not the handouts she received from her father. Reluctantly, she knew the time had come to sacrifice her independence and marry Bob. With money of her own (the dowry), she could remove Liane forever from her horrible milieu.

Having made the decision, Natalie wrote a long letter to Bob. Let us, she said, live in pursuit of our interests. Her idea was that, by maintaining a household that looked conventional from the outside, they would be able to safeguard its uniqueness. She posted the letter and held her breath, awaiting his reply. She didn't get a response, and in time realized that one would never come.

Bob, who felt that he had endured enough, soon became engaged to a woman who wanted a traditional life. Learning of his marriage through friends, Natalie felt simultaneously disappointed and relieved for herself, and happy for him. In her writings, Bob became the vague, nearly fictional fiancé of her youth.

JULES CAMBON, the French ambassador to the United States, knew the Barneys from Washington and Bar Harbor, and was among the family's frequent guests in Paris. A distinguished but fierce-looking fellow with a handsome mustache, he would prove a good friend to the Barney women over the years, providing helpful introductions and solving bureaucratic problems.

Natalie turned to Cambon now in her quest to find a worthy tutor of French poetics and classical Greek. One night late in November over dinner at Foyot's—then a haunt of artists, writers, and theatergoers—he introduced her to thirty-year-old Charles Brun, a literary professor and poet whose two slender volumes of classic verse, *Chants d'éphèbe* and *Onyx et pastels,* were well regarded. A prolific contributor to literary journals and a lover of folklore, this tall, thin, ink-stained man viewed the world through pince-nez that never rested long atop his bony nose before falling off. He agreed to become Natalie's teacher. To her pleasure, she soon found that he wasn't put off by the sapphic nature of her writing.

He may already have known about Natalie. She and Liane had attempted to be discreet, but word of the affair had slowly leaked out. Denizens of the demimonde were the first to know that de Pougy was involved with a young American woman who called herself Florence Temple-Bradford. *Gil Blas* referred sarcastically to the "loving soul who wants to be around [Liane] ceaselessly, the exquisite American girl who sings to her such delicious psalms . . ." It was disapprovingly murmured that Mlle. de Pougy was turning her back on entire fortunes for the sake of the young American woman, upon whom she bestowed her favors free of charge. It was no longer only Valtesse de la Bigne who lectured about her lack of professionalism. "Everyone tells me to let you go," Liane wrote Flossie. *"Everyone."*

People were saying the very same thing to Natalie. Around this time she was approached by a close friend of the Barney family, who considered it his "painful duty" to tell her "what they are saying." He repeated "things so repugnant," Natalie recalled, "that one has to pity the minds that have conceived them. Our feelings and our acts are cheapened by publicizing them and it's hard to restore our pure intentions once they have passed through certain brains."[18]

Soon enough, Albert learned about Natalie and Liane. Exactly how and when is unclear, since there are multiple accounts: he came across Natalie reading a love note from Liane, or a friend reported that he'd seen them in London, or he received a letter filled with salacious details. All these stories may well be true. In fact, it's entirely plausible that he heard the same rumor from a variety of sources. Perhaps he finally acknowledged what he had simply refused to believe for so long.

What's important is that he did confront his wayward daughter. According to the actress Charlotte Stern, a friend (probably a lover) of Natalie's around the century's turn, he was so enraged that he "pulled her by her hair, which was quite long, onto the sidewalk of avenue Victor-Hugo."[19] Natalie tried to convince Albert that she only wanted to be a friend to Liane and to help her, but he would hear none of it. He forced her to promise never to see Liane again (a promise she forgot about at the earliest opportunity).

Even as Albert exploded, the affair with Liane was entering a destructive stage on its own. Weary of Natalie's constant nagging and egged on by friends, Liane had returned to her courtesan's life with a vengeance. As far as she was concerned, all bets were now off, even with respect to promises about other women. "I was unforgivable," she recalled years later. "One day I . . . went into a bedroom with Valtesse, locked the door and refused her nothing, highly amused at the thought of Flossie speculating and suffering on the other side of the door."[20] Another time, according to Natalie, Liane brought her to a bordello and made her watch while she made love to one of the young female prostitutes. "That debauch without joy or beauty sickened me," Natalie wrote.[21]

When they came together now there was no talk of souls and higher purpose. Sex, punishing arguments, cruel remarks, and humiliation dominated the repertoire. Each time seemed certain to be the last. But, as Natalie observed, they weren't yet there. One day they'd end the relationship forever; the next they came back together with violent passion. In their writings, both used the same lines by Belgian poet Émile Verhaeren to explain their obsession:

> We are exhausted, we revive, we devour one another
> And we kill each other, and we complain
> And we hate it this way—but still we attract each other

Sometime that fall Liane traveled to Portugal with one of her protectors, the Duc d'Oporto. A long silence ensued, during which Natalie had no word from her. Bereft and alone, she entered a bleak, searching period. She kept to herself, either staying in her room to write poetry or taking long, lonely walks. She debated her future. The family friend had seemed certain that she'd be happier in her own world rather than the demi-world, but she knew that she belonged to neither. She belonged nowhere! What she needed, she realized, was to find a world in which she felt comfortable. She didn't quite know what that world might be, but she had a vague desire to ally herself with artists and creativity. She loved literature, after all, and entertained hopes for writing her own poetry. She was, by both upbringing and inclination, at home in the company of poets, writers, artists, musicians, dancers, dramatists, philosophers— anyone who felt the need to interpret and express the complexity of existence. Surely, with people such as these, she could find some sort of spiritual home.

Late that fall Liane finally ended her silence, sending Natalie a long letter crammed with high-blown phrases about love, joy, disillusion, and pale moonbeams.* Her fancy words couldn't disguise the fact that she had written a

---

*Liane included the entire letter in *Idylle saphique.*

kiss-off letter. "All that is born must die," she proclaimed to Natalie. "Even You and Me, and especially Us!"

Of course, her words, noble as they were, didn't end the relationship. The push-pull games between Flossie and Nhine would continue for years. As much as Natalie reveled in suffering while reading Liane's words, she knew that they hadn't yet exhausted their mutual founts of ecstasy and misery.

A few weeks later Liane wrote again. This time her tone was loving: nothing would please her more, she said, than to start the new century alone, at home, with Natalie. When no follow-up came, Natalie convinced herself that Liane had simply forgotten. Still, she made no other plans, hoping in vain that a note would arrive. On New Year's Eve she stayed home, alone, waiting. Finally, when the hour grew so late that she was forced to admit defeat, she undressed and crawled into bed.

Lying there, tossing, turning, and completely unable to sleep, she was haunted by the thought that she'd misinterpreted everything. Maybe Liane was at home, waiting for her—hurt and suffering because she hadn't come. Against all logic, she rose, threw a fur coat over her nightgown, and, "like a fool," went out. On the way to Liane's she ordered the fiacre to stop at a florist's, where she bought an armload of white roses. With beating heart she approached de Pougy's door and rang the bell, only to be told that Madame had gone out to dine with Monsieur, the baron.

Sick, Natalie glanced around the foyer. "What are all these trunks doing here?" she asked.

"Madame hasn't told you, Mademoiselle? She and the baron leave tomorrow for Monte Carlo." Catching sight of Natalie's expression, the sympathetic maid added: "Poor Mademoiselle!"

The humiliation of the moment lingered forever. "Condolences from a chambermaid!" Natalie fumed in *Mémoires secrets.* "It was too much. I fled. . . ."[22]

Distraught and humiliated, she returned home to greet 1900 alone. As dawn broke over Paris on New Year's Day, a few claps of thunder sounded. Soon a light, cold rain began to fall.

FIVE

Natalie and the Virgin

1900

> You may forget but
> Let me tell you
> this: someone in
> some future time
> will think of us.
>
> —*Sappho*
> *Translated by Mary Barnard*

My love is a selfish, glorious, god-like thing. It is very theatrical. It is very magnificent. It wields words with an eloquence that few people as sincere as I are capable of. It is tearful and tender, persuasive and despotic; it has its moments of genius.

> —*Natalie Clifford Barney*

ESPITE HER UNHAPPINESS over Liane, Natalie had kept busy. In fact, even before the humiliation of New Year's Eve, she had become involved with another woman.

While riding in the Bois one day in late November, Natalie had encountered two friends from her Cincinnati childhood, Violet and Mary Shiletto, with whom she had once studied French beneath the backyard lime tree. In the ensuing years the sisters had lived in Paris, where their father, Gordon, was the American representative of an Ohio company. The Shilettos were overjoyed to stumble on Natalie after so many years. When they learned that she'd been studying verse, they told her of another friend they had who wrote poetry. They invited Natalie to join them the next day for a matinee at the Comédie-Française, and promised to bring along their friend, Pauline Tarn.

Early the next afternoon, the butler informed Natalie that the Shilettos' comfortable open carriage, with its two fat black horses, was waiting outside. As she hurried out, he handed her a letter, just delivered, from Liane. Natalie hadn't heard from her in weeks, ever since she'd departed for Portugal on the arm of the Duc d'Oporto. She was desperate to tear open the envelope, but, already late, was forced to wait. Stuffing the letter in her bag, she dashed down the steps.

On the way to the theater Natalie found it impossible to focus on the conversation. She was so preoccupied by the letter that, as she later admitted in *Souvenirs indiscrets,* she was nearly oblivious to the Shilettos' friend: "I only pretended to listen when introduced to [Pauline Tarn] who, at first glance, seemed charming but too banal to hold my interest."[1]

Pauline had the opposite reaction to Natalie: her heart had momentarily stopped when the breathless Barney entered the carriage that day. She would forever recall "the thrill which went through me when my eyes met hers of mortal steel, those eyes sharp and blue as a blade. I had the strange feeling that this woman was telling me my destiny, that her face was the formidable face of my future."[2] For Pauline it was what the French know as *coup de foudre,* and what Americans call love at first sight.

At the theater Natalie was unable to concentrate on the play—she never could remember what she saw that day. Finally, during the second intermission, she couldn't bear the suspense a moment longer. Muttering apologies, she moved hastily to the back of the box, pulled the letter from her bag, and began reading in the dim light. In pretty words and graceful phrases, Liane had once again ended their relationship. Upset, Natalie folded the letter away and rejoined her friends.

Afterward, while the women took a leisurely drive through the Bois, Violet asked Pauline to recite one of her works. She complied in a soft and tender voice, without hesitation or false embarrassment. The poem she chose, "Lassitude," was about one of her major interests in life: death.

The haunting verse snapped Natalie to attention, and she examined Pauline anew. She saw a slender girl with a pretty face, straight light-brown hair, and brown eyes that, incongruously enough, were filled with laughter rather than the death wish her verse evoked. There was something about

Pauline that announced the very essence of a poet, one who was tragic, melancholic, and gifted.

The chivalrous knight in Natalie's soul picked up her shield, hoisted her sword, and stepped forward, wondering how she could help this fragile-looking woman. Perhaps she could awaken her interest in life—or, even better, in the life of Natalie Barney. There might, after all, be something gained by getting to know her better.

And so they began. Who could have guessed that such an inauspicious introduction would result in a drama that would be played out over the course of a century, right into our own time?

BORN IN 1877, Pauline Mary Tarn—known more commonly by her pseudonym, Renée Vivien—was the child of an American named Mary Bennett and John Tarn, an Englishman who was heir to considerable merchant-based wealth. The couple met and married in Hawaii and lived briefly in England before settling in Paris in 1878 at 23, avenue du Bois-de-Boulogne. In 1882 they welcomed a second daughter, Antoinette. The Shiletto clan moved into the same building not too long afterward, and young Pauline and Violet grew close.

Those years were relatively happy for Pauline. But her father's sudden death when she was nine left an absence in her life that would never be satisfied. Discussing the effect of this early trauma, one of Pauline's biographers noted that "during her life, she always sought the counsel or teaching of men and women who personified for her a certain authority."[3] He included Natalie Barney among them.

John Tarn's fortune was held in trust for his daughters until they reached the age of twenty-one, and his insurance alone didn't adequately cover his wife's extravagant ways. Beautiful but self-centered and emotionally cold, Mary Tarn reportedly lived a high-fashion life and kept fast company. By returning to England and putting her daughters in permanent view of her husband's kin, she hoped to keep their purse strings untied.

Pauline hated England and missed Violet terribly. France was her home; she loved everything about it, including the language, which she spoke and wrote like a native. Her relationship with her mother had never been good, and as the years passed it grew worse, particularly because Mary showed a marked favoritism for her prettier and younger daughter, Antoinette. Pauline turned inward. She was comfortable in solitude, enjoying literature, art, and music. She played the piano well and was particularly fond of Chopin; she might have become a musician had she not at an early age discovered a profound love of literature.

In her late teens Pauline began using a hypnotic drug, chloral hydrate, to help her sleep. She overdosed at least once. Interpreting this as a suicide attempt, Mary tried to have her committed to an insane asylum. The case ended up in court. Pauline won, became a legal ward of the state, moved from her mother's home, and was assigned a guardian who apparently treated her with fairness and generosity. In a tribute to the strength of the mother-daughter bond, Pauline and Mary continued trying to get along despite their fractious and at times hateful relationship. To please her mother, Pauline overcame her contempt for the idea of being "launched" into a society she thoroughly disliked, and in May 1897 was officially presented at court to Queen Victoria.

When her inheritance came through a year later, Pauline wasted no time moving back to Paris. She took a small pension on rue Crevaux to be close to Violet and Mary, who still lived with their parents on Bois-de-Boulogne. Daring for the time, she hired no chaperone, thereby forgoing the appearance of propriety. Like Natalie, she wanted total freedom and independence, though for quite different reasons. To Natalie, independence was the means to pursuing "a thousand follies." To Pauline it meant being left in peace to write poetry and see a few carefully selected friends. Unfortunately, the decision to exist sans chaperone made her persona non grata to the ultraconservative Shiletto parents, who were once described by their daughter Mary as "*un cochon et une vache*" (a pig and a cow). Since Pauline was forbidden to call on the Shiletto sisters in their home, they were forced to meet her on the sly, either at her pension or on outings to the theater and the Bois.

Contemporary accounts invariably dismiss Mary as pleasant but unexceptional (Natalie once referred to her as a half-wit), while focusing on Violet's extraordinary intelligence and spirituality. Mabel Dodge Luhan, who knew both sisters from boarding school days in New York City, wrote of Violet that she "completely understood and understanding, she forgave. I have never known any man or woman with such wisdom and such love as she had. She knew everything intuitively."[4]

By the time Pauline arrived in Paris in 1898, Violet had matured into a retiring but gifted young woman who knew Latin and Greek, read extensively in philosophy and religion, and was studying mathematics at the Sorbonne. As in childhood, she and Pauline—both quiet, sensitive, and deeply interested in the spiritual—had much in common. They renewed and quickly surpassed their childhood bonds, developing a deep and loving platonic friendship. Both women were not only virgins, but horrified by the idea of making love to men. In future years Pauline would make much of Violet's saintlike purity, contrasting it favorably with what she viewed as Natalie's evil carnality.

During her first year in Paris, Pauline was happy for the first time in her life, free to live as she liked and do only what she loved. So completely had her life reversed itself that she felt it constituted a form of rebirth, and so she renamed herself Renée Vivien, from the Latin for "renewed life."

A few years later, writing to a friend, she complained bitterly about the cruel turn her life took next. She had been so happy, so free, and then one day fate brushed against her, delivering her to the woman who would change her destiny forever: Natalie Clifford Barney.

FOR A WHILE Natalie and Pauline saw each other only in the company of the Shiletto sisters. There were the carriage rides, almost obligatory in those days, through the Bois. There were outings to the theater or the opera, and at least once Pauline, Mary, and Violet called upon Natalie and her family. This pleasant female foursome came to an abrupt end when winter's chill chased the Shiletto family southward to Cannes. Their train had barely left the station when Pauline invited Natalie to go skating at the Palais de Glace.

Not just any rink, the Palais was an elegant ice arena on the Champs-Elysées with a large round skate track and two stacked galleries from which visitors could enjoy hot tea or a rum grog while watching the skaters. "Here," wrote a contemporary chronicler, "one encounters the prettiest women of Paris . . . women of the world."[5] He was discreetly referring to courtesans, and, indeed, many such ladies were present on the day Natalie and Pauline visited. While Natalie sat watching Pauline's slender body gliding across the ice, she made a concerted effort to avoid the eyes of the various professional beauties she had previously encountered at Liane's. Even the stunning cocotte Emilienne d'Alençon couldn't succeed in capturing her attention.

From that point on, the two young women were inseparable. Natalie, sensing Pauline's timidity, courted her in a gentle, almost schoolgirlish manner. They giggled over nothing, discussed poetry, read aloud from their own work. They posed for photos, walked in the Bois, and sent each other daily notes accompanied by blossoms. Pauline's flower for Natalie was, ironically, the lily, a traditional image of purity that was also Liane's emblem.

The inevitable came to pass. One winter night Natalie visited Pauline in her tiny pension. Lit by dozens of candles, the main room was filled with a flickering glow that, to Natalie, seemed almost holy. White lilies were everywhere, crammed not only into vases and water jugs, but strewn over the floor and across the bed, illuminating by their whiteness the room's darkest corners. The evening unfolded with tantalizing slowness. Pauline played a set of graceful Chopin preludes on the piano. Then, in the "dazzling, suffocating" atmosphere of the room, transformed by the lilies and candles into "a passionate, virginal chapel," they kneeled before one another. In this position, as if praying, Pauline recited a poem she'd written for Natalie. Drunk from the heady words and the scent of lilies, Natalie pulled Pauline to her feet and embraced her. "It was in this way," she recalled, "that two young poetesses came together and began to love."[6]

To Pauline's disappointment, Natalie didn't stay the night, explaining that her family, whom she loved tenderly, would worry if she didn't return. A light snow was falling when Natalie left. As she walked along in the cold, her footprints left a distinct impression upon the whiteness, a track between Pauline's home and her own.

OVER THE COURSE of a century, the Natalie-Pauline relationship has become cemented into legend. We hear tales of Renée Vivien, the tragic poet who died for love of Natalie Barney, of Barney, the conquering Amazon, driving Vivien to suicide with her ceaseless romantic conquests. These legends, though at least partly true, define each woman from an endpoint rather than from the beginning.

It's important to remember how young they were at the start. Natalie had just turned twenty-three; Pauline, born nine months later, was twenty-two. Both had grown up in societies that shielded daughters from the world's realities, a custom that tended to keep them naive and dewy. Natalie, despite her many adventures, knew little about life's rigors. She still lived at home and was dependent on her parents for spending money, a situation that kept her a symbolic child. Pauline's financial independence allowed her to live on her own, but her upbringing had left her stunted emotionally.

Still, Natalie had led a cosmopolitan life, mingling in social, political, and art circles in Washington, Paris, Bar Harbor, and London. She was a highly social being, one who would rather do than be. Her childhood had its unhappy moments, certainly, but had held no great tragedies. For the most part, she always felt loved. Her parents and sister, her huge extended family, and her many friends loved and even adored her. All of this, along with the concomitant gift of absolute confidence, she accepted as her due.

Pauline's life had been quite different. Growing up, her world was tiny. Except for a short stint at a French boarding school, she had traveled little. She would always be withdrawn, shy, and self-conscious. She would far rather be than do. She had known two great tragedies: her father's early death and her mother's enmity. She felt deeply loved by her sister, Antoinette, and by Violet Shiletto, but rejected or treated indifferently by everybody else. This, along with the ever-present demon of despair, she accepted as her lot.

Pauline and Natalie were a mismatched love affair from the start, their individual beliefs and outlooks largely antagonistic. Where Natalie celebrated life, Pauline was drawn to death. Natalie was gregarious, while Pauline preferred solitude. Natalie's thought processes tended to be detached and analytical; Pauline's were ruled by emotion. For Pauline, nothing was more important than writing poetry, while Natalie wanted her life itself to be her greatest poem. Natalie loved her body, using it to participate in sports and enjoy sex; Pauline's lifelong abuse of her body, via drugs, alcohol, and anorexia, would result in a very early death.

Perhaps the most significant differences—certainly the most fatal—involved sex. Pauline wrote rhapsodically of their first evening together in the poem "À la femme aimée." However, despite the romantic backdrop of Chopin, candles, and white lilies, the night was not a sexual success. Pauline had probably never made love to anyone before and was unable to respond to passion. "With all my experience," Natalie confided in her memoirs, "I could do little to overcome her physical inertia. Her soul alone vibrated passionately to our union. As for my caresses, she murmured: 'Yes, it's very gentle, continue,' and I continued indefinitely without ever unveiling the woman who slept within the virgin, [a virgin with a] temperament uniquely transported by poetry: more sensitive to my verse and my words than to my kisses and caresses."[7]

The situation, which did not improve, was a constant punishment to Natalie, making her "irritable and cruel. I had the sad perspective of either becoming unfaithful to Renée or of renouncing a major part of myself."[8] Sensual and free-spirited, Natalie had little use for the concepts of fidelity and monogamy to begin with, and it wasn't long before she was exercising that "major part" of herself in other beds, including Liane's. She tried to convince Pauline that physical infidelity meant nothing and didn't take away from the essential beauty of their relationship. If anything, she said, such temporary passions made the heart grow fonder; it was monogamy that turned lovers into bored, unhappy companions.

But Pauline existed in an opposing dimension, one that wasn't ruled or perhaps even occupied by sexual passion. All she knew was this: she loved Natalie fiercely and wanted to possess every ounce of her. "I love her," she would write to Charles Brun, "with a passion so tenacious and so terrible that NOTHING can separate me from her—that I will brave all consequences—that I would choose craziness and death and desolation . . . rather than tear away from this unhappy love. I can support anything for her alone, the loss of her would throw me into an abyss."[9] That Natalie came equipped with a wandering eye and a frank approach to physicality shattered Pauline to the core.

The question begs to be asked: What did these two see in each other? One thrived on carnality and was incapable of fidelity; the other lacked sexual passion and sought a placid, faithful mate. The fact is that, despite their many differences, they also had some things in common. It was these commonalities—few in number, but highly significant—that accounted for the depth of their union.

First, each had a sense of humor. Many accounts of Pauline were written toward the end of her life, when, physically and mentally damaged by her excesses, she wasn't always lucid. But in the early days with Natalie she was still lively and fun-filled. In the 1950s Natalie would tell a friend that, even though Pauline had a morbid strain, her nature was essentially a happy one.[10] Others have remarked on her seemingly upbeat disposition. In any event, laughter—the ability to experience it, create it, and share it—was one of Natalie's great gifts. Pauline's gift for laughter wasn't nearly as profound, but it was nonetheless something they shared.

Second, they were both poets. From the start they spent vast amounts of time discussing, studying, reading, and writing poetry together, and for a while they even shared the same poetry professor, Charles Brun. Most important, they encouraged each other to write at a time when the artistic output of women wasn't taken seriously by most critics or the public. Their relationship acted as a kind of poetic tonic, inspiring in each a passion and dedication to verse. Natalie's first book of poems would be published the summer after they met. Pauline's, appearing a year later, was the direct and unequivocal result of her relationship with Natalie. In fact, without Natalie as an impetus, it's entirely possible that Pauline might never have pursued her poetic talent.

Third, each found in the other an intellectual equal who would listen, understand, and ease loneliness. "I belonged to everyone, she belonged to no one," Natalie wrote in her first book of *pensées*. "We considered ourselves quite different, and yet in our loneliness were alike." It's not difficult to think of the reclusive Pauline as lonely, but Natalie's crowded life seems to defy such a word. However, as we've already seen, she did possess a melancholic streak.

Natalie would always be intensely guarded about her thoughts and feelings, that inner life of the self, and tended to keep her own emotional counsel. So far she'd revealed her true self to only two people: Eva and Pauline. Her relationship with Eva, though important, was an outgrowth of childhood affection. It was thus with Pauline that the adult Natalie first shared her essential nature—or at least as much as she would ever be willing to share.

Fourth and last, Natalie and Pauline were connected by their feminist vision of a world in which women were not only as free as men, but superior to them as well. From the beginning, Barney's writing had a potent and positive feminist component. She was not one to bewail the lot of women. Instead, she celebrated everything female, extolling women's power, intelligence, and grit. She liked men, but didn't hesitate to decry masculine devices, such as war, that annihilated women's creations. She coldly analyzed the war between the sexes. She openly rejoiced in the beauty of lesbian love. Pauline took a different approach, reconstituting myths and legends to reflect a feminist bias. With the exception of her first book of poetry, she, like Natalie, forthrightly put her name to her sapphic poetry and prose. Natalie and Pauline were virtually alone among their peers in openly rejoicing in the love of women. "At a time when Krafft-Ebing classified homosexuality as a degenerate disease," wrote scholar and lesbian activist Gayle Rubin, "Vivien and Barney considered it a thrilling distinction. They responded to anti-homosexual disdain with insolent extremism."[11]

Laughter. Poetry. Mutual understanding. Feminism. In the end, it was these four shared qualities that united Natalie and Pauline.

AFTER YEARS OF POURING her feelings into poetry, Natalie was now gathering her best work and preparing it for publication as a small chapbook. Consisting mostly of love poems written to a variety of women, it would be published later that year as *Quelques portraits-sonnets de femmes*.

Pauline, too, was writing love poetry, although her works were directed to a single woman, Natalie, who fueled her literary and creative fires. Pauline turned out a new poem nearly every day, bestowing it on her "Loreley" like a precious gift. She buried poems amid floral bouquets and recited them at intimate moments. There were constant letters, often haunted by thoughts of Natalie's eyes: "They're blue, but they're also green, as if the sky had eloped with the sea and your eyes were proof of their marriage. Sometimes they're periwinkle, and other times they're violet . . . I love your eyes—I would die happily in their regard."[12] Natalie liked being admired but sometimes found such outright worship discomfiting.

At some point Pauline collected her love poems into an elegant handmade book, which she presented to Natalie. The book still exists, its white leather cover now spotted with age. On the front a lyre, exquisitely drawn in purple ink, is surrounded by white lilies. The words *Études et Préludes* wind back and forth between the instrument's strings. On the first of the heavy, gold-leafed pages are three words, *Pour Elle Seule* (For her alone). Ensuing pages contain verse written in Pauline's hand. Ten of the poems, with variations, would be included in her first published book of poetry, also entitled *Études et préludes*.

Natalie would always believe that life itself was more important than poetry. She believed that even now, at a time when writing poetry meant more to her, and came from a more impassioned place, than it ever would again. Pauline might have been content to stay home ceaselessly penning sonnets, but Natalie wasn't. She wanted to be out in the world, doing things. And in the early, blissful stages of their relationship, Pauline was usually happy to accompany her. Many of their outings evoke an almost palpable sense of 1900 Paris.

For instance, they attended the legendary Paris Exposition Universelle. Ten years in the making, the Expo opened in mid-April. Spread over nearly six hundred acres along the Seine, it would attract more than 40 million visitors from around the world during its seven-month run. Most came to witness the future's marvels: a demonstration of electricity, a magnetic recording tape machine, a moving sidewalk, wireless telegraphy, the most powerful telescope ever built, the world's first escalator. American ragtime music was presented to visitors by none other than John Philip Sousa. Auguste Rodin had his own pavilion, where everyone flocked to see the new sculpture of Balzac. At night, the city was ablaze with electric light. Some pavilions and other structures built for the event still stand, ranking among the world's greatest remaining Beaux Arts landmarks: the Grand Palais, the Petit Palais, and the Gare d'Orsay (now a museum).

On another occasion, Natalie, Pauline, and two other women friends donned male clothing at Carnival and slipped into the Moulin Rouge masquerading as a quartet of men on the town. Costumes, in fact, played a big role with these two. They loved dressing up and having themselves professionally photographed. In one such picture, Pauline, clad as the French revolutionary orator and journalist Camille Desmoulins, kneels before Natalie, who is wearing a revolution-era dress.

Their most amusing outing occurred when Natalie, her mother, and Pauline were guests at one of the first salon performances by Isadora Duncan. Not too long before, the California-bred Isadora had been living in near-poverty in a one-room Parisian studio with her mother and brother, Raymond. Invited to dance at an important salon, she had attracted the notice of the Princesse de Polignac, arguably the city's leading patron of dance and music. Soon, as a popular journal reported, "the only thing people are talking about is 'la petite danseuse.' You must go see Miss Duncan."[13]

Natalie, Alice, and Pauline ended up sitting in the front row. When Isadora learned that sister Americans were present, she asked her accompanist, an unknown twenty-five-year-old pianist named Maurice Ravel, to play the "Star-spangled Banner." She invented a free-flowing dance to match the music, and, at its climax, grabbed the skirt of her Greek tunic and lifted it high. Beneath the graceful, flowing white robes she was completely nude. Natalie was no doubt delighted by the unexpected ending, but Alice was shocked to the core.

Stunned, she turned to her daughter and sputtered: "Darling, do you see what I see?" Natalie collapsed with laughter.

Roughly the same age, Natalie and Isadora would be friendly from then until the dancer's early death in 1927. When Natalie started her own salon on the rue Jacob in 1909, it wasn't unusual for Duncan to make an appearance. She came once with her husband, Essenin, who recited his poetry in Russian, and on rare occasions she danced. Natalie would remember Isadora as being an egoist and a seductress, though not really beautiful. She might have been describing herself.

Among the salons Natalie enjoyed attending was the informal one hosted by her mother. Although Whistler refused to leave his Left Bank haunts to visit avenue Victor Hugo, plenty of other artists were happy to be entertained by the popular Mrs. Barney, who knew how to spark conversation, guide its flow, calm arguments, and make her guests feel comfortable and even brilliant. Upbeat and convivial, she had a gift for bringing out the best in everyone— which is exactly what people would say about Natalie someday.

Pauline, genuinely fond of Alice and Laura, liked visiting Natalie's home as long as it wasn't filled with company. However, she occasionally found herself trapped at one of Alice's convivial gatherings. Meeting Pauline at the Barneys', Charlotte Stern remembered her sitting in a corner, happy to be ignored. She was "dressed in black, her hairdo already outmoded, a little chignon, her hands crossed as if in prayer."[14] Small wonder that Alice, though she liked Pauline and had even painted her portrait, considered her "weak and meek."

Pauline's portrait was one of five watercolors of female heads that Alice completed, at Natalie's behest, for *Quelques portraits-sonnets de femmes*. Four are known with certainty: Eva Palmer, Pauline Tarn, Charlotte "Lottie" Stern, and Natalie's cousin Ellen Goines. Still cheerfully blind to her daughter's proclivities, Alice had no idea that some of the models were or had been Natalie's lovers.

Quelques portraits-sonnets de femmes was published late that spring by Librairie Paul Ollendorff in an edition of five hundred. The slender, sixty-six-page chapbook consisted of thirty-five poems, a preface, and a poetic dedication. Natalie so liked the Carolus-Duran portrait of herself as a Renaissance page that she used it as the frontispiece. The poems were addressed to various women in her life, although they are identified only by initials. A sonnet dedicated to "P.M.T." was obviously written to her current amour, Pauline Mary Tarn. However, "L"—Liane—still rated a couple of poems. Many of the high-society flowers Natalie had buzzed were also honored, as, for instance, "Comtesse de P." A poem was addressed to Sarah Bernhardt, whom Natalie admired, though it's not certain if they ever met. A handful were addressed to platonic friends, including Ellen Goines (E.G.) and the Princess Troubetzky, a popular turn-of-the-century novelist who published under her maiden name, Amelie Rives. Natalie had long had a passionate but unrequited crush on the older Troubetzky, who, with her husband, often stayed at Ban-y-Bryn as guests of the Barneys.

Most critics have dismissed the poems in *Quelques portraits* as formalized, conventional nineteenth-century verse, or as second-rate Mallarmé. "Poems were not her forte," Karla Jay tactfully admitted.[15] George Wickes described Natalie's verse as "frankly, apprentice work, and unfinished at that."[16] But whatever the poems lack in style, they make up in substance. With no hint of apology to anyone, let alone fear of scandal—her name appears on the cover and twice inside—Natalie openly and joyously celebrated her love for women in a way that hadn't been done since Sappho. As feminist historian Shari Benstock wrote, Natalie's book "addressed a subject that has been denied a literary tradition of its own. Although the external forms of this poetry were traditional, even clichéd, they enclosed a radical sentiment."[17] The scandalized attention drawn by *Quelques portraits-sonnets de femmes,* which we'll discuss shortly, underlines its historic importance. It doesn't matter how Natalie said what she said; the important thing is that she said it.

One day, when a large group of American society women gathered chez Barney, Laura recited from Natalie's just-published book. With mischievous intent, she read "The Song of Endymion," which disguised Liane as the goddess Diana. The recitation met with great success, and Natalie wryly noted that "even certain women in the American colony applauded, under the guise of myth, the liaison they had so strongly disapproved of."[18] The truth was, they hadn't understood the poems. Written in formal, old-fashioned French, they weren't easily grasped when read aloud; they demanded study. For the time being, at least, the book created little fuss.

IN EARLY JULY 1900, the Barneys, accompanied by Pauline, returned to the United States to spend the summer in Bar Harbor. Pauline's mother and sister may have traveled on the same ship (or else sailed behind them a short time later). The Barney and Tarn families had met in late winter or early spring. When Mary Tarn mentioned an upcoming visit to her siblings in America, the hospitable Barneys invited her to Bar Harbor. Mary and Antoinette stayed at the island's Malvern Hotel for a week or ten days before venturing off for long sojourns with relatives in Michigan and elsewhere; Pauline stayed on at Ban-y-Bryn.

On the voyage over, Pauline had "forgotten" to bring her evening gowns, which gave her a good excuse to avoid shipboard social functions. She was content to stay in her cabin each night, and before debarking in New York a dismayed Natalie learned why. Rummaging in Pauline's nightstand, she discovered empty chloral bottles, one for each night they'd been at sea. Natalie, who never used drugs and abhorred alcohol abuse, begged her to end the habit. Pauline insisted that the hypnotic did no harm. Over the next decade chloral and alcohol, a dangerous combination, would play havoc with her body.

Arriving at Bar Harbor aboard the ferry *Sappho,* they were greeted by Eva Palmer, whom Pauline hadn't met. Finding Eva's beauty astounding, she nicknamed her "the Sunset Goddess" in tribute to her red-gold hair. "[Eva] had the remote gaze of daughter of the Far North," Pauline wrote in her strange roman à clef, *A Woman Appeared to Me.* "Looking at her, I felt that divine and terrible trembling that a perfect statue inspires, a dazzle of radiant marble, a long-loved picture of infinite harmony."[19]

Most days the comely trio took off early in the morning and stayed away until late afternoon. Natalie and Eva delighted in showing off their childhood haunts and pastimes, taking Pauline to all the swimming spots: Frenchman's Bay, Eagle Lake, Witch Hollow Pond, and Somes Sound. They jumped the stones and looked for trout in Duck Brook, and explored the ferny paths of Green Mountain. In isolated spots, free from prying eyes, they removed their clothes to swim and lounge about.

That very year, 1900, the Kodak company introduced its first Brownie camera, selling it for one dollar. Cheap and easy to use, it transformed photography into a hobby for everybody. Natalie owned a Brownie, and the women posed nude. A dozen or so snapshots survive. Some show two women standing together while a third aims the camera, as when Eva and Pauline, clad only in big-brimmed straw hats, stand thigh-deep in water. Others are solo affairs: Natalie stretches out in tall grass, her hair lifting into a breeze; Eva Palmer stands naked but for her long coil of hair. Stripped of period clothing, they take on a timeless quality. They could easily be women of today, skinny-dipping and hanging out on a remote beach.

Needless to say, the lovely and independent threesome attracted the curiosity of almost everyone on Mount Desert Island. For months word had steadily drifted across the Atlantic about Natalie's "friendship" with a famous courtesan, and now, when she wasn't flirting outrageously with both sexes at the Kebo Valley Club, she was cavorting in the woods with two lovelies who couldn't keep their eyes off her. As if that weren't enough, a buzz was just beginning about her new book of poetry—containing, it was said, love sonnets to women. The talk about Natalie would grow louder and more frequent until it spread, as she wrote, "from Washington right up to the tiny islet of Bar Harbor."[20]

Undaunted, she pursued her social rounds and continued, despite her growing reputation for "vice," to be a popular belle. Pauline was free to come along, and, since Natalie had telegraphed for her missing gowns to be sent to Maine, she had no excuse not to. But, awkward in social settings, she usually declined, preferring to read and write in her room and await Natalie's return.

She didn't wait peacefully, however. She resented Natalie's gadding about, felt badly neglected, and suffered frequent bouts of jealousy. In a letter to Charles Brun she reported that, while Bar Harbor was beautiful, its occupants were unbearable. They were always "giving dinners and balls, making visits, dining and 'five-o-clocking' with deplorable relentlessness. I sequester myself from this daily maelstrom, but Mlle Barney is completely happy, followed by a crowd who never leaves her alone, riding her horse like an Amazon."[21]

Eva, too, disliked the social milieu, though for different reasons. Having grown up as a member of this privileged world, she was fairly confident of her position within it. It wasn't a feeling of inadequacy that drove her away; the inhabitants simply bored her. She once described society as the place "where one met the same people everywhere, but could talk to no one anywhere."[22]

With Natalie constantly away, her two lovers, both quiet, thoughtful, shy, and passionate about literature, turned to each other for company. Eva's enthusiasm for Greek inflamed Pauline with a desire to learn that language. Natalie, returning late at night from a ball at the Club, often found them in the roof turret of the Palmers' cottage, bent over a text and spelling out letters of the Greek alphabet. "Still feeling reckless from a night of waltzing," Natalie said, "I would carry [Pauline] off to bed."[23]

Early in the fall Pauline joined her mother and sister in Michigan to care for a dying cousin. Left on their own, Natalie and Eva were free to focus once more on their own complex relationship. Childhood friends long before they were lovers, they knew each other in a way no one else ever could or would. They were each other's "home port," a safe place to dock, replenish spiritual stores, and venture out again.

"I often look beyond those who are before me," Natalie told Eva, "[and] they become as glass through which I see you."[24] Or, as Eva said, "you are no longer outside of me but inside, touching the essence of me."[25] The nearly inseparable bond between these two would eventually snap, hurling them apart for decades. But for nearly seven years after that Bar Harbor summer, they were to remain a significant presence in each other's life.

Even at this early stage, most of the power in the relationship belonged to Natalie, and over the next few years Eva would scramble constantly to please and bend to her point of view—sometimes to the point of self-annihilation. She abetted Natalie's plans to seduce other women, delivered her love notes, and even pleaded her cause to various lovers. For such devotion she drew scorn rather than the love she sought; and was constantly berated for weakness and lack of initiative. Before their final break Eva confessed that Natalie's criticisms and fault-finding had caused her great suffering, removing any possibility that "I would perhaps change and become better for you [because] years of it have merely taught me the futility of such a hope."[26]

Beneath the constant criticisms and harping, Natalie needed Eva. She panicked whenever the red-headed beauty seemed interested in someone else, demanding—and getting—reassurance of her love. Natalie would drop anything, and usually anybody, for the time it took to tauten the bond between them. Once everything was pulled tight, she let go and turned her attention elsewhere.

That summer, though, there was still a lot of innocence between them. After Pauline left for Michigan in the fall, a lovely space of time ensued during which Natalie and Eva were free to simply enjoy each other. Natalie could pen a great love letter when she put her mind to it, as in this 1900 note to Eva:

> How pale is all reality next to the mere dream of you; my sweetest sunlit desire grows and is drowned and refound and lost again in the vibrating possibilities I feel in the looks of your half-closed eyes, and it is no longer my tongue but my soul that caresses you . . . ah, the warmness of being so together. I would have flame born of it—flame that is a sort of light! How it burns me with joy when I kiss you.[27]

Eva, who had been enrolled at Bryn Mawr from the fall of 1896 to spring 1898, decided to visit the college that fall, and Natalie received her parents' permission to go along. Once there, she sat in on classes given by feminist literary professor Mary "Mamie" Gwinn, who had lived for years with Bryn Mawr's president, Carey Thomas, in what was probably a lesbian relationship (the Thomas-Gwinn relationship played a big role in Gertrude Stein's novel *Fernhurst*). Natalie adored the dynamic professor. Once, gathering her courage, she showed her a few poems she'd written. Gwinn encouraged her to keep writing, and decades later the memory of her praise still had the power to move Natalie.

In mid-October Pauline joined her "cher grand Poète adorable et superbe" at Bryn Mawr. In *A Woman Appeared to Me,* she says that she enjoyed being there. The students seemed happy, Pennsylvania's autumn colors were glorious, and she liked writing poetry in the graveyard, where the quiet encouraged concentration. However, writing in *Souvenirs indiscrets* sixty years later, Natalie portrayed Tarn at Bryn Mawr as talking endlessly about death and spending hours in the local cemetery, where she wrote macabre poetry while lying atop gravestones and downing gin and chloral.

According to Barney, Pauline's depressive behavior was the direct result of her anguish over the recent death of Violet Shiletto. However, as discussed later in this chapter, Violet did not die until the spring of 1901. Voluminous post-marked correspondence makes two things certain. First, Pauline's American visit with Natalie occurred in the summer and fall of 1900—half a year *before* Violet's death. Second, Pauline remained in Europe for all of 1901. Natalie did travel to Bar Harbor in the summer following Violet's death, but without Pauline.

Given the length of time between the events and their retelling in *Souvenirs indiscrets,* Natalie's chronological error isn't surprising (she may have also erred, at least in part, with her take on Pauline's gloomy attraction at Bryn Mawr to gravestones and death, thus explaining the difference in their respective accounts). Unfortunately, her words have left an inaccurate depiction of Pauline, who at that point had not yet fully embraced the love of death.

NATALIE AND PAULINE returned to Europe in the late fall, stopping first in London. The Barneys had given permission for Natalie to take rooms with Pauline in Paris as long as they agreed to hire a suitable "lady's companion." In London they interviewed an Oxford graduate named Josephine Partridge, who agreed to enter their service in early December.

One day Natalie stopped into a London bookstore, Bodley Head, and purchased two books: Henry Wharton's 1885 translation of Sappho, which quickly became Pauline's favorite bedtime reading, and *Opals,* a first volume of poetry by a young Englishwoman named Olive Custance. Natalie enjoyed *Opals,* which she felt had sapphic overtones. Sensing a kindred spirit, she sent Custance an appreciative letter, along with a copy of *Quelques portraits-sonnets de femmes.*

The rapidity of Custance's reply inspired Natalie to try turning a long-cherished idea into reality. For years she had nursed the vision of forming a group of women poets for mutual inspiration. With herself, Eva, and Pauline she already had three muses; Custance could be a fourth. She wrote the Englishwoman again, sharing her idea and inviting her to Paris. Olive's reply was enthusiastic. She included her latest poem, inspired by Natalie's Carolus-Duran portrait in *Quelques-sonnets:*

> Her face is like the faces
> A dreamer sometimes meets
> A face that Leonardo
> Would have followed
> Through the streets.

Pauline read the poem and, perhaps spurred by jealousy, penned her own sonnet about the painting. Titled simply "Sonnet," and included in her 1903 collection, *Évocations,* it's a highly revealing character study of Natalie and a lucid description of her *"être double"*—the double being inherent in this child of witches and saints:

> Your royal youth has the melancholy
> of the North, where mist effaces all color.
> You mix discord and desire with tears,
> Grave as Hamlet, pale as Ophelia.
>
> You pass by, swept up by some beautiful lunacy,
> Like her, strewing songs and flowers,
> Like him, hiding pain beneath pride,
> But your eyes see everything.
>
> Smile, beloved blonde; or dream, dark lover;
> Your double-being attracts me like a double magnet,
> And your flesh burns with the cold ardor of a candle.
> My disconcerted heart is troubled when I see
> Your pensive princely brow and your blue virgin's eyes
> Now One, now the Other, then Both at once.

To Pauline, Natalie encompassed the natures of both Hamlet and Ophelia. She is at once female and male; soft and hard; light and dark; joyous and tragic. By embodying such disparate but alluring qualities, she escapes definition or understanding, becoming a never-ending journey into the unknowable. She is inscrutable, unsolvable, a mystery. She doesn't just attract, she attracts doubly. Indeed, "Sonnet" goes a long way toward illuminating the compelling allure Natalie had to so many.

AS THE YEAR CLOSED, the fallout from *Quelques portraits-sonnets de femmes* caused a major break in the Barney family. It had taken months for word of the book to develop a strong buzz, but by now many people had read or at least heard about it. Natalie generously bestowed copies on her friends, something she would do with all her books in the future. It may also have been sold in a few selected bookstores (an original copy at Yale's Beinecke Library bears a tiny "Brentano's Booksellers & Stationers" sticker). In addition, either Natalie or someone she knew might have sent copies to critics, because a tiny handful of reviews appeared over the course of summer 1900 and into the winter of 1901.

Most reviews were relatively positive. Nobody was about to confuse Natalie's sonnets with those of Shakespeare, but her first attempt as a poet drew mild compliments. "Miss Barney, a New American Poet," ran the headline of one small article. It went on to describe her as "a new poet of great talent . . . a belle of Washington and Bar Harbor fame . . . young and beautiful as well."[28] A respected American critic of the day, Henri Pene du Bois, so admired Natalie's "miraculous power to write French verse" that he honored it with two separate reviews.[29]

Some critics refused to believe that the poems in *Quelques portraits* were written to women. The *Washington Mirror* noted that one of the Barney daughters "has gone in tremendously for poetry. She writes odes to men's lips and eyes; not like a novice, either. She makes you thrill, grow hot and cold, turn pale, then crimson red, and stirs your soul while reading her verses. You wonder where in her childish heart she has heaped up such a wealth of tenderness and passion; where in her little mind she has stored away this mass of human knowledge. Yet it is so."[30]

Of course, the reporter may have been speaking in some sort of code, because by this time most of Washington knew how to read between the lines when it came to Natalie Barney. Even many who didn't know her personally knew about the book and, thus, her proclivities. More than a decade later a newspaper in West Virginia reminded readers of the brouhaha set off by Natalie's first book. "Those poems, *Quelques Portraits, Sonnets de Femmes* [sic], scandalized Washington. They were written in French. The French was very good, but the tone of the verse very unconventional, and the cave-dwellers were at the point of dropping their author. . . ."[31]

It's true that Natalie had been dropped by a few Washington society matrons, meaning that they refused to receive her in their homes. At least one family friend approached Natalie that summer, begging her to give up, for the sake of her parents, the course on which she was headed. Over time she would become persona non grata to many more in society, including members of the American colony in Paris. The painter Romaine Brooks recalled going to a Parisian reception toward the end of the century's first decade. In attendance were many American women "of the pouter pigeon variety." Brooks had not yet met Natalie, but knew all about her: "Everyone in Paris knew of Natalie Barney. Her spirit, her writings . . . and her poetry. But as usual it was her reputation rather than her gifts that was commented upon." Brooks was bored beyond belief by the women, who busied themselves with their tea, cakes, and card-playing. Suddenly, one of the pigeons announced that Natalie "will be received again in society [only] when she returns to her Mother's friends."

Romaine felt disgust. Glancing around "at these smug and puffed out members of society, I decided that Natalie Barney had doubtless made more inspiring friends elsewhere."[32]

Not only stuffy matrons viewed Barney with disdain. Writer Edith Wharton reportedly shuddered at the very mention of Natalie's name, dismissing her as "something—appalling"; she once warned her friend Blanche de Prévaux to "never go near" Barney.[33] Another who despised and actively spoke against her was the famed British stage actress Mrs. Patrick Campbell. In response to her critics, Natalie claimed that she didn't care whether or not Madame so-and-so deigned to greet her on the street. As she once said of Colette's first husband, Willy, "Not everyone is capable of knowingly creating a bad reputation for themselves."[34]

There was a certain hypocrisy to the way Natalie was treated. Then, as now, a certain percentage of women were lesbian or bisexual, and they existed in Natalie's social milieu to no lesser or greater degree than anywhere else. In fact, President Theodore Roosevelt's maverick daughter, Alice, a few years younger than Natalie, told a *Washington Post* reporter in 1974 that "lesbianism [was] very fashionable in those days, and it was quite acceptable. At least as far as I was concerned."[35]

Not everyone, of course, was that enlightened. Discretion (or, if you prefer, sexual hypocrisy) was considered a duty. Among Natalie's past and future conquests were socialites who, though they preferred the embraces of women, led ostensibly "normal" lives. As long as they married, had children, did charitable work, and managed fine homes, nobody much cared what they did behind closet doors. In the end, Natalie's greatest sin was not that she was a lesbian, but that she refused to be quiet and ashamed about it.

One day Albert Barney picked up the society gossip journal *Town Topics* and read a small but fatal headline: SAPPHO SINGS IN WASHINGTON.* With that single headline, his world exploded. Highly intelligent and far from naive, his suspicions about his beloved daughter had long ago turned to certainty. He knew that talk about Natalie had been simmering for quite a while, but until now—until her horrid book—the pot hadn't threatened to boil over.

The *Town Topics* piece, entwining his daughter's name with that of a perverted Greek harlot, fulfilled his worst nightmares of scandal. The fact that his wife had contributed the artwork to Natalie's book constituted a double knife-thrust to the heart. How, he wondered, would he ever live this down?

The timing and exact circumstances of what happened next are impossible to pinpoint. The entire episode wasn't one that anyone in the family wished to

*I have been unable to locate this article, which Natalie often mentions in her writing.

remember, let alone document. It's telling that Alice, who scissored from the newspapers each mention of her girls for permanent inclusion in her scrapbook, didn't bother to keep the big "Sappho Sings" article. However, some clues remain to indicate what happened. Natalie revealed some of the story herself, and over the years various friends added bits of information.

One of the puzzling pieces is where, exactly, Albert was when he read the infamous article. Some versions put him in Washington, claiming that he immediately sailed to Paris either alone or with Alice. In another version, he and Alice are already in Paris, staying at avenue Victor Hugo; if that's the case, perhaps a friend mailed him the article from the States.

What is true is this: Albert stormed into the editorial offices at Ollendorff in Paris to buy, and then destroy, the remaining copies and all printing plates for *Quelques portraits-sonnets de femmes*. His action doubtless accounts for the book's extreme rarity today.

He then brutally pulled the blinders from Alice's eyes about the meaning of the poems in *Quelques sonnets*. He berated her ceaselessly, and would until his death, for having so naively contributed paintings of Natalie's lovers to the book. How, he demanded, could they ever hold their heads up again?

The revelation about Natalie's sexuality stunned Alice. The evidence had been there for years, obvious to all, but she had been in complete denial. Now, forced to accept the truth, she was shocked and sickened. For perhaps the first time ever she was unable to apply the laissez-faire philosophy that had defined her approach to life.

In early January 1901 the Barneys boarded a ship to New York, leaving Natalie behind. Reluctant to return to Washington and endure the gossip, Albert rented rooms at Manhattan's Waldorf Astoria. Though weakened by illness, he constantly lambasted Alice, enumerating her countless sins, the greatest of which was the evil inherent in Natalie's character. As usual, she endured the abuse by politely ignoring him. Deep within, however, she was awash in conflicting emotions. She loved and admired her daughter, but was horrified by her lesbianism. Late in January, writing from the Waldorf, she made her feelings clear in a letter that must have devastated Natalie:

It has come at last. Your father is quite crushed by this and really very pathetic. How perhaps you, through your disregard for us and your callousness, may remember my disgust when you would speak of this forbidden sin—and realize that every right-minded decent person is condemning you and us—as they would of the greatest evil . . . I am too sick and ill to write more. I used to feel sorry for Mrs. Hoy when people said things of Mattie—and how small her sin was—if true—compared with yours, which you broadcast about, as if being evil is not bad enough.

But you must in every way, to every person, make yourself a horror and a danger. . . . Your only chance to redeem yourself is to change your life and writings and remember that in no way can you defend yourself—or reply to this [Town Topics] article. . . . For there is not the slightest loophole. You have closed every escape. This [article] is written by an able writer who knows the world and is ever ready to write against any reply which may be made by you or anyone else. . . . You have done a bad thing—a sin against law and mankind and I can only hope that your ideas have shocked and horrified instead of converting.[36]

It took months for Alice to accept Natalie's nature, but eventually the truth brought mother and daughter closer. No longer engaged in subterfuge and lies, Natalie's new relationship with Alice was easier, friendlier, and more honest. After her initial repugnance, Alice tried to see Natalie's sexuality as simply part of her nature—a nature similar in many other ways to her own. "How much of myself I've passed on to you," she wrote years later. "You're cultivated and I—not—but we've got the same traits, grabbing here and there, dashing from this to that. So much of the monkey in us."[37]

There would be many times in the future when Natalie and Alice didn't get along, but at its heart their relationship remained strong and loving. Each took pleasure in the other's accomplishments. "I'm terribly proud of you," Alice would write; or "I can't express my admiration, my child." They would collaborate in writing plays, visit each other, and always, no matter where they might be, there were the affectionate letters.

Only once, many years later, did Alice reveal the pain that Natalie caused her. It happened when Natalie made a casual observation. "Mother," she remembered saying. "You have so happy a temperament that I cannot imagine anything that has ever been able to cause you more than a passing sorrow."

Alice drew back as if struck. She appeared embarrassed, and looked away. Natalie laughed, curious to know what could possibly have shaken her mother's legendary equanimity, but Alice remained stubbornly and uncharacteristically silent.

Growing uneasy, Natalie pressed for an answer. Alice hesitated, gazing back over the years to a moment of sorrow so great that it obviously pained her to recall it now. And then, slowly, she faced her daughter, staring with profound sadness into those ice-blue eyes.

"You," she muttered, almost as if speaking to herself. "You . . ."[38]

AT RUE ALPHONSE DE NEUVILLE, Miss Partridge had proven too authoritarian and not very effective as a tutor. She was replaced by a former

French governess of Natalie's, Emmanuelle Lacheny. In her kinder moments Natalie described Lacheny as ignorant but useful; at other times she focused on her ugliness. Natalie was often cruel when discussing people's physical inadequacies, and never more so than with Lacheny; she once said it displeased her to have to look at the woman while eating. Pauline got on well with Lacheny, who so enjoyed typing Tarn's manuscripts, running her errands, and serving as her girl Friday that she stayed in her employ until 1907.

Life in this home of poets was pleasant at first. Laughter reigned. Friends called frequently. Natalie made fun of Pauline's "disgusting" habit of eating a daily sweetbread salad with mayonnaise sauce. Pauline banged out Chopin on the old piano in the salon, with Natalie accompanying her on violin.

They kept Charles Brun busy. Pauline was studying Greek and preparing her first book, *Études and préludes,* for publication in April. Natalie was completing two books: *Lettres à une connue,* her version of the affair with Liane, and *Cinq petits dialogues grecs,* a collection of short playlets. Aside from the ongoing tutoring in Greek and French verse, Brun helped in other ways. With his precise, calligraphic penmanship he recopied Natalie's scrawled manuscripts, edited drafts, and provided an introduction for Pauline to his own publisher, home of Verlaine, Sully Prudhomme, and Mallarmé.

Into this sweet existence one day in March came Olive Custance, visiting Paris for a month with her mother. They were accompanied by a twenty-one-year-old Norfolk neighbor, the Honorable Frederick Walpole Manners-Sutton. Known as Freddy, he was son and heir to the Viscount Canterbury.

Although from a conservative family, Olive had emerged with an independent outlook. Highly regarded as a poet, her work often appeared in the *Yellow Book,* an important British literary magazine of the 1890s. She was engaged to a man chosen by her parents, a politician named George Montague, but was in love with someone they loathed: Lord Alfred Douglas, the onetime lover and nemesis of Oscar Wilde. As Natalie quipped, Montague's career promised to be every bit as brilliant as Alfred's was scandalous. Olive would later suggest that Natalie form a *mariage blanc* with Douglas, after which they could all live in a free-spirited ménage à trois. It sounds like idle speculation, something they might giggle about in bed or over tea, but she may have been halfway serious. In 1901, at Olive's urging, Douglas made a point of getting to know Natalie.

At their initial meeting over tea at the Barney-Tarn household, Natalie was delighted with Olive's fresh-faced, dazzling complexion. "I have fallen quite in love with her," she confided to Eva. "How charming she is . . . [She] makes me feel that I should mount a charger and storm all the portals of her castle until I had succeeded in carrying her away."[39]

Natalie's attraction to Olive didn't escape the watchful Pauline, who by now knew all the signs of her lover's awakening interest in another woman. Before leaving that afternoon, the pretty English poet invited them to her lodgings the next day for "Lipton tea." The moment the door closed behind her Pauline delivered the opinion that Olive was "banal," and announced that she had no interest in going for tea. An argument ensued. Natalie reminded her that Sappho had been gracious and welcoming to women joining her circle, even those of whom she was jealous, and recited fragments of Sappho's poetry to prove the point. Pauline wasn't swayed, and relations remained tense all day.

That evening Pauline's jealousy was swept aside by a distressing telegram from Mary Shiletto, vacationing with her family on the Côte d'Azure. Violet was ill and asking for her; could she come immediately? Pauline reeled. Just before leaving for the south, Violet had confessed hurt and sadness at the gulf between them since Natalie had entered Pauline's life. Pauline knew it was true. She had seen less and less of her dearest friend, ignoring her for Natalie. Now, suffused by guilt, she packed hurriedly and took the next train south.

Upset over the argument with Pauline and the news about Violet, Natalie regretted the planned tea with Olive, her mother, and Freddy Manners-Sutton. Once at her destination, though, she forgot her problems. Natalie's charms were always at their glorious best when in pursuit of a new conquest, and so dazzling was she that afternoon that she unintentionally captured the heart of Manners-Sutton. Olive visited Natalie the next day, ostensibly to discuss poetry, and mentioned that Freddy had fallen in love with her.

"Tell him that I love you," Natalie replied.

"That wouldn't make any difference to him," Olive insisted. "He asks only that you agree to see him from time to time."

"But meanwhile," Natalie asked, "when will you come here again? Should we dine together tomorrow night, just the two of us?"

"Yes," Olive replied simply.[40]

That night, as moonlight poured in through Natalie's bedroom window, they commenced a brief liaison and much longer friendship. Through Olive, Natalie would soon meet a group of wealthy, worldly, and socially savvy lesbians. Among them was "Baby" Hohenlohe, the Austrian princess she had admired in Dinard two summers before. Married and the mother of two, Baby H. was frank and down-to-earth about her love life, and she and Natalie became good friends. Another member of the group was Olive's aunt, the aging but still-celebrated beauty Lady Anglesly, who, a decade or so later, would introduce Natalie to one of her greatest loves, the painter Romaine Brooks.

Olive also brought Freddy Manners-Sutton into Natalie's life. Once he overcame his initial crush on Natalie, he became a steadfast and devoted friend. At first, though, he was annoyingly lovesick, staring at her with devotion, peppering her with invitations, and praising her endlessly to others. Irritated by his constant presence, she suggested to Olive that they leave him behind and visit Venice accompanied only by a chaperone. The anticipated idyll turned into a disaster; struck down by malaria, they spent the trip confined to their respective beds.

In Cannes, Pauline learned that Violet had been hit by typhoid. Secluded in a clinic, she was feverish and often unable to recognize her parents or sister. Pauline spent hours with Mary at the Shilettos' vacation villa, Sunny Bank, worrying about Violet and talking over the past. When Mary told her that the liaison with Natalie had caused Violet unbearable suffering, the news intensified Pauline's already keening sense of guilt. She recalled every hurt she'd delivered to Violet, including turning down an invitation to accompany the Shiletto family on this very vacation. She chastised herself for consistently choosing Natalie over Violet, with little care for her old friend's feelings. When she compared the purity of her childhood friend against the frank, aggressive sexuality of her lover, she felt shame. Worse, even with Violet clinging desperately to life, she missed Natalie dreadfully. The realization sickened her.

Pauline spent a lot of time in her rooms at the Hôtel des Pins putting the finishing touches to *Études and préludes*. In late March, when Violet took a turn for the better, she made a quick trip to Paris to deliver the manuscript to her publisher. Her hopes of a happy reunion with Natalie were quickly dashed: she arrived just in time to say good-bye to Natalie and Olive, who were leaving for Venice. "They looked radiant," she wrote bitterly to Brun.[41] She returned, depressed, to Cannes, but came to Paris again on April 4 to drop off the corrected proofs. She stayed only a day before returning south. On April 8, shortly after her return, Violet suddenly worsened and died.

Natalie, back in Paris after her disastrous Venetian trip, was taken aback by Pauline's cable telling of Violet's death. Violet belonged to her earliest memories: learning French, driving the pony cart, spying on the gypsy camp. Natalie had known few grim losses, and the harsh realization that a friend had died sent her reeling. When she thought of Pauline's return from Cannes, she felt even worse. Her lover's hysterical scenes and tears had become commonplace, and Natalie expected to be on the receiving end of strong emotional storms. To her great surprise, Pauline's arrival brought no scenes. Scarcely acknowledging Natalie's presence, she shut herself up in her darkened room and wouldn't come out. Natalie heard her sobbing throughout the night.

How strange it must have been for Pauline when, on April 17, only nine days after Violet's death, *Études and préludes* was published. An event that should have been one of the happiest in her young life was now and forevermore mingled in her mind with death. Guilt, too: how could she feel pleasure from seeing her name on the cover when Violet moldered in a fresh grave? Her muddled emotions were compounded by the book's subject matter. Virtually every one of the passionate poems is about Natalie, for whose love she had ignored Violet until it was too late.

To Pauline's surprise, *Études and préludes* received a favorable welcome from critics.* Because she had published the book under the ambiguous name "R. Vivien," readers didn't realize they were reading sapphic verse, and Pauline received fan letters addressed to "Messr. R. Vivien." On one occasion she attended a poetry lecture with Natalie in which poet Charles Fuster earnestly praised *Études.* When he described its author as a young man consumed with passion for his first mistress, Natalie and Pauline ran from the room, collapsing with giggles when they were safely away.

Under the laughter, Pauline continued to mourn her dearest friend. She always would. Violet's death would mark a great change in Tarn. Death had always fascinated her, but until now she'd charted a careful course, one that merged here and there with the Shadow but always led back into Light. Now she took her first steps onto that long, lingering path leading to oblivion. Mourning became her raison d'être, the nurturance of grief her greatest joy, the cultivation of woe her most faithful lover. Whatever chance Pauline might have had for stability was now interred with Violet's bones.

---

*Besides Pauline's *Études et préludes,* two other significant, critically well-received books of poetry by women were published in France in 1901: *Occident,* by Lucie Delarue-Mardrus, and Anna de Noailles's *Le coeur innombrable.* That year marked a major turning point in France for the acceptance of women as serious poets.

SIX

Une Jeune Fille de la Société Future

1901–1902

Who was more 1900 than Miss Barney? And also, who was more exquisite?

—*André Germain*

"To Natalie Clifford Barney, Young Woman of the Future Society."
—*Pierre Loüys,*
writing in NCB's copy of
Les chansons de bilitis

D RAWN BY UPBRINGING to the arts in general and by nature specifically to literature, Natalie had always felt at home in the company of creative people. Early in 1901 she began making a concerted effort to enter artistic circles, particularly those inhabited by writers. She had little trouble being accepted. The general consensus among the city's young and creative set was that Natalie epitomized the very idea of a dashing, modern woman. Not only did she defy convention, but she was fiercely independent and highly intelligent. That she was also attractive, fun to be with, and extremely rich only added to her allure.

As aggressive in pursuit of friendship as she was of love, Natalie left nothing to chance. When she met someone she wanted to know better, she issued invitations to dinner, the theater, a canter in the Bois, or whatever seemed most suitable. Fully confident of her appeal, she didn't hesitate to call upon new acquaintances, intriguing them with her unusual combination of old-world manners and new-century daring. She sent beautiful flowers, wrote enticing notes, fired off witty *petits-bleus,* and presented inscribed copies of *Quelques portraits-sonnets de femmes.*

One of her earliest conquests on the Paris scene was the outrageous dandy Count Robert de Montesquiou, the model for Marcel Proust's Baron de Charlus. Effete and ultrarefined, Montesquiou was a living piece of performance art, staging his home, clothing, voice, and every action for maximum effect. People either adored his originality or despised his cruel wit, but he left no one indifferent. The Goncourt brothers described him best: "a crank, a literary lunatic, but endowed with the supreme refinement of an aristocratic race on the verge of extinction."[1]

Montesquiou was delighted by Natalie's forthright nature and nicknamed her "la Tribade* Triumphante," a title she considered exaggerated. "I am a lesbian," she explained to a friend. "One needn't hide it, nor boast of it."[2] Montesquiou introduced Natalie to some of the most glittering lights in Parisian society. In later years, when his excesses caused most people to turn their backs on him, she remained a faithful friend.

Another new friend (and brief lover) was famed opera star Emma Calvé, whose stunning sopranic voice had been influenced by her studies with the world's last acclaimed castrato, Domenico Mustafà. Composers wrote opera roles specifically for Calvé, and from 1890 until her 1908 retirement she was considered the world's foremost interpreter of Carmen. As late as 1997 a critic called her "the greatest Carmen of her, and probably of all time."[3] A 1900 photograph of the hefty Calvé features lots of dark curly hair, thick brows, a cupid's bow mouth, and big brown eyes.

One young woman Barney met around now was destined to become one of the century's most famous writers, though few would have guessed so at the time. Born and raised in Burgundy, Sidonie Gabrielle Colette had moved to Paris a few years earlier, following her marriage to the successful journalist Henri Gauthier-Villars, known as Willy, who was thirteen years her senior. Only twenty when she married, she stood in awe of her husband. Realizing that Colette possessed a talent with words, Willy encouraged her to write her childhood memoirs. The result was *Claudine à l'école,* which attained unprece-

*The word *Tribade,* which means lesbian, was in vogue at the time.

dented success when it was published in 1900—with Willy's name on the cover as sole author. Three more Claudine books followed in short order, all written by Colette. Eventually her authorship was revealed, and a brilliant writing career was born.

"We all learned in *Mes Apprentissages* the kind of life she led at that time," Lucie Delarue-Mardrus wrote later. "After reading that book I understood better the attitude she'd affected of a young woman perpetually poised to play Claudine for the one-hundredth time. 'She has the air of living on a postcard,' I used to tell my husband."[4]

Colette was still knuckled under Willy's control when she met Natalie, but even then she was high-spirited, insolent, and eye-catching. Horseback riding in the Bois, with its groomed parks, beautiful lakes, and tree-lined allées, Natalie had often noticed the feline-faced woman out "marching" her dog and cat. One day they exchanged a lingering glance, and not long after were formally introduced by Countess Armande de Chabannes. Within days Natalie called upon Colette and Willy in their home at 28, rue Jacob, a few doors from the *pavillon* where she herself would live for more than sixty years, and a lifelong spark was struck. In 1906 Colette would leave Willy and stay briefly at Natalie's home. The short affair the two women had at that time turned into a close friendship that ended only with Colette's death in 1954.

Occasionally Natalie's pursuit of a likely new friend came to nothing, but she simply accepted such failures and moved forward. For instance, when she learned that her neighbor was Edmond Rostand, author of *Cyrano de Bergerac*, she sent him a flattering note and suggested that they meet. He never bothered to respond. Undaunted, she tried the same trick with the celebrated writer Pierre Loüys. This time she hit a literary jackpot.

Loüys, then just over thirty, had achieved fame in 1894 with the publication of *Les chansons de bilitis*. Ostensibly a translation of erotic songs written by a contemporary of Sappho's named Bilitis, the book constituted one of the greatest literary hoaxes in history: Bilitis never existed and her songs were written by Loüys. With its extensive textual notes, scholarly bibliography, and adherence to ancient literary forms, the book fooled scholars and the reading public alike. When the truth was finally revealed, Loüys was widely admired for his brilliant coup.

Two years later he published a similar book, *Aphrodite,* one of the biggest successes Parisian publishers had ever experienced. Novels and a collection of short stories followed, and by the century's turn Loüys was famous throughout Europe and the United States. His close friend Claude Debussy set the *Bilitis* songs to music, and he became the confidant of other famed artists such as André Gide and Gabriele d'Annunzio.

In sum, Loüys was someone who mattered in the literary world. If he cared to, he could be a superb literary mentor to Natalie, greasing the wheels of publication and introducing her to important writers. She knew that, of course, but she had other reasons for requesting a meeting. Loüys's subject matter, sapphism, delighted her, and she anticipated that they would have much in common.

Natalie's boldness wrested an invitation to call at his home near the Parc Monceau and to bring the other poet she had mentioned, Pauline Tarn. It's hardly surprising that Loüys responded in a positive manner. He, too, thought they might have a good deal in common. Like everyone in Paris, he knew of Natalie's affair with Liane de Pougy. He would have been curious to form his own opinion of a young woman whose sapphic life seemed to echo his books.

Natalie exceeded his expectations. A few years before, when writing the dedicatory page of *Bilitis*—"This little book is respectfully dedicated to the young women of the future society"—he had in mind someone exactly like her. When they met, he was spellbound. He considered her the very embodiment of a modern woman. He admired her high-spirited nature and intelligence, and the fact that nothing he said shocked her or put her on the defensive. "It was above all the Amazon's character that attracted Loüys," Jean-Paul Goujon wrote in his published collection of Loüys-Barney letters. "This American, with her swift and caustic mind, her nature at once sociable and highly selfish, he found to be extremely agreeable."[5]

Natalie was drawn to Loüys as well. She liked the fact that behind his bad boy image was a gentleman of the old school, and she adored his quick wit. In fact, he was one of the few people she ever knew capable of matching her riposte for riposte.

Loüys didn't warm to Pauline that day and never would. Most critics consider Pauline far superior to Natalie as a poet, but Loüys preferred Barney's work. As he told Natalie, he saw under Pauline's talk of violets "a sort of instinctive defense against an imaginary malevolence that skulks about and lies in wait for her. . . . You, on the other hand, you were born having in your heart all that she lacked. You write with a heart as open as hers is closed. . . . She had as much of a devouring passivity as you are affectionate in the most active and beautiful sense."[6]

The day they met, Loüys presented Natalie and Pauline with autographed copies of *Les chansons de bilitis*. Before leaving, Natalie made an audacious request, asking the famous writer to review her manuscript for *Lettres à une connue*. He agreed to do so, but she was disappointed when his verdict came. *Lettres*, he said, was unpublishable as it stood. The characters were too easily identifiable, and it was written in a way that was "a little outmoded, overused by bad poets."[7] He added that there were excellent passages, and suggested that she rewrite the tale. If she did, he would consider giving her a preface.

Natalie ignored his advice. She didn't mind lightly editing a manuscript after it was professionally typed, but to her the idea of gutting a paragraph, let alone an entire work, was anathema. She believed that a writer's first impulse when putting pen to paper distilled the truth and should be left intact. The unfortunate result is that her large body of work is uneven. One is struck time and again in her unpublished manuscripts by passages of great, lyric beauty sandwiched between pages that, while decent enough, could have been good or even great if she'd worked them over rigorously.

Natalie felt that *Lettres à une connue* "vibrated with something sincere." Because the events related were written shortly after they occurred in real life, she considered the book to be an honest reflection of reality. She saw no reason to be discreet, as Loüys suggested, assigning pseudonyms or otherwise disguising characters. She had hid nothing in her writing so far, and saw no reason to start now. Instead, she made unsuccessful attempts to find a publisher in Belgium, where they weren't so squeamish about printing tell-all tales. She had no luck there, either, and eventually let the matter drop. *Lettres à une connue* would never be published.

To thank Loüys for his efforts, she sent a miniature Japanese cherry tree in bloom. Accompanying it was a copy of *Quelques portraits-sonnets de femmes* warmly inscribed in English: "To my favorite author and inimitable master, Monsieur Pierre Loüys. In remembrance of all the thanks I owe him. I wish I had something more worthy to offer. Natalie Clifford Barney."

Natalie has been criticized for so eagerly pursuing Loüys's friendship. "She questioned neither the methods nor the motives of this male homosexual who wrote lascivious works about women's sexuality," Shari Benstock observed. "She did not pose questions that a contemporary feminist would ask: what does it mean when a homosexual male describes erotic acts in the voice of a homosexual female? What unexamined psychological motives are implicit in such an act? . . ."[8] Indeed, even in Natalie's day there were those who considered Loüys's preoccupation with lesbians to be a bit strange. Rachilde, the doyenne of French literary criticism, puzzled over his "naïve and puerile insistence" in writing about lesbians and predicted, inaccurately, that he would bore readers.

But Natalie wasn't given to theorizing. It would never have occurred to her to question Loüys's motives or wonder if his writings embodied a subtle form of misogyny. Far from it. She thought it was for the best that someone, even a man, was writing about the beauty of sapphic love. *"Bilitis,"* she told him, "gave me more troubling ecstasies and more tender tendernesses than any mistress. If I now want to create books, it's to respond to *[Bilitis]* and . . . tell this old world, deaf to its own lies and blind to its ugliness, that already there are young women of the future society who appreciate what you have created for them."[9]

In addition to being inspired by *Bilitis*, Natalie simply liked Loüys. She viewed him not so much as a man but as a kindred spirit. From the first she felt that she could tell him anything about her life and her loves, and that he would understand.

While her feelings of friendship and affection for Pierre Loüys were genuine, that didn't prevent her from realizing how useful he could be. To this point her reputation had been based on scandal and her ability to shock. Now, grown friendly with a powerful literary figure, she would begin to develop another kind of reputation—that of the mind.

NATALIE AND PAULINE made plans to spend the summer of 1901 in Bar Harbor. At the last minute, however, Pauline wrote from Scotland, where she was vacationing with her mother. She would be unable to come, she said, because she was recovering from a minor accident.

That, of course, was just an excuse. Her true reasons for not coming were more complex. Foremost among them: she couldn't bear a repeat of the previous summer, in which Natalie had so often ignored her to run off and play the popular socialite. Also, as she revealed in an affectionate letter to Alice, Albert had made it brutally clear that her presence beside Natalie would create "disagreeable talk," and she had no desire to cause Natalie harm. "She has a very noble nature," Pauline assured Alice, "in spite of her little and big faults."[10]

In early July Natalie reluctantly sailed for the States without Pauline, commencing a separation that would forever change their relationship. Once in Bar Harbor, she issued a series of furious ultimatums, ordering Pauline to sail immediately for Maine or else. But with distance, safely removed from Barney's compelling presence, Pauline began to take a pitiless look at their union—and she didn't like what she saw. Natalie was a drug she desperately needed, but whose addicting habit she was equally desperate to break. If there was anything she desired as much as being with Natalie in Maine, it was not to be there at all. She expressed her inner battle in a letter to Charles Brun: "It was crazy to let her go," she said, "but it would have been worse to follow."[11]

Throughout the summer she wavered, pulled one day by feelings of deep love, and the next by anger and disgust over her inability to rid herself of those very feelings of love. Her letters to Barney ranged from furious rants about past hurts ("To see you twice a week, for 40 whole minutes, in the manner of last year!"), to affectionate cooing ("Don't you see that I love you with all my breath and being?"), to detached reasoning ("It's better [that I not come], for you as well as for me").[12]

Pauline began to look elsewhere for love. She probably had a brief affair with Olive Custance that summer or fall, and at some point may have had a liaison with Eva Palmer. She also tried entering the group of wealthy and aristocratic women, including Princess Hohenlohe and Lady Anglesly, who had embraced Natalie. While she was treated kindly enough, they always viewed her as an outsider, neither chic nor amusing enough to become a true member of their rarified circle.

Returning to Paris from a short trip to England, Pauline learned the latest gossip about Natalie from Lacheny: she was engaged to a young Frenchman, Count Chabannes de la Palice. The details of this situation are muddled and confusing. Chabannes did know Natalie, and some evidence exists that he hoped to obtain her dowry through marriage. There's a strong chance that he even traveled to Washington in pursuit of this goal. If so, Natalie might have encouraged rumors of an engagement to confuse the social gossips and appease Albert. Whatever the Chabannes story may have been, Pauline reacted violently. In a frenzied letter written on August 29, she called him a worm and Natalie a harlot, and declared that everything was over between them forever. "Go to men's embraces," she snarled. "They are the only ones you are fitted for."[13]

Obviously, it wasn't only Natalie's women who elicited Pauline's jealousy. To her, Barney's relationships with men seemed suspicious and threatening. Natalie may not have wanted to sleep with men, but she delighted in being a belle. She liked men, loved to flirt, and, possessed of a healthy ego, enjoyed the fact that men considered her attractive in all ways—including sexually. Natalie had close male friends all her life, even into her nineties. In one of those puzzling misogynistic remarks she occasionally made, she once admitted to often finding "the company of intelligent men far more interesting and agreeable than that of a pretty woman. In many men I confided quite freely. . . ."[14]

Conversely, Pauline had no use for men whatsoever. In fact, from her writings one might infer that she hated men. Certainly the idea of male/female sex disgusted her. In *A Woman Appeared to Me* she reveals that, when first learning about heterosexual intercourse, she felt "wholly revolted by the grotesque shame of human lust." At other times she refers to sex with men as "a crime against nature" and "abnormal," and the heroines in many of her poems are women who would rather mate with a monster than with a man. The foregoing may explain Pauline's vehemence when she heard the story about Natalie and the "worm" Chabannes, but even after her furious proclamation about the relationship being over, the love you/hate you letters to Barney continued.

Pauline needed and wanted to make the break, but she just couldn't bring herself to do it. It wasn't until autumn that she gathered her courage and took the plunge. On All Saints' Day, as if fleeing the witch born one day earlier, she moved from the shared apartment with Natalie. As she stepped into her future she seemed to symbolically embrace her past. Her new home, on the ground floor of 23, avenue du Bois, was in the same building where she had lived as a child, where Violet spent most of her life, and where Mary and her parents still resided. It was also the building in which Pauline would die.

Completely alone, Pauline threw herself into her writing. In the next two years, five new volumes of Renée Vivien's work would appear: *Cendres et poussières, Brumes de fjords, Évocations, Sapho,* and *Du vert au violet.* For better or worse, this prodigious output, which would continue without surcease until her death, had been set loose by Natalie. Pauline admitted as much. "You have been my inspiration," she wrote Natalie in July 1902. "You showed me my true path,—I found myself through you, came to know myself. You brought me strange flowers that I hadn't known, songs that I never would have heard, kisses that I never would have plucked. My thoughts and everything I write reflects all that."[15]

MEANWHILE, despite her worries about Pauline, Natalie had been caught up in the Bar Harbor scene. Some doors remained closed, but for the most part she continued to be accepted. In an August letter to Pauline, Laura expressed relief that Natalie had been received with "universal cordiality and enthusiasm." Writing to Natalie, Pauline repeated Laura's remark and added that anyone as brilliant and beautiful as Natalie could afford to walk "over the trim lawns and conventional geranium beds of society with impunity."[16]

She was right. There was something about Natalie that kept her from becoming a freak or a joke, even in this outwardly straitlaced society. Some might turn their backs and be nasty, and almost everybody gossiped, but it seemed to have little impact on Miss Barney. She refused to suffer or act ashamed for having chosen a different course. When snubbed, she reacted with regal disdain, and continued shining at the center of an adoring crowd. Natalie's unflagging popularity and obvious lack of guilt were a slap in the face to the self-righteous.

Most people who inhabited the world she grew up in liked and even admired Natalie. She'd always been different from other girls in her set: smarter, quicker with comebacks, bolder. It was she who'd been courageous or maybe just crazy enough to gallop across the island with another horse on lead; not even the bravest boy in her circle had been up to that. In everybody's earliest memories of the Barney girl, she'd always been brimming with caprice and pulling surprises from her bonnet. It had always been natural to expect the unexpected from Natalie, and so it became natural to accept the unnatural.

One day she visited the office of a close childhood friend, one of her old flirtations. Now married and a father, he had become the respectable vice president of a bank. When he caught sight of Natalie in the doorway, he smiled and gestured her inside. "Tell me what you've been up to since I saw you last," he said. "Tell me everything." He paused, reconsidering his words. "Well," he added, "maybe not everything!" And with that they both dissolved into laughter.[17]

The summer season was cut short when an assassin's bullet took the life of President William McKinley. The Barneys, along with the rest of social Washington, immediately closed up their cottage and returned to Washington for the funeral.

The change of scene was interesting for a while, but Natalie quickly grew bored. One day she received a packet from France containing a letter from Liane and a newly minted copy of *Idylle saphique.* She held the book in her hands with mixed feelings. Part of her was happy for Liane and pleased to see their love glorified, but she felt renewed disappointment that her own version of their tale, *Lettres à une connue,* had come to nothing.

"The Idylle has seen the light," Liane wrote, "and the public is scrambling, that's the word, for these scraps of us and our former desires. Everyone is writing to me; men and women, anyone with a soul who has been touched by our tenderness." Although Natalie reveled in the idea of being talked about in every fashionable corner of Paris, she worried that her family would learn about the book and discover her resemblance to Flossie.

She was right to worry. All of Paris knew who the book's real-life counterparts were, and word filtered swiftly across the Atlantic. It was probably the publication of *Idylle saphique* and the subsequent buzz it created in their circles that made Albert so stubborn about keeping Natalie in America, because no matter how much she wheedled he refused to let her return to Paris. When Lucie Delarue-Mardrus met Albert the next year, she was struck by the fact that he "felt severely about her having been the heroine of . . . Liane de Pougy's controversial novel."[18]

Natalie was working on her next book, *Cinq petits dialogues grecs (Antithèses et parallèles).* During her American exile she had carried on an extensive correspondence with Pierre Louÿs, who was helping ready the book for publication in 1902. His efforts went far beyond literary mentorship. He took a pivotal role, editing and revising the manuscript, correcting proofs, finding a publisher, and arranging for an excerpt to appear in the respected literary journal *La Plume*. He was motivated by a number of things, including his admiration and affection for the enticing Miss Barney and also his pleasure at having this exemplar of modern womanhood as a protégé. Nothing could have made him happier than Natalie's dedication of *Cinq petits dialogues grecs* to "Monsieur Pierre Loüys, par 'une jeune fille de la Société future.' "

Recalling Albert's rage over *Quelques portraits-sonnets de femmes,* Natalie decided to use as a pseudonym the initial "N." However, Loüys advised her that in France the letter stood for one thing only: Napoléon. He suggested Néanis, a Greek word that translated as *jeune fille.* She chose Tryphé, from the preface of Loüys's *Aphrodite,* wherein Odysseus encounters two virgins, Arete and Tryphé, equal halves of the goddess Aphrodite.

Cinq petits dialogues grecs consists of a short prologue and epilogue, three dialogues, two monologues, and a scattering of poetry. "Douce Rivalités," about three women caught in a web of infidelity and jealousy, was inspired by a delicate mission Natalie undertook to plead the cause of Baby H. to an angry lover. The most difficult aspect of this diplomatic endeavor, she found, was resisting the temptation to seize the princess's lover for herself. Since doing so would have caused the loss of Baby's friendship, Natalie used restraint. The tale contains a description of Sappho that sounds suspiciously like Barney herself:

> "Was she as irresistible as they say?"
> "She was irresistible as are all those who follow their true nature, as irresistible as those who have dared to live. She is as compelling as Destiny itself."
> "Why did she love only women?"
> "Because women alone are complex enough to attract and hold her. They alone know how to give her all ecstasies and all torments . . . [Sappho's] love is the gateway to eternity. Her love shines like a lighthouse across seas and time. . . . She is the flame which at the same time lights and destroys. Her approach dazzles and her flight consoles. . . . I believe her to possess more fidelity in her inconstancy than others with their constant fidelity. . . . When she sings, it seems that she exists for nothing but art; when she loves, we know that she lives for nothing but love."[19]

"Brute!" is an amusing dialogue that pokes fun at men and women alike. A woman addresses a man in high-blown prose about the nature of love. She claims to have sought the finest love on mountaintops, in temples, on the sea. After an interminable quest, she has finally found her man, for whom, at least in her soul, she has become virginally pure. After eight pages in this vein he utters his only four words in the dialogue: "I want your body."

Natalie's philosophies of love and life are evident throughout *Cinq petits dialogues grecs*. She celebrates paganism and contrasts it unfavorably to Christianity, believes that infidelity brings lovers closer than faithfulness, and counsels against jealousy. She also unwittingly allows an insight into her relentless future attempts to win Pauline back when Ione, speaking of her lover Myrelis, admits that "because she rejects me, I desire her even more."

TOWARD YEAR'S END Natalie learned that Pauline had become involved with Baronne Hélène van Zuylen de Nyevelt, one of the richest women in Europe. (In *Souvenirs indiscrets*, she claims to have known nothing of this affair until her return to Europe in late spring of 1902, but evidence disputes this.)

From Washington, Natalie tried to intercede in the new relationship. She asked Eva Palmer, then in Europe, to call on Pauline and plead her case, but that mission was unsuccessful. The next emissary was an unbelievably bad choice: Liane de Pougy. Pauline had always been jealous of Liane, and with good reason. When Natalie hadn't been sneaking off for assignations with the courtesan, she was celebrating their old love affair in *Lettres à une connue*. Not unpredictably, Mlle. de Pougy's visit resulted in failure.

In December Lord Alfred Douglas—Bosie to his friends—came to Washington to visit his cousin, Percy Wyndham, who was attached to the British embassy. The homosexual scandal involving Wilde continued to haunt Douglas, who was a frequent target of vicious barbs and cruel behavior in England. Natalie worried that he would be just as ill-treated in Washington. "Poor boy," she wrote Laura. "I fear he will have a hard time of it—through the narrowness or hypocrisy of this land of so-called free citizens who misname themselves Christians. . . . I cannot say how sorry I feel for the intensely vulnerable. I have been tormented in so many little ways myself that my whole heart goes out to them."[20]

That last sentence is revealing. Deep beneath her disdain for the opinion of the prudish and self-righteous, Natalie knew the pain of rejection. People who knew her often remarked on the queenly manner in which she turned her back to gossip, but she paid a price for doing so. Little by little, as the years passed, Natalie would harden her heart and narrow her vision until only the inhabitants of her circle held reality. The world at large would come to have little meaning for Natalie Clifford Barney. "I am fond of human beings," she noted in *Pensées d'une Amazone*, "but only one at a time."

Alfred Douglas and Natalie knew of each other through Olive Custance, and looked forward to meeting in the flesh. When her parents refused to receive him, Natalie—by now an expert at evading their scrutiny—found ways to spend time with him secretly. One of their favorite gambits was to go driving through the woods of Rock Creek Park on crisp winter days. Tucked in a cozy carriage, they talked for hours.

For Douglas, these meetings were a pleasant reprieve from the harsh treatment he received elsewhere in the capital city. As a titled English visitor, he'd been given an honorary membership in the exclusive Metropolitan Club, where, surrounded by some of the nation's richest and most powerful men, he'd been subjected to astonishing rudeness and repeatedly cut dead. Insulting remarks about Wilde were made in his presence, just loud enough for him to hear. "How abominably America has treated me!" he wrote Natalie. "Never even in the first days of the great [Wilde] debacle in '94 have I encountered such beastliness and such brutality."[21] To his credit, Douglas refused to be intimidated. He was supported in this by his country's ambassador, Julian Pauncefote, who made a point of escorting him to public events and even held a dinner in his honor.

Before his return home, Douglas presented Natalie with a set of gold hair pins that she wore for years. Rumors circulated that they were engaged, but, as usual, they weren't true. In fact, that coming March, Douglas and Olive Custance married against her family's strong objections. A year later, Natalie and Freddy Manners-Sutton became godparents to their first child, Raymond. Their combined gift, a set of round opals to be used as marbles, paid tribute to Olive's first book of verse.

Despite the distraction of Douglas's visit, Natalie worried increasingly about Pauline. The commanding tone that marked her earlier letters to Tarn had long since disappeared, replaced by a note of increasing desperation in which she begged Pauline to remember their love. In return came only silence. Finally, in April, Pauline sent a telegram brutally announcing that everything between them was completely finished.

If only she could return to Paris, Natalie knew, she could make everything right.

IN LATE SPRING Natalie's worries about Pauline were shoved aside when Albert had a heart attack—his second. The first had occurred the previous summer, when he had collapsed on the golf links, but after plenty of bed rest he had seemed like his old self. This time around the attack was more severe, and may have been precipitated by his concerns over the deepening involvement of Laura and Alice in the Baha'i faith.

From the late 1890s on, Laura's letters to her parents addressed issues such as martyrdom, the soul, universal love, and her desire to serve humanity. Obviously seeking something to wrap her soul around, Laura found it in 1900, in Paris: the Baha'i movement, whose tenets included absolute equality between the sexes; the absence of formal creed, rituals, ceremonies, and clergy; and a belief in the oneness of God and humanity. She soon converted to the religion, and shortly thereafter, so did Alice. In early 1902, when a leading Baha'i teacher came to Washington with a group of followers, Alice assumed their rent at a downtown property. When he learned of this, a furious Albert bought out the lease and closed the Baha'is down. Shortly afterward his heart gave out.

When the doctors declared him fit to travel, Natalie was assigned the task of taking him to Europe to recover in his beloved spas. In late May they sailed to England. After Albert rested for a few weeks, they came to Paris en route to Bad Nauheim, Germany. After settling into the hotel, Natalie took a carriage to 23, avenue du Bois, only to discover from the concierge that Pauline was not home. She stood outside wondering what to do, when suddenly Pauline drove up in an automobile. Catching sight of Natalie, she leaned forward, gave the chauffeur an order, and the car raced off.

Writing to Loüys about the incident, Natalie quoted Browning: "I know how much I love her/I know it now I've lost her." The lines sum up Natalie's unresolvable attitude about love, which was guaranteed to frustrate and keep her searching forever: she only desired what she didn't have; what she had, she didn't want.

Accompanied by Freddy Manners-Sutton, Natalie and Albert departed for Nauheim. Albert was happy to have Freddy along, viewing him as a strong contender for a son-in-law. Not only was he a future lord, which appealed to Albert's love of all things British, but he genuinely liked Freddy, who returned his affection. "[Freddy] was fond of my father," Natalie wrote, "who favoured his suit."[22]

Even in failing health, Albert focused his attention on Natalie's propensity for scandal. In Nauheim he went on a tear, grumbling over her evil deeds of the past and speculating about those to come. In a letter to "Muz-Buz" (Alice), Natalie complained that "Papa was in one of his moods last night, and so insulting as ever over bygones that I could hardly stand him—drinking again, I suppose, from the care he took all day to avoid his doctor. I tell some of this so that my letter may serve as an antidote if he writes trying to worry you. Even before F Manners-Sutton he told such a whopper that neither of us could help from shrieking from laughter."[23]

According to Albert, he had been approached by lawyers for a woman who intended to publish love letters from Natalie in American newspapers unless paid a great deal of money. Natalie told Alice that the woman in question, "though wicked in some ways I believe to be incapable of selling such things." She added that Albert's story "alarmed me a good deal for I loathe notoriety of that sort, but on my asking him to show me the words of warning he had just received he said he wouldn't, and so I was immediately reassured. Of course he has received no such things and only wanted to be nasty and worry me."[24] To Laura she noted with bitter humor that "Papa is pathetic and tyrannical by turns, severely pathetic at night and tyrannical in the morning."[25] In another note to her sister, she said: "I almost wish I had no reputation left, then [Papa] might pension me off the way they do old soldiers that have come out of the fight wounded—and so leave me alone."[26]

Once back in Paris, Natalie called on Mary Shiletto, who lived in the same building as Pauline. Glancing out the window of Mary's apartment, she spied Pauline in the garden below talking in an intimate way with her new lover, Baronne Hélène. Fourteen years Pauline's senior, Hélène had grown up in the grand, ancient style of the early nineteenth century. In fact her mother, Baronne Salomon, was reportedly the last Parisian to be driven about in a brougham pulled by a team of horses.

Both of Hélène's parents were Rothschilds, and as a young woman she had caused a minor quarrel in her Jewish family by marrying a Christian. Her husband was the equally wealthy Baron van Zuylen de Nyevelt, a polo player and early automobilist with whom she bore two children. It's not clear when Hélène ceased living *en famille,* but by the time she met Pauline in the winter of 1901–1902, at the home of Lady Anglesly, she was on her own.

Natalie was unkind to Hélène in her writings. She nicknamed her "la Brioche" for her puffy body and rounded topknot, and described her as ugly, ungainly, and socially awkward. But by all evidence, Hélène was a woman of formidable personality, vigor, and intelligence. She was worldly and well traveled. As an early automobile enthusiast, she had even raced her own cars in trans-European runs. True, she wasn't a lithesome beauty, but she had other gifts. What she offered Pauline was stability, strength, kindness, and, most important after Natalie, fidelity. An emotional shelter, she helped protect the unstable Pauline from her fearful inner storms and, in particular, from the temptation that Natalie would always present. Hélène could be controlling and she probably had other negative qualities as well, but she wasn't the monster she has so often been made out to be. Pauline was not head over heels in love with Hélène, but she felt safe and knew contentment. This is evident from her astonishing production as a poet during their years together.

For Natalie, Hélène's great crime—aside from "stealing" Pauline—was that she had been born with a thick, graceless body and was way short on beauty. Compounding that villainy was the fact that, after separating from her husband, she often dressed like a man, once reportedly appearing at her theater box in a tuxedo while sporting a fake mustache. It was one thing to go about gaily masquerading as a page, Natalie believed, but something altogether different to be a serious cross-dresser. She loved the feminine and was at a complete loss to understand why a woman would want to look like a man. "In the days of the Amazon's youth, and of my own," recalled Liane, ". . . we loved long hair, pretty breasts, pouts, simpers, charm, grace; not boyishness. 'Why try to resemble our enemies?' Natalie-Flossie used to murmur in her little nasal voice."27

Gazing into the garden from Mary's apartment window, Natalie was horrified. The idea that Pauline would choose someone like Hélène over her was so baffling that she convinced herself it was all a mistake, or "some hideously incomprehensible physical attraction."28 That Pauline would turn from her own blond magnificence to the masculine frumpiness of the Baronne decimated her pride. "Instead of being beaten down," she recalled, "I was obliged to show what I was made of."29 Pauline refused to see her? Very well! She would do everything in her power to be noticed.

Natalie pulled out all the stops. She took to riding horseback before avenue du Bois decked *en amazone*. Baronne Magdeleine Wauthier always remembered her first sight of Natalie, wearing "a Seventeenth Century riding costume, a long habit with black facings, and on her incredibly blond hair a felt hat rebelliously plumed with ostrich feathers."30 Back and forth this magnificent personage rode, until not only Pauline but the entire neighborhood took notice. During these excursions Natalie's competitive spirit raged, spilling onto anyone who got in her way. Once, trotting past Pauline's window, "another mount tried to pass me, and my horse and I, as one, took off at a crazy gallop to avoid being overtaken."31

Perhaps the most sensational escapade of the campaign to retrieve Pauline involved Emma Calvé. One night Natalie and the world's foremost soprano stood beneath Pauline's French windows costumed as street singers. When Calvé began singing Gluck's aria for the grieving Orpheus, "J'ai perdu mon Euridyce," an enthusiastic crowd gathered to toss coins. Natalie, scion of millionaires, stooped to gather the money while keeping her eye fixed sharply on the window. At last Pauline appeared. Natalie tossed a bouquet containing a poem she'd written that begged Pauline to see her. By this time Calvé had been recognized and the two street singers slipped away. The romantic serenade, alas, didn't work. The flowers and poem were promptly returned by Mlle. Lacheny with a note: Pauline, it said, wished to be left alone.

Over the next few months, Natalie wrote ceaselessly, begging Pauline to see her. When Pauline bothered to respond at all, it was with unequivocal rejection. Sometimes she dictated notes, but more frequently she asked Lacheny to respond on her own. Once, referring to the "stations" Natalie made before the building and the roses she'd thrown on the balcony, Lacheny said: "It's punishing to her. If you really care for her, leave her alone."[32] Another time she noted that Natalie had "charm and grace, but more often you are imperious and despite yourself you do bad things."[33]

At a loss for what to do, Natalie turned to her sister. "Pauline won't even hear of or from me," she despaired. "I'm at the end of my strength and hope. You *must* do something about it, you alone are direct enough, big enough and far-seeing enough to be able [to get me] out of this misunderstanding."[34] When Laura came up empty, Natalie resorted once again to sending other emissaries to plead her case. The subsequent visit of Pierre Loüys enraged Pauline. "Why did you send [him] as a plenipotentiary minister?" she fumed. "Do you believe . . . the words of a man would persuade me? . . . I'm astonished that you don't sense how humiliating it is to have intermediaries (above all of the masculine sex) between us and our poor mutilated love. You alone could have reconquered me, if it were possible, and not your ambassadors."[35]

She also demanded to know why Natalie showed such jealousy toward Hélène. She explained that she would never love Hélène, or anyone, the way she had once loved Natalie, that such agonizing and heart-rending feelings could only occur once in a lifetime. "Ah! Natalie! Natalie! If only you had loved me before shattering all my beliefs and illusions, how many regrets you would have spared us!"[36]

Natalie suffered greatly over Pauline, it's true—but that didn't stop her from consoling herself with other women. She had a pleasing fling with a woman she described as a "robust romance writer."[37] This was followed by a brief affair with Baby H., which both women immediately regretted. They were too much alike, Natalie thought, to the point where their affair seemed downright incestuous. Almost embarrassed at what had occurred between them, they moved on quickly, deciding it was best to be friends rather than lovers. Agreeing to henceforth aid each other in any way possible on the battlefield of love, they half-jokingly fooled around with a plan to kidnap Pauline and confine her in the princess's Austrian castle, where the hunting dogs would prevent her from leaving.

THAT SUMMER Natalie met a recently married couple, Lucie and Joseph-Charles Mardrus. Often referred to in the plural as *les Mardrus,* they would, along with Loüys, be vital to Natalie's acceptance by the Parisian literary elite.

Joseph-Charles, whose initials earned him the nickname "Jesus Christ," was known as an "Orientalist," someone who possessed a scholarly knowledge of the East. Today he is best known for his sixteen-volume translation of *Arabian Nights,* which began appearing in 1899. A huge success, it appealed to the rising taste for exotica. Some criticized his translation as coarse and sloppy, but others, such as Edmond Jaloux, praised his naturalism, with its "odors of the bazaar . . . leather, mixture of people, fruity cuisine."

Arriving in Paris as a young man, J.C.'s good looks, saucy dark eyes, and charismatic personality hastened his entry into the clique at the *Revue Blanche,* an important magazine that published literary and artistic works by Marcel Proust, André Gide, Guillaume Apollinaire, Émile Zola, Paul Claudel, Jean Cocteau, Pierre Bonnard, Édouard Vuillard, Henri de Toulouse-Lautrec, Suzanne Valadon, and others.

Mardrus was well known as a critic when he met Lucie Delarue, one of six daughters of a wealthy Parisian shipping lawyer. Born in 1874, Lucie's childhood summers were spent at the family's beautiful country estate on the Normandy coast. The girls were allowed free rein of the place, but were schooled by governesses and kept aloof from other children. This robust and outdoorsy childhood turned Lucie into a woman who was "honest, charming and almost naively healthy."[38]

She was also beautiful. A visitor to the Delarue household, meeting Lucie for the first time, turned to her parents and exclaimed: "Your daughter is simply ravishing!" And, indeed, that was the opinion most people had of the tall, thin, small-breasted young woman. "She was the most beautiful of the four poetic muses of my youth," recalled writer André Germain (the others were Renée Vivien, Anna de Noailles, and Mme. de Régnier). "Everything about her charmed me: her thin body . . . her large eyes . . . that languid Norman beauty . . . [and] above all, her soft voice."[39]

From a young age Lucie had been attracted to women, but confided her emotions solely to poetry. Eventually she would become one of the most famous and sought-after writers of her day, turning out more than seventy books of fiction, poetry, memoirs, and plays (two of her novels were made into films). She was painted by Odilon Redon and sculpted by Rodin. André Gide dedicated *The Prodigal's Return* to her. Gabriele d'Annunzio had a perfume mixed especially for her, and a Lebanese millionaire once poured a fortune of pure rose essence into the wake of her departing ship. She met kings and queens, lectured throughout Europe and the United States, and once appeared in the pages of *Le Tout Paris* as a "famous personality," akin to being on the cover of *Time.* Today she is best remembered for a few lines of poetry evoking her beloved Normandy: "In the smell of an apple I held my native land."

Lucie met J. C. Mardrus in the summer of 1900, when he attended a dinner given by a mutual friend. At some point Lucie was urged to read her poetry, as yet unpublished, to the influential critic. J.C. turned a pitiless eye upon her while she bravely recited. Almost immediately, his expression changed from cynicism to surprise, and then he listened with rapt attention. "You are the greatest poet of your generation!" he exclaimed. Declaring himself hopelessly in love, he proposed that same night and the next day asked M. Delarue for Lucie's hand.

They were married three weeks later. The wedding party was transported to the church in automobiles, of which there were still so few in Paris that the procession caused a sensation. At the ceremony, Lucie wore the current bicycling costume of Zouave trousers, a checked top, and a straw boater, and her hands were lavishly covered with jewels presented by her new husband. Once established in their own residence, J.C. assumed management of the household. It was he who hired and fired servants, gave the daily orders, arranged the menu—all so that Lucie, whom he sincerely believed to be a great poet, wouldn't waste her time on such trivialities.

Natalie met this unusual duo through Pauline, though in a roundabout way. Lucie's first volume of verse, *Occident,* had recently been published to acclaim. Among the book's many admirers was Pauline Tarn. Hoping to meet Lucie, Pauline sent a copy of her second volume of poems, *Cendres et poussières.* Lucie liked the poems and said so in a thank-you letter. A time was arranged for Pauline to call at the Delarue-Mardrus villa, La Roseraie.

Both Lucie and J.C. were disappointed in Pauline, finding her timid, hesitant, and spilling over with trite conversation. But they were impressed by her poetry, and for this reason accepted an invitation to dine at her apartment. Present that evening was Eva Palmer, whose beauty stunned the couple. Lucie recalled her as "a thin and superb creature, a veritable heroine out of Dante Gabrielle Rosetti . . . I didn't have eyes big enough to take in this woman from another time, beautiful as a poem."[40] Eva invited les Mardrus to share her box at the theater the next night.

As fate would have it, another young woman was in the box with Eva, one whose presence was so powerful that Palmer's beauty faded by comparison. "It was in that loge," Lucie remembered, "that I saw, for the first time, Natalie Barney, who was, is, and will always be one of my dearest friends."[41] Lucie—quite aware of Natalie's reputation—was charmed to discover that the scandalous Flossie blushed so easily.

The moment Lucie stepped into the box, Natalie took cool note of her beauty and tall, slender frame. Her first thought was that, seen in the nude, a body like Lucie's would not disappoint. Her unapologetic gaze would have conveyed this thought clearly; the blush suffusing her face would have excused it; and the whole package would have been irresistible to Lucie, with her life-long but repressed attraction to women.

The evening was a great success. J.C. was entranced with Natalie's lively intelligence and found her good-natured frankness appealing. She, in turn, loved his humor and stories. One day she would pay him the ultimate compliment, saying that she never once heard him utter a cliché.

Les Mardrus readily accepted Natalie's invitation to dine later that week. "I can see her again as she was when we arrived," wrote Lucie, "dressed in pale blue chiffon, playing the violin while she waited for us. The remarks she made during that dinner, in a voice that she never raised (and which has always remained thus), her ironic smile, her ease of manner, her quiet and curious epigrams soon revealed that we were in the presence of a real person. Three days later she was at La Roseraie, all her seductions in play."[42]

Situated on the unpaved banks of the Seine in the Parisian suburb of Neuilly, La Roseraie, home to les Mardrus, was named for its lush, rose-filled gardens. The property also contained a handsome grape arbor where lunch was served on sunny days. A henhouse was headquarters for two roosters named Ali and Baba, a harem's worth of chickens, a few golden pheasants, and a score of huge Toulouse geese. In addition to this menagerie were a tame gazelle, a goat, a few angora rabbits, and an alley cat that wandered in one day and became part of the family. The villa's interior contained thousands of books, handsome Arabian carpets, and practical American-style furniture.

On her first visit Natalie arrived by carriage, accompanied by Albert. He planned to drop her off, take a leisurely afternoon carriage drive, and return to pick her up. But to her father, Natalie said, the couple appeared bizarre and otherworldly. He was reluctant to leave her in the clutches of the dark-complexioned J.C., with his suspicious Eastern manners. J.C.'s opinion of Albert is unknown, but Lucie categorized him as "an elegant Washington club-man . . . who understood nothing about his daughter."[43]

Finally, albeit reluctantly, Albert took his leave. When he returned hours later, he found his daughter not only safe but unusually happy. She stepped into the carriage, her arms filled with books and roses, her talk bubbling over with love of literature. As they drove away, the shocked Albert asked Natalie if she thought J.C. lined his eyes with kohl.

One of the great pleasures shared by Natalie and Lucie was horseback riding, particularly along the Seine. Natalie always dressed *en amazone,* but Lucie liked to wear American cowboy garb, riding astride with her long hair tucked beneath a ten-gallon hat. Young boys, concluding that she was a man, shouted "He's as pretty as a woman!" and other, probably far more insulting, remarks.

Natalie always passed by haughtily, but the quick-tempered Lucie would pivot her horse and trot in their direction. Once she rode toward a taunting bicyclist who panicked and fell to the ground. Although he was unhurt, his bike was damaged. "We took off at a gallop," Natalie said, "leaving the bad boys fretting and reduced to silence."

The two women spent long hours in La Roseraie's living room, which J.C. never entered until dinner. Alone, they were, as Lucie said, "two sweet allies, two poems, two women." But not two lovers. Barney's attempts at seduction had thus far failed. It wasn't that Lucie didn't desire Natalie; she did, and passionately. But, the product of a conservative Catholic upbringing, she was immobilized by feelings of guilt and shame. Despite her comfortable place in the literary avant-garde and her friendships with many homosexual writers, she thought her feelings for Natalie were simply wrong. Her crushes on women had thus far been innocent: meaningful glances, the exchange of poetry, a stolen kiss here and there. As long as flesh was never involved, she hadn't sinned.

But it was clear to Lucie that Natalie was all about sins of the flesh, and about enjoying them. The dilemma would have to resolve itself, one way or the other. In the meantime, Natalie, as always, enjoyed the chase, spurred on by the need to possess what she couldn't have.

IN OCTOBER Albert asked Natalie to accompany him once again to Nauheim, but this time she begged off. Between her new passion for Lucie, the continuing worries about Pauline, and the upcoming publication of *Cinq petits dialogues grecs,* she felt pressured and pulled to pieces. Anyway, Albert seemed to be in far better shape than he had been immediately after his most recent heart attack. Nauheim, she felt, was something he could tackle on his own.

He seemed even better when he returned from Germany, but soon developed pleurisy and took to his bed. His constant coughing resulted in the doctor cupping his lungs twice.* The treatments didn't help much. He felt bad and looked worse, and Natalie doubted that he was strong enough to return to the States in early November, as he'd planned. She urged him to rest for a few months in the warm south of France, an ideal place to spend the winter.

He refused to listen. He was anxious to return home to curb Alice's spending, which he believed had gotten out of hand. According to him, she was frittering away a fortune on a new Washington residence. "This house business of

---

*An ancient treatment for drawing blood, cupping is no longer used.

hers will ruin us all!" he informed Natalie. She found his letter so amusing that she forwarded it to her mother. "Poor Dad!" she scrawled on the back. "Have you been so careless with his and your sheckles?—Please don't, for I love money & need it for I haven't so far found a profession—nor do I see my way to becoming self supporting."[44]

Despite objections from all quarters, Albert insisted that he was well enough to sail on November 8. However, after another downward turn, he reluctantly admitted that he was too sick to make the voyage home. In the care of a nurse whom he particularly enjoyed, he journeyed south to Monte Carlo. Natalie worried about him, but convinced herself that nothing was seriously wrong. After all, he had never yet failed to recover after enough rest.

With her father resting in the south, Natalie turned her attention to the abysmal situation with Pauline. She sought help in arranging a tête-à-tête from Eva, who finagled an invitation for herself to share Pauline's private box at the Nouveau Théâtre for a performance of the *Manfred Overture*. However, it was Natalie who showed up. Pauline appeared happy to see her, and they listened to the Schumann music arm in arm. The atmosphere must have been a little strained, because Mlle. Lacheny was also in the box (as well as the artist Levy-Dhurmer, who had recently painted Tarn's portrait). When they parted, Pauline promised to see Natalie again the next day.

But next morning Natalie received a telegram from the concierge of Albert's Monte Carlo hotel, advising her to come immediately because her father was seriously ill. Distraught, she made reservations for the next train. She cabled Alice, telling her that Albert had taken a turn for the worse and that she was leaving to join him. Since the train didn't leave until late afternoon, Natalie decided to meet Pauline as planned. When she failed to show up, Natalie phoned, only to learn that Pauline had thought things over and decided not to come. "One cannot play one's life over again," Pauline said.

Natalie told her of the telegram. Pauline hesitated. "If his condition becomes alarming," she said with obvious reluctance, "and you have need of me . . ."

"I don't need anyone," Natalie replied, stung, and hung up "with death in my soul."[45]

Arriving early the next morning at Monte Carlo, she was met by Albert's nurse with the unexpected news that her father had suffered another heart attack and died. At the Grand Hôtel, she gazed at Albert, still stretched out in his bed, and was overwhelmed by sadness. He had been strict, even harsh at times, but he had loved her deeply and she had loved him in return. Now, with so much left forever unsaid between them, he was gone. Until that moment she had never stared death in the face and was surprised at how peaceful he looked. "This is the only untroubled moment," he seemed to say, "the only quiet ever known. Keep the memory of it and do not mourn."[46]

According to the nurse, Albert had worried about Natalie until the end. The night before his death he dreamed that he was standing in a room filled with flowers for her wedding. "Right up to his last breath," Natalie said, "my poor father had dreamed of seeing me married to an English lord."[47]

Once again Natalie cabled Alice, this time with the news that Albert was dead, and then traveled with her father's body back to Paris, where she was met by Eva and Freddy. The next few days were taken up with the distracting details of death. As was the custom, she had a photograph taken of Albert in his shroud. On foot, she followed his bier to Père-Lachaise Cemetery, where he was cremated. Then, still accompanied by Eva and Freddy, she boarded a ship at Le Havre for New York. They were met at the dock by Laura and Alice, who was swathed in black crêpe. Natalie, her emotions raw, embraced her mother and delivered the urn containing Albert's ashes into her hands.

Later, when the will was opened, the Barney women learned that Albert's estate of about $9 million ($162 million in today's dollars) was to be held in trust, with the considerable yearly income divided equally among them. Natalie was now a very wealthy woman in her own right.

IN LATE JANUARY, Natalie returned to Paris. For a few months she lived in hotels, but on April 1 she and Eva moved into the apartment Freddy Manners-Sutton had bought at 4, rue Chalgrin, a small street near the Bois. Until the place was perfectly decorated, he preferred staying elsewhere on his visits from London. Natalie and Eva, not so fussy, were happy to make do. The place was elegant enough—every room had its own marble mantelpiece—but contained only a few chairs, a sofa, and a stunning Louis XIV Boulle table. Natalie and Eva rented beds, purchased curtains, and shared the price of a tapestry. Laura was told that a spare room awaited her visits, as well as a maid to dress and cook for her.

Natalie and Eva lived here on and off until the next summer, when each took a small house in Neuilly. Natalie moved into a property at 56, rue Longchamps; Eva lived on the adjoining street, rue Bois de Boulogne. After a spot of trouble with thieving servants, Natalie settled down with "an old cook called Virginie; an honest garçon, Swiss and innocent, Léon; and a deaf maid who when I call for shoes brings me boas."[48] The Seine was just at the end of her street, and she took to walking along the river each day.

For twenty-six years Natalie had been dependent on her father for support. And he had, though not without complaining, allowed her a handsome lifestyle. In return for this generous outlay, she had been forced to offer the appearance of living up to his values and expectations. Now, with an enormous yearly income of her own, everything had changed. She was completely independent. No matter what she did or said or wrote, she would never again worry about money. With her father gone and her mother in Washington, there was no longer a need to conform or toe an imaginary line. She could do anything she wanted to do.

And, starting now, she would.

SEVEN

The Heiress

1903–1908

The isles of Greece, the isles of Greece! Where burning Sappho loved
and sung.

—George Gordon, Lord Byron

My joy and my pain
My death and my life
My blond bitch!

—Lucie Delarue-Mardrus

*B*Y EARLY 1903 Natalie was known widely in Paris as the heroine of
Liane de Pougy's *Idylle saphique* and the inspiration behind Renée
Vivien's *Études et préludes*. Three, as they say, is a charm, and when
Colette's *Claudine s'en va* was published later that year, depicting her as an
unapologetic and flirtatious lesbian, she was forever branded a moral outlaw.
In this final Claudine book, Natalie, as Miss Flossie, is accompanied by a friend
whose red hair and American identity peg her as Eva Palmer:

> Miss Flossie, when she refuses a cup of tea, utters such a prolonged, gut-
> tural "No" that she seems to be offering her whole self in that throaty purr.
> Alain (why?) does not want me to know her, that American woman, supple

as a piece of silk, with her sparkling face glittering with tiny gold hair, her sea-blue eyes and her ruthless teeth. She smiled at me without a trace of embarrassment, her eyes riveted on mine, till a curious quiver of her left eyebrow, as disturbing as an appeal for help, made me look away. At that, Miss Flossie gave a more nervous smile while a slim, red-haired young girl huddled in her shadow glared at me with inexplicable hatred in her deep eyes.

Maugis—a fat music critic—his protruding eyes flashing for a second, stared straight at the two Americans so insolently that he deserved to be hit and mumbled almost inaudibly as he filled a claret-glass with whisky:

"Some Sappho . . . if that sort of thing amuses you!"

By now Natalie had come to rather like being viewed as disreputable, and was fond of saying that she had the most respectable of bad reputations. She meant by this that, no matter what anyone might say about her, they couldn't deny her excellent family background, her exquisite manners, or her money. This "respectability," combined with her strong will and sharp intelligence, allowed her to spurn conventional regard. She insisted on being accepted for what she was. If there were those who didn't like it, well, they probably weren't her sort to begin with. "Withdrawn from high society before it could withdraw from me," she said, "I ended up seeing only those of my choosing and of an inexhaustible variety."[1]

Indeed, turn-of-the-century Paris was home to countless exciting, talented, and brilliant originals. Natalie wanted to know them all, and most were eager to meet the blond American everyone was talking about. Introduced under the impeccable auspices of les Mardrus and Pierre Loüys, her circle quickly expanded. She became friends with many literary movers and shakers of the day, including André Gide, who had celebrated hedonism in his novels *The Fruits of the Earth* and *The Immoralist,* the prolific poet-diplomat Paul Claudel (brother of the great sculptor Camille Claudel), and many others. "I am beginning to meet worthwhile people," she reported to her mother.[2]

Natalie reacted to the sudden influx of new faces like any other highly social twenty-six-year-old woman: she gave parties. She had always enjoyed balls, costume dances, cotillions, private musical performances—in short, any excuse for a fête. She herself had previously hosted only small dinners. Now, blessed with money, a charming home in Neuilly, and fascinating new friends, she set about transforming herself into a hostess extraordinaire.

To entertain, according to most dictionaries, means to amuse, to divert, to exhibit hospitality. Whatever the definition, one thing is certain: whether a grande dame overseeing the season's most splendid society ball or an adolescent throwing a slumber party, any hostess worth her salt strives above all to entertain. To this end, guests must not only enjoy themselves but believe with-out question that all has been arranged for their pleasure. A gifted hostess may spend weeks in preparation, but during the revels she will appear completely relaxed. Events, no matter how elaborate, seem to unfold effortlessly while she concentrates only upon her guests.

From the start Natalie was a superb hostess, combining a stage manager's precision with the showmanship of a Barnum. She came by such gifts natu-rally. Her grandfather Pike had mastered the art of entertainment as an opera impresario, passing his abilities on to Alice, who could concoct a celebration for hundreds as easily as most people plan dinner for four. Observing her mother from childhood on, Natalie assimilated the Pike flair for festivities.

It was in Neuilly—then a small village just outside Paris—that Barney's famous salon really got its start. Her petite villa, sometimes described as a lodge, seemed made for parties, with its huge living room and separate maisonette for visitors. The extensive wooded grounds held formal gardens, fountains, and a swimming pool. The entire property rested on the unpaved banks of the Seine and overlooked the long, narrow island of Puteaux, which at the time housed an exclusive tennis club.

Natalie used Neuilly brilliantly, transforming it into a gathering place for artists, writers, musicians, and forward-thinking aristocrats. Amusing and often costumed events were always afoot, including dinner parties, theatricals, and poetry readings. The conversation was invariably lively, and usually some-thing unconventional would occur, providing fodder for the next day's gossip.

ONE UNFORGETTABLE FESTIVITY took place in June 1905 on a balmy afternoon. Upon the lawn, a green expanse surrounded by trees and dotted with fountains and statuary, stood a mostly young and fashionable set. The men were clad in handsome, light-colored suits and sporty bowlers. The women wore long, billowy dresses, carried delicate parasols, and upon their heads were perched hats with enormous brims. Servants walked to and fro, offering trays filled with glasses of champagne or punch.

The hostess stood serenely in the midst of the crowd. Dressed completely in white, her long hair glinting in the sunlight, she held herself with the straight back and self-assured regality that would still be remarked upon in her tenth decade. She made a point of talking to everyone at least once, focused upon each her ice-blue eyes, variously described as kind or cruel, depending on how one felt about her. She spoke in a soft murmur, never raising her voice, and her infectious, melodic laughter rang out often.

It was on this day that novelist and literary critic Edmond Jaloux encountered Natalie for the first time. They were introduced by a mutual friend, Joachim Gasquet, who had himself recently met the *"très jeune et très belle Américaine."* During the carriage ride from Paris, Gasquet bubbled with enthusiasm about their hostess, predicting that Jaloux would find her to be "the rarest and most intelligent woman of our time." Skeptical, Jaloux remained silent.

Arriving at Neuilly, the two men entered Natalie's gardens. And then, Jaloux recalled, "I saw coming toward us, between the lawns, a girl thin as a sword, the pre-Raphaelite type so common among the Anglo-Saxons at that time. Her beautiful blonde hair framed a pink face in which gleamed her extraordinary eyes; eyes of steel, piercing, a little hard, with a pitiless clairvoyance . . . [but] I have never known [Miss Barney] to be anything but soft, good and charming."[3] Instantly enchanted, he became one of Natalie's most ardent admirers.

Natalie did not rush events on that long-ago day. Instead, she allowed her guests time to enjoy the gardens, sip champagne, flirt, and stroll beside the water. Just as these preliminaries reached their height, she set the entertainment in motion.

The first event was a dramatization of Pierre Loüys's *Dialogue at Sunset.* This short playlet has lines that seem absurdly precious now: "When I take thine hand, why dost thou tremble?" Or: "I should be ashamed to act like Naïs, or like Philyra or Chloë, who did not wait for their wedding day to learn the secrets of Aphrodite. . . ."

The dialogue was enacted by Eva Palmer as Melitta, the young and beautiful virgin; and Colette as Arcas, the randy goatherd. Eva was the embodiment of femininity with her masses of red hair twisted into ropes around her head and a long blue-green tunic silhouetting her slender body. The athletic Colette was clad in a short tunic the color of terra-cotta, leather sandals with straps winding up her calves and, atop her head, a flowered wreath that looked more Tahitian than Greek.

The play commenced, with musical accompaniment by violinists partially hidden behind a large boulder. Loüys, in the audience, paid careful attention to the interpretation of his words. Colette's career as a music hall performer lay in the future, and on this day both she and Eva were so paralyzed by stage fright that they forgot the slow, careful enunciation they'd rehearsed. Instead, each fell back upon her respective accent: twangy, slightly nasal American and rough, rolled-R Burgundian. According to Colette,

Eva Palmer, white as a sheet, stammered out her words. I was so stiff with stage fright that the rolling r's of my Burgundy accent became positively

Russian. Pierre Loüys, author and guest, listened. Or perhaps he did not listen, for we were undoubtedly pleasanter to look at then to hear. But we believed that the whole of Paris under its sunshades and its hats, which were immense that year, had its eyes upon us. After the performance I plucked up the courage to ask Loüys if "it hadn't gone too badly."

He answered gravely: "I have experienced one of the greatest emotions of my life."

"Oh! dear Loüys!"

"I assure you! The unforgettable experience of hearing my work spoken by Mark Twain and Tolstoy."[4]

"I was terribly hurt," Eva recalled years later, "and only some time afterwards I reflected that if I was as much like Mark Twain as Colette was like Tolstoi, I need not mourn over the resemblance."[5]

After a brief interlude came the day's second entertainment. At Emma Calvé's Natalie had recently met a dancer new to Paris, Margaretha Geertruida Zelle, whose stage name was Mata Hari. She hired her on the spot. Now, at Natalie's, Mata Hari suddenly appeared from a hiding place in the woods. Dressed as Lady Godiva—that is, nearly naked—she sat comfortably on the back of a white horse harnessed with an intricately tooled leather bridle heavy with turquoise cloisonné. She rode slowly into the gardens, dismounted, and began one of her now-legendary Javanese dances.

Paris took note of the day's events. "On a quiet street in Neuilly," reported *La Vie Parisienne,* "electric automobiles brought from Paris divorced princesses, very Parisian writers . . . such as the Willys and Montesquiou, musicians and artists [such as] Emma Calvé . . . if Oscar Wilde were still alive, he would have been there."[6]

In a sense, Natalie's Neuilly theatricals constituted a sort of informal repertory company. She often used the same actors, performed works by her friends as well as herself, and enlisted help from those she knew for the many tasks involved with a production. Pierre Loüys came by to critique stage direction. Raymond Duncan choreographed the dances. Eva Palmer gathered costumes and props (one such list in her handwriting calls for a harp, turtle shell lyre, sandals, and flowers). As the performance day drew near, everyone concerned grew excited with anticipation. Since audience members tended to be friends, relatives, or lovers of the actors, the performance itself, no matter how amateurish or silly, was greeted with enthusiasm.

Typical of such collaborations was the performance in June 1906 of Natalie's *Équivoque.* The actors were all familiar faces in Natalie's circle: professional actress Marguerite Moreno (Sappho), Colette (a maiden), famed actor-playwright Sacha Guitry (the husband-to-be), and Eva Palmer as the girl who abandons Sappho for marriage—which, as events would soon bear out, was remarkably fateful casting. Within a circle of columns on the lawn stood a five-foot wrought-iron brazier wafting incense toward the audience. The barefoot or sandaled actresses, clad in gauzy white floor-length Greek robes, danced to Aeolean harp music and traditional songs performed by Raymond Duncan and his Greek wife, Penelope.

Les Mardrus were playing a big role in Natalie's life in early 1903. Small wonder, since Natalie and Lucie had finally commenced a blazing-hot affair. The liaison probably began the previous November, but was stopped short by Albert's death and Natalie's subsequent trip to the United States. Upon her return, they picked up where they left off.

Until Natalie, Lucie's sexual appetites were unexplored territory. It was generally accepted among their friends that the Delarue-Mardrus union was sexless, a *mariage blanc*. According to André Germain, J.C. delighted in showing visitors the twin beds that he and Lucie slept in, and then announcing: "My wife is still a virgin."[7] In *Mes mémoires* Lucie wrote that J.C.'s love for her was completely intellectual and that "his garden interested him much more" than whatever she was up to with Natalie. "For him I remained above all and perhaps only: The Poet."[8]

Under Natalie's touch, Lucie exploded with passion. Sex was such a revelation that she felt as if thrust into a new existence. Fully alive for the first time, her creative juices overflowed, as evidenced by the intensely erotic verse she wrote at this time, the lines burning with love and longing. Twenty-eight years old and in the throes of her first love, Lucie grew obsessed. "I think of you every second," she scribbled to Natalie. "I live for the idea of seeing you again."[9]

J.C. surely knew, or at least suspected, what was going on between Natalie and his wife, but he didn't interfere. Intelligent and worldly, he had a wide-open view of human sexuality. In addition, he was extremely fond of Natalie himself. She returned his affection, not only permitting him to call her by an impudent nickname, "Blonde," but to address her with the informal *tu* rather than the more formal *vous*. In those days such an address indicated deep intimacy, and Mardrus *tutoyered* Natalie often—too often for some. André Germain, who despised J.C., wrote that "he . . . violated her with his frequent tutoyers."[10]

J.C. very much wanted a child. This, obviously, was an insurmountable obstacle in a *mariage blanc*, but even if he and Lucie had enjoyed a vibrant sexual relationship he wouldn't have wanted her pregnant. Not only was she far too delicate and fragile for childbearing—in his opinion, anyway—but he intended for her life to be dedicated to literature, not babies.

Natalie, on the other hand, he judged to be perfectly suited for birthing. One day when they were alone, he made a proposition. "Blonde," he said, "I'm going to put your friendship to the test." He led up to his request by first talking about Lucie's poetic genius and the fact that her work demanded much of her. For this reason, he said, he couldn't ask her to bear a child. "But you," he said in the most natural way possible. "[You're] idle, young and as healthy as one could wish. You could carry the infant for us which I would propagate with you, showing you all the esteem and affection I could."[11]

Natalie regarded him somberly, trying hard to keep a straight face. She managed to tell him that, though the idea was extremely flattering and would probably have a very interesting result, she couldn't bring herself to do something so completely against her nature. Later, when she related the conversation to Lucie, they were consumed by laughter. In published writing Natalie said that J.C. accepted her rejection with grace, but in her memoirs she revealed that he sulked for more than a week.

With Natalie now living in Neuilly, she visited La Roseraie almost daily. During the day she and Lucie spent hours undisturbed in the living room, which they jokingly referred to as their harem. It was a harem in which everything was reversed, since the females were sexual partners to each other instead of to a man. In the evenings, when J.C. joined them, the harem reconfigured itself more traditionally to make him its center. He presented both women with roses from the garden, directed the serving of the evening meal, and entertained them with intricate Arabian tales.

Since Lucie dated most of her poems, she inadvertently provided a timetable of the affair from its joyous beginning to its inevitable unhappy end. The first poems, starting in late November 1902, are gentle. Soon, however, a disquieting note creeps in:

> Your soul of fleeing water and my soul of thirst
> Where to find the double kiss that stems the flow?
> How do we join
> if you run off like an agile spring
> clear water, ah! I want to drink you!

Yes, Natalie was as maddeningly elusive as ever. She could be tender and warm, but she had many other interests, including whatever casual dalliance came along. Worse, she made it clear to the point of callousness how much she yearned to win Pauline back. When Lucie read aloud verse inspired by their own relationship, Natalie's thoughts often drifted to her former lover—and she said so. Once, knowing how much Pauline admired Lucie's poetry, she sent Lucie to avenue du Bois with a note that pleaded for a meeting. Recalling this incident decades later, Natalie wrote with mournful insight: "Why is it that one always loves elsewhere, always elsewhere?"[12]

As the months rolled by, Lucie became haunted by Natalie's other loves. She began to sound on occasion like Pauline, accusing Natalie of "taking into your arms all the women who pass by [while] I wait . . . alone." Her poetry echoes these feelings: "Despite the night of joy and the closed doors/I'm not alone with you!/Gomorrah burns around us!" The poems gradually reveal her knowledge that she is simply another of Natalie's conquests. Though her passion was unabated, she began to feel oppressed by her love.

Her emotions were compounded by guilt, since Lucie suffered over the transgression of her marriage vows. True, there was neither passion nor sex with J.C., but she loved him in a quiet way and was grateful that he'd promoted her career so selflessly. Pulled between guilt and desire, when she was with J.C., she agonized about Natalie; with Natalie, she was torn by thoughts of J.C. Being true to one meant betraying the other. The lack of balance, she later said, filled her with such terror that she was afraid to write, talk, or think.

Lucie's guilt was nothing compared to the humiliation she felt over Natalie's constant infidelity. Humiliation turned to anger, and near the affair's end Lucie's poetic rage is frightening: "I will attack you/I will cripple you!/The beautiful and brief light/Made by a blade . . ." After this come poems of realization, sadness, and resignation, until finally, in the last poem (August 1903), she acknowledges that the affair is over: "The love has died/gone home/or gone anywhere you want."

For a while, trying to gain stasis, Lucie simply refused to see Natalie. In what had now become her pattern, Natalie was excited by the rejection and tried winning her back. Lucie, however, saw no value in continuing to suffer. She remained firm. "You ask me, Natalie, why I won't see you," she wrote crisply. "It's quite simply because I don't want to." In a final thrust she added: "You, who always say we should only do what pleases us in life, can better than anyone understand my reasoning."[13]

Alarmed by Lucie's depressed behavior, J.C. decided that it was best to take her away. He planned a trip to Arabia, and in March 1904 the couple departed on a long journey. Visiting them in Tunis shortly afterward, the Duchesse de Clermont-Tonnerre admired Lucie's boyish beauty and the way she "wore an

Arab horseman's costume, a practical one for her rides into the desert." Some months later André Germain ran into them in Egypt, where by now Lucie was traveling on a camel she had named Sarah Bernhardt.

When les Mardrus returned to Paris, Natalie felt that Lucie had regained her equanimity. "I do not believe she has ceased caring," she observed coldly to Eva, "but it no longer gets in my way."[14] In yet another example of Natalie's pattern, fiery passion had been replaced by a strong friendship—one that would remain close until Lucie's death in 1954.

But the insightful Lucie would forevermore view Natalie with a jaundiced eye. Years later, in her roman à clef *L'ange et les pervers,* she disguised Barney as the rich and selfish (though not unkind) Laurette Taylor, who relentlessly toyed with women and lived for seduction in a life "born of idleness, wealth, and too many novels."[15]

Natalie and J.C. also remained friends until his death in 1949. But something, probably the brutality she exhibited to Lucie, changed his uncritical fervor for "Blonde." According to André Germain, J.C. began to belittle Natalie behind her back and spoke of her in bitter terms. But, Germain noted, such words "turned against him, and couldn't but attest to the unheard-of charm . . . of that incomparable young woman."[16]

IN THE MEANTIME, Eva Palmer had been trying to forge a stage career, but hadn't encountered much luck. At one point Sarah Bernhardt hired her for a play, more for the beauty of her hair than her acting ability, but the production never opened. She finally got a big break when invited to join the acting company of Mrs. Patrick Campbell, the temperamental but popular English actress for whom George Bernard Shaw wrote the role of Eliza Doolittle in *Pygmalion.* Unfortunately, the prudish Campbell attached a harsh condition to Eva's employment, making it clear that "I should have to give up a friend of mine in Paris of whom she disapproved."[17]

In other words, if she wanted the job she could never see Natalie. There must be an open and permanent break. Campbell lectured Eva for being "careless about the people with whom I was seen and . . . [told me that] this carelessness was bad for my reputation." If Eva joined her company, Campbell pointed out, she would probably go on to a successful stage career. If she turned down this big chance, she would remain just another rich dilettante, "an amateur smatterer on the outside fringe of the theater."[18] Eva refused to give up Natalie.

When not in New York or London, Eva had been living in her own tiny Neuilly pavilion, privy to every nuance of Natalie and Lucie's relationship. All three were good friends, and it wasn't unusual for Eva to hang out in the harem. In many ways, their get-togethers echoed that poetic trio from the 1900 summer at Bar Harbor. Natalie retained her position as the group's Sappho; Eva firmly held on to her role as beloved confidante; and Lucie had replaced Pauline as the gifted poet/love.

By now it was apparent that Natalie was drawn to the number three, at least in relation to *affaires de coeur*. She sometimes wrote about the human love triangle. Two chapters from her unpublished book, "La troisième," appeared in the May 1912 edition of *Le Manuscrit Autographe*. More than a decade later she reworked the material into the lyrical opening chapter of another unpublished book, "Amants féminins ou les troisième."

Renée Lang observed years later that Natalie was happiest when positioned between two loves—one in the midst of a painful and reluctant departure, the other making a joyous entry onto the scene. For decades, a running joke among NCB's friends referred to the incoming lover as the *"nouvelle amoureuse"* (the one who is newly in love), while the latest cuckold became the *"nouvelle malheureuse"* (the one who is newly unhappy). When Lang asked Natalie whether she cared that one of the two always suffered, she shrugged her shoulders. "She didn't care," Lang acknowledged.[19]

Eva was more of a "continual" than a "nouvelle" *malheureuse*. She was stuck in a state of permanent unhappiness regarding Natalie, who took her for granted. She could be cruel, chastising Palmer for being too gentle or not smart enough. Natalie could be heartless, using her to carry notes to, or plead her case with, other women. There were, certainly, moments of joy, times when Natalie was soft and attentive. Whenever she feared losing Eva, or needed Eva's unconditional love to tide her over a passing heartbreak, Natalie didn't hesitate to pull out all the stops, displaying all her charms and retightening that bond between them. Palmer put up with all of it, believing that her love for Natalie would win out in the end. If any two women could forge something beautiful in this world, she told Natalie, they could.

Although the years hadn't diluted Eva's love for Natalie, she had long since overcome her reluctance to indulge in other affairs. She acted with great discretion, because, although Natalie claimed for herself the privilege of multiple lovers, she reacted badly when Eva took one. If the other woman was someone Natalie knew, trouble was unavoidable.

In mid-decade Natalie, Eva, and Baby H. were in Bayreuth for the yearly festival. Out motoring one afternoon in the princess's Mercedes, they discovered a small pond buried in the woods, removed their clothing, and jumped in. Later, lazing about in the altogether, the usually blasé Natalie was shocked to see a tiny heart tattooed on Eva's body. Peering closely, she realized that it bore the initials *B.B.* "That enterprising Princess had seduced her!" Natalie fumed. Afterward, when they were alone, she berated Eva so ceaselessly that she ended up having the tattoo painfully removed "to prove to me that I alone had rights to her body."[20]

This small anecdote, slipped innocuously into the pages of Natalie's memoirs, reveals a confused feminist philosophy. While most of Barney's ideas about women are progressive and liberated, she doesn't always follow through on a personal level. Her writings consistently defend a woman's right to control her own body and life; nonetheless, she sees nothing wrong in proclaiming ownership of Eva's body.

Today we might define this as a "control issue." Natalie liked and probably needed to control. Many who knew her believed that her quest for new lovers was motivated by a need for dominance. Her close friend Bettina Bergery once said: "I never quite understood the motive behind Natalie's love of conquest. I believe her passions were mostly cerebral and that her strongest desire was to dominate—in a velvet-glove way."[21]

LATE IN 1903 Natalie traveled to Washington to spend time with her mother, whose formal year of mourning was ending (one journalistic wag described Alice's dramatic black costumes that year as "ultra mourning"). Laura later said that her mother began to change radically at this time, becoming quite "bohemian."[22] If Alice was changing, it was doubtless due to the fact that she, like her oldest daughter, was no longer held in check by the conservative Albert. Free to act upon her impulses, she did so.

The first evidence of the new Alice was her unusual new home off Sheridan Circle at 2306 Massachusetts Avenue, designed to serve as both a private residence and a public meeting place. She called it Studio House, and in the years to come it would be the site of theatrical productions, art exhibitions, teas, and dinners to further artistic and charitable causes.

The austere façade of the Spanish Mission–style house was vastly different from those of the ornate mansions nearby. In a photograph-laden article, *Town & Country Magazine* noted that it was "conspicuous among the handsome houses which have sprung up within the last few years on the shores of Rock Creek . . . the palatial residences owned by multimillionaires." The bemused reporter noted that Alice had invited the construction workers and artisans to her housewarming party: "The affair was unique in local annals and created widespread comment."[23]

Compared to other wealthy homes, Studio House was small. It had two basements, one containing servants' quarters, a kitchen, and the laundry. The first level held an entrance hall, an octagonal dining room, a library, and a large room with a built-in, elevated stage. Among the rooms on the second floor was the huge, two-story "Studio Room." Meant for exhibitions and entertainment, it contained a musicians' gallery and a quote from Goethe stenciled in gold leaf: "The highest problem of art is to produce by appearance the illusion of higher reality." The remaining floors held Alice's studio, five bedrooms (some with attached sitting rooms), and three baths. A trellised roof garden over-looked Rock Creek Park and the distant Virginia hills.

Natalie settled in, planning to remain until the spring. As she unpacked, Laura, who had been with Alice since Albert's death, prepared for a trip to the Middle East. While away she would acquire a working knowledge of Persian and, after spending time in Palestine with the Baha'i leader, Abdul Baha, pro-duce an important book about the faith, *Some Answered Questions*. The timing of Natalie's arrival and Laura's departure indicates mutual concern for their mother. Despite her unhappy marriage, Alice had shared two children and nearly three decades of life with Albert. For a while his death snuffed out her gaiety.

Natalie fell into the familiar Washington routine. She also read, wrote, helped with Alice's latest exhibit, and was diverted for a time by Emma Calvé's visit while on a performance tour. But, as usual when away from Paris for any length of time, she felt bored and restless.

When a fire destroyed large portions of Baltimore in early February, Natalie decided to emulate her mother by holding an entertainment to bene-fit people who lost their homes. Unfortunately, her idea of entertainment was more suited to a Parisian literary salon than to a Washington stage. A hopeful blurb appeared in the paper a few days beforehand: "The benefit perform-ance planned by Miss Natalie Barney for the Washington and Baltimore Fire-man's fund . . . will be the social event of Thursday afternoon when Walter Damrosch will give his lecture on *Parsifal*."[24] The lecture attracted a few big names, notably Mrs. Theodore Roosevelt, but most seats remained empty. Stung by her colossal failure, Natalie thereafter left fund-raising activities to her mother, who seemed to accomplish such work far better than any-one else.

Proof of this came soon, with Alice's benefit to aid the families of sailors killed in an explosion aboard the battleship *Missouri*. She wrote and produced the evening's centerpiece, *The Dream of Queen Elizabeth*, describing it as "an extravaganza in 2 acts and 3 scenes." With full confidence, she hired the Lafayette Square Theater to hold the expected crowds and finagled the Marine Corps Band to play during intermission. She snared a Russian countess and an admiral's widow as the play's stars, and had her sketches of Queen Elizabeth printed as posters and placed in shop windows all over town. As performance day neared, she invited visiting celebrities such as Calvé to rehearsal, along with reporters and photographers.

The Dream of Queen Elizabeth was a smashing success. It attracted a cosmopolitan crowd, including the president's wildly popular daughter, Alice. The $5,000 profit was deemed a hefty sum. The fact that the production was torn to pieces by the critics seemed beside the point (one uncharitable review was headlined "The Queen's Nightmare").

In the spring Natalie and Alice returned together to Paris, and soon accompanied Calvé to London, where she was engaged to sing *Carmen* at Covent Garden. They sailed across the Channel in high style, taking along Calvé's chauffeur and new automobile. The vehicle was "the latest type, rather high to step into and entered from the rear, like a Roman chariot. It was the first to be seen in London [and] threw consternation into their midst . . . a-lack-a-day!"[25]

One day the three women grabbed a young Italian tenor and set off on an automobile jaunt into the countryside. All day long Calvé and her high-spirited lead—Enrico Caruso—tried to outdo each other with song, bursting out with one aria after another. According to Alice, the laughter never stopped until they returned to the hotel and exited their chariot.

DESPITE NATALIE'S extraordinarily busy life—Lucie Delarue-Mardrus would accuse her, only half-jokingly, of having "twenty-five appointments in all corners of Paris at the same time"[26]—she continued to pine for the one thing she couldn't possess: Pauline. Then, unexpectedly, the relationship sprang temporarily back to life in the summer of 1904.

In *Souvenirs indiscrets* Natalie wrote that she received a surprising telegram one day from Baby H., informing her that Pauline was at the Wagner festival without Hélène. In reality, Natalie had learned that information earlier, and from Pauline herself. In a letter to Alice, Pauline mentioned that she would be going alone to Bayreuth; Alice passed the information on to Natalie; and Natalie wrote Pauline asking if it was true. "I wasn't lying to your mother, my Tout-Petit, when I wrote her that I was going to Bayreuth alone," she replied. "I repeat to you that I'm going alone."[27] Though not explicit, her words were a clear invitation to meet.

Natalie talked the ever-faithful Eva into accompanying her. Once in Bayreuth they managed, though the festival was under way, to obtain tickets in the balcony. From high above, Natalie kept an eye on Pauline throughout the first act of the tetralogy. At intermission, Eva and Pauline traded seats, and Natalie happily held her beloved's hand for the rest of the night, and for the remaining performances of the festival. But, "as I aspired to retain her outside that Wagnerian communion, I brought her the first part of a long prose-poem I composed with the intention and in the hopes that she would be touched and feel how much I missed her . . . to the point where I could win her back."[28]

The poem was "Je me souviens." This haunting work, which would be published in 1910, glorifies their past relationship. By frequent repetition of the title phrase "I remember," Barney produces a feeling of lyricism: "I remember her on the balcony with all the stars of the night and the darkness of the sky in her hair. I remember how the earth, covered with a blanket of snow, reminded me of our virginal bed of love and how everything seemed made for the memory of our love . . . I remember those red nights, where we devoured one another, insatiably hungry."

When Pauline failed to respond to the poem's sentiments, Natalie sent another work describing a sad, lonely garden in the center of town and asking that they meet there. The night before leaving Bayreuth, Pauline came to the garden. Whatever Natalie may have done or said seems to have worked, because Pauline agreed to meet her at the end of the month in Vienna, from where they would travel together to Lesbos. Natalie said in *Souvenirs indiscrets* that she would have been happy to go anywhere; Lesbos was Pauline's idea.

Half expecting to be stood up, Natalie traveled to Vienna and was overjoyed when Pauline arrived as promised. Soon enough they were chugging away aboard the *Orient Express,* the legendary luxury train that ran between Paris and Constantinople (today's Istanbul). They rode to the end of the line, and stayed for a few days at a hotel, probably the Pera Palas, on the city's rue de Pera. In an unusual display of independence, Pauline left Natalie at the hotel and went to visit a woman with whom she'd corresponded but never met. Kérimé Turkhan-Pacha resided in a harem, and during her visit Pauline had the strange experience of being guarded by two imposing eunuchs.

A few days later Natalie and Pauline boarded an Egyptian tramp steamer, the *Khedive,* for the second leg of their journey. This steamer routinely plied the waters between Constantinople and Alexandria, stopping along the way at Mytilene on Lesbos, then a Turkish possession. At dawn they stood on deck, straining to catch their first sight of Sappho's ancient home. The island appeared slowly, its mountains, trees, and beaches emerging gradually from the dark. Having dreamed of this moment for years, they were thrilled by its fulfillment and by the thought of stepping onto holy ground consecrated by the great poet herself. But as they grew closer the beautiful moment was destroyed by a popular French song blaring from a wind-up phonograph. According to Natalie, Pauline turned pale with horror at the words, considering them an indignity to women: "C'mere darling, here, my pet, c'mere!"* Another dose of reality hit when they drove through town: the modern women of Lesbos, they agreed, had little in common with Sappho's beautiful companions.

The situation quickly improved, thanks to a rustic hotel whose attractions included a talky parrot, terra-cotta water jugs, and tasty food cooked in olive oil. The interpreter, brought along from Istanbul, found them an isolated rental property. It consisted of two villas connected by a fig and peach orchard, a garden dense with "an orgy of roses" and the heavy scent of jasmine, a giant parasol pine, and a pond whose frogs croaked throughout the night. Cages, suspended from the trees, were filled with colorful birds. Across the dusty dirt road a stone staircase led to the sea, where big banks of soft seaweed dotted the sand. Pauline declared that she planned to stay forever and moved into the larger villa; Natalie took the smaller.

Lesbos was exactly what they had both hoped for, a halcyon existence of lazy days and ecstatic nights. During the day they read, wrote letters, and worked on their verse. They walked on the beach, toured the island by carriage, and once traveled by boat to Smyrna (now Izmir) on the Turkish mainland. Rich and elegant, they attracted comment among the island's residents. Years later, Mytilan residents could recall their splendid clothes and a particularly beautiful amethyst necklace that belonged to Natalie.

In bed the first night, Pauline responded at long last to Natalie's caresses. In fact, the immensity of her passion so overwhelmed Natalie with happiness that she found herself smothering a "cry of victory triumphant." She had never imagined, she later wrote, that their bodies and souls could unite so deeply. Pauline must have agreed. Long after, in a letter to Natalie, she recalled "that marvelous first night at Mytilene" when they were reunited and rejoined.

Natalie took to stretching out in the garden, gazing heavenward to equate the number of stars with her joys. Pauline insisted that she would stay in her villa writing poetry for the rest of her life; if Natalie, the restless one, needed to leave every now and then to get her necessary dose of the world, Pauline would patiently and lovingly await her return. They also revived their favorite fantasy of starting a community for female poets, believing that the villas, with their lush gardens, would provide a perfect backdrop.

Viens poupoule, viens poupoule, viens!

Toward the end of August this paradisiacal existence was brought to an abrupt end. One day they traveled into Mytilene for the mail, only to find a letter from Hélène. She missed Pauline and, believing that she had come to Lesbos alone for some sort of research, wanted to join her. To prevent her arrival, Pauline sent a telegram announcing her own immediate return.

During their stay, Pauline had promised Natalie to end the relationship with Hélène, and now she insisted that it was something she must do in person. Once that painful duty was done, she and Natalie could return to the island together. But, she warned, this final break would take time to arrange. Hélène wouldn't accept the news easily. She was powerful and she could be difficult. In the interim, Pauline and Natalie would be sustained by their strong mutual love.

They enjoyed a last, lingering lunch in the fruit orchard. From the old tree they picked figs warmed by the sun. They played with the servant's dog, walked one last time on the beach, and reluctantly traveled into town to meet the *Khedive*. In Constantinople, putting off the moment of separation, they decided to sail to Athens instead of taking the *Orient Express*. One last night, spent visiting the Acropolis with a Baedecker and a Brownie camera, and they parted: Natalie to Paris, Pauline to meet Hélène in Utrecht.

At the beginning Pauline probably intended to follow through on her promises. She wrote to Natalie within days, reporting her tears and misery on the train that had carried her away. She expressed her love in strong terms, praised their journey, and asked Natalie to find a small studio in Neuilly "not too far from you."

Natalie rented a place separated from her own by a fence and began impatiently awaiting Pauline's arrival, but all she received was letter after letter filled with excuses for the delay. Pauline's old jealousies began to pop up. Learning that Freddy Manners-Sutton was visiting, she became irate. Sutton, she declared, was a "second-rate little cad!" and had only "second-hand smartness." Later that day she wrote again, apologizing for her outburst. She spoke of her jealousy. "I love you unreasonably," she admitted. She was unable to curb herself. A short time later it was Baby H. against whom she took umbrage.

Away from the bliss of Lesbos, Pauline, as time went by, began to see only misery for herself in a life with Barney. She knew that, underneath her temporary good behavior, Natalie was and always would be absolutely incapable of fidelity. She loved Natalie passionately, and always would, but now she weighed the scales. Was it worth sacrificing her own small measure of inner peace and the happiness she had forged with Hélène for an alliance that would eventually bring bitter disillusion and heartbreak?

Apparently not. Shortly afterward, Natalie received a letter from Pauline ending their relationship. In it, she referred to herself as the "thing" of Hélène, who "is my strength and my will. I depend on her, I live through her, I breathe through her. I can't live without her. . . . A single being possesses my heart and my body. She alone."[29]

While it sounds as if Pauline and Hélène were involved in some sort of sadomasochistic situation, they probably were not. It's more likely that Pauline was simply using Hélène as an excuse to avoid Natalie. Yes, the Baronne was a strong and dominating figure, but she wasn't a jailer: Pauline traveled extensively during their years together, often on her own. Hélène wasn't a censor, either: many of Pauline's published poems in that decade centered on her passion for Natalie, which was apparently fine with the Baronne. In the years ahead, Pauline and Natalie not only continued to correspond, but also saw each other from time to time (probably platonically). Sometimes Hélène was present on these occasions, but only as an emotional protector—not a controlling keeper—and probably at Pauline's behest. Without Hélène, Pauline might have lost her resolve and succumbed to her love for Natalie, something she absolutely did not want to do.

The fact that the Baronne was fourteen years older than Pauline and the mother of two children also played a role in their relationship. Despite her tuxedos and fake mustaches, Hélène had a woman's heart and knew how to protect younger, vulnerable souls. In the title poem of À l'heure des mains jointes (1906), Pauline says of Hélène: "My sweet! I love you with simplicity." She speaks of security, of sloughing off fear, suspicion, and artificiality, of being healed beneath "the friendly roof of your good home."

> Your fingers have knotted around my rough heart.
> And with a stammer, a naive cry
> Of inexperience and gratitude,
> I will tell you how, fatigued from the rough sea,
> I bless the anchor at the port where my skiff is docked.

Security, healing, gratitude, the end of fear: this relationship wasn't the storm-tossed sea Pauline had traversed with Natalie. It was calm and peaceful, providing a sheltered cove to dock and rest. Hélène was a mother figure to Pauline, who had never known her own mother's comforting love. Why she chose to portray the Baronne as a sadistic controller is difficult to fathom. In the future, the portrayals become darker, more frequent, and increasingly bizarre. Perhaps she had some deeply recessed need to feel controlled by a "master," wanted to add drama to her life, or simply required a ready excuse to avoid seeing people without hurting their feelings. Whatever the reason, Pauline did Hélène a great injustice.

But Natalie, reading Pauline's letter, knew nothing of these psychological complications and emotional subterfuges. Even if she had, she would have impatiently dismissed it all as nonsense. "I want her," she would have said. "That's all that matters." But now, even for Barney, all the signs were evident: the end had come. If they had failed to make a go of it after Lesbos, they never would succeed.

Was it finally over, at long and painful last? Yes—and no. It would *never* be over. As long as they lived, Natalie realized, they would be obsessively drawn to, and then pulled from, each other. "I couldn't live with or without her," she wrote. "I don't know what was more punishing to me: our unhappy encounters [or] our separations. . . . Perhaps death was the only thing that would end it."[30]

As Natalie's relationship with Pauline reached a new turning point, one of the most secure underpinnings of her life—the relationship with Eva— collapsed. The end had begun back in 1905, when Eva became friends with Isadora Duncan's brother, Raymond, and his wife, Penelope. Always drawn to Greek literature, she was fascinated by the couple, who dressed in the style of ancient Greece, with white robes, sandals, and long flowing hair.

For a while the Duncans lived in Eva's *pavillon* at Neuilly, where Raymond built a loom. Everyone got along, and eventually the couple invited Palmer to join them on a trip to Greece.

On a sun-kissed Greek island Eva met and became involved with Penelope's brother, Angelos Sikelianos. Ten years her junior and a onetime law student turned poet, he was obsessed with the idea of reviving the ancient Greek spirit. Nothing could have suited Eva better. By the time she returned to Paris with her new love in tow, she had gone Greek, deciding never again to wear anything but white robes and sandals. Natalie thought she had lost her mind. "Unless it gives you exquisite pleasure," she wrote frostily, "do not go through the streets of Paris dressed as an Ancient Greek: *cela detourne,* also I cannot see the advantage derived from it—neither the beauty."[31]

To Natalie, the simple and earthy Angelos seemed little better than a peasant. She treated him with shocking disdain, disparaged his talents as a poet, and delivered her opinion that he was "ridiculously affected" and "quite unworldly." She finally came right out and asked Eva to send him away. Later, realizing she had gone too far, she tried to make amends. It was too late. Eva responded that Angelos hoped never to see Natalie again. "He went to Paris ready to care for you," she said, "and it was your manner to him that made him dislike you."[32]

Underneath Natalie's bad behavior was an overwhelming fear of losing the bond that had united her with Eva since childhood. Time and again Eva explained that she could never have for Angelos the love she felt for Natalie. "I love his country, his people, his language, and most of all his dream," she explained. "My punishment is that I don't love him. His punishment is that I have lied to him, and told him I cared more for him than for you."[33]

Eva made a conscious decision to marry Angelos, whom she admired more than she loved, in order to live a life dedicated to poetry, literature, and the arts. She explained her decision to Natalie in a way that made clear how much she still loved her. "I simply had no more strength or courage for the life you liked me to lead," she wrote, "or rather for the effort toward it I was always making . . . I showed or I had my misery, that's about all I've ever done for you, and you seemed to be tired of both ways, and I loved Greece—loved it, loved it—not for a day or a trip or a holiday, but for as many days as one may be on its earth. . . . You ask me dear, dear—oh, hands that I have loved, eyes that I have followed, hair that I have sobbed to touch . . ."[34]

Eva begged Natalie to be happy for her. Instead, Natalie tried to make Eva jealous with accounts of the goings-on in her own life. Eva's reply was devastating:

> . . . the same tiresome little people you brought me to, the same eternal little intrigues and passions you chose to live among when you had me to mold as you chose. We were both as free as the wind, we might have gone to any beautiful place and done any noble thing, and . . . you tried to fit me into a private and public life that were both to me like an ill-fitting shoe. I walked after you for years like a high-heeled woman whose feet hurt but who is too proud to say so; I was too affectionate, too weak to say so, but now that I have said, now that I have taken the gag of loyalty out of my mouth and have come to air where I can breathe, you ask me if I would come back to you if you needed me . . . I am tired of you and all the little things you care for. You are as drugged with all your little passions and your little memories as all the takers of morphine and chloral and valerian and absinthe whom you see.
>
> You say you want to believe I still care because I cared. But my caring was a determined effort on my part to make the best of a very miserable life, and there was never an art or ambition of yours that my soul loved; so now that I see your hot-house grass as artificial and odourless, what is there left? Simply nothing, unless your persistence were to make me remember your hardness and injustice, in which case I should feel resent-

ment . . . Last summer Mother told me that you had said the only way to treat me was like a dog, and I protested vehemently, swearing that you would never have thought such a thing . . . and as I talked I wondered in my heart if you had said it.

But I'm tired of the thought of it all. I have protested so many times to myself and to others that you were the most kind, the most generous; and after all those years it somehow needed just this stupid letter from you to make me cry out like the child in the story: 'Why, he's naked!' You remember the King's clothes . . . the tailors came and dressed him elaborately, the people expected and saw the most gorgeous clothes . . . So I see the unpardonable: you are stupid. And so the fantasies melt all away, like the snowforts we used to build; no more ice, and no more glistening. But the sun, the sun—the spring. Eva.

Eva and Angelos married in 1907 in Bar Harbor. Like so many other women Natalie knew, she adopted a hyphenated surname (Palmer-Sikelianos). The couple went to live in Greece, devoting themselves to revitalizing ancient Greek drama, dance, and music. Perhaps their greatest accomplishment was to reinstitute the Delphic Festival and encourage the return of classical Greek tragedies performed in ancient theaters. Angelos would also become known as one of the most important Greek poets of the twentieth century, while Eva, having discovered the secrets of ancient weavers, garnered acclaim for the spun cloth and traditional garments she created.

The bond between the two women was eventually repaired, and the day would even arrive when Eva thanked Natalie for the role she had played in her life. "Looking back," she wrote decades later, "I wonder what would have happened if, 35 years ago, you had left me alone. Would I have ever found my own open road where I follow my soul leaping and racing as your greyhound used to leap and race around your carriage? . . . Would [I have lived] so freely if you had not twisted me into a knot of pain for—how many years? Were you the mystic and only gate which led to my distant mountain?"[35]

NATALIE STARTED LOOKING around for a new place to live sometime in 1908, and in the fall she learned through Lucie of a small charming house and gardens available in the Left Bank. She toured the place, delighted with everything about it—particularly the mysterious Grecian-style temple, dedicated to friendship, tucked behind the *pavillon* (house). Natalie wasn't the only one hoping to rent this forested oasis in the heart of Paris. The place was in hot demand, but somehow, possibly through the influence of Jules Cambon, she ended up the new tenant of 20, rue Jacob.

There were those who thought Natalie was crazy to leave fashionable and modern Neuilly for an old, dusty part of the city. In fact, it's not really clear exactly why she moved. In *Souvenirs indiscrets* she hoped that Pauline would feel more comfortable visiting her in a place with no unpleasant connotations. In *Mémoires secrets* she claims to have finally realized that, with Pauline consumed by Hélène, she must symbolically move on. Elsewhere she stated that Neuilly represented old habits of her youth that needed to be destroyed. It all boils down to the same thing: it was time for a big change.

There may been yet another reason for the move, one that Natalie never wrote about. According to a 1909 article in the *Dayton Journal* (deemed worthy of huge, above-fold headlines in the Sunday edition), Natalie grew furious at her landlord's criticisms of the sapphic plays enacted on her lawn, which he felt "followed nature too closely. Miss Barney waxed indignant that a mere layman should dare to object to her beautiful creation. She cancelled her lease, paid for the remaining term of years, left the villa in high dudgeon, shook the dust of Neuilly off her feet, and took up her quarters in an old ivy-colored house. . . . Whether it was the incense fires or the strange marriage ceremony or the frisky dances . . . or the vague knowledge that Sappho wrote erotic poetry, or all combined, which induced the landlord to become aggressive against the American girl it is hard to say. But he met his Waterloo. Miss Barney is honored, not only for her poetry but for her stand against insolent landlords."[36]

The newspaper couldn't resist an opportunity to quote liberally from *Quelques portraits-sonnets de femmes,* wryly adding: "After penning lines like these it does not seem strange that Natalie Clifford Barney should have selected the legendary Greek poetess for the heroine of her first classic drama."

Natalie hired someone to oversee the move and departed for Russia in late December. She was in pursuit of her current amour, Henriette Roggers, "one of the most beautiful young actresses, with the brightest future, of her day . . . red-haired, exciting, with green eyes and an impetuous, playful nature."[37] Performing at St. Petersburg's Théâtre Française, Roggers was the toast of Moscow. She was pursued by a bevy of titled male admirers, one of whom eventually followed her back to Paris. "Henrietta is quite the belle of the season," Natalie wrote to her mother on January 1, 1909, "and a great success theatrically—I am glad for she deserves it."

Despite these brave words, Natalie was miserable. She had recently written Eva that "Henriette makes me happy mostly, and seems to care for me perhaps as much or even more than I do for her."[38] Now, standing on the sidelines while Henriette was adored by the multitudes, she tried to make the best of her heartbreak.

A Russian friend gave Natalie a copy of Voltaire's *Candide* to help her get through this latest crisis in love. Apparently the cure worked: deciding to till her own gardens, she returned to Paris on January 15, earlier than planned. Her possessions had been moved into her new home while she was gone, and as soon as the place was arranged to her liking she took up residence. Natalie was thirty-two years old on the day she moved into rue Jacob and she would live there almost until her death sixty-three years later.

EIGHT

The Salonist

1909

In a Salon you can't be ponderous, egocentric. Anything other than a
lucid, witty, graceful style is simply not allowed.

—Evangeline Bruce

Courage after love: She dared to die . . . I dared to live.

—Natalie Barney

*P*ERCHED ON THE EDGE of the ancient Latin Quarter and close
by the Church of St. Germain-des-Prés, rue Jacob is a short, quiet, narrow street graced by elegant seventeenth- and eighteenth-century
buildings. Known in the Middle Ages as Chemin du Pré aux Clercs, the street
had been home to an exceptionally creative group of people over the centuries.
Among them were the Duc de Saint-Simon, author of a monumental and personal history of Louis XIV's reign; the Duc de La Rochefoucauld, coinventor of
the maxim and friend to Molière, La Fontaine, and Corneille; writers Racine,
Mérimée, and Prudhomme; and painters Ingres and Delacroix.*

Natalie was by no means the street's first American resident. Benjamin
Franklin, who lived there in 1777, may have been the first. President-to-be John

---

*Delacroix inhabited Natalie's *pavillon* in 1824.

Adams came along in 1784, followed nearly two decades later by Washington Irving. Thomas Paine, though never a resident, avoided arrest by French police in 1783 by hiding his "seditious" writings in the rue Jacob hotel room of a friend.

When Natalie took up residence in 1909, the street was—as it is now—elegant, low-key, and largely residential. Two small hotels were located down the block (the Orléans-St.-Germain, the Daniloc), and among the handful of expensive shops were Challamel, a purveyor of antique maps, and the bookseller Haar & Steinert.

One entered No. 20 by walking through the huge, dark green double doors described by writer Paul Morand as *"la porte cochère Balzacienne."* Beyond was a covered, cobblestoned area once used by carriages. On the left, a four-story apartment building fronted rue Jacob. Straight ahead, across the cobbled courtyard, stood Natalie's small *pavillon.*

What made Natalie's two-story, seventeenth-century house so unique was this: adjoining it was a wooded oasis, the last remnant of forests that had once stretched to the edge of the Seine. A huge and ancient chestnut tree towered over all the others, spreading its branches across the *pavillon* and courtyard, and ivy grew thick over the enclosing walls. Here, in the very heart of Paris, a wild woodland offered its own winding path, wrought-iron chairs, marble fountain, and a deep well long fallen into disuse.

To many visitors, the garden wasn't nearly as fascinating as the small, circular, four-columned Doric temple, complete with stone steps and sculpted double doors, tucked away on the *pavillon's* far side. Carved into its stone lintel were the words *Temple à l'Amitié* (Temple of Friendship), surmounted by a crown of laurel and two snakes with open mouths. At the very top was a small round medallion with the letters *DLV,* which may stand for *Dieu le veut* (God wants it).

Four stone steps lead into the temple, with its tiny, round, windowless room, small fireplace, faux marble columns, and rounded cupola with skylight. Little is known of the temple's history. Many experts believe it was built during the First Empire, while the present owners say it is the sole survivor of half a dozen Freemason temples built in the fifth and sixth arrondissements during the nineteenth century.

No formal record of ownership exists for the *pavillon* itself until about 1750, when it was owned by a silversmith. For years it was said that two women famous in French history, Ninon de Lenclos and Adrienne Lecouvreur, had resided here at different times, but that story has since been discounted.

Nonetheless, it's interesting that Barney moved into a building associated, rightly or wrongly, with two such progressive women. De Lenclos (born in 1620) was known for her intellect, nimble conversational epigrams, and espousal of an early version of feminism. Her salon was attended by Molière, La Fontaine, La Rochefoucauld, Madame de Maintenon, and many others. The actress Adrienne Lecouvreur, who debuted at the Comédie-Française in 1717, is credited with bringing a more natural acting style to the French stage. She was a close friend of Voltaire, and it was in her honor that Francesco Cilea wrote the opera *Adriana Lecouvreur.*

The rooms in Natalie's *pavillon* were few but large. Beyond the front door was a small entry hall leading to a narrow hallway dividing the first floor. To its left was a kitchen with an ancient stove and a charcoal cuisinière for heating bathwater. To the right, the large, connected living and dining rooms, which faced the garden (early on the view was somewhat obstructed by a glass-walled conservatory, later removed). The dining room, where the salon would usually be held, was square, with an alcove beneath a domed ceiling. A circular recess beneath held four paintings of nymphs by Albert Bernard, each representing one of the four elements. An unconfirmed but delightful story has it that Natalie once gave a Persian dinner; on a ledge beneath the dome she supposedly concealed a small boy who, at the appropriate time, showered her guests with rose petals.

Upstairs were Natalie's private quarters. Her blue-walled bedroom was floored with ancient parquet, covered in part by a white polar bear skin, a gift from Liane de Pougy. Furnishings included two Empire-style chaises, a black marble table, a small desk facing the garden, and a piano. French doors opened onto a faux balcony. There was also a second bedroom for guests.

The furnishings, mostly so-so antiques Alice picked up at an auction house, suited Natalie just fine. She was completely indifferent to the concept of decor, and, once the frumpy old furniture was set in place, she was done decorating. *Forever.* Art Nouveau was all the rage when she moved in, minimalism was popular sixty years later when she moved out, but Natalie neither noticed nor cared. She wasn't interested in furniture, or, for that matter, most possessions. "I am beginning to have a healthy dread of possessions," she wrote. "If we are bothered by possessions we cannot really live either from without or from within; we are the possession of our possessions. All wars and most loves come from the possessive instinct."[1]

Soon after moving in, Natalie did some reconstructive work to the temple, setting off another round of stories in American papers. "Miss Barney Rebuilds the Temple of Love," announced the *New York American;* "Authoress of Forbidden 'Sapho' Reconstructs Famous Retreat Set up by Adrienne Lecouvreur."[2] The article rekindled the Neuilly landlord tale and noted that Natalie wrote poetry with a "Grecian spirit." Natalie didn't know it yet, but she, her mother, and Laura were on their way to becoming major tabloid fodder.

A big change came when Natalie sold her carriage and horses, replacing them with a Renault Cabriolet automobile. As she told Eva, a motor vehicle cost "far less than horses, and . . . it doesn't get tired or cross like horses and coachmen."[3] She had a garage built directly in front of the temple, but it, too, would later be torn down. By the way, Natalie did not drive, and nothing indicates that she ever wanted to learn. She almost always employed a chauffeur.

The *pavillon's* floors were not sturdy, and Natalie had been warned to be careful about giving large dancing parties. This set her to thinking about quieter ways to entertain, and she slowly developed the idea of hosting literary get-togethers. Meanwhile she confined her big, festive parties to the garden. At first these affairs resembled her Neuilly fêtes. There were masquerades and theatricals, with musicians strolling through the garden or standing on the temple steps. Gradually, a different kind of gathering began to dominate. Always held on a Friday, its important element was conversation. People came to talk, usually about literature, although anything of interest might get tossed around: the arts, music, philosophy, current events, gossip, even, at times, politics. Though she always referred to these events as her "Fridays," Natalie was actually holding a salon.

WHAT EXACTLY *is* a salon, anyway? American dictionaries have trouble with this distinctly French invention, tending to define the word in haughty and exclusionary terms. To the folks at American Heritage, a salon is "a periodic gathering of people of social or intellectual distinction." Merriam-Webster thinks the word means "a fashionable assemblage of notables (as literary figures, artists, or statesmen) held by custom at the home of a prominent person." Here's my own definition: a salon is an organized get-together at which people discuss artistic, political, or other intellectual subjects of mutual interest.

The salon's origin stretches back two and a half millennia to the ancient Greeks. We hear a lot about how democratic life was in those days, but in reality only male citizens enjoyed freedom. Most women led a constricted life, rarely leaving their homes or spending time in the company of men who weren't relatives. This left a void for discourse between the sexes, one ably filled by the hetaerae.

These cultivated, high-priced courtesans were known not only for their sexual abilities but for intellect, wit, and skills such as dancing and singing. A few also sponsored gatherings centered around lively rhetoric. Perhaps the best-known hetaeric hostess was Aspasia, the mistress of Pericles and the friend of Socrates. Another, Phryne, is believed to have been the model for Praxiteles' legendary marble sculpture, the *Aphrodite of Cnidus.*

Leap forward to sixteenth-century France and a young woman named Louise Labé. The daughter of wealthy Lyonnaise ropemakers, Labé wrote poetry, played an excellent lute, and was fluent in Italian and Latin. When she began inviting writers and artists to regular conversational gatherings at her home, it was considered a social innovation. In Paris at roughly the same time the Duchesse de Retz, one of the few women allowed by Henri III to seek higher education in the Académie du Palais, also opened her home for discussion with accomplished men and women.

With few exceptions, all the great salonists who followed Labé and de Retz would be women. This is understandable when you consider that, for centuries, such gatherings provided the only acceptable way a woman could exercise her love of literature, music, politics, or art.

Salons really took off in the seventeenth century. Around 1610, Catherine de Vivonne, Marquise de Rambouillet, a young aristocrat in the court of Louis XIII, began hosting major literary figures. She was deeply interested in questions concerning the content and form of language, which led to her being satirized by Molière in his 1659 play, *The Ridiculous Young Ladies*. In those early salon days, guests tried to sway others to their point of view with banter and wit. A well-turned phrase evoked accolades and appreciative laughter, and could even spark the kind of flirtation that evolved into something more serious—but a clumsy rejoinder brought mockery. Delicious food was served at the gatherings, accompanied by excellent wines, rare teas, and, when it became available, the exotic concoction known as coffee. A party for those with an intellectual bent, the salon was quickly seen as a refuge from worldly intrigue and political rivalries. It wasn't long before others followed in the footsteps of Rambouillet.

The Marquise de Sablé's salon launched an entirely new form of French literature, one for which Natalie Barney would become known: the short, witty, truthful saying known as a maxim or epigram. The maxim was born when de Sablé and her friend the Duc de La Rochefoucauld began taking ideas bandied about at the salon and transforming them into sentences so sharp they could wound. One of de Sablé's most famous remarks: "If we took as much trouble to be what we should be as we take to deceive others by disguising what we are, we could appear as we really are without having the trouble of disguising ourselves."

Both Mesdames Rambouillet and de Sablé had a profound influence on literature. "It would be difficult," wrote one historian, "to overestimate the benefits conferred by the Salons upon French literature, language, and even thought during the first half of the seventeenth century. . . . In the linguistic field the constant influence of . . . Mme de Rambouillet and Mme de Sablé upon most of the great writers of the day gradually transformed the picturesque and over-rich legacy of the sixteenth century into the clearest and most elegant medium for conveying abstract thought known to the modern world."[4]

Other salons were equally important. Madame de Maintenon, who hosted important figures such as Ninon de Lenclos and Racine, eventually became the second wife of Louis XIV and strongly influenced him in religious and political matters. The Marquise de Sévigné, perhaps the most famous letter-writer in history, regularly brought together the most politically important figures at the time of Louis XIV. However, her comment—"The more I see of men, the more I admire dogs"—doesn't say much for her esteemed guests. Speaking of men, one of the few who held a salon was Valentin Conrart, secretary to Louis XIII. When Cardinal Richelieu suggested that he transform the meetings into an official society, the Académie Française was born.

By the early nineteenth century, certain salonists themselves were so famous that it was considered an honor to attend their gatherings. Madame de Staël, who welcomed the most powerful figures of her day, was celebrated throughout Europe for her brilliance. Madame Récamier, whose portrait in an Empire dress symbolized the Age of Napoléon, hosted Chateaubriand, various Bonapartes, Delacroix, de Tocqueville, and Balzac. The salon of Baronne Dudevant, better known as the prolific novelist George Sand, was attended by Liszt, Chopin, and Hugo.

But as the twentieth century neared, the salon had lost its spontaneity, becoming formalized and formulaic. Lively gatherings could still be found, but they were becoming rare. More typical was Madame de Caillavet's salon, which centered around her lover, Anatole France, who could pontificate endlessly. "His conversation was that of a superior but crashing bore," George Painter complained. People came there for the lavish cuisine, or, as the Duchesse de Clermont-Tonnerre believed, because it was "profitable . . . Certain Salons become a sort of exchange [and] Madame de Caillavet was a very industrious woman."[5]

Salons of a different type began to pop up: more casual, less fussy. The matronly Rachilde, with her no-nonsense haircut and gruff ways, gathered a vivacious crowd in the offices of the literary review *Mercure de France*. She attracted many people Natalie knew or would come to know—Pierre Loüys, André Gide, Remy de Gourmont, J. C. Mardrus, and Colette's husband, Willy. Major musicians, dancers, and artists flocked to Misia Sert's relaxed gatherings on quai Voltaire. And soon after the century's turn people began crowding into the Left Bank home of American siblings Gertrude and Leo Stein to drink tea and study their bizarre collection of modern paintings. In the late 1960s, a journalist for the *New York Times Book Review* asked Natalie how she had gone about establishing a literary salon. "I was an international person myself," she explained, "and as I had a nice house I thought I should help other international people meet. The other literary Salons weren't international. Newcomers who didn't know what to do with themselves could come here. Americans found translators for their work. I gave afternoons to French or American poets so others could get to know them."[6] On another occasion, she remarked: "I didn't create a Salon; a Salon was created around me."

She made it sound easy, but it wasn't. Running a successful salon required a rare mix of qualities. It wasn't enough to command great intelligence, unruffled self-confidence, and a lightning-quick wit; one must also possess a willingness to let others take the spotlight. Evangeline Bruce, the quintessential mid-century American hostess, once said that women were better than men at running salons because they were more likely to suppress their own egos and "take the time to be sure that everyone shines." Since Natalie's salon was destined to be "one of the main centres of intellectual commerce in modern Paris,"[7] it's fair to say that she had what it took to carry it off. As Richard Aldington put it: "Her world was that meeting place of society and literature which is better understood and organised in Paris than anywhere. . . . Many women in Paris attempt to found a salon; Miss Barney succeeded."[8]

As we've seen, Natalie had been in training her entire life to take on this role, learning from her own mother how to wow a crowd. Beyond this, she had an intuitive sense of how to make people feel special. She instinctively found and stressed commonalities, put shy souls at ease, and gave flight to the wit and brilliance of others. Most people who met Natalie for the first time walked away feeling that they had made an exciting new friend—one who appreciated their best qualities.

André Germain, one of Natalie's close and long-term friends, met her in 1909 or 1910 when brought to the *pavillon* by Lucie. "I'll remember that first meeting all my life," he wrote. Instead of the usual stiff and formal introduction, Natalie took one look at him and said, without preamble, "Who is this pre-Raphaelite?" And then, "imperiously, she took possession of me . . . Her antenna were as wondrous as her coquetry . . . she felt my soul and began to play with it."[9]

Natalie had an above-average quota of ego, but she knew how to keep it under wraps. Nowhere was this more obvious than at her Fridays. She never dominated conversations, didn't interfere when others spoke, and introduced guests to people they might find interesting.

She also promoted people. When she spotted new talent, she did what she could to help, to introduce, to publicize. Her tastes in music and literature were strictly nineteenth century, but that never stopped her from helping or trying to appreciate the work of artists with a different viewpoint. Some of the more unlikely recipients of her monetary aid and other assistance would include surrealist writer Louis Aragon, revolutionary composer George Antheil, and madman-playwright Antonin Artaud.

As finely honed as Natalie's people skills might have been, they don't account for the extraordinary power and longevity of her salon. The credit for that goes to her incredible presence. Despite her small stature and quiet voice, she dominated any room. Even though she was willing to shine the light on the poet of the hour or the newest inductee into the Académie Goncourt, at the end of the day there was never any doubt about who was the focus of all eyes. Few could resist Natalie, even when they wanted to. That long blond hair, described by so many as resembling moonlight. Those "very blue eyes . . . Natalie had extraordinary eyes, very sparkling, with stars in them; the irises had a delicate marking like the little round petals of pompom dahlias."[10] Her voice, which "sounded like crystal, it touched and caressed you like the wind passing over flowers, it dazzled with femininity."[11]

And then there was her unique intellect—quick, penetrating, insightful. Her "luminous intelligence spares no one—not man, not woman, nothing. It's not that she's hard, or sad, or mistrustful. It's just that she always speaks the truth, and she does it in a paradoxical fashion, even a comic fashion. But that truth is so just, so exact."[12]

While Natalie could be devastatingly truthful, she was slow to judge, a tendency that dated back to childhood and was one of her finer qualities. In *L'ange et les pervers,* Lucie Delarue-Mardrus is often harshly critical of Natalie, but nonetheless extols her ability to withhold judgment. As one of the characters tells Barney's fictional counterpart: "I am sure that if I, or another of your friends, were arrested one day, let's say for theft, you would be there, and it would not affect your friendship in the least because you are capable of loving someone just as they are, even a thief."[13] People appreciated Natalie's acceptance of them, foibles and all, and felt free to tell her their secrets.

Natalie also claimed to hold no opinions, reasoning that she couldn't limit herself to a single opinion when there were two or even two hundred sides to every question. "The person who speaks 'against' has nothing to say," she wrote. "Why destroy when one can surpass? One limits oneself to what one attacks, and proves nothing thereby save one's limitations."[14] Or, more succinctly, "Conclusions: delusions?"[15] She had plenty of opinions, of course; she just knew it was best to keep them to herself. As Ward McAllister, the late-nineteenth-century suzerain of New York society, once said, "the highest cultivation in social manners enables a person to conceal from the world [her] real feelings. [She] can go through any annoyance as if it were a pleasure." Such concealment, he added, was "the ladder to social success."[16]

The last and absolutely not least quality that contributed to Natalie's success as a salonist: wit, that rare collaboration of intelligence and humor. "Natalie was very, very funny," her close friend François Chapon told me. He glanced away, thinking back across the decades, and suddenly burst into laughter. "Yes, indeed, she was very funny." Jean Chalon felt the same way. "Natalie always laughed—oh, she had a marvelous sense of humor," he said. "You laughed with her like you could with no one else."[17]

Capturing wit on the page is a bit like trying to trap a sudden breeze in handcuffs; both wit and breeze slip easily away. Just as one must be there when the breeze rises to feel the air freshen and hear the willow trees rustle, so must one be present to experience the myriad emotions—surprise, comprehension, the uncontrolled upwelling of laughter—resulting from a witty comeback. That said, here is one small example of a Natalie-ism. During a visit to Washington in the 1940s, she mentioned to William Huntington that she would be attending that night's performance of *The Tempest,* an innovative version that played fast and loose with Shakespeare. According to Huntington: "I remember saying to Natalie the next day, 'Did you enjoy *The Tempest?*' and she said, 'It was not correctly named. It should have been called *The Tea.*' "[18]

Natalie's wit, at its best, went far beyond such clever but simple humor, as she excelled at the difficult art of delivering ripostes via epigram. She had the ability to hear a remark, grasp its essence, transform it into a succinct and amusing epigram, and send it hurtling back at the speaker—all within seconds. So stunningly accurate and speedily delivered were her comebacks that people sometimes stood open-mouthed when one of these startling gems popped from her lips. In the explosive laughter that followed, her own silvery, infectious laugh rang out loud and clear. Even Laura, known for her dour and humorless personality, was constantly laughing around her sister. That astonishing wit of Natalie's won over skeptics, made her Fridays lively, and sent people home happy.

Natalie's salon managed the difficult trick of being both exclusive and inclusive. Although she was much too polished to ever come right out and say so, Miss Barney had definite standards of admission. Requisites included at least one of the following: worldly accomplishment, extraordinary intelligence, celebrity, love of life, a sense of humor, and, in the case of women, beauty and style. Eccentrics were welcome, but the dull and boring need never return. Another standard—it applied to *everybody*—was that you had to possess excellent manners and leave any tendency toward vulgar speech at the door. Inclusivity lay in the fact that, if you passed the initial test of merit, nothing else about you mattered, including your political views, sexual persuasion, nationality, or religion. In those days, such democratic assimilation was rare.

One of the most unusual aspects of the salon was its international flavor. As discussed in greater detail in a later chapter, until the 1920s the only place in Paris where writers and artists of different nationalities could mingle socially was at rue Jacob. "The universe came here," wrote an observer, "from San Francisco to Japan, from Lima to Moscow, from London to Rome."[19] For this reason alone Natalie's Fridays filled a void in the world of Parisian letters.

Another rarity: the sexuals (hetero-, bi-, and homo-) mingled at the *pavillon* with a transparent ease that was remarkable for the time. It's often said that Barney ran a "lesbian Salon," but that's simply not the case. She ran a *salon*, period. Many lesbians attended, as did straight men and women, male homosexuals, and plenty of others who ranged the considerable territory in between. The implicit understanding—the triumph of Natalie's Fridays—was that it was okay to be who you were. Such casual, guilt-free mingling was unheard of back then; it's not always easy to pull off even now.

It's important to remember that this was a time when psychologists like Krafft-Ebing and Havelock Ellis promulgated destructive theories that classified homosexuals as perverted, ill, and something apart from the rest of society. In other words, to be homosexual meant being the Other. Almost everybody, including many homosexuals, agreed with this point of view. Natalie did not. Her embrace of her sexuality was both joyous and matter-of-fact. As she often said: "I am a lesbian. One needn't hide it, nor boast of it." Such an attitude imparted strength to her lesbian friends. "The image of lesbians in both literature and life was constructed around notions of illness, perversion, inversion, and paranoia," Shari Benstock wrote in *Women of the Left Bank.* "Natalie Barney dedicated her life to revising this prevailing image."[20]

Nobody ever expressed this better than Radclyffe Hall. In her novel *The Well of Loneliness,* the tortured and self-hating lesbian character, Stephen Gordon, attends the salon of Valerie Seymour, who is closely modeled on Natalie. Stephen is surprised to observe homosexuals interspersed with the "normal" guests. Miraculously, they don't seem to feel as if they bear a "stigma," because "Valerie, placid and self-assured, created an atmosphere of courage; everyone felt very normal and brave when they gathered together at Valerie Seymour's."[21]

NATALIE MAY HAVE been cutting a swath through literary Paris and racking up conquests of the heart and mind, but her mother was still capable of teaching her a thing or two about how to get things done.

In the years since Albert's death Alice had brought new dimension to the word "busy." Her most startling accomplishment was that she had—with no precedent, no warning, not a clue that she could do so—won four patents from the U.S. Patent Office. Three were awarded in 1902, the first two for improvements to clothing wardrobes and parlor-car chairs, and the third for a device that fastened chairs to one another for alignment in rows. In 1903 she received a patent for an automatic stirring device known as a fluid agitator.*

But inventing arcane mechanical objects was just a side hobby for this woman. Alice's major efforts had gone into her art, which had been the subject of shows at prestigious galleries such as Washington's Corcoran, New York's Knoedler, Boston's Walter Kimball, London's Modern, and the Bernheim Jeune in Paris.

In her spare time she had toured southern Europe and Egypt and put on numerous musical entertainments at Studio House. She brought to Washington the avant-garde dancer Ruth St. Denis, who shocked audiences with her bare feet and naked midriff. She produced an outdoor pageant for charity, styled after an eighteenth-century pastorale once given at Versailles. She became active in a charitable welfare agency for needy families called Neighborhood House, bought it a headquarters in southwest Washington, and later added a child-care center. She taught classes in silk tie-dying. She teamed up with composer Harvey Howard to write an opera, *About Thebes,* and danced the leading role before a packed audience, which included President and Mrs. Taft. She wrote another play, *The Bridal Veil,* which regaled the summer crowd at Bar Harbor. Finally, in 1909, she wrote a theatrical piece, *The Man in the Moon,* whose profits were to benefit Neighborhood House. Ticket sales soared when word got around that she would star as the torrid, jealous Spanish dancer.

It was during rehearsals for *The Man in the Moon* that Alice met twenty-two-year-old Christian Hemmick. Just back from Europe, where his father had been serving in the U.S. diplomatic corps, Hemmick was polite, cultivated, well-educated, and extremely good-looking. Tall and slender, with blond hair and a serious demeanor, he was popular with the day's debs.

In those moneyed circles, participation in Alice's productions was considered not only good form but great fun. And so, like many of his friends, Christian sought a small role in the production. Despite the three decades that separated them, the young amateur thespian was bowled over by the middle-

---

*The patents for improvements to various devices are Nos. 697,778 (Wardrobes); 723,977 (Fluid Agitators); 697,777 (Parlor Car Chairs); and 712,898 (Fastening Devices). The official patents are stored at the Smithsonian Institution.

aged artist/dramatist/director/producer/inventor/socialite/flamenco dancer. "According to both Christian and Alice," wrote Jean Kling, "it was love at first sight. Christian was her Greek god; she was his queen. Night after night he stood in the crowd and watched her move to the seductive rhythms of flamenco, knowing that she danced just for him."[22]

Widow Barney and young Hemmick were constantly together, but, though it seems impossible, nobody who knew them suspected a thing. She kept him late for special rehearsals at her home, portrayed him as a noble god in her paintings, and allowed him to accompany her to social functions. While dancing as Narcissus in yet another theatrical she'd written, she even dared to kiss him on the lips before a packed audience. Indeed, there were clues aplenty, but so outside the bounds of acceptability was their love that even those who knew Alice best couldn't gaze past the well-trimmed trees of Studio House into the wild forest where she secretly gamboled.

As one of the newspapers put it after the scandal broke, "due to the fact that Mrs. Barney is exceedingly popular with the younger set, no special significance was attached to his attentions to her . . . and the difference in their ages precluded any [hint] of an engagement."[23]

But all that fuss was in the future. For now, Alice and Hemmick were blissfully alone, thrilling to love's first blush.

MEANWHILE, IN PARIS, things had taken a bad turn for Pauline Tarn. A pervasive myth has it that, after Natalie broke her heart, Pauline gradually lost her life force, pined away, and died. She did all that, but in between Natalie and the wasting away were a few years of intense accomplishment and activity. It was almost as if she were trying to squeeze in as much as she could, while she could.

For instance, Pauline became quite the traveler. She visited Lesbos often, usually accompanied by Hélène; they always occupied the property where she had been so happy with Natalie. Between 1906 and 1908, she traveled to Jerusalem, Egypt, Constantinople, Hawaii, and Japan. She took to vacationing in Nice and liked it so much that she rented a villa where friends, including Colette, came to visit.

She also had a few lovers. She may have been faithful to Hélène during their official liaison, but in 1907 the Baronne left her for another woman. After a period of depression, Pauline turned into a minor seductress. Among her lovers were two courtesans—one of whom was Emilienne d'Alençon (who really got around!). Despite their new amours, Pauline and Hélène remained close.

The never-ending constant in Pauline's life was her writing. Her total oeuvre, produced between 1901 and 1909, amounted to fourteen volumes of poetry and seven of prose. In addition, she probably wrote additional works under the pen name Paul Riversdale.

All this time Pauline and Natalie had maintained a wary friendship. They sent notes, kept up through friends, and occasionally visited. Natalie sometimes attended social events in Pauline's apartment. Natalie and Hélène got along in a civilized manner. The Baronne scribbled convivial messages to Natalie on Pauline's letters, and once even invited her to visit them on Lesbos.

Nonetheless, the situation continued to cause Natalie heartache, or maybe just damaged pride. Writing to Eva, she remarked huffily that Hélène "apparently cannot live without [Pauline] a single day, for my morning walks (usually solitary) are harassed by the sight of their coupe and steppers—which makes me take to running with all the agility of outraged solitude and vanity."[24]

Somewhere in these frenetic years Pauline became derailed, and nobody realized what was happening until it was too late. The two people who knew and loved her best—Hélène and Antoinette Tarn—were busy with their own lives. They probably noticed on occasion that Pauline was drinking too much, or not eating enough, or seemed a little dopey, but undoubtedly considered it a passing problem. And then, just like that, the reality: Pauline was seriously alcoholic, intensely addicted to drugs, and refused to eat.* In addition, her behavior was becoming increasingly erratic.

Once under way, Pauline's disintegration was not a secret. She was, until nearly the end, highly visible. She entertained, gave interviews, and could be spotted walking or being driven about. People had plenty of opportunity to observe her, and a few left written records about her bizarre behavior.

Colette lived nearby and visited often, and in *The Pure and the Impure* she wrote the definitive description of Pauline's last years. She told of the huge rooms, dark and airless behind curtained windows. She described the heavy scent, a combination of funereal-like incense, too many flowers, and overripe fruit. Once, sickened by the odor, she tried to open a window, only to find it nailed shut. She wrote of the mysterious notes Pauline received, supposedly from Hélène, summoning her immediately away ("I'm requisitioned," Pauline would say. "*She* is terrible at present.").[25] Colette found Pauline's dinner parties particularly disturbing. While her guests ate, Pauline drank heavily, tossing down glass after glass of exotic liquors. On one occasion, when Colette came right out and called her an alcoholic, Pauline was furious.

On her first visit to Pauline's, Romaine Brooks was struck by the other-

---

*The word *anorexia* was not used in 1909.

worldly atmosphere of the dark, heavily curtained room, with its "grim life-sized Oriental figures propped up on chairs, phosphorescent Buddhas glowing dimly in the folds of black draperies [and] . . . perfumed incense. A curtain draws aside and Pauline stands before us in Louis XVI male costume. Her straight blond hair falls to her shoulders, her flower-like face is bent down; she does not lift it even to greet us. Though I know that she is a very gifted poetess, it is difficult to detect other than a seemingly affected and childish personality. . . . We lunch seated on the floor Oriental fashion and scant food is served on ancient Damascus ware, cracked and stained. . . . What possible affinity is there between these ugly surroundings and the poetical images of our pale hostess?"[26]

In the summer of 1908 Pauline tried to kill herself with an overdose of laudanum, a derivative of opium. From there everything went swiftly downhill. By early 1909, her state of health was in crisis, involving amnesia, partial paralysis of her limbs, dysentery, and problems with her eyes. Hélène took on the job of caring for her. She begged Pauline to see a doctor and to eat, but she refused to do so. Despite her ailments, she continued drinking, going out, and even traveled to London to visit her sister.

That summer, a shocked Louise Faure-Favier observed Pauline on the street. "She was walking feebly, supported by a cane on one side and on the other by her maid. It was only through the latter's presence that I recognized her, as she herself was unrecognizable. She looked like an old woman passing by, and she was only thirty-one!"[27] Pauline would have agreed. Writing to her sister around that time, she said: "You see, my chérie, I'm thirty-one, and I have the sense of being very old, and I only want peace."[28]

By late October 1909 Pauline could no longer leave her bed and could scarcely move her limbs. With the end clearly in sight, Antoinette arrived from London. On the tenth of November Pauline asked that a priest be called. She converted to Catholicism, just as her beloved Violet had shortly before her own death. On the fourteenth she managed to obtain and drink some alcohol, resulting in a paralysis of her larynx.

On November 18, around seven in the morning, Pauline Tarn died. She was thirty-two years old and, it is said, weighed about seventy pounds. The official cause of her death was lung congestion (pneumonia), but those who knew her considered her passing a long, slow suicide. Natalie disagreed. "More than any other," she wrote, "she was the priestess of death, and death was her last major work, for that amorous virgin died in accord with herself. . . . It wasn't a suicide: those who love life kill themselves; those who love death allow themselves to die. . . . All her life had been an evolution toward that final and undeniable hope."[29]

Pauline's early death became one of the great legends behind Natalie. Even the way Barney received the news of her former lover's death lends itself to legend—though the true tale isn't exactly as she related it. According to Natalie, she learned that Pauline was ill upon returning to Paris from St. Petersburg and her doomed pursuit of Henriette Roggers. The next morning, carrying a bouquet of violets, she walked to Pauline's apartment and was met at the door by the butler. He announced matter-of-factly that Mademoiselle had just died. Natalie, shocked, handed him the flowers and staggered away, collapsing onto a sidewalk bench.

The broad outlines are true: the violets, the butler, the shock. However, Natalie did not learn about Pauline's illness after her return from Russia, which occurred on January 15. Pauline died on November 18, ten months later. During the intervening months, Natalie had been busy settling into rue Jacob, buying an automobile, and planning her first entertainments. She knew through mutual friends that Pauline was extremely ill, yet no record exists of any visit to her old lover's bedside.

With spooky synchronicity, Natalie picked the very morning of Pauline's death to finally pay her respects. When she rang the bell, she had no idea that Pauline was dead, nor that people who disliked her intensely were weeping over her corpse. Antoinette, in particular, blamed Natalie for her sister's deterioration—and, thus, her death. Natalie was not wanted in that residence or beside that deathbed, and it is a logical probability that Antoinette or Hélène refused her entry, ordering the butler to send her away.

Pauline was buried alongside her father in the cemetery at Passy, steps away from Natalie's eventual gravesite. In time, Hélène constructed atop her grave a tiny, neo-Gothic chapel with a granite altar and a pretty stained glass window. The walls inside are inscribed with lines from Tarn's poetry. The epitaph, on an outer wall, is one she wrote for herself. It's engraved as written, in French, but time and weather have nearly rubbed it smooth. Here is an English translation by Natalie, which appeared in a literary review:[30]

> Here the door through which I passed
> —Oh roses mine and thorns, both mine!—
> What matters now to me the Past?
> Who sleep and dream of things divine?
> My ravished soul, from mortal breath
> Appeased, forgets all former strife,
> Having, from its great love of Death,
> Pardoned the crime of crimes—called Life.

NINE

The Amazon

1910–1913

You, Amazon, belong to the race of conquerors. You do not permit
things to resist you, to oppose your will to conquer, and you will not
endure to be loved against your will.

—*Remy de Gourmont*

In reality, she was an Amazon long before Remy de Gourmont christened her so.

—*Eva Palmer*

T HE YEAR 1910 BEGAN with torrential rains. As January progressed
and the downpour continued, the Seine rose above its banks for the first
time since 1746, the Métro flooded, and water gushed crazily through
the streets. At its height the flood threatened to spill into the Louvre, putting
the treasure of centuries at risk. When the waters finally receded at month's
end, they left more than $200 million damage.

For Natalie, the flooding marked a symbolic start to a year destined to
overflow with import and activity. Two significant people would enter her life,
Remy de Gourmont and the Duchesse de Clermont-Tonnerre. Three of her
books would be published, including the first, a collection of epigrams, to gar-
ner serious attention. She would be injured in a motoring accident that killed

her chauffeur. She would be involved in yet another bicontinental scandal, although this time it would be caused by Laura; and her mother would lay the foundation for an even greater disgrace the following year. On a lighter note, she would learn to dance the tango and have the unusual experience of seeing her former lover become a princess.

Natalie didn't know it—no one did—but she would be dancing that tango at the edge of a dying world. This wonderful year and the three to follow were to end the prosperous, peaceful era that had given rise to the glories and grace of the Belle Époque. An ugly, brutal war was coming. When it ended, the gentle world that Natalie had known would be gone.

IN THE FIRST two decades of the century, a man named Remy de Gourmont held a unique position in the French literary world, that of a revered recluse. His entry into Natalie's life—or, more accurately, her entry into *his*—gifted her with precious intellectual cachet. He also bestowed upon her a nickname that she would carry for the rest of her life and, considering that it's engraved on her tombstone, into eternity.

Born in Normandy in 1858, Gourmont had studied law at the University of Caen before moving to Paris in 1883. He took a job working with ancient manuscripts at the Bibliothèque Nationale, "which was to make him one of the most learned men in Europe."[1] In 1890 he became a founding member of the literary journal *Mercure de France,* which for years introduced many of Europe's best writers to the public. A writer himself, he eventually produced more than one hundred works of fiction, poetry, science, sexology, erotica, anthropology, essays, psychology, and literary criticism. Handsome, outgoing, and popular with women, Gourmont led a satisfying life as an intellectual man-about-town.

All that changed when he developed lupus sometime in his early thirties. The disease scarred and disfigured his face terribly. Unable to deal with the shocked or sickened glances directed his way, Gourmont largely withdrew from the social whirl. It's often said that he was a hermit, but that's not quite true. While he didn't mingle in society—no glamorous balls, theater openings, or big races at Longchamps—he remained connected to the larger world. Most afternoons he stopped at the *Mercure*'s offices; he liked to read, write, or talk with friends at the Café Flore; he occasionally dined at the Restaurant Duval on boulevard Saint-Michel; and he was fond of browsing for treasures among the *bouquinistes* whose bookstalls lined the Seine.

Gourmont even entertained in a modest manner. On Sundays a small group of close male friends, including the poet Apollinaire, illustrator André

Rouveyre, and publisher Edouard Champion, dropped by for conversation in his sixth-floor apartment on rue des Saints-Pères. Invitations to a newcomer were exceedingly rare; to a woman, even rarer.

In 1910 Gourmont was fifty-two years old, in declining health, and physically weak. Natalie was a robust and athletic thirty-three. It seems unlikely that two people as different as the young party-giver and the middle-aged, reclusive scholar would even meet, let alone become friends. "One would have said he was an owl in love with a fairy!"[2] quipped André Germain, and everyone who knew them agreed.

In fact, the relationship began in the only way it could have: through the pen. Natalie had long wanted to meet Gourmont, but, wary as he was of being judged ugly by a beautiful young woman, he had to trust her first. Only then would he consider sliding from the page and into life.

The right opportunity presented itself when their mutual friend, Edouard Champion, sent Gourmont a copy of Natalie's new book of short plays and poems, *Actes et entr'actes*. Gourmont liked what he read and in early April sent a note telling her so; he added that her verse would soon appear in the pages of the *Mercure*. "From then on your book will be launched toward glory," he noted.[3] Indeed, publication in the *Mercure de France* was considered a coup. As promised, four of Natalie's poems appeared in the *Mercure* on the first day of May.

Toward the end of June, Natalie sent Gourmont another of the three books she would publish that year, *Éparpillements,* and tucked a flattering letter inside. He replied immediately, expressing pleasure with the book's noble, delicate spirit. Soon afterward came an invitation to one of his Sunday get-togethers.

And so, one afternoon in late June or early July, Natalie accompanied Champion to Gourmont's scholarly lair. It was a comfortable place, where he lived "surrounded by his tools—a lamp, pens, paper, cigarettes . . . and a vase full of seasonal blossoms. . . . Three sides of the wall were lined with books, packed tightly together from ceiling to floor. A casement-window from which one could look over a perspective of Parisian roofs and see the windows on the courtyard lighting up towards evening. It was pleasant, warm and remote in this monk's cell."[4]

On that fateful first visit, Gourmont opened the door and held out both his hands in a warm welcome. Nervous, Natalie could never recall exactly how she greeted him. She took little notice of his scarred face; instead, she was struck by the intelligence in his pale eyes, his shy but spontaneous manner, and his obvious, though repressed, joy for living. They hit a melodic note, and Gourmont let her know that she was welcome at future Sundays.

A correspondence of daily notes developed, and Natalie began to appear at the Sundays. By August she felt on friendly enough terms with this literary lion to suggest an evening automobile ride in the Bois. The invitation presented a dilemma for Gourmont. He feared being exposed to the pitiless glances of strangers; he was nervous about spending time with Natalie in uncontrolled circumstances; and he dreaded breaking away from the safety of routine. But at the same time he was anxious to go, as he already possessed a breathless fascination for the blond American.

In the end, he went, albeit sulkily. Natalie's chauffeur fetched him from the sixth floor. Once outside he climbed slowly over the wide running board, settled into her Renault cabriolet, and sat beside her in complete silence. Others might have responded to his taciturnity with nervous conversation, but Natalie countered him, brilliantly, by echoing his silence. Finally, in the acacia-scented Bois, with moonlight shimmering on the lakes and backlighting the huge, graceful trees, he heaved a deep sigh and spoke haltingly of his loneliness. Natalie confided that she, too, was lonely, and had been since the death of Renée Vivien. The odd couple had found a mutual meeting ground of the emotions.

There was something shameless and even utilitarian about Natalie's confession. While she may have been distraught in the wake of Pauline's death, her life was crowded and busy. In fact, a day after the drive in the Bois she traveled to Évian with a new lover. Gourmont wrote her there a week or so later. Using the formal *vous*—a habit which he almost never broke with her—he boldly stated that he had treasured their evening, and that his memory was haunted by the ironic music of her voice. He admitted that she intimidated him, despite her natural ease and unaffected nature. He had, he hoped, found a friend to play at life with now and then, when she could waste the time. He closed with: "I kiss your hands. Remy de Gourmont." A bit coy, a trifle fussy, but clearly the man was hooked.

The friendship quickly intensified. By autumn Natalie had been granted virtually unlimited access to Gourmont, and he had taken to calling on her at rue Jacob, which was only minutes away. They took tea, walked in the gardens, and talked.

Talk, in fact, was the never-ending constant between them, the lifeblood of their unique association. They spoke not only of literature, but of being and existence, sex and love, myth and metaphysics, Schopenhauer and Scheherazade. His Renaissance intelligence blended well with her wide-ranging interests; though his knowledge had far greater depth, her quicker and more intuitive mind anticipated his points. Stimulated by her intellect, Gourmont began writing essays that further explored their conversations or introduced new topics.

Natalie once said that she was drawn to Gourmont for his brilliant mind and free opinions, and that in exchange she liberated his joy by persuading him to mix once again with the living. This was not the first time that Natalie played the rescuing knight and it wouldn't be the last. Part of her intriguing duality was that, despite her strongly self-centered existence, she also possessed a genuine desire to help others. And so, as she had once tried to persuade Liane into another profession and attempted to turn Pauline from thoughts of death, she now hoped to rescue Gourmont from loneliness. In large part, she would succeed.

Altruism aside, there's no denying that the chase and capture of Remy de Gourmont had a self-interested edge, one that Natalie expeditiously honed. She knew that friendship with such a man would transform her, in the eyes of others, into a woman of substance. Anyone who doubted her intellectual weight would be forced to admit that her mind was capable of holding Gourmont's interest. By taking Natalie seriously as a writer, he placed her in the ranks of other writers he admired; by welcoming her Sunday visits, he made her a member of a highly select literary set.

Janet Flanner once remarked that Natalie's association with Gourmont "was not a very valid qualification for her literary reputation, was it? . . . I've always thought that was an unfair advantage that fate and chance took of Natalie, to place [Gourmont] in her path."[5] Flanner missed the point. Fate didn't put Remy in Natalie's path. Natalie was her *own* fate. She made a conscious decision to swerve onto *his* path and make it her own—in a part-time way, of course.

Many saw Barney's conquest of Gourmont as cold-blooded. Describing Natalie as "an American who burned with an appetite for conquest," Maurice Martin du Gard concluded that she "had an almost hypnotic, if not supernatural, power over Remy de Gourmont."[6] Others simply couldn't understand the relationship without assigning it a sexual basis, and the many rumors to that effect have lingered: a 1968 treatise about Gourmont claimed that "an American poetess, Nathalie Barney, became for a time his mistress."[7] Anything's possible, of course, and the only two people who could tell us what that relationship was really about are long dead. But chances are that Natalie spoke the truth when she said that she never gave in to Gourmont's desires. "When you want to make someone crazy," she added, "you must not give in."[8]

While Natalie and Gourmont probably never touched sexually, they nonetheless joined repeatedly in an orgiastic intercourse of the mind. That alone gave the relationship an unusual intimacy, a closeness often lacking in more traditional couplings. "In friendship as in love, can one say exactly where lie feelings such as ours?" Gourmont asked her. "Where they begin? Where they end, if there is an end? They exist, we feel them, that is enough. One should ask no more, neither interrogate nor cross them. Let them live freely."[9]

Natalie was the last great love of Remy de Gourmont's life. The fact that she was a lesbian didn't dim his ardor in the slightest. If anything, her sexuality intrigued him, turning her into the double-being she had always considered herself to be, part man/part woman. He gave her a nickname to capture this dual nature: Natalis. "Natalis is a charming being," he told her in early December. "Natalis enchants me." He included a poem he'd written, inspired by the old Carolus-Duran portrait that hung at rue Jacob:

> Natalis was already a page,
> Natalis was already a woman.
> He remained both page and woman,
> She remained both woman and page.
> She may be a page to women,
> She is woman enough for a page.
> If I were young, were I a page,
> I would love in Natalis the woman.
>
> Put on a doublet, put on a bodice,
> You will not change your soul.
> You will not fool my soul
> By the form your bodice takes.

Natalie's immense regard for Gourmont can be seen in how willing she was to act against type, exhibiting a generosity of self that few others ever saw. "Despite that cruelty that made up part of her charms," observed André Germain, "Lorély rarely tormented her old and lovesick friend. She even developed, for his sake, the kind of virtues she seemed least capable of: patience, a tender gentleness, a sort of fidelity."[10]

She made a point of bringing Gourmont, whenever feasible, into the kind of activities from which he'd long been absent. One June night about a year after they met she held a masked outdoor ball against the backdrop of *pavillon*, temple, and gardens. She included Gourmont in the planning; for instance, she wrote an invitation in verse that he edited and arranged to have rotogravured in her handwriting. Such a clever invitation attracted notice, and at least one poetic response: Surrealist poet Guillaume Apollinaire sent his own versed regrets. His petite poem remained unpublished until 1965, when

Natalie discovered it buried in a drawer. It quickly appeared in *Le Figaro Litteraire*.

The garden was beautiful on the night of the ball, its ancient pathway lit by colorful Japanese lanterns. Masked, costumed revelers strolled about. Natalie's neighbor, Jean de Bonnefon, arrived costumed in the red robes of a cardinal. Couturier Paul Poiret was disguised as a Buddhist monk. Calvé, her heavy body stretched across an ancient sedan chair, was delivered to the garden by four exhausted porters.

Wanda Landowska had arrived early to supervise the installation of her harpsichord beside the French windows in Natalie's second-floor bedroom. From there she played the graceful rococo music of seventeenth-century composer François Couperin. A theater piece, a two-act comedy entitled *Le ton de Paris* (also known as *Les amants de bonne compagnie*), was performed by Génia of the Comédie-Française and Francis de Miomandre. Written in 1787 by the Duc de Lauzun, who was guillotined shortly afterward, the play wasn't published until 1911 (by Edouard Champion). The production of this lost-and-found gem in the gardens where Racine once strolled was considered the last word in chic.

Gourmont was transformed by Natalie into an Arabian prince via a mask, one of her embroidered robes, and a turban made from an old green silk stocking. She appeared in the whimsical guise of a Japanese firefly chaser, carrying a collection of tiny lit bulbs in a wicker basket to give the illusion of fireflies. She stayed by Gourmont's side all night long, disappearing only once or twice, briefly, to take care of hostess details. With his scars hidden from sight and his goddess by his side, that soft summer night was a happy one for Remy.

Another adventure Natalie asked him to share was her August 1911 cruising trip on the Seine. Chartering a "smart little yacht," the *Druide,* she invited friends to meet her at different ports along the way, accompanying her for a day or two on her river journey. Gourmont was invited for a three-day voyage from Nogent-sur-Marne, which necessitated taking a train from Paris and then waiting hours on the dock for the *Druide* to appear. But he thought the trip was well worth it, sailing peacefully along the placid summer waters beside Natalie with little to do but talk, read, and eat. "How natural it felt to live beside you," Gourmont wrote as soon as he returned to Paris. "How I love looking at you, listening to you, cherishing you!"[11]

One day on her way home from horseback riding, Natalie stopped at Gourmont's for a brief visit. She marched up the six flights of stairs still dressed *"en costume d'amazone,"* carrying a cane and wearing the customary bowler hat and black bow tie. She burst into the room, still excited from her ride, and Gourmont jokingly addressed her as *"l'Amazone."* He soon realized that it was an apt nickname for her—not for her riding clothes so much as her equestrienne skill, her reputation for romantic conquest, and her kinship with the legendary female warriors of ancient times.

From then on Remy occasionally referred to her as "the Amazon." It was a name that would soon bear literary fruit.

THE OTHER IMPORTANT PERSON Natalie met in 1910 was a woman widely admired throughout France. "If ever a great lady existed on this earth," wrote Gabriel-Louis Pringué, "it's the Duchesse de Clermont-Tonnerre, née Elisabeth de Gramont."[12]

Known as Lily to her friends, Gramont was born in 1875. A descendant of Henry IV, she was the daughter of the Duc de Gramont and the Princesse de Beauvau-Craon. Wealthy and privileged, she experienced in her youth the most gilded excesses of the Proustian Age. Proust, in fact, consulted her while writing *Remembrance of Things Past* to be sure he'd gotten the details right for the Guermantes' grand dinner—the exact rigidity of the asparagus, the precise scent of its accompanying sauce. In fact, many sources say that Lily Gramont and the Princess Greffulhe were Proust's two primary models for the Duchesse de Guermantes.

When Lily was growing up it seemed perfectly normal that, when her mother left the house, she would always be preceded to the waiting carriage by a bevy of bowing footmen. The family maintained horses to match their various equipages: very large horses pulled the barouche; medium-sized were attached to the landau; sleek high-stepping beauties were paired with phaetons and victorias; and a comfortably steady "night horse" belonged to the carriage that took them to the theater. Gramont once estimated that her parents entertained more than ninety thousand people at balls and lavish dinners during their marriage. "As a child," reported *The New Yorker*, "[she was] saluted as princess by peasants on her farm who begged her not to clean her shoes before entering their houses."[13]

What made the Duchesse admirable was that she grew up to be resolutely unimpressed by her aristocratic birth. Time and circumstance caused the demise of her fortune, but, rather than bemoan her lost privilege and wealth as did so many others, she transformed herself into a twentieth-century woman. She earned a good living as a writer, and her four volumes of memoirs were praised by critics, historians, and the general public alike. "Few memoirs written by French aristocrats bewail aught except the good old times," Janet Flanner noted. "This lady is valuable in having been modern and accurate before either were the style. She looks backward with a shrug rather than a sigh."[14]

Modern is certainly the word to describe Lily Gramont. Practically alone among her high-born peers she embraced socialism as the answer to mankind's troubles, earning the nickname "Red Duchesse" (when she finally witnessed theory in action in Russia, she lost her Socialist fervor). The composer George Antheil recalled that, at the 1926 premier of his Second Symphony, "my concierge and the Duchesse de Clermont-Tonnerre, both equally formidable old ladies, had by some strange coincidence secured seats side by side and later gave me mutually complimentary reports about each other."[15]

Many have said that Gramont resembled a Gainsborough portrait with her billowy white dresses, blue eyes, and rosy-pink complexion. Lucie Delarue-Mardrus described her as "ravishing, with a rose complexion beneath her huge black-plumed hat, exactly how one imagined Marie Antoinette at her most beautiful."[16] Extremely nearsighted, she peered at the world through a lorgnette. "It was always in her hand," Pringué recalled. "She would plant herself in front of you and examine you as if you were under a microscope. She studied the world with the manner of a vivisector, and to that surgical precision she added much poetry—for the Duchesse de Clermont-Tonnerre was bathed in both dream and reality."[17]

In 1896 Lily married the Duc de Clermont-Tonnerre, a union that produced two daughters. Although Gramont kept resolutely away from the personal, never writing about her own marriage, she did address the repression common to married women of her class and time. "A woman's husband then was only a more or less cruel jailer," she said. "Frenchwomen were subject to their husbands to an incredible degree, possessing the right to dispose neither of their time nor their opinions nor their money. . . . The direct effect of this subjection on its victims was a total incapacity for dealing with the realities of life."[18] Perhaps we can believe Marcel Proust, who told his housekeeper that Lily's husband "was violent and led her a life of hell. He spared her nothing."[19]

Of all the big loves in Natalie's past and future, only Gramont would match her at having a positive outlook, intelligence, objectivity, humor, and refinement. The two women were so much alike that sometimes a description of one sounds uncannily like the other. François Chapon wrote that, within the Duchesse, "independence and tradition had formed a lively character . . . with a rare gaiety . . . quick to seize the best among the hazards of existence, to dismiss sadness and cares, especially if they were personal."[20] He could have been describing Natalie. Lily even spoke in Natalie-like epigrams: "Civilized beings," she once told Pringué, "are those who know how to take more from life than others. That is what the non-civilized cannot and will not pardon."[21]

Natalie and Lily met through Lucie Delarue-Mardrus, probably in the spring of 1910. Lily had met lesbians in her wanderings through social and lit-

erary Paris and had been theoretically intrigued; Natalie carried her from theory into reality. According to Natalie, May 1 was the day of their first kiss, by
which she probably meant the first sexual encounter. The date took on almost
mythic overtones for them. For the rest of their lives, except when separated by
war, they insisted upon being together on the first of May. Part of the ritual
they developed for this anniversary was to eat half a dozen plover's eggs each,
which usually had to be shipped from England.

The beginning of their lifelong liaison was marked by immense passion.
Lily, who had led a traditional life, found sex with another woman exciting.
Decades later, telling Renée Lang about the start of her affair with Natalie, she
said: "She showed me . . . It was a new planet for me."[22] To Natalie, Lily represented everything she loved about France—elegance, sophistication, intelligence, spirit.

Eventually Lily's husband figured out what was going on and forbade Lily
to have anything to do with Natalie, including written correspondence. Such a
stricture was easily overcome by using trusted servants and hand-delivered letters. Natalie and Lily continued to meet, though often weeks went by between
adventures. Most meetings involved elaborate planning, with dozens of forbidden letters zipping back and forth. In one rushed note Natalie gave the
name of their favorite meeting spot in Trouville, the Hôtel des Roches Noires,
and said she would be listed under the name of Breslow.

The situation was agonizing to Natalie, although it was the sort of lovesick
agony she enjoyed because it added excitement and complexity to her life. She
began to obsess about having Lily all to herself, and by 1912 was begging her to
ask for a separation. Recalling their last meeting, she wrote of "your wonderful
arms about me, and your eyes and your voice, and the whole maddening sweetness of you close, at last close. And my love and your love together, safe, for an
hour! Sweet, when will you come again, and when will you come forever?"[23]

At one point Lily left her husband and stayed temporarily at rue Jacob. I
believe it was from this experience that Natalie wrote the undated, privately
printed mini-story "The Woman Who Lives with Me." It's generally presumed
that she wrote this piece back in 1904 to woo Pauline, but that's unlikely. For
one thing, the story addresses an unnamed married woman with two children
who has left her husband and who is "older than I." Lily was born the year
before Natalie, was married, and had two children.* Pauline, a year younger
than Barney, was horrified by thoughts of childbirth and sex with men; Natalie
would have chased her away by assigning her the role of motherhood.

---

*The story speaks of two little boys, but Lily had two daughters; perhaps this was an attempt at disguis-
ing Lily's identity.

Additional factors point away from Pauline and that 1904 date. For example, the author is obviously addressing someone she considers a complete equal in all respects; Natalie never felt that way about Pauline. Also, the poetry Natalie wrote for Pauline was of the love-struck variety. "The Woman Who Lives with Me" is clipped, straightforward, and slightly callous: "Perhaps I told her that I loved her. I do not remember, I say these words lightly, for me there is no meaning left in them." This is not the hopeful, fresh-spirited exuberance of *Je me souviens*. It's harsher and almost jaded, wrought from experience on the battlefield of love.

And, finally, there is the fact that Natalie did not include "The Woman Who Lives with Me" under "Other Works by the Same Author" when *Éparpillements* was published in 1910. However, it appeared on the list in *Pensées d'une Amazone* ten years later. It's reasonable to assume that Natalie had not written "The Woman Who Lives with Me" when *Éparpillements* was published.

Lily and her husband finally separated and eventually divorced in 1920. In Radclyffe Hall's *The Well of Loneliness,* Lily appears as the Comtesse de Kerguelen, who has left her husband for Valérie Seymour (Natalie). The Comtesse is "dignified and reserved, a very great lady, of a calm and rather old-fashioned beauty . . . She had left all for Valérie Seymour; husband, children and home had she left; facing scandal, opprobrium, persecution. Greater than all these most vital things had been this woman's love for Valérie Seymour."[24]

At any rate, from the time they met and for the next few years, Lily was the major, though of course not the only, love of Natalie's life.

NATALIE INTRODUCED HER two new friends, Lily Gramont and Remy de Gourmont, and was pleased that they liked each other. Gourmont seemed at ease in Lily's company, so Natalie sometimes brought her along on visits and felt free to ask him to dinner at rue Jacob when Lily was there. André Rouveyre did a charming, cartoonlike drawing that shows them in conversation. The Duchesse sits on the floor with her legs bent to the side, while Natalie and Gourmont lounge amid the sofa's pillows. The title: *Le Philosophe chez ses amies en 1913.*

Conversation continued to be the lively focal point of the Natalie-Remy friendship. André Germain's belief that Natalie was "the most intelligent woman I have ever known" was one with which Gourmont was in complete agreement. "You are the only person," he told her, "to whom I have ever submitted . . . intellectually."[25] Alone after their talks he further developed the ideas they discussed, wrote them up, and sent them off to Natalie. In effect, these letters continued their conversations.

Toward the end of 1911 he decided to re-create their discussions in the form of letters addressed to an imaginary friend and then publish them in the *Mercure de France.* Considering the project as a form of collaboration, with his writings inspired by Natalie's thoughts and conversation, he decided to give this imaginary being the nickname he'd used since seeing her dressed *en amazone.*

In late December Remy showed Natalie the first "Letter to the Amazon," watching breathlessly while she read. The first "Letter" ran in the *Mercure* on January 1, 1912. It began dryly enough: "An idea or a problem of the emotions often arises between us, my dear friend, and the chances of conversation make us neglect it." Then, suddenly, Gourmont switches gears. The detached, scholarly tone becomes a loving evocation of, and tribute to, an intellectually and physically powerful woman—an Amazon:

> You see, you are the cause of absent-mindedness in me! When I am near you I forget every one of my plans, except that of gazing at your face. I lose myself in your eyes. They absorb my thoughts, my soul and all my projects. . . . Ah! What an excellent thing is presence of mind, how much I admire it in you, the proud Amazon never taken unawares, always ready to seize the horse's mane, to leap into the saddle and to draw the bow to your tanned breast!

The *Letters,* thirty-two in all, appeared bimonthly until October 1913, when they were gathered into a book. They centered on topics such as Memory, Chastity, Love, Survival, Physics, Forgetfulness. In most, long and complex passages are interspersed with doxologies to the "Amazon more happily born than all other women" (Letter IX), a "Conqueror . . . with the bow bent under your naked foot [with] all the power of womanhood in your heart" (Letter XI).

"The friendship with the Amazon was a rejuvenation [for Gourmont]," Richard Aldington wrote in the preface to his 1931 English translation of *Letters to the Amazon.* "These letters . . . are at once a record and a homage. . . . I do not know any other book where all the shades of an ambiguous affection and relationship have been noted with such delicate accuracy."

But without the Amazon at their heart, these letters would have simply been another of Gourmont's highly respected, but largely unread, philosophical creations. By addressing his ideas to a strong and willful goddess, his philosophy became infused with a compelling humanity. Elisabeth Gramont likened Natalie to an Egeria, a female adviser, who freed Gourmont's sensibility. "His mind," she wrote, "poured itself out into a masterpiece of . . . tender abandon."[26] Once a lonely man scribbling abstractions, Gourmont was now viewed as a passionate being who celebrated the play of power between lover and beloved.

Natalie had often been called an Amazon, by herself and others. As a child at Les Ruches, she frequently used the term in letters to her parents. Eva referred to her as an Amazon when they were young teenagers. Pauline Tarn's first book of verse, *Études et préludes*, included a poem about Natalie entitled "Amazon." But all those previous uses of the word had amounted to just another affectionate nickname for Natalie, no different from Flossie, Moonbeam, Loreley, Nat-Nat, or Blonde. It was Remy de Gourmont who made her *l'Amazone*—the one and only Amazon. It was a name she would carry proudly for the rest of her life.

This dazzling Amazon persona was so ideally suited for the modern age that many women claimed to be, or referred to themselves as, Gourmont's Amazon. A puzzled Remy once told Natalie of a woman he hardly knew who wrote to ask why he'd chosen her to be the Amazon. "She's the fourth one who's had that illusion," he added, "not counting those who haven't said anything."[27]

However, as everybody in and beyond the French literary world knew, there was only one woman to whom that title belonged. "When one speaks of the Amazon," wrote Edmond Jaloux, "one is speaking of Miss Barney. The virility of her character and her mind have earned her that surname."[28] Denise Bourdet agreed: "Natalie Barney well deserved this appellation, not only because of her taste since childhood for horseback riding, but above all for the precision with which she let fly her arrows."[29]

With *Lettres à l'Amazone*, Natalie began to enjoy a new kind of renown. As Remy de Gourmont's Amazon she became a formidable presence in the literary world. Nothing sums this up better than a letter from her mother. "Tell me, my dear child," Alice asked. "What did you do, since you've known this old gentleman, to be talked about this way all over Europe?"[30]

There is no record of Natalie's reply.

IN EARLY JULY 1912, while motoring to Switzerland with two friends, Natalie was involved in an accident that killed her chauffeur, Achille. She flew "skyward like the last firework on the 4th of July,"[31] landing so hard in the middle of the road that her gold hairpins, the long-ago gift from Lord Alfred Douglas, lay scattered on the pavement. In shock and unable to move, she remained conscious and observant. Finally a doctor appeared with a shot of morphine, and she was taken by ambulance to a hospital sixty miles away.

Natalie's detached shoulder and torn hip muscles required a week's hospital stay and a lengthy healing process at home. For her, the confinement was akin to punishment. "I have never been so still before," she complained to Laura, "and find it hard and whimper a little nights because I want to move. . . ."[32] When sciatica later developed near the damaged hip, she blamed it on the accident.

Upon hearing the news, Lily rushed from Paris. Later, in her unpublished novel, "Accident," Natalie turned her visit into a dreamy and surreal love story. The characters have no names, but are obviously she and Gramont. At one point the two women hold a private ball "for the two of us only, and where I danced with her alone. Musicians in the next room couldn't see us. I held her against me, my limbs against her limbs, following along together, each movement of her body rhythmically following the music, breathing with love."[33]

One passage illustrates the care Natalie took, as a lesbian, to appear decorous. Visiting England, the two lovers are shown one hotel room with separate beds. They insist on separate rooms. The only other room available contains only a sofa, but the manager agrees to make it up as a bed. That night, "content that we'd saved appearances," the lovers leave the sofa bed empty.

Natalie's accident had also inspired a flurry of writing from Gourmont, who penned his "Letter to the Amazon XIII (Mechanisms)" as a direct response. It ends with a "revived Amazon . . . I have seen your smile again, I have seen once more your ever radiant soul; I know now that the Greek sculptor was right and that a wounded Amazon is still an Amazon."

THREE BOOKS BY Natalie Clifford Barney were published in 1910: *Éparpillements, Je me souviens,* and *Actes et entr'actes.* Although she hadn't published a book since 1901 (*Cinq petits dialogues grecs*), and despite the fact that another decade would pass before her next book appeared, Natalie wrote constantly. She was a "born writer" in the sense that she felt compelled to scribble, to record, to create something out of nothing with a pen. She was absolutely fearless about genre, trying her hand at whatever intrigued her: poetry, dialogue, memoirs, character sketches, or essays. She even undertook drama, writing herself or coauthoring with Alice at least half a dozen full-length plays.

From her earliest years, Natalie always had a notebook going in which she jotted down anything and everything: her scattered thoughts, the opening lines of a story, a book's preliminary chapter, the draft of a difficult letter, a snatch of dialogue overheard at a party. She also used the notebooks as a kind of haphazard filing system, sticking stray bits of this and that between the pages and then forgetting about them.

When Natalie grew serious about a work, its creation moved onto sheets of full-sized paper. When she was composing slowly, her penmanship was controlled and small; if words tumbled faster than her hand could move, her writing grew huge. A hired secretary later transformed the written sheets into a typed manuscript. Natalie did, at most, a light editing. After changing a word here and there, or occasionally crossing out one sentence and inserting another, she was done.

This cavalier approach toward writing and the editing process led many, including her close friend Ezra Pound, to consider Natalie a lazy writer. She agreed, though she also believed that revision destroyed spontaneity without necessarily improving the finished product: "Erasure of worse, or better?"[34]

There is a deeper significance to the way Natalie abruptly finished and moved quickly from her work, one that illuminates her approach to love. "At first, when an idea, a poem, or the desire to write takes hold of you," she said, "work is a pleasure, a delight, and your enthusiasm knows no bounds. But later on you work with difficulty, doggedly, desperately. For once you have committed yourself to a particular work, inspiration changes its form and becomes an obsession, like a love-affair . . . which haunts you night and day! Once at grips with a work, we must master it completely before we can recover our idleness."[35] In other words, be it the creative process or love, if it obsesses you enough to remove you from life's peaceful flow, it must be done away with. Consume it, possess it, master it—and be gone!

All three of the 1910 books were written in French. Of Natalie's twelve published books, only one would be written in English *(The One Who Is Legion);* a second *(Poems & poèmes)* was bilinual. Natalie preferred writing in French. Perhaps this was because, as one of her characters states in *The Color of His Soul* (a 1928 play coauthored with Alice): "it is the only language in which an artist can express himself on certain themes."

Let's take a brief look at two of the books published that year, *Je me souviens* and *Actes et entr'actes.* We'll pay closer attention to the third and most important of the three, *Éparpillements.*

Je me souviens was the long, lyrical prose poem that Natalie presented to Pauline at Bayreuth in August 1904. That original bore a parchment cover; and the poem itself was probably copied from Natalie's manuscript by a professional calligrapher. Pauline ended up carrying it around in her purse. One day when they were on Lesbos she upended the purse and out popped *Je me souviens* with its parchment bearing traces of cold cream.

"Before I ruin it any further," Pauline said, "let's get it published."

Natalie protested. "I wrote it for you alone."[36]

And there the matter stood for six years. It was doubtless Pauline's death that impelled Natalie to publish this work. If she meant it as a tribute to her former lover, she succeeded. It's a handsome, well-conceived little book that rests comfortably in the hand. To read it, you must first remove a delicate glassine slipcover, which seems a metaphor for the uncovering of Pauline's fragile heart. Beneath the title are two lines from Pauline's translation of Sappho: "Lato and Nioba were very tender companions," and "I believe that someone in the future will remember us." The poem is gentle, dreamy, loving, and very personal. Natalie wrote it with the sole intention of reawakening Pauline's love for her, and she used a tender hand to call up memories from the past. Some critics have called it her best verse.

Actes et entr'actes was a collection of short, formal verse plays and poems written over the previous few years. One of the plays was *Équivoque*, the "Sapho" that may have resulted in Natalie's departure from Neuilly. It reverses the legend that Sappho jumped to her death from a cliff over love of a man, Phaon, who left her for another woman. In Barney's version, the leap is made because Sappho is in love with the woman Phaon is marrying. Two other plays were *Autour d'une victoire,* in which Barney exhibits anger over inequality between the sexes, and *La double mort,* which incorporates many of her feelings about Pauline's death. The poems (which include the four published by Gourmont in the *Mercure de France*) have a strong feminist basis, showing women triumphing over adversity.

The third book, *Éparpillements,* which translates as "scatterings," is the first in a series of three collections of Natalie's *pensées*—cleverly expressed thoughts about life, love, art, and human foibles. The *pensée* had long been a traditional literary style in France. Among its earliest and most brilliant practitioners were the Duc de La Rochefoucauld ("We all have enough strength to endure the misfortunes of other people"); Mme. de Sablé ("To be too dissatisfied with ourselves is a weakness; to be too satisfied with ourselves is a stupidity"); writer Jean de La Bruyère ("As long as men are liable to die and are desirous to live, a physician will be made fun of, but he will be well paid"); and philosopher/mathematician Blaise Pascal ("Men never do evil so completely and cheerfully as when they do it from religious conviction"). By the end of the *ancien régime,* such clever remarks were the common language of the court. This led Carlyle, in his 1837 *History of the French Revolution,* to remark that "France was long a despotism tempered by epigrams." (In English, the *pensée* is most commonly known as an epigram, aphorism, or maxim.)

As discussed earlier, Natalie was renowned for her epigrammatic wit. Renée Lang, who regularly attended Barney's salon in the 1950s, told me that "Natalie didn't talk much. She would sit comfortably, listening to the conversation. But every once in a while—Ziiiiip! She'd swoop down and make a witty, insightful remark—often a devastating remark."[37] An earlier habitué of those

Fridays, Gabriel-Louis Pringué, remembered that "Miss Barney's epigrams, enunciated in a quiet voice—nearly murmured—were sharp and incisive."[38]

After social events, Natalie always scribbled her favorite comments into a notebook, onto the back of an envelope, across a dressmaker's invoice—whatever came quickest to hand. Eventually she'd gather these "scatterings," those she could find, anyway, and pull them into a book. Over the course of her long life, three such volumes were published: *Éparpillements* (1910), *Pensées d'une Amazone* (1920), and *Nouvelles pensées de l'Amazone* (1939). Of all her published works, *Éparpillements* was Natalie's personal favorite; it was through this book, she claimed, that she conquered Gourmont.

Today many of the *pensées* remain insightful or funny, as: "To have or have not, which is worse?" Others seem dated at first, but then, with a little thought, become modern. For example, take the line: "Weak as I am, I have strength only for passion!" It's quite ho-hum on first glance, but if you consider the historical context and the method of delivery, the line comes alive.

Imagine that it's 1910, and a dozen guests at rue Jacob are arguing over the relative merits of the fair and masculine sexes. A "manly male"—let's say it's Dr. J. C. Mardrus—announces that the great muscularity of men makes them superior to women, who are physically weak. Silence falls as the group's feminists, men and women alike, struggle to rise above this vulgar truth with a suitable riposte. Suddenly—in her low-toned cello of a voice—Natalie speaks up. "Weak as I am," she drawls, "I have strength only for passion!" From Miss Barney, whose passions and conquests are legendary, such a statement demolishes the very idea of a weaker sex. With one sentence she has destroyed Mardrus's argument by simply agreeing with him.

At once intellectual and accessible, *Éparpillements* was well received by critics and readers alike. It was a book to be savored. You could leave it on your nightstand, picking it up at random to read one or two bon mots, which you might repeat to their author or within her circles as a mark of your intellectual acumen. The *Paris Herald* honored it as a "Book of the Week" and noted that the epigrams "are reflections, not in the manner of Pascal whose serenity they lack, nor in that of La Rochefoucauld, because they don't lash out . . . it is charm that characterizes the Scatterings of Natalie Clifford Barney, a charm which conceals subtle observations of herself and of others and also, of life."[39] London's popular *Tatler,* after describing Natalie's "wonderful figure and crown of fair hair," raved about the book's amusing sarcasm. "Oui, mon oncle," the article ended, "decidement *Éparpillements* is a volume to travel with."[40]

In many ways *Éparpillements* was a subversive work. Natalie once again refused to hide her sexual proclivities, openly celebrating her love for women with dozens of straightforward, joyful epigrams. A good example: "When she lowers her eyes she seems to hold all the beauty in the world between her eyelids; when she raises them I see only myself in her gaze." Another: "Loving her: having leaps of joy."

The book is doubly subversive by being a strongly worded objection to the traditional woman's role. Barney underlines her antipathy toward marriage and childbearing with remarks such as "To be married is to be neither alone nor together," and "The most beautiful life is spent in creating one's self, not in procreation."

The *pensées* were also shorthand proof, to those who needed it, that literary and intellectual substance existed beneath Natalie's golden hair and charming ways. Miss Flossie could bite.

Read today, *Éparpillements* has one disturbing element: its handful of anti-Semitic epigrams. This seems odd coming from Barney, who exhibited pride in her Jewish heritage and had many Jewish friends. This dichotomy testifies to the great flaw in Natalie's intelligence: her glibness.

Natalie had a lightning-quick mind, an ability to instantly perceive the essence of a situation, and a talent for distilling complications, but she resisted plunging deep and long into an idea. Instead, she preferred a brisk sail across its surface. When you add to this inclination Natalie's oft-voiced pride in having no opinions, it's evident that any subject could become fodder for her epigrammatic mill. In short, she gave little or even no thought to the underlying significance of her remarks and didn't think anybody else did, either. "She secretly thinks that people do not look beyond the surface of a jest," Eva Palmer noted.[41] For Natalie, a witticism was an end in and of itself; any means could be used to accomplish it.

In the climate of the time—decidedly anti-Semitic both in Europe and, to a slightly lesser degree, in the United States—nobody thought twice about epigrams such as Barney's. Far harsher comments were common in everyday conversation, let alone in literature and poetry. While many people had the largesse of heart to question such obvious bigotry, Natalie did not. In fact, her anti-Semitic remarks, as we'll see in a future chapter, would become more frequent.

IN THE DECADE'S first years, two events rocked the Barney family, scandalized Washington, and resulted in many nasty newspaper stories. For once, Natalie wasn't the cause. The spotlight of infamy now shone on her sister and mother.

Laura, always so proper, seemed the least likely of the Barneys to create a stir. Though known primarily for her governmental endeavors and work with the Baha'i, Natalie's younger sister was a woman of many talents. She read, wrote, and translated Persian, authored short stories, and was a good painter. But it was her considerable ability as a sculptor that caused all the trouble.

In the summer of 1910 Laura shipped her latest sculpture from Paris to Alice's Washington home, Studio House. The work, *Reclining Nude,* was of an unclothed woman stretched out and cradling her right arm beneath her head. A note to the caretaker accompanied the statue. Laura asked him to keep it outside covered with canvas, and to sprinkle it every day with water (made of plaster of Paris and cement, it would harden each time it was wet down and allowed to dry). He did as asked, leaving the heavy sculpture to cure where it had been delivered near the front entrance of Studio House.

One windy day in October, the canvas cover blew away and the sculpture was revealed for all to see. This work would raise few eyebrows today, but American culture was so conservative at the time that various state legislatures were considering laws requiring clothing to be placed on nude statues in museums. Consequently, the sight of a nude cement body lying outside Studio House created a sensation. Someone telephoned the newspapers, and reporters came running. As soon as their stories appeared, "sightseeing automobile managers [made plans] to make regular stops in front of the Barney residence to show strangers the statue and tell them through megaphones all of the interesting things about it that they could think of."[42]

Soon tony Sheridan Circle was overrun with tour buses, automobiles, and countless pedestrian gawkers. Members of the Watch and Ward Society, a women's organization devoted to upholding the city's moral values, unanimously concluded that *Reclining Nude* was a moral threat and must be taken away—immediately. They brought their complaints to chief of police Richard Sylvester, who, hoping to stem the crowds, covered the statue with a pup tent. "Barney Statue Shocks Artistic Police Chief!" blared a headline in the *Washington Times.* Another paper reported that he had ordered the cover because "his chivalrous nature revolted against letting the statue of a lady lie exposed to the wind and rain, and because he didn't think it was an out-of-doors work of art anyhow." The *Press* observed that the statue "has attracted the rabble as well as the art-loving, and the rabble is the most numerous among the sightseeing crowds. The comments of the rabble are offensive to the ears of delicately matured women on Sheridan Circle, where the crowd is intensively objectionable."[43]

According to newspaper estimates (probably exaggerated), 25,000 people came the next day to view Laura's work—visible once again because a crowd of drunken rowdies had moved the statue from its pup tent to the pedestal of General Sheridan's sculpture. The story became front-page news around the country, made the leap from the *New York Herald* to that paper's Paris edition, and soon hit English-language newspapers across Europe.

Despite vigorous denials by Alice, who had been in Europe since June, most articles insisted that Natalie—called a "society girl" in one newspaper— posed for the sculpture. "It is simply scandalous," Alice is quoted as saying, "the statement that the figure is that of my daughter. . . . My daughter was not the model. Too much emphasis cannot be placed on that declaration."[44] The *New York American* ran a cabled story in which Laura, too, denied that Natalie posed for the work. Her sister, she noted reasonably, is delicate and graceful, while the sculpture shows a model who is tall and muscular.

Some of the articles focused on Natalie herself, bringing up old scandals and generally raking her over the coals. "Miss Barney's role of model," wrote one reporter, "is only one incident of a remarkable career which has at times set two continents a-talking. At the age of twenty—that was in 1901—she caused a genuine sensation by publishing a book of poems in French which she called 'Portraits-Sonnets de Femmes' . . . It was a book of Lesbian voice— it recalled Sapho. The sheer audacity of the poems pleased the world of society and Miss Barney's name was on every tongue."[45] The *Bar Harbor Record* reminded readers that Natalie "is a remarkably beautiful woman, both in face and figure . . . [but] her wit alike charms and frightens her acquaintances . . . her Portrait Sonnets of Women . . . were not poems that the ordinary American girl of twenty would write, and they drew from one French critic the remark: 'That woman has lived.' "[46]

The nude sculpture story simply wouldn't die. For years Alice would be identified in newspaper articles as, for example, the woman "whose name was brought into prominence by the newspaper accounts of the statue. . . ." A 1911 article in the *New York Times,* about the mansions that had lately sprung up on Washington's Sheridan Circle, identified Alice as the "ever versatile and delightful Mrs. A. C. Barney, she of the statue and art fame." One confused reporter wrote that she had turned the Studio House garage into a Greek temple dedicated to Love when "the chief of police of Washington made [her] move a classic undraped figure from the lawn in front of the Temple away from the public gaze."[47] In the 1960s, when Laura was in her early eighties, she visited Washington, D.C., to approve the Smithsonian's new site for the statue. A photograph was taken in which she symbolically draped the work with a canvas tarp.

Was Natalie the model? Most of the Barneys' friends believed she was, and at one point the Smithsonian's National Museum of American Art listed in its collection a sculpture by Laura dated 1910 and entitled *"Reclining Nude— Natalie."*[48] On the other hand, in a 1961 letter Natalie referred irately to "that stupid statue of my sister's that is neither a representation of art nor of myself."[49]

THE SECOND BARNEY SCANDAL hit with great fanfare a few months later when, in the spring of 1911, Alice shocked everyone she knew by marrying young Christian Hemmick in Paris. She had come alone to France the previous summer, probably viewing their long separation (until spring) as a practical test to determine if their love would remain strong.

She also wanted time alone with her daughters to prepare them for the unexpected gift of a stepfather much younger than they were. She suspected they might be upset, and she was right. Practical Laura, the family's money manager, was convinced that Christian was no more than a gigolo. Pointing out that she herself was eight years older than Hemmick, she warned that social humiliation, if not outright ostracism, would be her mother's lot. Natalie's objections took a more feminist perspective. After years of marital imprisonment, she said, Alice was finally a free woman. Why entrap herself once again? Both daughters finally accepted the upcoming marriage when they realized how happy their mother was.

Laura, too, was planning to marry. The idea of a double wedding was first broached by Alice, but Laura and her husband-to-be, Hippolyte Dreyfus, were agreeable to the idea. Born in Paris in 1873 into a wealthy and artistic Jewish family, Dreyfus became a lawyer and practiced before the city's Court of Appeals. In 1900 he converted to the Baha'i faith, and soon afterward met Laura. He gave up the law a few years later to study Arabic and Persian, intending to translate Baha'i scriptures into French. A fervent Baha'i adherent and a compassionate human being, Hippolyte's interests dovetailed perfectly with Laura's. In addition, he had the ability, like Natalie, to make the serious Laura lighten up. It was common knowledge among Natalie's friends, however, that Laura and Hippolyte had entered into a *mariage blanc.*

In February, a month before Christian was to leave Washington for Paris, word broke of the impending marriage. The newspapers went—there is no other word to describe it—berserk. "Rich Widow, 61, To Marry Man of 26," trumpeted one.* "[He] Swears to Love for Rich Widow," sang another. The *New York Times* slyly revealed that "Mr. Hemmick has been active in the younger set, and Mrs. Barney has been a leader in her own circle," and then rehashed the infamous statue incident, which "brought Mrs. Barney and her two grown daughters . . . into international notoriety." Somewhat uncharita-

---

*Their actual ages were fifty-three and twenty-three.

bly, the *Club-Fellow and Washington Mirror* of March 15 wondered "how the Barney girls will accept their new papa. They cut loose from Mama's apron strings . . . years ago and have been following their several bents, but . . . they may not take to [Alice] presenting them with a father younger than they themselves are, for neither of the Barney girls will ever see thirty again."

Not everyone was so negative. Writing in *Washington Society* on March 4, Hobart Brook admitted that, though a significant age difference existed between the betrothed couple, "if the same standard that is applied to a man that he is only as old as he feels, should be applied to Mrs. Barney, she would be counted young, indeed, for she is as buoyant in spirit as a girl of sixteen and as full of life and as keen for enjoyment. She has truly found the fountain of perennial youth, this gifted woman, and will be quite as likely to make her young lover happy as would a woman nearer his own age."

But such an enlightened approach was rare, and Alice found herself chased through Paris and constantly bedeviled by pesky reporters. In late March, hoping to be left alone, she informed a Paris correspondent for the *Boston American* that she wasn't engaged to Hemmick "or anybody else . . . According to some newspapers, marriage . . . is my ceaseless ambition. I wish they would turn their attention to something more interesting to the public."[50]

Meanwhile Hemmick endured nasty insinuations, from friends and newspapers alike, that he was marrying Alice for her money. He responded by proving his love with a grand gesture: he rejected her wealth, offering to sign away any rights. After seeking legal advice, Alice placed her $3 million inheritance from Albert into an irrevocable trust for her daughters. She and Christian would live on the income.

At this news the headlines grew even more frenzied. "Widow, 61, Gives Away $3,000,000 to Wed Boy!" proclaimed the *Chicago Journal*. After referring to Alice as the woman "who turned explorer Stanley's hair white," the article focused on her latest outrage: "Mrs. Barney . . . has transferred her fortune of $3,000,000 to her daughters, Natalie and Laura, so that gossips might not declare that her youthful suitor had married her for her money."[51]

Despite worldwide attention, the double wedding went ahead as planned on April 15. The *New York Times* reported the event at length the next day under the relatively dignified headline, "Mrs. Barney Weds Young Hemmick— Wealthy Widow of Albert Barney, Aged 61, Married to Youth of 26 in Paris." By that time the young couple—one in years, the other at heart—were already enjoying their honeymoon in Venice.

Laura and Hippo did not emerge unscathed by criticism, either. Their sin, as far as the gossips were concerned, was in adopting a hyphenated surname. Upon marriage, each became known as Dreyfus-Barney, which was highly unusual at the time. "Just what Laura thinks of her [husband]," one newspaper opined, "may be judged by the manner in which Laura now styles herself—Dreyfus-Barney, if you please. The Barney eccentricity is ever uppermost in mother and daughters alike."[52]

ALICE WASN'T THE ONLY woman in Natalie's intimate sphere to marry a younger man that year. In June, still achingly beautiful at forty-one, Liane became the wife of a twenty-six-year-old Romanian prince. She had met Georges Ghika of Moldavia, whose aunt was Queen Nathalie of Serbia, in a sanatorium, where Georges was recovering from a failed suicide attempt over his unrequited love for an actress.

The young prince was physically tiny but quite handsome. Sensitive, dreamy, and a poet, he was much different from the powerful men Liane had known. Taking up with a man so much younger resulted in mockery within the demimonde and in the journals. In *La Vie Parisienne,* Colette wrote that she'd caught sight of Liane walking with Georges, looking like a happy young mother out with her grown son. The cruel remark so angered Liane that she nursed a rancor toward Colette for the rest of her life.

There had always been those who felt compelled to let a courtesan know that, despite beauty and wealth, she was still just a whore. The more successful the courtesan, the nastier the abuse she must occasionally endure. Liane had long been used to certain "proper" women turning away when in her presence. The newspapers that praised her beauty one day would just as willingly revile her the next. And even the tattiest bourgeoise walking down the street felt free to hiss unpleasant words in her direction.

It was to save Liane from such treatment that Georges proposed marriage. One day in the spring of 1910, he and Liane had a pleasant lunch with a female friend in St.-Germain-en-Laye. Afterward, they browsed antique shops. The fashionable Liane was wearing a futuristic hat by the high-society milliner Lewis; most women still wore huge hats crowned with ostrich plumes, but hers was very small and decorated with white lace. As the trio strolled about, they happened to pass two big-plumed women who didn't hesitate to make loud fun of the cutting-edge hat—and then moved on to a critique of Liane herself.

"Just look at that hat!" one cried.

"It's Liane de Pougy," said the other, "the Paris tart."[53]

They broke into laughter. Georges advised them that, before mocking others, they should first look in the mirror. The women's husbands had been following behind. One of them hit Georges who, his hands filled with packages, couldn't return the favor. Liane and Blanche sought help. The police came, and eventually the matter was resolved in court.

Georges's reaction was to accomplish what Natalie had so longed to do years before: he removed Liane from the life she'd been leading. She accepted his marriage proposal. In spite of her past, she wanted a Catholic ceremony (her first husband's death meant that she could be considered a widow, not a divorcée). Her confession just before the wedding mass was a simple matter. She informed the priest that, except for murder and robbery, she'd done everything.

The prince and the courtesan were married on June 8, 1910. Eighteen-year-old Marco, Liane's son from her short-lived and brutal marriage, was living in Australia and thus unable to attend the wedding. However, one of her brothers, his wife, and their two children were present. Georges's family, furious about the union, refused to attend; they would later pretend the marriage had never taken place. The worst blow was delivered by his aunt, Queen Nathalie, who forbade anyone in the family to speak to Liane. She also cut off Georges's income, making him dependent on whatever small amounts his mother chose to dole out. This was no problem for the newlyweds—at first, anyway. Shrewd with money, Liane had invested her earnings well. She was also smart enough to ask Georges to sign a prenuptial agreement separating their property.

Everyone, it seemed, had a hard time accepting the transformation of Liane de Pougy, Queen of Love, into Anne-Marie Ghika, Princess. In high-society parlors, even on her husband's arm, she encountered cold shoulders, upturned noses, and averted heads. The journals and newspapers never let up. *Fantasio* bewailed her marriage, calling it the symbolic end of the demimonde. "And now she's a princess," snorted *La Vie Parisenne* shortly after the wedding day.[54] A few months later the same paper noted nastily that "the Prince and Princess Ghika went to see their racehorses at their trainer's, Raoul, since the Princess, after having run through Tout-Paris, now wants to run the thoroughbreds . . ."[55]

Gossip and nastiness made life so difficult for the couple that, in the winter of 1911, they decamped for Algeria and took a long-term lease on a villa. Here, safely removed from wagging tongues and mocking glances, they would remain until the spring of 1913.

Natalie did not attend Liane's wedding. She did, however, send a gift: a copy of her recently published paean to Renée Vivien, *Je me souviens*. Liane received it gracefully. In her thank-you note she mentioned that the prince loved Natalie's writing and looked forward to meeting her.

DURING THE CENTURY's early years, Natalie, and almost everyone she knew, had been mesmerized by a dance called the tango. Probably born in the bordellos of Buenos Aires early in the century, the tango had leaped across the seas to become the rage of fashionable Europe—one of its early fans, it was said, was the grand duchess Anastasia of Russia.

Parisians in particular loved the dance, responding to its throbbing music and sexy yet formalized moves. In restaurants, a dessert called Bananas Tango was every bit as popular as Peaches Melba; Argentine orchestras, genuine and otherwise, drew enthusiastic crowds; tango parties were in vogue. When Natalie mentioned to Gourmont that she wanted to learn the dance, he imposed on one of his close friends, André Rouveyre, to teach her how. Reluctantly, only to please Gourmont, Rouveyre called upon Barney.

Thus began one of the most important friendships of Natalie's life. André Rouveyre—close friend of major French literary and artistic figures such as Apollinaire, André Gide, and Henri Matisse; a talented artist and writer; a legendary ladies' man—became one of Barney's closest friends and confidants until his 1962 death. He was often at rue Jacob, and Natalie made frequent visits to his home at Barbizon, near Fontainebleau. Few people knew Natalie better than Rouveyre, and even to him she remained something of a mystery. He once said that, by combining decency and dissolution in equal measures, she represented an inconceivable paradox.

True to Gourmont's promise, Rouveyre taught Natalie and one of her current loves, the Baronne Ilse Deslandes, to tango. "In that sacred dance," Rouveyre recalled of their first lesson, "I guided the uncertain feet of Mlle. Barney."[56] But, an apt pupil, Natalie soon tangoed with style. For a while she seemed always to be rushing off to a tango party, or sponsoring one, or teaching someone else how to make the sensuous moves. She wasn't alone in her enthusiasm. The whole world, it seemed, was moving to the tango beat, with its dotted rhythm, 4/4 time, and dramatic posturing. It was irresistible, it was fun, it was magic.

When the music abruptly ended, everyone was taken by surprise.

TEN

The Great War

1914–1919

It's raining my soul, it's raining, but it's raining dead eyes.
—*Guillaume Apollinaire*

Viewed as a drama, the war is somewhat disappointing
—*D. W. Griffith*

THE WEATHER IN PARIS was absolutely perfect on that last Sunday of June 1914. It was hot, clear, bright, and sunny, and people were out in droves. All across town they strolled the broad avenues, walked sedately through parks, rowed about on lakes, or simply lay on their backs in tall grass, watching clouds move with languid grace across the sky.

At the Parc des princes, a crowd of hundreds cheered cyclists departing on the month-long run of the twelfth annual Tour de France. Nearby, at Longchamps racecourse, Baron Maurice de Rothschild's Sardanapale narrowly won the yearly Grand Prix. Most racing-goers, though, were far more interested in the scantily clad couturier mannequins who "fluttered about with butterfly brilliance in fashions which made the ordinary person gasp from sheer wonder at the courage they showed in daring to wear things in which an angel might have caught a cold."[1]

That day the restaurants of the Bois shimmered in a kind of golden glory that would be remembered years later with a sigh. In the sumptuous gardens of Pre-Catalan one heard the buzz of moneyed voices, the pop of champagne corks, the harmonious tinkle of crystal glasses joined in a toast. At stylish Armenonville, formally suited men and big-hatted women in long narrow skirts danced round and round to an orchestra. The cafés dotting the park served up far more glasses than usual of lemon pressé and eau de minerale, and the dusty allées were crowded with leisurely walkers.

The Duchesse de Clermont-Tonnerre would recall the day's luxuriously slow pace. She had gone with a few friends to Marly, outside Paris, where her family possessed a huge, old, very rusty key to the gates surrounding Louis XIV's ancient forests. The group wandered lazily among ruins of the king's Twelve Zodiac Pavillons, destroyed in the Revolution. They marveled at the hydraulic machine that had once raised water from the Seine and sent it on, via an aqueduct, to Versailles. They peered into a stand of impenetrable brush, hoping to spot remnants of the king's once-renowned Théâtre de Verdure. Later, after lunch, "we were talking of one thing and another in the scant shade of a chestnut-tree . . . making idle plans. . . ."[2] So peaceful, so calm were their surroundings, that someone mused aloud: "Perhaps while we are sitting here carefree and lazy, something is happening. History may be taking place and momentous events looming."[3] The comment seemed amusing, the world far away.

Indeed, it was a very pleasant day, that June 28 of 1914. It might have been a completely forgettable day, too, if not for a single event that occurred far from the fashionable racecourses and concert halls, the sparkling lakes and manicured parks, the exquisite ruins of another time. In a place few of the day's revelers knew or cared about, a husband and wife were murdered. In many ways they were as unremarkable as one of Tolstoy's happy families: they had married for love, given birth to three children, and by all accounts were satisfied with life and each other.

His job, however, made them more than just another happy couple: he was the Archduke Francis Ferdinand, heir to the Austro-Hungarian throne. That day they were making a formal state visit to Sarajevo, Bosnia. The archduke, fitted out in a splendid military uniform, his cocked hat topped by long green plumes, was being chauffeured through the streets in an open Graef und Stift sports car, his beloved Sophie beside him. Suddenly a young man stepped from the crowd and threw a bomb. It rolled off the car and exploded in the street, leaving the royal couple unharmed. The motorcade sped away from danger toward its destination, the town hall, and then slowed down. Suddenly, unbelievably, another man ran up to the automobile, drew a gun, and fired twice. Sophie died immediately; the archduke, a short time later.

Their deaths on that otherwise peaceful June Sunday would lead directly and almost immediately to the first great war of the modern age. And with its arrival the last graceful vestiges of the nineteenth century disappeared forever.

NEXT DAY, the *New York Times* headline read: "Heir to Austria's Throne Slain with His Wife by a Bosnian Youth to Avenge Seizure of His Country." The first three pages were devoted to the assassination, and most major newspapers around the world reported the slaying in similar fashion. The story was of monumental importance to journalists, diplomats, politicos—anybody, really, who possessed a savvy understanding of Europe's pressure-cooker politics.

But to many intelligent people the events meant little. American writer and hostess Muriel Draper had a typical reaction: "A man in Sarajevo—where was Sarajevo?—killed an Austrian Archduke . . . shot him and his Duchesse as they sat in the archducal motor-car on the way to the Town Hall of Sarajevo. Why? Doubtless . . . another of those remote Near East problems!"[4] Soon, like millions of others, she came to understand the impact those "remote" problems would have on her life. "The Golden era," she admitted, "was at an end."[5]

The empire's reaction to the murder of its Archduke was slow but fateful. On July 23, nearly four weeks after Sarajevo, Austria-Hungary submitted ten humiliating demands to Serbia, threatening to take military action unless all were met. On the twenty-fifth, Serbia accepted eight demands but rejected two; three days later, Austria declared war against Serbia.

Across the continent, other nations rattled metaphoric sabers and issued threats. Old resentments sprang to life, ancient hatreds seethed anew. Alliances were made, or broken. In a classic domino effect—propelled by economic rivalries, imperialist notions, and territorial claims—the great powers fell, one by one, into war. As the situation progressed, more and more countries joined in. Eventually, thirty-two nations around the globe were involved in the tangled and impenetrable mess that would be known as the Great War.

France's chief concern from the beginning was Germany, which was hungry to establish itself as the foremost power in Europe. On August 3, marching through Belgium, Germany declared war on France. Through August, the Germans managed to advance into and capture France's Lorraine region. The French fell back to the Marne River, with the Germans in hot pursuit. At that point few doubted that the Germans would take Paris, and the French government fled to Bordeaux.

The situation looked bleak until, on September 6, after the Germans had crossed the Marne, the French army circled around Paris and attacked. In this, the First Battle of the Marne, the French halted the German army's advance.

More than half a million French and German men lost their lives in the week-long battle, the bloodiest in history to that point. By year's end, both sides had established their positions. They dug in, built trenches, and scarcely moved for the next three years. It was a new kind of war, one in which soldiers died through slow and painful attrition rather than heroic action in battle. But they died nonetheless.

As HOSTILITIES HEATED UP, Natalie was urged by friends to return to the United States. At first she agreed. She packed her bags and traveled north in early August, intending to sail home from Britain. At the last minute, however, she was undecided and remained on the north coast. With her trunks sent ahead, she ended up "going about in sneekers and an old black dress!"[6]

After the first panic wore off, she realized that she couldn't bear to leave Lily, and that, in any event, France had become her country just as much as the United States. She had an unrealistic notion that "being an American I risk less than others and can protect them more—I have a flag and will wave it over the heads that are dear to me here."[7] However, she knew that it was dangerous even for an American to remain in Europe, and for that reason had a new will drafted.

When it looked as if the Germans would take Paris, more than half a million Parisians retreated to their provincial hometowns or summer dwellings. Lily moved into her charmingly cheerful, slightly down-at-the-heels lodge in Honfleur. Lucie took up residence nearby, at her Pavillon de la Reine, a tiny but pretty house built in the eighteenth century for a visit by Marie Antoinette. For a while Natalie divided her time between them while deciding whether to live through the war's "stupidity and uselessness" in Bordeaux. When it became clear that the Germans were stuck indefinitely on the Marne, she returned to Paris. The French government officially returned to the capital on December 11.

On a war footing now, Paris was a very different place. Cafés, bars, and restaurants were forced to close by 10:30. There were no buses, the Métro stopped running early in the evening, and at night the streetlights stayed dark and windows were blacked out. Writing to her mother, Natalie noted that, despite the war's hardships, everybody continued to enjoy life. "What a blessing a nice nature is," she said, "and here it is a whole nation's nature! I'd rather live with the French even in time of war than with any other nation in time of peace."[8]

To many, the city seemed a better place—not least because most of those pesky, free-spending foreigners had disappeared. "Four months earlier Paris belonged to the Americans," wrote a wartime resident. ". . . American money was the dominating factor of external Parisian life. Without a word of warning she became French."9

In between the daily bombings, Paris developed a peaceful hush. To Alice's old friend, Elizabeth Nourse, "Paris is too beautiful now, so quiet, so exquisite in the pale autumn sunshine. And the nights! Nights of beauty—with the most wonderful effect of light and shade—because there are so few street lamps, and the great masses of shadow—the moon beams like silver—all like a wonderful painting—painted by God."10

Another quality that braced everyone's spirits was the great feeling of patriotism. A popular entertainer, Madame Chenal, sang the "Marseillaise" to raise money for war charities. "She was magnificent," remembered Pearl Adam. "She did not disdain to be theatrical—wore a white Greek robe, an Alsatian bow with a tricolour cockade, and when she lifted her arms the dress became a French flag. She also carried a tricolour. She kissed it. At the end, she rolled it around her, and drew from the folds of her dress a sabre encrusted with jewels which she held aloft while the curtain fell."11

To Natalie's surprise, the war transformed most of the privileged women she knew into angry Amazons intent on firing arrows at the enemy. Liane turned her home into an infirmary. Colette worked first as a nurse and then as a journalist on the front lines. Lucie, now divorced from J.C., undertook nursing at the Honfleur hospital and donated money for an expensive X-ray machine. Lily Gramont worked as a nurse at the rail station that received wounded soldiers, dealing with endless litters of anguished men, mangled bodies with missing limbs, the smell of gangrene, and constant screams of pain. She also helped raise funds for medical supplies.

Liane, Colette, Lily, and Lucie were part of an enthusiastic and patriotic trend among women. Many had never worked a day in their lives, but with the outbreak of hostilities they eagerly aided the war effort. Some did what they knew best—producing fêtes and teas to raise money, or gathering with friends to knit warm gloves and sweaters for soldiers. Others endured grueling, often punishing tasks without complaint. They nursed the wounded or ran canteens, and the most daring drove ambulances right onto the battlefield. Lily wasn't the only titled gentlewoman of Barney's acquaintance who willingly dirtied her hands. The Duchesse de Rohan transformed her mansion into a military hospital in which she labored "body and soul . . . all her time . . . consecrated to the sick and wounded."12 Lady Westmacott joined the ambulance corps. The Princesse Marthe Bibesco worked as a nurse. Princesse Edmond de Polignac helped Marie Curie establish clinics where her radium therapy could be used on wounded soldiers.

Many American women in France rushed to aid the war effort, including some who were or would become friends of Natalie. When a bad back dashed Romaine Brooks's hopes of driving an ambulance, she established a fund to care for artists wounded in battle (and was later rewarded with a bronze plaque by the French government). Gertrude Stein and Alice Toklas delivered hospital supplies in the south of France. The future owner of the bookstore Shakespeare and Company, Sylvia Beach, worked as a Red Cross secretary. Elizabeth Nourse collected money for refugees and artists. Laura Dreyfus-Barney worked tirelessly for the American Ambulance Corps, the American Red Cross, and the Refugee and Repatriation Service. Toward war's end she was instrumental in establishing a children's hospital in Avignon. For her efforts, she would be honored in 1920 with the Médaille de le Reconnaissance Française.*

And Natalie? Clearly, laboring on behalf of anybody was incongruous with the Amazon's worldview. A woman so imperious that she described herself as *"plus royaliste que le roi"* wasn't about to murmur comforting words to gangrenous soldiers or flex her fingers with knitting needles. Besides, her deep loathing of that "gross stupidity," war, prevented her from being proactive. To Natalie, participation in the war effort was akin to supporting the very concept of war itself. Someone had to hold fast at the gates of civilization, protecting art and love and beauty. Why not her? The opening stanza of a poem she wrote during the war, "Apology," attempts to explain this outlook:

> While blue and khaki share the heroes' mud,
> And women tend in white or weep in grey,
> Though all expressiveness seems over-dressed,
> Yet must some wear the colours of their hearts
> Upon their sleeves, like troubadors, of old;
> And sing, and sometimes write their singing down.

Natalie turned herself into that troubadour, becoming a kind of early peacenik in the process—one with feminist underpinnings. She believed that love, the province of women, demanded far greater heroism than war, the creature of men. To love was life-embracing; to kill, the opposite. She hated the fact that women raised children, only to see them die in war. "Women would not waste so readily and uselessly the lives they had such care and pains in bearing," she wrote. "Why should they submit to the massacre of the innocent, one generation after another . . . and allow them to be brought up as live-stock for the inevitable killing?"[13] She came to such theories painfully,

---

*Laura would receive at least two additional honors from the French. In 1925 she became a Chevalier de la Légion d'Honneur; in 1937, an Officier de l'Ordre de la Légion d'Honneur.

because she saw many grieving mothers in her own life, even among former lovers.

In early December Liane's only child, Marc, was killed in battle. An early aeronaut whose flying adventures in India and Indochina had made headlines, he was considered one of the best pilots of the age.* The prince personally delivered the news of his death to Liane, who sank into a long, deep depression. She recovered, but Marc's death haunted her forever. "I did not love my son enough when he was alive," she despaired. "I was all woman—woman, not mother. My love was not able—didn't really want—to make a place for itself in his gloriously beautiful, excessively independent life. Oh how I have regretted it, how I have wept and been punished!"[14]

Natalie's wartime salon turned into a meeting ground for peace lovers. At rue Jacob there was no need to keep up the kind of chauvinistic pretense required in the larger society. It was perfectly acceptable to say that war was hell. There were those who criticized Natalie for continuing her Fridays at this time, but by doing so she offered a profound sense of continuity to people whose lives had become disconnected and chaotic.

According to Magdeleine Wauthier, anyone present at those wartime Fridays remembered them as a respite "where the intellectual atmosphere was more important than material cares, where one's mind could recompose itself in a calm, beautiful atmosphere [in which] liberty of thought, of opinion, of expression reigned. . . . Only around the little Temple of Friendship, hidden in a garden, was it permitted to [say]that the war was cruel, horrible, and that the political errors which prolonged it were unpardonable. It didn't solve anything, but it was a relief. . . . The weeks, months and years passed, mournful and sad. But the Fridays which brought me there were good days for me. I found there the courage to live and a spiritual enrichment which has never left me."[15] Or, as Gabriel-Louis Pringué described those days: "One came to Miss Barney's feeling tired and harassed, but left reinvigorated."[16]

Another visitor who sought solace at the salon was a young American poet, Alan Seeger. A friend and classmate of T. S. Eliot's at Harvard, Seeger moved to Paris after his 1910 graduation. He came to know Natalie before the war, and particularly enjoyed their conversations about Pauline Tarn, whose work he admired. Inspired like many young men by grandiose notions of heroism, he joined the French Foreign Legion in 1914. "I have the feeling of being in an

---

*A book detailing the adventures of Marc and a fellow pilot is *Deux grands chevaliers de l'aventure: Marc Pourpe et Raoul Lufbery* (1937).

immensely magnified boys' camp," he confided to a friend, "where work is play, war a sport, and everyone is joyous and light-hearted." On leaves to Paris he continued his visits to rue Jacob, occasionally attending a Friday—a charming retreat from the war's brutality, he believed. Seeger died in battle on July 4, 1916, something he may have foreseen in his most famous poem, "Rendezvous":

> I have a rendezvous with Death
> At some disputed barricade,
> When Spring comes back with rustling shade
> And apple-blossoms fill the air—
> I have a rendezvous with Death . . .

Oddly enough, among rue Jacob's peaceniks were a few high-ranking diplomats actively engaged in the war. Most important among them was the handsome, self-assured Philippe Berthelot, France's secretary general of foreign affairs (equivalent to the U.S. secretary of state) and a major designer of the postwar peace accord. Berthelot, who appreciated creativity in others, knew many writers and artists (he and painter Marie Laurencin were lovers at one time). He was close friends with Natalie, who once said that he "protected" her and the salon during the war. Two other diplomats often present were Oscar Milosz, a Lithuanian who represented his country in Paris, and Paul Claudel of France's foreign service. Diplomats like those two, excelling at both statesmanship and literary creation, don't exist anymore. Claudel was a respected poet and playwright, while Milosz was renowned for his mystical and elegiac poetry (he was also the cousin of Czeslaw Milosz, 1980 winner of the Nobel Prize for Literature).

There was nothing passive about Natalie's pacifist stance, since many of her gatherings were pointedly against war. She once honored Henri Barbusse, author of a bitter, shockingly graphic antiwar novel, *Le feu* (The Fire), which won the 1916 Prix Goncourt. On another occasion a French translation of Goethe's *Faust* was read aloud to candlelight while the city was bombarded by German bombs. In July 1915 she hosted an "Heure Commémorative," an afternoon to honor the dead. It was held before the Temple of Friendship, which was "lighted up for the sacred ceremony like an ardent chapel."[17] The day included a performance of Paul Dupin's *Canon for Four Voices,* a dance recital by Armen Ohanian with harp and flute accompaniment, and the reading of poetry written by deceased friends such as Robert d'Humières and Renée Vivien. Present that day was the sculptor Auguste Rodin.

An interesting side story is connected to the Heure Commémorative. Back in June 1912 Natalie had hosted "An Hour of Poetry in Memory of Renée Vivien." Pauline's sister, Antoinette, was furious when she learned about the event. She immediately penned a frosty letter to Natalie, addressing her as "Madame" and forbidding her ever again to use Pauline's pen name in such gatherings. Failure to comply, she added, would result in legal action. The Heure Commémorative allowed Natalie once again to pay public tribute to Pauline without worry of Antoinette, who could take no action with the war waging.

On New Year's Day 1916, approximately one hundred wounded soldiers came to rue Jacob for a matinee of luminous pictures (lantern slides). It was, Natalie thought, "most impressive. Most of them were armless or legless and had the croix de guerre—some fine intellects with amputated hands—fortunately the house was dark for the pictures—so the horror of all this seemed less obvious."[18] She was struck by the sincere and unresentful way the soldiers sang the "Marseillaise."

The most significant wartime event at rue Jacob was the Women's Congress for Peace, attended not only by Natalie's Parisian friends, but by women from many countries and professions. The mostly female speakers ranged from the director of a munitions factory to a political economist. One prominent attendee was a French writer and political theorist, Marie Lénéru, whose works were strongly pacifist. Scarlet fever had left her deaf and partly blind, but she nonetheless participated in numerous antiwar activities. Another attendee was a "gentle, white-haired little woman who turned out to be Mrs. Pankhurst,"[19] whom Natalie had first met while a student at Miss Ely's. Almost sixty when she visited rue Jacob, the English suffragist had temporarily turned her attention from the feminist movement to furthering a peaceful solution to the war.

Natalie listened attentively to all the speakers, but was disturbed by the way grand ideas seemed inevitably to dissolve into petty arguments. In the end, she decided that this would be the "last time my literary salon took on the colours of political enquiry [sic] . . . And I now felt like [saying] that whatever my passions had been, they were no-wise political. . . ."[20]

What she didn't realize was that her antiwar and feminist views could not have been more political. For example, her belief that the only way to stop the wars created by men was for women to become stronger was completely antithetical to the status quo. "Perhaps a reign of powerful women is necessary," she wrote, "to make, or unmake when need be, powerful men. . . . If the voices of women are hushed up like children's—they the courageous mothers of men—if they have no worthy representatives for their cause, if they cannot rule equally with men over the lives they together created, should not the stronger in the instinct of race preservation prevail; and the Matriarchal again dominate the Patriarchal? If, through all these centuries of patriarchal rule, this war-curse has not been averted, but increased and made more terrible, is it indeed madness to hope that women might stop this madness?"[21]

SOMETIME AROUND THE START of the war—they never could remember exactly when—Natalie met the painter Romaine Brooks, probably the greatest love of her life. Their relationship would last for more than fifty years, until Romaine broke it off for good when both were over ninety.

Born Beatrice Romaine Goddard in 1874, she was the third and last child of a wealthy American family. Her father, an alcoholic who died young from liver complications, separated from her mother soon after Romaine's birth. She was thus left to the care of a deranged mother who hated her to the same degree that she worshiped her only son, an epileptic named Saint Mar. Romaine's childhood was extremely unhappy and emotionally abusive. Her biographer, Meryle Secrest, described her upbringing as "an atmosphere of supernatural evil . . . of childish terror, of adolescent suffering, of the inner anguish that accompanies the death of hope, and the correspondingly valiant struggle not to be overwhelmed by life."[22]

There is no denying that Romaine Brooks's childhood gouged deep scars into her emotional makeup. All her life she was plagued by depression, crippling insecurities, and a profound distrust of people that often veered into paranoia. All these emotional peculiarities she blamed on her upbringing. "My life is certainly . . . quite incomprehensible to most people," she once told Natalie. "But as I was a child-martyr I can't be like others [and now] seek peace and quiet away from nasty people."[23]

After a series of Dickensian childhood experiences, nineteen-year-old Romaine Brooks came to Paris in 1893 to study art and music on a grudgingly given, barely sustainable allowance from her mother. She tried to bide her time, waiting for the money she would receive at her majority, but, restless and unhappy, decided to strike out on her own. She studied voice for a while and was good enough to appear on a cabaret stage, but then decided to pursue art studies in Rome. Still a virgin, she fell in love with a fellow student, a young Englishman named John Fothergill.

In the summer of 1899 Romaine visited the island of Capri, which harbored a community of creative expatriates. Many, such as writers Somerset Maugham and Norman Douglas, were homosexual. The atmosphere was tolerant, at least to foreigners, and one could get along cheaply with only a bare income from home. Romaine lived and painted in an abandoned church in the poorest part of Capri, with a view of the sea spread far below. She became close friends with a handsome homosexual Englishman named John Brooks, and received her first commission as a painter. For the first time in her life, she felt that she had a home. When her mother died in 1902, she inherited millions, and, for reasons that have never been understood, married Brooks. When they separated a year later, she gave him a small allowance. In 1905, after maintaining her own studio in London, she moved to Paris.

Although Brooks was attracted to and had affairs with women, one of her most profound relationships was with a man. In 1910 she met Gabriele d'Annunzio, the Italian writer and heroic soldier whose prowess as a lover was legendary (his most famous conquest was actress Eleonora Duse, Bernhardt's only rival). Their emotional connection was filled with passion and anguish, although it's not clear if the relationship was sexually consummated. The friendship that developed would last until d'Annunzio's death in 1938.

As a painter, Romaine Brooks had the uncanny ability to see, and the artistic courage to reveal, what lay beyond a sitter's surface. Early on she adopted a primarily black, gray, and white palette, and by pairing her sober colors and unique psychological perceptions, she produced haunting, cruelly accurate portraits. Her subjects gaze uncompromisingly at the viewer, their innermost pith emphasized by unrelieved monochrome.

A critic observed in 1926 that "in [her] portrait of the most à la mode young writer in France, Paul Morand, one again gets a gust of despair. It is almost as if Morand had just realized how thin was the veneer of his present popularity, and how hollow the volume it covered."[24] Lily Gramont described Romaine's work as "excellent, dismally excellent, likenesses of her sitters at the very moment when some secret bitterness gives their countenances the nobility of regret."[25] Count Robert de Montesquiou dubbed her the "Thief of Souls." Such paintings, at once attracting and chilling viewers, brought acclaim. Brooks's first exhibit, at the prestigious Galeries Durand-Ruel in 1910, won high praise.

One of the few portraits by Romaine Brooks that manages to convey warmth is her 1920 portrait of Natalie, *l'Amazone.* In this work Barney sits quietly, wrapped in a fur stole. On a table to her left is a small sculpture of a galloping horse meant to symbolize her Amazon-like qualities. To the rear, barely visible through a soft and snowy haze, is the *pavillon.* Natalie stares somberly, almost without expression, at the viewer; few people ever saw this quiet, slightly pensive side of Barney. The painting now forms part of the collection of, and is on permanent display at, the Musée Carnavalet in Paris. Fittingly, the museum resides in the former home of Mme. de Sévigné, one of the most famed of Natalie's salon predecessors.

Romaine had long been aware of the Amazon. During her brief friendship with Pauline Tarn, she had grudgingly listened to endless complaints about

Barney's wicked ways, but she "found little interest in listening to endless love grievances which are so often devoid of any logical justification."[26] She frequently heard Natalie discussed in American circles—sometimes maliciously, as with the "pouter pigeons" discussed earlier. But it seemed to Romaine that, for every nasty remark, a laudatory comment was not far behind. Such a schism made her curious, and she had long wondered what Natalie, whom she often spotted walking or riding along the chestnut-lined allées of the Bois, was really like. Oddly, although they had friends in common, they had never managed to meet.

That changed one day when Lady Anglesly invited Romaine to a reception at her Versailles home. Introduced to Natalie at long last, Brooks considered her "a miracle. Though she had lived . . . among many dark unhealthy people, she remained uncontaminated, as fresh as a spring morning. . . . Her 'esprit' was used neither as a weapon of defense nor of attack, but rather as a game wherein she found few opponents worthy of her subtle repartee. She never ruffled anyone. . . . Her rebellion against conventions was not combative, as was mine. She simply wanted to follow her own inclinations."[27] Natalie offered Romaine a ride home from the party, and their relationship began.

Natalie was thirty-seven when she met Romaine. Relatively young, she was still slender, still tossing around that long mass of blond hair, piercing people's souls with her icy blue eyes, and drawing attention with her electrifying presence. Romaine, too, had a strong charismatic appeal—although, as opposed to Natalie's inclusionary magnetism, hers was all about exclusion. Nobody captured this quality better than English writer Compton Mackenzie, who knew her on Capri. He and his wife, Faith, were living there in August 1919 when Romaine visited, and he was bowled over by her commanding aura. "The lesbian dovecotes were fluttered by the arrival of Romaine Brooks," he recalled.[28] Among the doves were pianist Renata Borgatti and a beautiful, aristocratic Italian named Mimi Franchetti. They, together with Romaine, would serve as the real-life models for three major characters in Mackenzie's 1928 novel, *Extraordinary Women,* a farce centering around a group of lesbians living on Capri during the Great War.

Romaine, called Olimpia Leigh in the novel, "never had a misgiving about the power of her genius and personality to compel recognition. She was not beautiful . . . but her body though little was not shapeless and her throat though tawny as the nightingale's was beautifully modeled, and her eyes as dark and bright, yet not like the bird's apprehensive. Olimpia seemed a big name for so small a person until one heard her speak, and then it could no longer be felt that she was overweighted by it."[29]

Faith Mackenzie confirmed Brooks's personal power: "Romaine was a painter of established reputation, and to me a figure of intriguing importance, because for the first time I met a woman complete in herself, isolated mentally and psychically from the rest of her kind, independent in her judgments, accepting or rejecting as she pleased movements, ideas and people. The arrival of this striking personality was a sensation. . . . Feverish bouquets of exhausted blooms lay about [Romaine's] big studio; letters and invitations strewed her desk, ignored for the most part, while she, wrapped in her cloak, would wander down to the town as the evening cooled and sit in the darkest corner of Morgano's Café terrace, maddeningly remote and provocative."[30]

In short, Barney and Brooks could not have been greater opposites. Natalie was given to bountiful, easy laughter; Romaine rarely smiled. Natalie was a model of energy and health; Romaine was constantly abed with real and imagined illness. Natalie was a highly social and utterly confident being, seemingly impervious to slight and insult; Romaine was happiest in solitude and found offense in the most casual remark. They even *looked* opposite: blond Natalie with her impenetrable blue gaze; brunette Romaine, whose big brown eyes possessed fathomless depths. "One could say that Romaine and Miss Barney were completely different," Natalie's longtime housekeeper said. "One was completely black, and the other completely white; one laughed, and the other . . ."[31]

In a sense, their union was a real-world embodiment of Romaine's black and white palette—a living chiaroscuro. Whatever one was, the other wasn't. Where one concaved, the other convexed. Perhaps in the end it was those very hollows and hills that brought them together, neat and tight as a hand in a glove.

A profound and nearly unshakable love existed between these two from the beginning. To Natalie, Romaine was an artistic genius plain and simple. If Romaine chose to hold herself apart from and above the mass of humanity, Natalie thought she had every right to do so; that, after all, was exactly where she belonged. To Brooks, Natalie was the kind of woman she herself wanted to be in her secret heart, the woman she thought she might have been had she not emerged twisted from her crushing existence as a "child-martyr."

As in all the best relationships, these two brought out unexercised aspects of one another. As gruff as she might be in social situations, Romaine was capable of immense softness toward her "Nat-Nat." As controlling as she might be with others, Natalie let loose the reins with "My Angel." Their union, at its best, was characterized by affection, caring, and laughter.

Not that things were always easy. Romaine could be overbearing and harshly judgmental. She liked the world to be clean and simple, and the complexities of Natalie's life exasperated her. Soon after they became involved,

Natalie wrote Romaine to finalize arrangements for an upcoming trip with friends. Her letter was a confusing maze of stratagems regarding cars, trunks, dates. When should the maids go? So-and-so wants a lift partway, but in that case, where would Mlle. X sit? This one and that one are already partway there, so perhaps we might pick them up on the way? And we mustn't forget Laura's special request to do such-and-so once we arrive! The letter gave Romaine a headache and put her to bed. "The complications of your life are too much for me," she responded. "This morning . . . I received your dreadful letter. If life means detailed complications to you, for me it means hell or rather death a thousand times. Please go to Aix les Bains on your own; I shall go as I wish either by train or car . . . I'm tired of the whole affair."[32]

In Romaine's eyes, Natalie possessed two big negatives. First and foremost, she objected to almost all of Barney's chosen companions, considering them to be silly, vain, useless, parasitical, back-stabbing, and a complete waste of time. She would never change her mind, and, if anything, her feelings on this subject only grew stronger with time. The second negative was, not surprisingly, Natalie's infidelity. Romaine hated it, but usually handled it far better than most of her predecessors. With few exceptions, she tended to ignore the other loves, sometimes purposely leaving town when Natalie was in the throes of a new passion.

Actually, one of the major factors in the relationship's duration was Romaine's geographic restlessness. For most of her life she maintained a home in Paris, but also kept a changing array of residences elsewhere (in one ten-year period she made fifteen moves). Between her various homes and pleasure travels, she was forever on her way to somewhere else: Capri, New York, London, Nice, Venice, Florence, Fiesole, Santa Margherita. The frequent separations acted as a stimulant to Natalie. Rather than growing bored with Romaine through overexposure, she constantly anticipated her return. Their relationship was in some ways a constant series of new beginnings. Natalie's *pensée* "I re-read you, always for another first time," could easily have been directed at Brooks.[33]

Natalie did have one lover whom Romaine could neither avoid nor belittle: Lily Gramont. From the beginning Natalie made it clear that Lily came with the relationship. Simply put, if Romaine wanted Natalie's love, she had to get along with the Duchesse. Brooks managed to do so. She didn't always like it, but Lily, the soul of graciousness according to everyone who knew her, made it easy. The three women were often together in Paris, for dinner at one another's homes, theater outings, visiting friends, and so on. They even occasionally vacationed together.

Tension existed, though, and it pops out now and again. Lily took an occasional high-handed swipe at Romaine in her writings. "Mrs. Brooks," she observed in *Years of Plenty*, "puts little bars on the windows of her various establishments in order to keep out the disappointing human race, and now no longer knows who the prisoner is."[34] And in her monumental 1924 painting of Lily, *Elisabeth de Gramont, Duchesse de Clermont-Tonnerre*, Brooks manages to convey Gramont's nobility of character while hiding her charm, warmth, and Watteau-like beauty.

HAVING ANOTHER MAJOR new love didn't end Natalie's "demi" liaisons or more fleeting encounters. Among the longest of her short-term loves at this time was Armen Ohanian, known widely in Paris for her lyrical "dance-poems." Ohanian had been reared as the privileged daughter of a wealthy Armenian family living in Russia, until, when she was fifteen, her father was murdered by Cossacks and Tartars. Her widowed mother, stripped of money and possessions, soon gave the girl in marriage to a brutal man. Unable to endure a life in which she was beaten and forced to address her husband as "My Master," she ran away.

Ohanian's autobiography reveals her as quite a free spirit. She became a courtesan for a while, and later spent a happy year as consort to the "Queen of Crowns," a debauched Persian princess and drug addict. The two women enjoyed smoking opium through a jeweled hookah while lounging about on Oriental carpets.

Eventually Armen settled in Paris. She was painted by leading artists of the day, and her memoirs, published during the war, were prefaced by none other than Anatole France. Natalie delighted in the book's "odd Eastern points of view about all of us."[35]

The Barney-Ohanian affair was under way long before the war. Germaine Beaumont recalled dining at Colette's one summer night in 1913 when the two women arrived in a carriage pulled by white horses, both dressed in white saris embroidered with pearls. In his journal, Paul Claudel wrote of seeing Armen at rue Jacob in March 1915, performing "the dance of death, the soul alone and imprisoned . . . the bracelets on her ankles made a sound like death and dry leaves . . . despair, defiance, desire. On her knees, her tense and quivering body trying to pull away from itself. A dance of the veils, a woman between two loves, her body goes and comes, moving back and forth."[36]

Lily Gramont was present that night. At least five years into the relationship, she had by now reluctantly accepted Natalie's *fidèle/infidèle* nature, contenting herself to be the Amazon's constant friend and sometime lover. Still, she must have watched Ohanian—one of her lover's other lovers—with mixed feelings. Worldly, Lily would have appreciated the dance; kind, she would have told Ohanian so; human, she must have suffered at least a bit. "I have been told," Liane de Pougy confided to her blue notebooks, "that [the Duchesse] has shed bitter tears over Nathalie, but nowadays they have a very close and tender friendship."[37]

BY THE WAR'S START, Natalie's relationship with Remy de Gourmont had lost its original fervor—for her, at least. She would often be criticized for neglecting him in his last years, and there were those who insisted that her negligence hastened his death. Such criticisms are unfair. It's true that her visits to the bookish sixth-floor lair had lessened, but she nonetheless continued to call, never stopped inviting him to gatherings, and made a concerted effort to look out for his interests.

Through the American poet Ezra Pound, whom she met in 1913 when he was brought to rue Jacob by a mutual friend, Natalie helped get an English translation of Gourmont published. Pound revered Gourmont, completing several translations of, and writing numerous essays about, his work. Since Pound, in his turn, became a strong influence on many younger American writers, it's fair to say that some little part of Gourmont came to reside in the work of, say, Ernest Hemingway. Natalie also took pains to ensure that Remy meet one of her friends, a man with whom he had much in common: Anatole France. Only a few years from receiving the Nobel Prize, France was the most prominent literary figure in the country. When they met, he praised Gourmont's writing highly.

The Barney/Gourmont relationship was—as our own best intimacies often are—extremely complicated. Neither one was perfect. Natalie was a good albeit inconsistent friend to Gourmont; he was a good but demandingly possessive friend to her. The friendship persisted despite its problems for one reason only: they loved each other, each in a different way.

Of everyone who knew and wrote about Natalie, only Magdeleine Wauthier seemed to truly appreciate the depth and complexity of her relationship with Gourmont. "In the Amazon," she wrote, "he found a faithful friend [and] a constancy of heart and mind which made that platonic union a miracle of love on his part, a miracle of friendship on hers. . . . She was profoundly attached to him, but he *loved* her. . . . She was 30 years old . . . she led a life complicated by pleasure, risk, caprice and all the fantasies of a young woman, free and rich, in Paris. She had everything. He had nothing but her . . . [but he

was] dear to her and became dearer still. . . . At the age she was then, surrounded and courted by others, always busy, her faithfulness represented a
constancy, a charity of friendship, a great and beautiful thing."[38]

Remy de Gourmont suffered a stroke and died on September 27, 1915.
Natalie was in Normandy at the time, and it's not known when, exactly, she
learned of his death. She didn't attend his funeral, but she probably wouldn't
have whether she'd known about it or not—she'd already developed a philosophy about death that ruled out her presence at such occasions. The dead
remained alive for her; little matter that their bodies were gone.

There were and would continue to be mutterings about Gourmont dying
without his Amazon beside him. Natalie ignored such talk. Years later, writing
about Remy's death, she said: "Each of us has our own form of piety, our own
fashion of living with our dead and keeping them alive in ourselves."[39] And
then, recalling how he used to stand on the landing of his apartment to watch
her descending the stairs, she wrote one of the prettiest passages that ever
emerged from her pen:

> He could see only my hand on the banisters, polished by long use, or my
> smile ascending back to him between the gas lights of the spiral staircase,
> interminable as that of a tower. The walls glided smoothly between the
> floors, with no roughness other than the Gas Company boxes. Arriving in
> the courtyard (where a rabbit nibbled peacefully beneath a solitary tree), I
> glanced upward one last time. He was there. Moved at feeling so discreetly
> followed, I left. I never saw his door close. . . .[40]

Remy de Gourmont may have died, but his door remained open to Natalie
forever. And, until her own death, she continued to visit.

BY 1917, Lily Gramont had left her husband, moving into a small but beautiful home in the Passy area of Paris. By coincidence, Romaine lived nearby.
With her two major loves in the same neighborhood, Natalie had all the excuse
she needed to vacate rue Jacob for a while, thereby removing herself from the
intense bombing at the city's heart. She ended up in an apartment on rue des
Vignes, the same street where Pierre Loüys lived.

Natalie and the Passy group—Lily, Romaine, Loüys, and assorted others—
often came together during air raids, finding shelter beneath a nearby train
station or in the secret passage under Lily's home. By this time Parisians were
on intimate terms with air raids. When the sirens screamed out the warning
that German airplanes or zeppelins were arriving, everyone ran for the nearest
shelter. Snuggled securely below the streets, friends and strangers alike hud-

dled together, listening to the explosions above, while trying to keep up a brave front. When the danger passed, buglers tooted the merry notes of "La Berloque" as an all-clear signal, and life returned to its normally surreal wartime state. The whole process, though dangerous and heart-pumping, had become a routine.

Natalie worried about Loüys walking home at night after air raids or social events. His eyes had begun to fail badly, and she thought the streets were dangerous for him to navigate with the lamps unlit and windows blacked out. But, though he could scarcely see, he insisted on doing his gentlemanly duty by accompanying her home. They would meander slowly to her door and say goodnight. She would enter the building. Loüys would walk away. A few moments later she would reemerge and tiptoe silently behind him. Once he was safely through his own gates she returned home.

Like Natalie, Lily always had interesting people milling about. One day in the spring of 1917, the novelist Francis de Miomandre presented her with a copy of a poem written by a friend. Entitled "La jeune parque," it related a tale about the youngest of the Three Fates after she is bitten by a poisonous snake. It was, said Miomandre, the finest poem he'd ever read. Despite its extreme length, he vowed to learn it by heart and promised to recite it aloud in her garden some night. But first, he said, why don't you drop by my house and meet the author, my close friend Paul Valéry?

Lily did so and ended up inviting Miomandre, Valéry, Natalie, and a few others over for an evening. On that night, as promised, Miomandre stood in the garden, reciting all 512 verses of the poem: "Who is that weeping, if not simply the wind/At this sole hour, with ultimate diamonds?" When he was through, Lily's guests and numerous neighbors hanging out their windows shouted praise. Today Paul Valéry is considered the greatest French poet of the twentieth century, so the listeners that night showed a good deal of prescience.

At the time Valéry was "unpublished and profoundly ignored, except by a few friends and future academics."[41] Among them was his old and close friend, Pierre Loüys, who tried to interest Natalie in his work. "You just read 'La jeune parque,' " he wrote her, "and I'm sure you have a sense that it is 'a thing of beauty and a joy forever.' Think about it. Talk about it. And fête my old friend. He is a great poet."[42]

Natalie didn't need any convincing on the subject of Valéry. She had wanted to meet him for a few years, ever since reading his audacious short story "La soirée avec M. Teste" in *Vers et Prose*. "At some party or other," Lily recalled, "I heard Miss Barney praising [M. Teste] and asking, 'Who is this Paul Valéry? It would be interesting to know him.' "[43]

As it turned out, Valéry also lived in Passy, just a stone's throw away. After the night in Lily's garden he began dropping in on Natalie, and soon they were frequent companions. They had much in common, including a reverence for the Symbolist poet Stéphane Mallarmé, whose Tuesday-evening gatherings Valéry had attended back in the 1890s. Natalie and Valéry even took a pilgrimage to Mallarmé's former country home at Valvins, near Fontainebleau. They crept up a mossy old stone staircase, past tiny trailing roses, to stand reverently beside "the Master's" living quarters while observing his view of the slowly moving Seine. After a visit to Mallarmé's grave at nearby Samoreau, they hopped in the river for a swim.

Natalie once wrote that she and Valéry were similar in their dilettantism. Like her, she said, he was interested in many things, and found it easier to discuss ideas than to commit them to paper. She describes their conversations as creative works, with idea building upon idea, leading here and there and onward and upward. Of course, for Natalie to equate her variety of dilettantism with Valéry's is self-serving. His lifelong oeuvre might be tiny, but it is brilliant, and he suffered mightily over his creations. "La jeune parque" alone took him four years to write. Natalie, on the other hand, tried hard to dispense with creative suffering altogether.

At Valéry's request, Natalie began translating some of his works into English. After succeeding with one or two short poems, she eventually completed the first-ever English translation of "Monsieur Teste," which was published in the *Dial* in February 1922.

Another new friend who came into Natalie's life during the war was Bernard Berenson, at that time the world's foremost expert on Italian Renaissance art. After being introduced by a mutual friend, Salomon Reinach, Berenson began writing affectionate notes to the "responsive, appreciative and zestful" Natalie. "I ought at my age to be more indifferent," he observed, "but I cannot resist . . . I bless the gods that brought us acquainted and I pray to them to continue their kindness." A few days later he admitted that they had become "greater friends in two or three hours than with others in so many hundreds."[44]

To certain friends Berenson later revealed that he had loved Natalie deeply, and he told her as much in the mid-1950s. He confided to literary agent Jenny Bradley that he'd had no idea Natalie was a lesbian until she introduced him to Romaine Brooks, who was dressed in a severely cut jacket and wore a top hat. He once told Sir Harold Acton that he and Natalie had engaged in a passionate affair, but Acton didn't believe him. The story got around, though, and still makes its way into print as legitimate fact (a 1994 biography of Edith Wharton, herself a close Berenson friend, lists Natalie among the women with whom he had an affair). The Barney-Berenson friendship deepened further during

World War II, when, exiled in Italy, they lived near each other, and only ended at his death in 1959.

THE WAR'S GREATEST SPY scandal involved an old acquaintance of Natalie's, Margaretha Zelle. Years before, as Mata Hari, she had mesmerized the guests at one of Natalie's Neuilly garden fêtes in a Godiva "costume." The two women had maintained a distant contact since.

During the war's early years Mata Hari had many lovers among the Allied high command. Eager to bed a woman whose name was synonymous with seductive glamour, they were happy to answer her seemingly naïve questions about troop movements and weapons. The information she received was allegedly passed along to the Germans. In 1917 the French accused her of espionage and threw her in jail. She was court-martialed, found guilty, and shot.

Until the end, Mata Hari hoped that her sentence would be commuted. When that didn't happen, she bravely accepted her fate. At five in the morning on October 16, 1917, she drank the glass of rum prescribed by law for all prisoners leaving to face death. Accompanied by two Sisters of Charity and a priest, she was taken in an automobile from Cell No. 12 at St. Lazare prison and brought to the parade ground at Vincennes, where a firing squad stood waiting. She requested that her wrists be left unbound, and, "giving proof of her courage to the end, refused to wear an eyeband."[45] She faced forward, coolly observing her executioners. A young French noble, his saber held high in the traditional manner of honoring one about to die, later recalled trembling at the sight of her. Nonetheless, he issued the command to fire and "she went to her death calmly, on her lips a shadow of the smile that for years fascinated famed beauty admirers in every European capital."[46]

Mata Hari's tale captured the public imagination and has never let go to this day. It's a story that has everything: a beautiful woman, sex, spies, glamour, power, and an old-fashioned moral comeuppance at the end. Mata Hari has inspired dozens of books. At least nine separate films have been made about her, the first in 1919 (*Mata Hari: The Red Spy*) and the most recent in 1985 (*Mata Hari*). The greatest film version of all, made in 1931, starred cinema legends Greta Garbo, Lionel Barrymore, and Ramon Novarro.

Neither Natalie nor her friends had ever held the dancer in much esteem. "She really had very little charm," Natalie recalled. "We were all rather embarrassed by her dances. She was just an ordinary woman who shot into fame through her espionage career."[47] Liane de Pougy's opinion was harsher: "Mata Hari, so beautiful in her body and so ugly in her soul . . . never was I able to feel friendly towards her, and it's the truth. There was something too hard in her which I found tedious and off-putting. She had a loud voice and a heavy manner, she lied, she dressed badly, she had no notion of shape or colour, and she walked mannishly."[48]

Still, Natalie considered her an acquaintance and felt that, whatever the woman's transgressions in life, she had redeemed herself with a courageous acceptance of her fate. Consequently, she hated the demeaning gossip and ridiculous rumors that followed her death. One story—that Mata Hari had faced the firing squad wearing a full-length mink coat over her nude body— she found particularly troublesome. Some sources claim that Natalie paid someone to find out the truth, and that she then passed the information on to Janet Flanner. No evidence exists to support this story. However, Flanner did report in her *New Yorker* column that Mata Hari "died wearing a neat Amazonian tailored suit, specially made for the occasion, and a pair of new white gloves."[49]

ONE MORNING in March 1918 Parisians woke up to an unpleasant surprise. Howitzers—shortish cannons that deliver hits via a high trajectory—began to shell the city from a distance. When the first of these new bombs fell, nobody knew what they were. "At seven a.m.," a witness recalled, "loud, determined, short noises burst out of an empty sky at twenty-minute intervals. They were not loud enough to be factories blowing up; and, besides, factories don't blow up by timetable; they didn't reverberate like bombs, and besides there was no barrage and no noise of aeroplanes. The telephones everywhere tinkled like mad with people asking other people what on earth (or under the earth) was happening. . . . When the afternoon papers came out we learned that we were being bombarded by a gun that carried 75 miles! Of course, we did not believe it. Who could?"[50]

The howitzer's huge shells were wildly inaccurate, but they managed to inflict great damage whether they hit an intended target or not. By the war's end, 303 shells would strike Paris, killing 256 and wounding 620. The guns quickly earned the nickname "Big Bertha" for Bertha Krupp, wife of the German arms manufacturer whose factory produced them.

Finding the big guns nerve-wracking, Natalie and Romaine took off for a respite at d'Annunzio's home in Italy, a "dear little house on the bay of the Cote d'Argent. Books, quiet, pine trees and nice servants, all awaiting his glorious return from the war."[51]

Not long after Natalie and Romaine returned from Italy, the bloodiest, most meanly fought war in history finally ended. "First day of Peace," Natalie

*A*lbert Clifford Barney in 1876, the year
Natalie was born. He is twenty-six.
(Smithsonian Institution Archives, Acc. 96-153)

*A*lice Pike Barney in 1880.
At twenty-three, she is the mother
of two young daughters.
(Smithsonian Institution Archives, Acc. 96-153)

*N*atalie at about one year of age.
(Private Collection)

*S*isters Laura and Natalie Barney, circa 1881.
(Collection of the Author)

𝒩atalie with her pony,
Tricksy, 1883. She is six
or seven.
*(Smithsonian Institution
Archives, Acc. 96-153)*

𝒩atalie at eleven, as
painted by Charles E. A.
Carolus-Duran. She is
dressed in the costume
of a page—an apprentice
knight.
*(Smithsonian American Art
Museum, Acc.1971.181.2)*

*L*aura, Alice, and Natalie Barney, around 1889. Natalie is just entering her teens. *(Smithsonian Institution Archives, Acc. 96-153)*

*T*he front entrance of Ban-y-Bryn, the Barneys' summer "cottage" in Bar Harbor, Maine. *(Bar Harbor Historical Society)*

Natalie in Fur Cape, by Alice Pike Barney (1896), was selected for the 1897 Salon and highlighted in the catalog. Natalie's regal bearing and cool self-possession seem remarkable in a young woman of nineteen or twenty.

(Smithsonian American Art Museum, Acc.1951.14.74)

*E*va Palmer (left) and her sister, May. The exact date is unknown, but Eva is probably in her late teens. *(Collection of Gina Sikelianos)*

*P*auline Tarn in Nice, circa 1905. *(By kind permission of Imogen Bright)*

*N*atalie Barney, Forest Nymph of Bar Harbor (summer 1900).
(Private Collection)

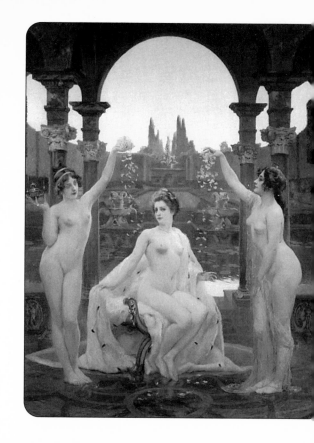

*L*es *Grâces Florentines*,
a 1903 painting by Gervais,
used three premier
courtesans as models: Liane
de Pougy (on the left),
La Belle Otero, and Cleo
de Merode. Today the
painting hangs in the Salle
Blanche of the Monte
Carlo Casino.
*(Courtesy of Archives Société des
Bains de Mer)*

A popular Liane de Pougy
postcard of the late
nineteenth century.
(Collection of the Author)

LIANE DE POUGY

*L*ucie Delarue-Mardrus, circa 1900.
(Courtesy of George Wickes)

*N*atalie at twenty.
(Collection of the Author)

*A*n outdoor fete at Natalie's home in Neuilly, sometime around 1905. The woman in white facing forward at the right is probably Natalie (but possibly Laura); her right hand is clasping that of Eva Palmer. The dancing maidens surround a raised platform where a woman is orating while two others play a flute and lyre.
(Smithsonian Institution Archives, Acc. 96-153)

*T*he Temple of Friendship, circa 2000. In Natalie's day there was no wrought iron or lawn furniture. Two five-foot marble pillars at ground level held small sculptures.
(Photograph by Janice Lynn Matthews)

*T*emple interior in Natalie's time.
(Courtesy of George Wickes)

*L*ily Gramont, the Duchesse de Clermont-Tonnerre, in 1904. She was twenty-nine.
(Collection Jean Chalon)

*N*atalie at twenty-five, a "young woman of the future society."
(Collection Jean Chalon)

A portrait of Rémy de Gourmont by Henri de Groux. The painting originally belonged to Natalie but was auctioned after her death to her friend, writer Philippe Jullian. At François Chapon's urging, he left it in his will to the Bibliothèque Littéraire Jacques Doucet.
(Bibliothèque Littéraire Jacques Doucet)

*N*atalie and Romaine during the Great War.
(Courtesy of George Wickes)

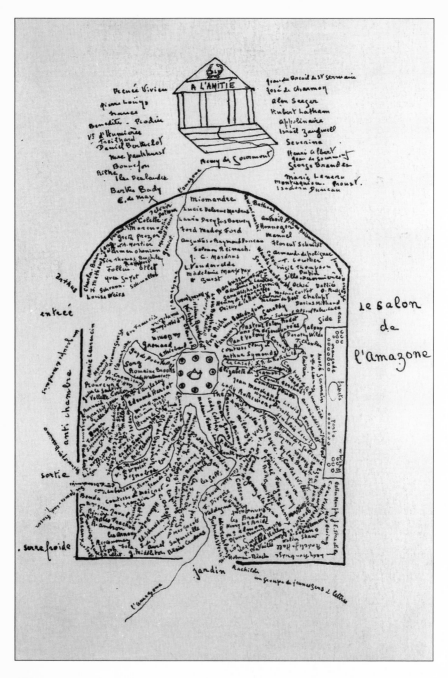

*T*he salon "map" Natalie drew for publication in *Aventures de l'esprit* (1929). Names closest to the temple include Renée Vivien, Pierre Loüys, Anatole France, Apollinaire, Alan Seeger, Isadora Duncan, Marie Lénéru, Montesquieu, Proust, Mrs. Pankhurst, and Rilke.

(Courtesy of George Wickes)

*T*he infamous nude sculpture by Laura Barney (resting briefly outside Studio House in 2001). Natalie was widely believed to be the model.
(Photograph by Suzanne Rodriguez)

*N*atalie at sixty.
(Collection of the Author)

*N*atalie and Romaine in Florence, toward the end of World War II.
(Courtesy of George Wickes)

*N*atalie at eighty-eight, with her close friend Jean Chalon.
(Collection of Jean Chalon)

NATALIE CLIFFORD BARNEY
ECRIVAIN
1876 · 1972
ELLE FUT L'AMAZONE DE RÉMY DE GOURMONT
JE SUIS CET ÊTRE LÉGENDAIRE
OÙ JE REVIS N.C.B.

ET SA SŒUR

LAURA CLIFFORD BARNEY
OFFICIER DE LA LÉGION D'HONNEUR
1879 · 1974
VEUVE D'HIPPOLYTE DREYFUS
MEMBRE
DE
LA COMMUNAUTÉ BAHA'IE

*T*he shared grave of
Natalie and Laura Barney.
*(Photograph by Janice Lynn
Matthews)*

prefaced a letter to Alice on November 11, 1918, the day the Armistice was declared. More than ten million people had been killed, and twice that number were wounded. Such statistics led many to feel as Natalie had all along—that war was revolting, stupid, and senseless. The idea of a multinational disarmament pact became popular and the newly formed League of Nations gathered support.

The Treaty of Versailles, signed on June 28, 1919, returned the world to a peacetime footing—officially, anyway. Three of the major powers that signed it were dissatisfied with its terms. Defeated Germany bitterly resented its lost territory and costly reparations payments. Victorious Italy felt cheated by the small amount of territory it was awarded. Another victor, Japan, was angry at not gaining control of China. The governments and people of France, Great Britain, and the United States were pleased: the war had reduced Germany's military might to nothing, and Europe had been reorganized in a way that reduced the possibility of future conflict. If all went as hoped, the Great War would be the last major conflict ever fought.

IN THE FIRST WEEK of August, with the world at peace, Natalie and Lily sailed for the United States to visit New York and Canada, as well as to spend time with Alice in Bar Harbor and Washington. Lily marveled over America's wonders, particularly the smoothly paved roads and easy availability of gasoline. Upon her return, she told a reporter from the *Excelsior* that the experience of motoring around the countryside had been almost magical.

Alice's marriage had deteriorated in the last few years, and she was now separated from Christian. The final straw for Alice had been to learn of Christian's "involvement" with a young male actor. She had been just as blind to her husband's proclivities as she once was to Natalie's, even though rumors had been rife for years. "Does Christian Hemmick make it a point to use perfumed notepaper," a snide newspaper columnist asked in 1915, "or was it just by accident that some of his wife's sachet powder got mixed up with Christian's stationery the other day when he wrote to a man friend? At any rate, much amusement was expressed upon receipt of the odoriferous epistle."[52]

Ceaseless newspaper attacks had added to the stresses and strains of their marriage. Everything was fair game: the difference in their ages, his idle and luxurious life, her constant gadding about. Not surprisingly, they began to argue, and toward the end of the war Alice gave serious thought to divorce. Times had changed, the stigma of a divorced woman had greatly lessened, and her daughters fully encouraged her to make the move. Laura's letters were filled with legal strategies geared to helping Alice rid herself of Hemmick at minimum cost. Natalie advised making a clean, cold break, no matter the cost: "Do it and don't be done by it," she wrote.

They were right, and Alice knew it. She had suffered enough in her first go-round with marriage. This time she would be quick to disentangle herself. When she offered Christian a lump sum of $10,000 to end their union, he accepted.

When Natalie and Lily returned to Paris in early 1920, a new era had begun.

ELEVEN

Years of Glory:
The Salon

THE TWENTIES

Dinners, soirees, poets, erratic millionaires, translations, lobsters, absinthe, music, promenades, oysters, sherry, aspirin, pictures, Sapphic heiresses, editors, books, sailors. And how!
—*American poet Hart Crane,*
describing 1920s Paris in a postcard

What did you see in the Salon? I saw—that I was seen.
—*Natalie Barney*

*T*HE TWENTIES ROARED into Paris, briskly extinguishing the last lingering glow of the Belle Époque and launching the world into a new era characterized by speed, flight, and youth. Those at the forefront of this new world, the Moderns, were roughly the same age as the new century. Everything about them was different. Where their parents had been drawn to the curved, graceful lines of Art Nouveau, they responded to ugly cubes and harsh angles. Where once conversation turned on clever phrasing and an arched brow, now bitter plaints and ironic sneers held the day. Subtlety had been replaced by artless assertions, soft voices by vulgar shouts. Breeding, manners, elegance, respect for one's betters—all gone!

Or, at least, that's ho⌐   ⌐d to survivors of a gentler era.

But the Mo⌐   ⌐neration before or since, were simply the sum of ⌐   ⌐r short lives had been shaped by the rise of a huge ⌐   ⌐movements, the increasing independence of women, the ⌐   ⌐ birth control, Freud's theories, the mobility afforded by auto-⌐⌐iles and airplanes, the popularization of moving pictures, and a lot more. Many had squandered their youth on a filthy war that put them on intimate terms with poison gas, starvation, and the death of friends. For them, a life of curved and graceful lines was hypocrisy, that of cubes and angles merely truth.

Nothing symbolized the great divide between generations so much as the changes in younger women. Many, having risked their lives at the front as nurses or ambulance drivers, were simply unwilling to return to second-class citizenship after the Armistice. And, as the 1920 passage of the Nineteenth Amendment to the United States Constitution made clear, they didn't have to. The hard-won right of American women to vote was a symbolic declaration to women everywhere that they were equal to men.

The modern women flooding postwar Paris were confident, self-assured, even brazen, lounging openly in cafés or racing low-slung automobiles through the streets with cigarettes dangling rakishly from their lips. "These days," La Vie Parisienne noted, "one is always running into young women who leave autos outside that they've driven themselves, and who walk in smoking a cigarette!"[1] A pretty Pole named Tamara de Lempicka became a success in these years with her innovative Art Deco paintings of the new, sleek, fast-moving woman.

Even the way women looked underwent a major turnaround. During the Belle Époque the hallmark of femininity had been a fleshy, zaftig body. Swathed in floor-length skirts and stuffed into constricting undergarments, women were forced to move gracefully and slowly. But the postwar, lightning-paced world demanded a streamlined body and simple, no-nonsense clothing. With a snap of the fingers, full-figured Rubenesque was out, Modigliani-thin was in. Corsets and ankle-length skirts disappeared, replaced by drop-waist, short-skirted dresses.

"These short skirts," Natalie fumed, "so many women showing their legs without being asked ... Poor legs one meets in the streets, knock-kneed, wanting in padding and training. What has become of that dance, that rhythm, that gait?" She wasn't alone in mourning the long skirt's demise. "What a charming gesture it was to lift the skirt just enough to excite desire by suggesting the rest," pined Liane. "[Now that] skirts are short, no more need to lift them."[2]

With this simplified dress came the first signs of class leveling. "Today, except on court occasions," said Coco Chanel, "who could pick out a king from a commoner; as far, that is, as costume is concerned? Or a lord from a laborer on a holiday, or a lady of the highest rank from the ranks of near-ladies about her? . . . The world as a whole now looks pretty much alike to an outsider . . . any costume that would, in everyday life, differentiate classes from masses is not to be found."[3]

Many decried these changes. Sniffed Liane: "Washerwomen wear silk stockings. My butcher has bought herself a car. . . . Women nowadays are so commonplace!"[4] Paul Morand, observing a table of "pure nouveaux riches" at La Perouse, noted contemptuously that, balanced atop their fine silk robes and ostentatious diamonds, the women had "faces like housemaids . . . [they] exchanged their jewelry on a napkin and tried it on. A huge emerald, necklaces."[5] He practically choked when they paid their large check with five-franc notes.

There were those who delighted in the new class disguises, as characterized by a cartoon in *La Vie Parisienne*. In one panel, a courtesan sits in a barber's chair and says, "Make me look like a lady." In the next panel, a lady says, "Make me look like a courtesan."[6] That a lady could play at being a courtesan said something about society's updated outlook on propriety and morals. Throughout the Western world, and especially in Paris, it had become much more acceptable to be a maverick. "Things that were long ago taboo," mused Salomon Reinach, "are now the object of everyday conversation."[7]

As if by magic, Natalie was now fit company in parlors where she'd once been considered a pariah. As André Germain observed, "little by little, the condemnation of which she was the object has been transformed into a sort of moving curiosity, even an official esteem."[8] She had become acceptable. "After the war," commented Romaine, "when point of view had broadened, [Natalie] actually became popular and this was a sore disappointment to me. It was not long before I was again meeting at her house the very hornets I had hoped to escape for ever."[9]

Concomitant with all these glorious changes to womanhood was a less divine truth: the young sprites of 1900 were middle-aged. Bodies had thickened, steps had slowed, hair had grayed.

Natalie turned forty-four in 1920. Though she still played tennis, enjoyed long walks, and loved to dance, she had left her girlish athleticism behind. No longer did the sight of the blond Amazonian sylph, cantering along the leafy

240 WILD HEART: A LIFE

paths of the Bois, strike passersby with admiration. In fact, she rarely rode now, and her days of hiking mountain paths and energetic rowing had also passed.

The lack of robust exercise combined with her hearty love of food had begun to add heft. She wasn't happy about this; Amazon or not, she was Everywoman when it came to coping with the advances of time, and she wasn't above trying the fad diets making the rounds. A photo she sent to Laura at this time showed the two sisters looking decidedly plump and scrawny-necked. On the back Natalie penned a ditty:

> The worst we can look.
> The camera took us necks and all.
> We never fall so low in beauty—so worn in duty!
> Oh what grins and ravaged chins!
> Your "acid" diet—Must we needs try it?[10]

Despite her increasing girth, Natalie retained a good deal of her youthful freshness at the decade's start. She was heavier, yes, but not yet stout. Her skin was unlined, her eyes clear, her wit untempered, her lust for life and love undimmed. She also retained that crown of glory, the thick mass of blond hair celebrated by friends and lovers alike. It was thus quite a shock when, sometime in the early 1920s, she began to sport a practical bob. With a few scissors-snips and the storing away of Natalie's legendary tresses into boxes, the ethereal, captivating Flaxenflower ceased to exist.

Her friends were horrified. "Straw-colored silvery wisps crowning the Amazon's forehead," Colette despaired. "How many crops mowed down through caprice, fashion?" But it wasn't caprice or fashion that caused Natalie to cut her hair; it was simple acceptance of the fact that life was moving on, and she along with it. As she stated in one of her epigrams, "Her hair stayed too young for her face." She wasn't about to make that mistake.

ALONG WITH BARNEY'S updated look came a changed attitude toward her place within the literary firmament. She was at an age when most people begin to question the meaning of life and ponder the significance of their role within it, and she had few illusions about her literary talents. A clear-eyed American stoic, she knew that she could be a much better writer if she worked harder—but even then, her chance of attaining the highest ranks of belles lettres was slim. No matter how mightily she labored, she would never be considered a literary genius.

On the other hand, she was a marvel as a literary salonist. Her only peers existed in centuries past—women like Catherine de Rambouillet, Madame de Sévigné, and the Marquise de Sablé. As a writer she would never be a Valéry, a Colette, or a Gide. As a salonist, however, she could play a very important role in the lives of such writers. They, and many other writers of their caliber, not only treasured Natalie's friendship, but respected, honored, and even courted her because she wielded a certain power in the literary world. Natalie Barney could, if she chose, be immensely helpful to a writer's career.

Barney's Fridays already played an important role in Parisian letters, bringing together an eclectic, multinational mix of writers in a setting that stimulated creativity, talk, and friendship. That sounds easy, but it was a considerable accomplishment for that time and place. Despite modernity's upheaval, the formal standards of introduction still held: most people met through mutual friends or not at all. The French, who tended to shun outsiders, were particularly ingrown. The presence of an Anglophone at a French salon, even one who spoke French well, was rare.

What made Natalie's salon unique and exciting was that she wanted a true literary melting pot from the beginning. As she put it: "I wanted to form an intellectual and international elite, an understanding that bridged diverse languages [and offered] receptivity to the similarities and differences in the great family of minds united beyond borders."[11] While most guests tended to be French, American, or British, you had a fair chance of meeting writers from anywhere on the planet. By the 1920s she had welcomed visitors from India (notably Sir Rabindranath Tagore, winner of the 1913 Nobel Prize for Literature), Germany (poet Rainer Maria Rilke, who came often in the early 1920s), Lithuania, Russia, China, Poland, Scandinavia, Chile, Egypt, Peru, and on and on.

One of Natalie's most likable qualities—her sincere desire to help people fulfill themselves—was a great boon in running a salon. She had a justified reputation for providing practical solutions for authors in need, and particularly loved being the catalyst for friendships and literary connections. Can't find a publisher? Need a recommendation for your translating skills? Desperate for an introduction to so-and-so? Whatever the problem, chances were that Natalie had a solution. Even in her later years she continued to go out of her way to be helpful. In 1954, when Marguerite Yourcenar experienced frustrating complications in renewing her American passport, seventy-eight-year-old Natalie got on the phone and straightened out the problem with dispatch. "What happens to the hundreds of people who don't have a Natalie Barney battling for them on the telephone?" the grateful Yourcenar asked.[12]

Natalie took sincere pleasure in being helpful, but she also enjoyed having clout. The fact that she could make things happen for people was an undisputed sign of power—and she loved it. After the war, though, Natalie sought something deeper: the recognition and satisfaction that came from making reputations. She thus began to be far more active on behalf of chosen writers and, occasionally, musicians.

The first person to whom she devoted such effort was Paul Valéry. She hadn't been able to do much for him while the war raged, but afterward she found publishers for translations, talked him up among her friends, and introduced him to important contacts. In June 1920 she devoted a Friday to Valéry's work, in which he read four poems ("Palme," "Anne," "Aurore," and "Narcisse"), followed by Natalie reading her own English translations. During his recitation Natalie ensured the proper respect and quiet by stationing herself "upright, at the threshold of the room, like the two-faced genie of welcome and vigilance, who will welcome the latecomers while protecting the poems."[13]

Five years later Valéry was elected to the Académie Française, succeeding to the chair of the recently deceased Anatole France. "It was commonly conceded in literary circles around Paris that Miss Barney had very largely 'made' Valéry in the first place," Samuel Putnam wrote. "For reputations, I found, were still being fashioned in salons like this, and what you heard in the drawing room one day you would not be surprised to read a day or two later in Le Figaro."[14]

IT WAS THE DESIRE to further Valéry's career that brought Natalie to collaborate with Ezra Pound on an endeavor known as Bel Esprit. When Pound moved to Paris from London in 1920, these two strong-minded and quirky Americans began seeing each other frequently. They're an odd match on the surface: Imperial Natalie and Hectoring Ezra. But something about the opinionated, ever-lecturing Pound twanged a forgotten midwestern chord within Natalie, while he admired her hardheaded, unshockable aplomb and considerable refinement. If he didn't have a wife and she weren't a lesbian, who knows? They might have married, had a passel of unorthodox children, and led a happy-but-argumentative and oddball life. But he did and she was, so they played tennis, gossiped about writers they knew, and shared eccentric opinions about the world's ways.

Pound was a busy and influential man in these years. It was he who had convinced James Joyce to move to Paris in 1920. Their presence, together with that of Gertrude Stein, turned Paris into the world capital of English-language Modernism, attracting scores of writers during the decade to come. Pound was also involved with leading exponents of French Modernism, including Cocteau, Brancusi, and Stravinsky. He espoused the ideals of the Dadaists, and, when they faded away, the Surrealists. He was involved with many of the English-language literary reviews so popular at the time, such as the *Dial*. He worked tirelessly to promote the work of Americans, or at least American men. One of the criticisms leveled at Pound is that he largely ignored women writers. Natalie saw this long ago, noting that Ezra "did less for women. He didn't approve of women writers."[15]

One of the few female writers Pound sought to help was Natalie. He took an interest in her work, attempted to edit it, and tried when possible to get it published. He helped get her translation of Valéry's short story "An Evening with M. Teste" into print (*Dial*, February 1922). He translated portions of her *Pensées d'une Amazone* into English for publication in *This Quarter* (1929). He edited—the word used in print was "arranged"—two NCB poems for the October 1924 *Transatlantic Review*. One of them, "After Reading Chinese Poems," sounds more Poundian than Natalienne:

> On the first day of May I lie reading poems,
> They mount on the fumes of jasmine-scented tea
>   A friend has prepared
>   —After the heavy hours of meals—
> In cups like the shells of plovers eggs.
> No newspapers pass through the budding garden
>   Into the quiet house:
> How still and restful are the days of revolution!
> . . . . . Red flags are leading dingy crowds,
> Thoughts of pleasant tints are leading my dream-mind
>   Back to the dynasties of the delicate,
>   Who value a poem and a friend
>   As the deep possessions of their lives
> And hold all the rest as gold-dust under their feet
>   —That but touch the earth that they may spring from it!

The *Transatlantic Review*'s editor, Ford Madox Ford, had a certain selfish interest in publishing these poems, because on a few occasions it was a financial contribution from Miss Barney that helped his magazine stay afloat.

Natalie and Ezra cooked up numerous literary schemes, though most came to naught. With Ford, they talked of starting a bilingual literary review; at one point they even dreamed of having Sinclair Lewis, soon to win both the Pulitzer and Nobel Prizes, as their coeditor. This planned review was probably "Le Livre d'Heures de l'Année." Described by Natalie as a yearly "review of reviews," it was intended to gather and present the past year's best writing from various literary magazines published in English and French. "If you had dropped from the moon," declared her draft advertising copy, "or just returned from around or out of the world, you [would] need to know what to read to catch up with the times."[16] Unfortunately, this interesting publication—which would have covered not only literature, but art and science—never evolved beyond the planning stages.

Natalie and Ezra's grandest attempt was Bel Esprit, designed to ease the financial problems of worthy writers and leave them free to work without distraction. The idea was to corral well-to-do literary friends into subscribing shares on a yearly basis. There would be thirty shares, each costing 500 francs, amounting to a grand total of 15,000 francs. The money would be awarded to a carefully selected writer, who would, in turn, give each member a specially printed edition of any work resulting from the stipend. Lots would be drawn by the "shareholders" for the actual manuscript.

Two writers were to be chosen, one working in French, the other in English. Natalie's choice was Valéry, whom she hoped to free from his job as private secretary to the director of Agence Havas, the French press association. Pound selected an American, T. S. Eliot. He worried that Eliot, who was employed by a London bank, didn't have enough time to write poetry, even though he had produced two volumes of verse, *Prufrock and Other Observations* (1917) and *Poems* (1920), and was working on a third, *The Waste Land.**

Working enthusiastically to bring the project to life, Natalie and Ezra wrote, designed, and circulated a prospectus outlining Bel Esprit's fundamentals. They talked it up among their wide circle of literary friends, and in his monthly letter in the *Dial* Pound brought the endeavor to the world's attention: "The society of Bel Esprit has been founded in Paris, a sort of consumer's league to pay for quality rather than quantity in literature and the fine arts."

Unfortunately, Bel Esprit had one gigantic flaw: Valéry and Eliot weren't interested in receiving charity. Eliot simply refused the award. Later that year, after publication of *The Waste Land,* he attracted a traditional patron and left the bank to become a full-time poet. As for Valéry, the French literary world had begun taking an interest in him, and the *Nouvelle Revue* wanted to take over from Natalie the responsibility of raising funds to assist him. She resisted as long as possible. Eventually her opponents won out, agreeing to subsidize Valéry with 15,000 francs per year, the same amount she had proposed to raise via collective patronage.†

---

*Eliot would win the Nobel Prize for Literature in 1948. In 1971, when a facsimile of the original *Waste Land* manuscript was published, it was evident just how much the final poem owed to the extensive revisions made, at Eliot's request, by Pound.

†Many years later, Natalie had a revised or perhaps time-altered view of what had occurred. "We saved T. S. Eliot from his bank and Paul Valéry from his government profession," she told a reporter in 1965.

Natalie claimed to be happy with the outcome. Valéry's financial freedom corresponded so completely to her design, she said, that she was satisfied to let the others take charge. Still, it must have hurt her pride to be stripped of a project into which she'd invested much time, enthusiasm, and not a little money. Though Valéry continued to attend the Fridays, a chill descended on the friendship.

Bel Esprit was an innovative, well-conceived, and businesslike plan for which Natalie deserves credit, but it has sometimes been rudely dismissed. Ernest Hemingway wrote contemptuously about it in *A Moveable Feast*. However, he was in no position to criticize. At Pound's urging Hemingway had solicited funds for Bel Esprit, later blowing what he'd collected at the racetrack on a losing horse. As Natalie remarked: "How badly brought up was Hemingway!"[17]

ONLY A YEAR OLDER than the century, young Ernest was one of many Americans who had first discovered Paris during the war. Many Yanks, having survived their stints as soldiers, nurses, or ambulance drivers, stayed on after the Armistice. Others returned home, discovered they could no longer endure a life of Rotary Club values, and couldn't get back to Paris fast enough. As a smash hit of the day put it, "How 'ya gonna keep 'em down on the farm, after they've seen Paree?"

They didn't *have* to stay on the farm. The economy was burgeoning in the United States, with growth fueled by rapidly increasing industrialization, technological improvements, and boundless consumer optimism that translated into carefree spending. France, on the other hand—like most of Europe—was struggling to repair an economy destroyed by the Great War, and its franc was depressed. Americans quickly discovered that a tiny allowance from their prosperous but Babbitt-infested homeland easily afforded a happy, café-sitting, bourgeois-bashing life in France.

"Oh, dear folks at home," a popular guidebook informed readers. "If you knew what they are saying about you in the Latin Quarter studios, your ears would burn. Your smug follies, your stupidities, the badges you wear in your coat lapels, your Prohibition, your Ku Klux Klan, your childish concern with religious questions which intelligentsia thought were settled fifty years ago, your insensibility toward modern masterpieces . . . Philistines!"[18]

To the young expats, with their updated outlook on propriety and morals, Natalie no longer carried the stigma of scandal. In fact, to many she seemed like an antique with her formal manners, her friendships with the Duke of this and the Princess of that, and her aloofness from Left Bank bohemia.

"Natalie was inclined to know the conventional French and was already considered a bit too Right Bank and smart, outside our group," wrote the English poet Bryher. "She would never turn up in a café at six in the evening. Whereas we had one coffee at the Dome or the Rotonde and it had to last an hour or two. There was a great gap." Richard Aldington agreed: "I suppose Miss Barney has at some time been in a café, but she is not the kind of person you would think of inviting to such a place."[19]

It's true that Natalie wasn't given to café and nightclub life. She preferred the theater, opera, fine restaurants, afternoons in the Bois, and leisurely evening walks. The debutante who used to dance through the night and then go horseback riding at dawn had evolved into a middle-aged woman who retired at an early hour. A morning person, Natalie disliked staying up late.

Still, she did occasionally venture into the city's *boîtes de nuit.* She had a passing knowledge of Left Bank cafés, and once in a blue moon entered the city's more disreputable hotspots. She could be a wet blanket, though. A scene in Radclyffe Hall's *The Well of Loneliness,* based on a real-life night in 1926, shows Natalie on an evening's trek with friends, going from one dingy homosexual joint to the next. When one character hears that Valerie (Natalie's counterpart in the novel) will be coming along, she "supposed that Valerie would drink lemon squash and generally act as a douche of cold water . . . sure to grow sleepy or disapproving, she was no acquisition to this sort of party."[20]

And that's exactly what happens. Most of the group drinks champagne or wine, but Valerie confines herself to a lemon squash, insisting that it be made with fresh lemons. She sits "calm and aloof, her glance roving casually round the café, not too critically, yet as though she would say: 'Enfin, the whole world has grown very ugly, but no doubt to some people this represents pleasure.' "[21] A few of the women get up and dance. Valerie watches them with an enigmatic expression and then announces that she preferred life "when we were all martyrs!" Everyone sees that Valerie is bored, bored, bored.

Luckily, Natalie's salon took place in the late afternoon when she was wide awake. And, whether or not they viewed Natalie as an antique, many young English-speaking expats were more than happy to make the trek to rue Jacob. Natalie kept up with reputations, and never hesitated to ask those she thought had merit or might prove interesting. When particularly intrigued, she asked people to lunch. That was the case with Scott and Zelda Fitzgerald, whom she liked well enough. The manner in which Scott teased a kitten, however, sticking it in his jacket pocket, convinced her that he had a cruel streak. The Fitzgeralds also attended a Friday in the company of etiquette maven Emily Vanderbilt.

The youngsters came for the same reason people had always come: to have a good time while making contact with other literary folks. Walking into the dimly lit *pavillon* in the 1920s, you stood a fair chance of meeting some of the most important and/or popular French writers living (Colette, Paul Valéry, André Gide, Pierre Loüys, Anatole France, Paul Claudel, Lucie Delarue-Mardrus), as well as edgier scribblers like Max Jacob, Louis Aragon, and Jean Cocteau. You were always sure of meeting English-speaking expats; during this decade, frequent visitors included Janet Flanner, Mina Loy, Djuna Barnes, Gertrude Stein, Ezra Pound, Ford Madox Ford, Solita Solano, and Anna Wickham. Less often through the door: T. S. Eliot, Nancy Cunard, Peggy Guggenheim, Somerset Maugham, George Antheil, and Virgil Thomson. Also known to attend, though likely only once or twice: Bob McAlmon, Caresse and Harry Crosby, Sinclair Lewis, Sherwood Anderson, Thornton Wilder, William Carlos Williams, Hart Crane, the Sitwell siblings, and Edna St. Vincent Millay. James Joyce came once, perhaps twice, but he and Barney weren't each other's cup of tea. Some claimed to have seen Hemingway, but Natalie once said that he had never attended a Friday.

Isadora Duncan made an occasional appearance, sometimes dancing just for the fun of it. Duncan's brother, Raymond, and his wife, Penelope, came more often, showing up in their flowing Greek robes and offering a touch of exoticism. Liane de Pougy's frequent appearances in the 1920s created a sensation. Bookstore owner Sylvia Beach was a regular in those years. Painter Marie Laurencin, a good friend of Natalie's (and probably a brief lover), remained a permanent fixture until her death in 1956. Another painter, Tamara de Lempicka, came a few times on the arm of her lover, the Duchesse de la Salle.

As salon time drew near, it wasn't unusual for neighbors to gather on the sidewalk or gaze into the courtyard from apartment windows. One never knew who might show up at Miss Barney's: titled nabobs in chauffeured limousines, beautiful women walking arm in arm, a famous actor from the Opéra Comique, eccentrics in ancient Greek clothing, members of the Académie Française, that infamous fin de siècle courtesan, the poet who . . .

A young American artist married to a Frenchman, Elizabeth Eyre de Lanux, watched each Friday afternoon from her third-floor perch, fascinated by the flamboyant-looking guests making their way to the *pavillon*. This harmless spying went on for a couple of years until she happened to attend the first-ever reading of *Ulysses* by James Joyce at Adrienne Monnier's bookstore. Natalie was there and introduced herself. "I believe we are neighbors?" she asked, and issued an invitation to her next Friday. From then on, de Lanux was a regular guest. She and Natalie also engaged in a casual, on/off affair that lasted for a few years.

Guests made their way through the courtyard to the *pavillon*, where they were usually met by one of Natalie's servants. In the early 1920s, the role was held by a Chinese butler. But after 1927, Berthe Cleyrergue—Natalie's housekeeper for more than fifty years—became the official greeter. The number of attendees changed from week to week. The average Friday hosted perhaps thirty or thirty-five people. However, it wasn't unusual to see a crowd of fifty to one hundred, and special events, such as the 1927 Friday honoring Gertrude Stein, brought as many as two hundred into the garden. A consistent group of "regulars," usually good friends, formed the salon's backbone, but new blood was constantly circulating. Celebrities passing through Paris, particularly writers, were always welcome. Newcomers were often brought by an invited guest. Sometimes the Amazon met people in a friend's parlor, took a shine to them, and said, "Why don't you come 'round to my next Friday?"

Usually the salon was held indoors, but in nice weather people wandered around the gardens and into the Temple of Friendship, which held a nicely banked fire in its petite hearth on cooler days. Sometimes, especially with very large groups, events took place outside, with talks and readings given from the temple's steps.

In the early years Natalie mingled, but as time went by she began to sit. The chairs on either side of her were highly sought-after for what she called her tête-à-têtes, "where I can pick someone's brain. [I] scalp them to see what's inside, palpitate the contents, graze on the authentic substance."[22] Other chairs encircled the room, so that conversation could flow freely. Anyone reading aloud would stand in the small alcove at one end, easily visible to all.

A generous feast was always laid on the large central table. Natalie had an excellent cook for fifteen years named Maria, who prepared an astonishing spread each week. After her death in the early 1930s, Berthe Cleyrergue took on the fearsome responsibility for laying on the Friday fare and succeeded beyond measure. Everything she put on the table was homemade. In the center was always a huge platter of chicken, ham, cucumber, and roast beef sandwiches. Cakes and pastries were so beloved by regulars that they were often described in memoirs; the half-vanilla, half-chocolate cake, meringues, éclairs, almond cookies, and cheese twists were famous. Punch, tea, and hot chocolate were served, along with champagne, whiskey, and mixed drinks. Natalie drank little alcohol herself, but didn't mind serving it. "Always," Morrill Cody said, "champagne and cocktails flowed generously."[23]

Food played a subtle but very important role in a salon. If a regular gathering could be depended upon to be entertaining and filled with powerful and interesting personalities, people would probably come. If you added absolutely wonderful food, they were certain to come. In other words, a great spread could make a salon. "If the literary salon disappears," Natalie's friend François Chapon mused recently, "one of the primary reasons will be that there are no good cooks left, cooks like Berthe. She was a marvelous cook."[24]

After most guests had departed, any close friends remaining stayed for dinner. Natalie was filled in on what she might have missed while engaged in one of her tête-à-têtes. Everyone replayed the afternoon's events, nodding with appreciation over a reading, laughing at someone's puffed-up foibles, or enthusing over another's unusual dress. On Saturday mornings, Natalie might rehash the events once more. Once that was done, the Friday officially ended.

NATALIE, WHO LOVED MUSIC, knew many composers personally, including Maurice Ravel, Igor Stravinsky, and Florent Schmitt. She often incorporated music into her Fridays, hiring violinists, pianists, or others to play discreetly in the background. Once in a great while a musician had a starring role at a Friday, as when Virgil Thomson played his composition *Four Saints in Three Acts,* based on a work by Gertrude Stein. Without question, the single most important musical performance at Natalie's salon took place on New Year's Day, 1926, when the young avant-garde composer George Antheil made the official debut of his radical First String Quartet, which Barney had underwritten.

Antheil is famous for the groundbreaking *Ballet mécanique,* which made liberal use of sounds from an airplane propeller, sirens, anvils, automobile horns, and a mechanical piano. At its 1926 premiere at the Théâtre des Champs-Elysées in Paris, the strident, disturbing cacophony of sound enraged concert-goers, whose screams were drowned out by the music. Natalie, having helped fund the piece, was present on this memorable evening.

Natalie met Antheil in the summer of 1923, when he was brought to the *pavillon* by Ezra Pound. The two men had met only hours earlier at a party given by painter Francis Picabia, and Pound, fascinated by Antheil's revolutionary philosophies about music, wanted to hear him play. Since neither of them had a piano—Antheil had just moved to Paris—they came to use Natalie's. Although she felt that Antheil "seemed to turn more noise than music out of my Bechstein," she allowed them to use the instrument all summer long.[25]

As he did with so many writers, Pound took the iconoclastic musician under his wing and helped to promote his work. It was probably at his urging that Natalie agreed to her first hosted debut of an Antheil piece, *Symphony for Five Instruments,* in January 1924. A reporter described that performance as "a weird mixture of jazz and discords, almost barbaric in the effect it produced [and which] baffled the . . . distinguished gathering of prominent Americans and Parisians."[26] Florent Schmitt could only find one word to describe what he'd heard: "Interesting."

Such music wasn't Natalie's thing, either, but she understood its relevance, appreciated Pound's enthusiasm, and probably enjoyed Antheil's notoriously engaging company. According to Antheil scholar Mauro Piccinini, her financial backing paid among other things for cutting "the piano rolls of his *Ballet Mecanique*," an expensive undertaking.[27] Through Natalie, Antheil met Lily Gramont and Romaine Brooks, who also underwrote some of his work.

Two years later Natalie debuted Antheil's First String Quartet. January 1 of 1926 was a Friday, and she held her salon in conjunction with, and at the much larger home of, Lily Gramont (the day's offerings also included a display of recent lithographs by André Rouveyre).* With Antheil's piece Natalie hoped to do away with the annual New Year's Day "mawkishness," and she succeeded. There is nothing even remotely sentimental about the First String Quartet. Ezra Pound considered it "something new in violin writing and violin playing," though admitting that violinists with solid reputations thought it was simply bizarre.[28] As even its composer admitted, the Quartet was "by no means a mild number."[29]

Natalie's interest in Antheil was long-lasting. In 1930, she and the Duchesse traveled to Frankfurt for the opening of his opera, *Transatlantic.* She liked it so much that she tried to help him arrange a performance in Paris, but the idea was dropped due to the project's steep cost.

As for Antheil, he remembered Natalie as having been among the first to encourage him. In a letter to her a few years later he said that some of his happiest experiences had taken place at rue Jacob. This was partly polite beneficiary blather, but he really did value her patronage. Evidence of this can be seen in notes for his autobiography, *Bad Boy of Music.* On a huge sheet of tracing paper he penciled a timeline of his life with prominent events enclosed in circles. On the 1926 segment, just after his marriage, he drew a circle, enclosing the words: "1st String Quartet—Barney."[30]

Ironically, the First String Quartet almost missed its debut on New Year's Day. "Having finished the work," Antheil wrote, "I left it in the taxicab. Fortunately, however, I still had the majority of my pencil sketches [and] was thereby able to construct it . . . I was nearly dead [on January 1] for want of sleep."[31]

MARCEL PROUST IS often associated with the salon. In fact, he and Barney met only once, alone, late one winter night in 1921. At the time he was working on *Sodom and Gomorrah,*† the fifth volume of his epic *Remembrance of Things Past.* Knowing of Natalie's reputation, he believed that she might help him

---

*A playbill for the First String Quartet, written for a Carnegie Hall performance a year later, indicates that it is dedicated to "Nathalie Barney." Natalie, and possibly Lily, underwrote the piece.

†Published in English as *Cities of the Plain.*

depict the novel's lesbian characters. He asked a mutual friend, diplomat and writer Paul Morand, to approach Miss Barney on his behalf.

"I haven't seen you in ages," Morand said to Natalie one night at a charity ball, and proceeded to spill out a half-dozen similar clichés. Natalie considered Morand's platitudes an unfortunate augur, but agreed to meet the reclusive genius anyway. At Morand's suggestion, she sent Proust a copy of *Pensées d'une Amazone* and invited him to visit her Temple of Friendship.

For Proust to leave his cork-lined room on the boulevard Haussmann was no small concession. Long notorious for hypochondria, he was actually quite ill and would die the next year at the age of fifty-one. Suffering from asthma and hay fever, he took great pains to avoid pollen, dust, and similar irritants. The windows in his apartment were closed tight as a drum, which made the scent of his medicated vapors overwhelming to visitors.

Proust agreed to call, but that was only the start of protracted negotiations. First they had to find a mutually agreeable hour. Since Natalie retired early, about the time his day began, that presented great problems. After a long flurry of correspondence, they compromised on a midnight rendezvous. Next came letters discussing the Proustian need for warmth. The Temple, he decided, should be reserved for a summer visit. It now being winter, they should instead meet in a room easier to heat though perhaps less aesthetic. In other words, Natalie's drawing room, in which he required the temperature to reach exactly 70 degrees. Such heat wasn't easy for the *pavillon*'s rickety old wood furnace to produce, but Natalie agreed to try.

Once the details were resolved, the visit was repeatedly postponed by Proust's colds, fevers, and other illnesses. Natalie grew discouraged, even irritable, about the endless planning, but was determined that they should meet and get it over with. Only half-joking, she warned Proust that they might meet the first time for the last time. He replied that, since he believed each day would be his last, he hoped to meet her before he died.

Finally the big night came. Proust arrived exactly on time and found his hostess wrapped in an ermine robe. The two settled down for a long talk and . . . nothing happened. The conversation fizzled. They had nothing to say to each other. Proust, perhaps nervous in Natalie's presence, chattered snobbishly about high French society and dropped aristocratic titles left and right. Natalie considered him stiff and artificial and felt that his "conversation" had been rehearsed in advance. She tried leading him to talk of love between women, the ostensible purpose of his visit, but he continued to "take refuge" in inane chitchat. It would have been easier, she thought, to interrupt a Sorbonne lecture than to try to add a word to anything M. Proust had to say.

An infrequent correspondence between them continued until Proust's death in November 1922. As Natalie had predicted, though, their first meeting was their last. The great writer's demise produced an outpouring of emotional tributes in the newspapers, where Natalie was amused to read another of Morand's inexhaustible platitudes: "He leaves a great void."

When *Sodom and Gomorrah* was published Barney was horrified by the abominable sapphic characters, who, in Proust's words, "felt that to be seen would add perversity to their pleasure, and chose to flaunt their dangerous embraces before the eyes of all the world . . . [and they] crowed and chortled and uttered indecent cries." Colette asked: "Was he misled, or was he ignorant?—when he assembles a Gomorrah of inscrutable and depraved young girls, when he denounces an entente, a collectivity, a frenzy of bad angels . . . with all due deference to the imagination or the error of Marcel Proust, there is no such thing as Gomorrah."[32]

Proust's lesbian women were, Natalie agreed, completely unrealistic. And if anyone in Paris knew whereof she spoke on that topic, it was certainly Natalie Barney. What a pity Messr. Proust didn't stop talking long enough that night to hear what she had to say!

IN 1927 NATALIE brought sexual politics to the salon by instituting the informal Académie des Femmes, a none-too-subtle reproach to the all-male Académie Française.*

The idea of forming such a group had been kicked around for years by Barney and many of the women writers she knew. Early in the century she had talked of forming a coalition of women poets, whose nucleus would be composed of herself, Renée, Eva, and Olive Custance. A few years later, she and others debated the idea of a "French academy for women." Their discussions were serious enough to make news in the United States. On October 17, 1909, the *Los Angeles Examiner* ran an article cabled from Paris by the Marquis de Castellane. Headlined "Women Shut from Halls of Fame Commence an Immortality Factory," it read:

> A strong movement is on foot in France for the establishment of a "French academy" for women. The eminent body of men known as the Forty Immortals will admit no women to share their immortality.
>
> When Cardinal Richelieu established the French academy there were too few literary women to be taken into consideration, but now the women

---

*The Académie Française did not admit a woman to its ranks until 1980, when Natalie's friend Marguerite Yourcenar became a member.

of the French republic intend to put men and themselves on a literary equality. The movement is headed by Comtesse de Noailles, the young Duchesse de Rohan, and the Duchesse d'Uzes . . . [and] your compatriot, Mrs. Clifford Barney [sic], the poetess, who writes both French and English verse.

The future "forty immortelles" argue that literature is neither male nor female; that Belles-letters cannot be divided into two sections; that the question should resolve entirely into one of merit and not of sex. There is good logic in this, for we have indeed many excellent women writers.

Obviously, the idea for a coalition of women writers wasn't new, but it was Natalie who eventually put a plan in motion with the Académie des Femmes. She envisioned an association in which English and French women writers could meet, read their works, and honor one another. As she pointed out, "women of letters scarcely know one another, except sometimes by name."

Unlike the Académie Française, Natalie refused to discriminate against the opposite sex: men were welcome to enjoy the festivities. Inviting men was a clever move. By their mere presence men couldn't avoid doing something they had never done before: honor the accomplishments of women writers.

To truly appreciate the académie, it's necessary to consider that, as a general rule, women writers were not taken seriously at the time. Most reviewers and literary opinion-makers were men, who tended to ignore or condescend to books by women. Male critics considered gutsy, muscular writing to be so completely the province of men that they didn't know how to deal with someone like American writer Djuna Barnes. When her *A Book* appeared in 1923, much was made of the fact that the bleak, dark tales were written by a woman. When *Ryder* was published in 1928, the *Saturday Review* called it "the most amazing book ever written by a woman." *Transition* felt it was "a work of grim mature beauty [that] no women, and few men, have succeeded in giving us." The *Argonaut* considered it "vulgar, beautiful, defiant, witty, poetic, and a little mad . . . the most amazing thing to have come from a woman's hand."

Colette and Gertrude Stein were among the first to be honored by the academy. January 14, 1927, was devoted to Colette, who performed scenes from her *La vagabonde* with couturier Paul Poiret and her best friend, Marguerite Moreno (who, since Bernhardt's death four years earlier, had become the country's most renowned stage actress). Incidentally, this was the play's second performance at rue Jacob. In 1922, before *La Vagabonde* made its official public debut, Colette played several scenes before an appreciative audience at one of the Fridays.

On February 4, Gertrude Stein, whom Natalie had met the year before, was given two introductory tributes. The first was by poet Mina Loy, who described Stein as "the all-American innovator . . . [who] is not a writer in any sense of the word as it is understood at present." Loy was followed by Ford Madox Ford and his "Homage to Gertrude Stein." Natalie then read two passages she'd translated into French from Stein's *The Making of Americans*. This was no small feat; as Loy had said moments earlier, Stein's works were untranslatable even in their own language. Next up came the star of the day herself, reading her work in English. And, finally, the irrepressible Virgil Thomson played the piano and sang "Susie Asado" and "Preciosilla," two Stein poems that he had set to music.

A young American artist, Matthew Josephson, later recalled that day:

> A great tea party in Miss Stein's honor was given by Nathalie Clifford Barney. . . . This party really marked the coming out of Miss Stein, formerly somewhat retiring. . . . The ceremonies took place in the garden, where some two hundred guests from every walk of life were gathered. . . . Miss Stein, a solid block of a woman, was there in the midst of the crowd, talking with many of us, taking everything in with her characteristic aplomb. . . . A formidable woman, in short, and with quite an ego.
>
> The crush of Americans was so great that most of Miss Barney's aged French writers . . . soon beat a retreat. . . . Miss Barney entertained her guests not only with excellent food and tea, but also with liberal quantities of champagne. The Americans relaxed more and more; the sound of jazz music filled the stately house in the Rue Jacob. As I left my last glimpse was of a small salon where some young women, transported by literature and champagne, danced madly about in each other's arms.[33]

One writer honored, Anna Wickham, is little known today. Born in England in 1884, she trained for an opera career before marrying and becoming a mother. After a brief confinement in a mental institution, she began to write poetry addressing the constraints imposed upon women (her work was included in Louis Untermeyer's 1920 book, *Modern British Poetry*). After moving to Paris, Wickham had a brief affair with Natalie and was devastated when it ended. According to Berthe, she developed an unhealthy obsession with Barney, coming uninvited to the *pavillon* so often that orders were given to turn her away. She took to stationing herself on rue Jacob, hoping to catch sight of Natalie coming and going. "Because she was a little unbalanced," wrote Cleyrergue, "Miss Barney was apprehensive."[34] Others, too, considered the poet unstable. Sherwood Anderson, present on the day she was honored at the Académie, referred to her as a "derailed freight car." In 1947 Anna Wickham would die by her own hand, leaving behind nearly one thousand poems forged on her conflicting joy and bitterness toward a woman's lot.

Other writers honored by the Académie included Lucie Delarue-Mardrus, Rachilde, Aurel, Elisabeth de Gramont, Mina Loy, Djuna Barnes, and—in memoriam—Renée Vivien and the antiwar dramatist Marie Lénéru. Romaine Brooks and her paintings were also given a day of tribute (many were startled to see the unsociable Brooks get up and sing, accompanied by four harpists).

Later that year Natalie told Alice that she'd been asked to speak on the radio "about the representative women I celebrated here this year. I don't know if the radio goes as far as California—if so, and if you hear it, you may have heard a familiar voice."[35] She did write an account of the year's events—which, unfortunately, has disappeared—but, feeling that Laura's trained speaking voice carried better, asked her to handle the broadcast.

The Académie des Femmes is one of Natalie's major achievements. It was one of the first-ever attempts to organize women writers into a cooperative and supportive environment, and for this alone it stands as a significant contribution to feminist and literary history. After 1927, the academy faded away, but by then it had accomplished its purpose: to unite, honor, and draw attention to women writers.

ONE MAJOR WAY in which Natalie differed from most hostesses of a literary salon was that she herself was a writer,* and this decade saw publication of three of her books. In late winter of 1920, her sixth and seventh books were published a month apart. *Poems & poèmes: Autres alliances,* a French-English collection of romantic verse, appeared on Valentine's Day. *Pensées d'une Amazone,* her second gathering of aphorisms, was published on March 15. Her eighth book, *Aventures de l'esprit,* would appear in 1929.

Poems & poèmes has been largely ignored. The few mentions one finds decry its antique phrasing, wandering syntax, and occasional triteness. George Wickes felt that, after living in France for more than twenty years, Natalie had lost touch with her native idiom and was thus "inclined to translate some expressions literally from the French or to quote clichés as if they were epigrams."[36]

Ezra Pound would have agreed. When Natalie began pulling the manuscript of *Poems & poèmes* together, she offered to pay him to critique and help improve her verse. She didn't realize how seriously he would approach the task

---

*Other exceptions to this general rule among Natalie's contemporaries included Rachilde, Princess Bibesco, and Gertrude Stein (whose gatherings were really more about art than literature).

nor how extensive his recommendations would be. Pound was good at such vetting, and writers who adopted his advice, most notably T. S. Eliot and Ernest Hemingway, were invariably grateful.

If Natalie had made the suggested changes, the poems would doubtless have improved. For reasons mentioned earlier—mostly laziness and the desire for spontaneity—she chose to keep the verse as it was. In this particular situation she might also have felt that the problem was with Ezra, that her poetry just wasn't modern enough to suit him. One of her *pensées,* "Regular verse, a game of patience/Irregular verse, game of impatience," suggests her disdain for modern poetic forms. She'd been trained to write classical poetry, and saw no reason to change. After all, what was good enough for Mallarmé was good enough for her.

In *Poems & poèmes,* as was usually the case with Natalie's romantic verse, subject took precedence over style. But now, in the postwar culture, the subject matter caused scarcely a ripple. The poems themselves are a mixed bag, with most written over a period of many years. Some suffer from obscurity; they're muddled and unclear. One isn't really a poem, it's the versified invitation to the masked ball attended by Gourmont in 1911. Still, there is much about *Poems & Poèmes* to admire. Many of the poems are good, and some are lovely. One, "How Write the Beat of Love," is pleasantly erotic.

A charming feature of *Poems & poèmes* is its versified *éparpillements.* A few pages in both English and French compile various lines Natalie had scrawled on scraps of paper in her usual slapdash manner. Retrieved and pulled together, these scatterings on the subject of love evoke Sappho's fragments:

> Pale with the spring-time,
> Wandering without you—
> Sick with love-sickness!
>
> •
>
> What beauty in the way the light fell on her eye-brows . . .
>
> •
>
> As through the air
> Her little fan-shaped feet

Poems & poèmes affords a glimpse into Natalie's love of romantic suffering, evident in phrases such as "the weeping face of love," "the mouth of bitterness," "hearts that weep," and "hateful lovers." One poem, "I Built a Fire," is a veritable feast of lovesick drama. Natalie also pays respects to a favorite theme, the double-being. In "The Love of Judas," she is "an infidel in thought and word and grief/A double heart and a promiscuous soul!" In "Suffisance" she refers to a double-being who is at once one's male and female lover. A third poem,

"Double Being," seems to be about Romaine, who possesses "a northern mind, a face from Italy . . . A brow of genius and a lonely heart."

FAR MORE INTERESTING is *Pensées d'une Amazone*, arguably the finest of Natalie's books. It's also the most frustrating. It could have been a great philosophical treatise if only she had battled that damnable proclivity toward laziness. Provocative and innovative ideas are presented throughout with a flourish and then dropped. Rarely are they developed, and even then only partially. As Natalie herself proclaims in its pages, "I never go to the end of an idea—it's too far." One can't help but wish that she had, just this once, completed the journey.

Despite its flaws, *Pensées* is an extremely powerful document, one which is vehemently antiwar and vigorously profeminist. The sentiments espoused in its pages are far ahead of their time. The observant reader is put on notice of Natalie's deftly aimed arrows even before opening the book: the yellow cover displays as decoration a round circle with a dot in the middle, like the single breast of a warrior Amazon.

The first section, "Sexual Adversity, War, and Feminism," opens with a quote from Anna Maria van Schurman, an early (mid-seventeenth-century) proponent of women's right to education, and is followed by a conversation between Portia and Nerissa from William Shakespeare's *The Merchant of Venice:*

NERISSA: How like you the young German, the Duke of Saxony's nephew?

PORTIA: Very vilely in the morning, when he is sober, and most vilely in the afternoon, when he is drunk: when he is best, he is a little worse than a man, and when he is worst, he is little better than a beast.

Thus, Natalie gives warning of what follows in the pages ahead: an angry commentary-via-epigram on the role of men and women in the Western world. Simply put, her thesis was that war is a natural outgrowth of mens' militant nature; because they are drawn to war, they are unable to fully love life ("Those who love war lack the love of an appropriate sport—the art of living"). This masculine need for battle extends to every aspect of human life, resulting in the conquering of women and the destruction of women's work—children, love, and hope. ("War—men's childbirth. They give birth to death, as women do to life, inevitably and with courage.")

Women, Barney says, operate from a foundation of love, which is completely opposed to war ("We who touch life only with our hearts"). Because love has no need to conquer, women are seen as weak. But, she argues, as it takes far more strength to love than to kill ("Love, that outmoded heroism"), women are the truly strong and should be recognized as such ("We should adopt home rule in a universal sense," because "It's necessary to liberate man from man"). The result of these conflicting masculine/feminine natures: continual strife between the sexes.

Oddly, scattered amid the staunch feminist ideas are a few epigrams that sound inexplicably misogynistic: "This catastrophe, being a woman." "Sentimentality is lady's work." "Rape is perhaps not the least desirable way of pleasing." "The flighty female: the child who has been raped walks away sucking happily on a stick of barley." Why would Natalie, who had repeatedly espoused a woman's right to control her own life and body, toss off a remark lightly dismissing rape? This may have to do with that fatal flaw in her intellectual outlook, glibness, wherein she believed that a desirable end (i.e., a successful witticism) justified any means—even, if necessary, a deplorable comment.

Reaction to *Pensées d'une Amazone* varied from angry denunciation to admiring praise, most but not all of it breaking along sex lines. Women loved it. "George is reading Nathalie's book and criticizing it heartily," wrote Liane. "As for me, I'm prejudiced in its favour."[37] In *Years of Plenty,* Lily complimented Natalie's "bitter observations on the human soul in . . . *Pensées d'une Amazone.*"[38] Future literary scholar Renée Lang, then an adolescent living in Geneva, remembers being simultaneously shocked and intrigued by the daring epigrams, which had a strong influence on her. Alice Barney adored the book: "I'm terribly proud of you. I want everyone to see these wonderful things you say and say so finely, Natalie. How can you, whence does it come? I can't express my admiration."[39]

What many men disliked was not Natalie's opinion of their sex, but the cold and detached (i.e., unfeminine) manner in which she presented her arguments. J. C. Mardrus decried the book's sense of futility and Natalie's pedantic voice. "But the greatest reproach," he added, "the fault without hope, the mortal sin, is that in these pages there is no smile, not the trace of a smile, not a single smiling pensée." In a similar vein, Edmond Jaloux declared that few *pensées* were "as pessimistic as those of Mlle. N.C.B Barney." Ditto Francis de Miomandre: "Mlle B. is so pessimistic!" And the *New York Evening Post's* Vincent O'Sullivan complained that Natalie was so detached that "one finishes the book without knowing anything about [her]"—not the case, he claims, with other *pensée* authors such as Pascal and Schopenhauer. "They built a house stone by stone, and made it come to life by living in it. Miss B. built her house stone by stone, but she seems to live elsewhere."

Natalie took their comments in good stead, but she was upset by Ezra

Pound's "Paris Letter" in the *Dial:* "Natalie Barney . . . has published with complete mental laziness a book of unfinished sentences and broken paragraphs, which is, on the whole, readable. . . . The *Pensees d'une Amazone* contain . . . at least one sublime sentence running I think 'Having got out of life, oh having got out of it perhaps more than it contained.' " Ordinarily slow to take offense, she fumed over his comments for the rest of her life. In 1966 she told journalist Mary Blume, as if the offending *Dial* had been published the previous day: "I was thinking of how wrong Pound is. How lazy it is to write *a lot.* If you can put a whole novel into a few sentences, why not?"[40]

Many men did admire the book. The nation's leading man of letters, Anatole France, bestowed high praise: "Amazon, I kiss your hands with a sacred terror," he wrote after reading *Pensées.* Rainer Maria Rilke sent a note saying that the book, his current bedtime reading, reaffirmed his pride and affection in their friendship. Max Jacob described *Pensées* to friends as "delicious." *La Lanterne*'s V.S. called it "ingenious, spiritual, bold . . . it's the book of a woman who is an Amazon, that is, a superwoman." Maurice Privat thought that Natalie's "love of beauty . . . enriches our French literature," Charles Rappoport admired the way she married "American positivism with French finesse," and to Alexander Arnoux "her thoughts . . . are like arrows planted in life, quite surely." Although he disliked Natalie's pessimism, Jaloux admired the thinking behind it: "We do not lack thinkers, some padding Pascal, others pirating Montaigne; but not in all their bombastic passages is there a quarter of the real observation that I find in the formulas of NCB, so succinct and almost always elliptical."[41]

Natalie couldn't have been more delighted with the fact that her book had agitated so many men. She gathered up a representative sampling of their critical comments into a twenty-four-page booklet entitled "What the Men Think," had it illustrated with scenes of Amazons battling Greek warriors, and distributed it liberally. In 1921 she brought out a second edition of *Pensées d'une Amazone* and included the booklet's text as an appendix.

She also expanded the second edition by an additional thirty-nine pages. Most of the added heft was an expanded subsection about homosexuality, in which she interspersed historical writings on the subject with her own commentary. In the first edition, this section is titled merely "Le Malentendu" (Misunderstanding); in 1921 it became "Le Malentendu or Sappho's Lawsuit (Fragments and Witnesses)."

PUBLISHED AT DECADE'S END, *Aventures de l'esprit* is considered one of Barney's most "readable" books. The title, which translates into English as

"Adventures of the Mind," loses its complexity in the process. In French the word *esprit* has intricate layers of meaning involving intellect, wit, and spirit. To really appreciate the title, one needs to examine English definitions for all three words. *Wit* can refer to intelligence, learning, or "the ability to perceive and express in an ingeniously humorous manner the relationship between seemingly incongruous or disparate things." *Spirit* offers more than a dozen meanings, including strong loyalty, a person characterized by vigor and animation, or "the part of a human being associated with the mind, will, and feelings." As for *intellect,* one of its definitions is "a person of great intellectual ability."[42]

Intellect. Wit. Spirit. It's almost as if the word *esprit* had been invented to capture Natalie's elusive essence—and in fact, it's a word frequently used to describe her. And it's the intangibility of *esprit* that Natalie celebrates in *Aventures*—not her own, but that of writers whom she has known.

The book is divided into two parts. The first discusses her friendships or encounters with a baker's dozen of male writers, including Pierre Loüys, Anatole France, Remy de Gourmont, Marcel Proust, Rainer Maria Rilke, and others. One of the most delightful portraits is of Oscar Wilde. She had remembered little about meeting him except that, after rescuing her from a bunch of mean little boys, he'd sat her on his knee and told her a story. Preparing to write, she quizzed Alice about the encounter. "I must have been at least three," she wrote. "Where was it? Saratoga? A watering hole on the Atlantic?"[43]

The second half of *Aventures de l'esprit* is devoted to the Académie des Femmes and its honorees. Each woman is celebrated in a chapter of her own. Some chapters include the spoken introduction from the day a particular woman was honored; some contain Natalie's personal recollection of the event; and all treat their subjects with humor, affection, and—most important—respect.

Something that scholars have found helpful is the book's foldout salon "map." Natalie had originally asked Romaine to come up with an illustration symbolic of the Fridays, but for Brooks, who didn't much like the salon, it was an impossible task. Natalie ended up doing it herself.

On a piece of paper she wrote, "Le Salon de l'Amazone." At the top she drew an outline of the temple and its columns. Below came a larger shape representing her *pavillon* (with, inside, a teapot and cups atop an octagonal table). A winding pathway led from the garden, at the bottom edge, up to the temple. Crowded in tiny handwriting along the way were the names of some of the people who had attended her Fridays up to the late 1920s. It's a compelling historical document.

Publication of *Aventures de l'esprit* brought a letter from Eva Palmer-Sikelianos. "Your mission has quite clearly been to make others change," she wrote. "No one has done this as heroically as you. . . . From the beginning you must have had an apostolic certainty, an interior justification, which never failed you."[44]

TWELVE

Years of Glory:
The Amazon's Tribe

THE TWENTIES

When it comes to friendship, I am very lazy; once I confer friendship, I never take it back.

—Natalie Barney

True friendship is never serene.

—Mme. de Sévigné

*J*UST AS THE SALON reached its apotheosis of greatness in the 1920s, so too did Natalie's relationships with women. Lovers, friends, mother, sister: the Amazon's world was completely intact. Never again would this intricate web of female associations be as consistently rewarding. Never again would she be surrounded by so many vital and extraordinary women. Even her rare adversaries—Aurel, say, or Edith Wharton—possessed such indelible character that their enmity could be brandished proudly, like a badge of honor.

In the giddy, champagne-popping atmosphere of 1920s Paris, where life seemed like a continual fête, Natalie's complicated approach to love and friendship worked more smoothly than it ever had—or ever would again. It was as if she had gathered together a tribe of women finally able to experiment in small and large ways with her long-held philosophies. They were a varied lot: lesbian, straight, bisexual; old and young; proper and not; even one or two foes. They possessed one great commonality. By virtue of love, or friendship, or antipathy—and sometimes all three—they belonged to the Amazon's world. They were members of her tribe.

THE OTHER AMAZON QUEEN

Since 1903, Gertrude Stein had lived at 27, rue de Fleurus, only a few blocks from Natalie. The two women, however, never met until the mid-1920s. That seems odd, as they surely knew about each other. Both were Americans, writers, and lesbians, and they shared many mutual friends such as Sylvia Beach, Ezra Pound, Marie Laurencin, and Virgil Thomson. Obviously, their slowness to meet was a matter of deliberate choice.

Perhaps their reluctance had something to do with the way each experienced her lesbianism. Gertrude had been settled since 1910 in a committed relationship with Alice B. Toklas, while Natalie was notorious for being the most restless of free agents. The opposing Stein/Barney interpretations of what it meant to love women are a strong indication of just how limiting labels—in this case "lesbian"—can be.

Gertrude and Alice, from the perspective of their happy domesticity, disapproved of Natalie's womanizing ways. Evidence of this can be gleaned from a comment Alice once made, half-joking to a friend that Natalie picked up her lovers in the toilets of a department store. She may have meant to be humorous, but the statement reveals the Stein-Toklas perspective on Natalie's active sex life: it was dirty.

Natalie, hearing about Gertrude and Alice from mutual friends, probably developed a dismissive viewpoint of her own. She would have determined that, aside from the fact that Stein and Toklas were women, they were joined in the kind of conventional marriage she had preached against all her life. They even took on traditional male-female roles. Gertrude talked to husbands about literature; Alice shared recipes with their wives. Alice ran the household, overseeing the kitchen and the help; Gertrude concentrated on the important business of writing.

Natalie might have overcome her antipathy toward Stein's domestic setup if only Gertrude had other gifts to offer; that is, if she were even minimally soignée and/or talented. But to Natalie's sensibilities, Stein was a no-go on both accounts. With her blunt Roman senator's profile, her squat body, and her corduroy peasant clothes, Gertrude could hardly be deemed fashionable.

As for talent, Natalie never understood Stein's work and did not believe in it. That she promoted it later was a matter of politics, writerly sisterhood, and the friendship that did eventually develop between them.

Barney and Stein finally met, probably in 1926, at a party given by Lady Rothermere, the patron of T. S. Eliot. At long last scrutinizing one another in the flesh, perhaps each woman thought, "Well, she's not so bad. Maybe we should try to strike some sort of détente." Soon after, Natalie and Romaine encountered Gertrude and Alice at the Russian ballet. Natalie invited them to her next Friday, which, according to Toklas, "was the beginning of a long and warm friendship."[1] From then on Stein was often seen at Natalie's gatherings, "the permanent occupant of right wall center. With her stout tweeds, her sensible shoes, she seemed like a game warden scrutinizing the exotic birds."[2] The friendship was cemented forever when Natalie honored Stein at the Académie des Femmes in 1927.

Because both Natalie and Gertrude held influential gatherings in their homes, some have called these two women rivals. That's hardly the case. Natalie's Fridays centered on literature and writers. Gertrude's "afternoons" may have attracted notable writers, but the real purpose of her socializing was to promote modern art (or at least her contribution to it vis-à-vis her early, prescient collection of works by Picasso, Matisse, Gris, and other Modernists). Virgil Thomson, who knew them both fairly well and often attended their gatherings, once remarked that no rivalry existed between them "because they weren't doing the same thing."[3]

It's not certain how warm the relationship really was. Each was formidable, liked to have her own way, and was used to being at the center of a talented circle. They might just as easily have waged war on each other, but, probably due to Natalie's outgoing nature and desire to be helpful, they settled into a wary friendship. François Chapon summed up the matter succinctly: "Between Natalie and Gertrude," he said, "there was a kind of armed peace."[4]

The *Amazone de Joie* Rejoins the Tribe

Though Natalie maintained a distant friendship with Liane, they rarely saw each other. This bothered Liane, who penned a subtle reproach in a 1920 Christmas card:

> O brilliant moon
> We see each other better
> From afar. . . .

Natalie responded with a phone call shortly after the holidays, and came to call the same day. "Charming surprise!" Liane scribbled happily in her blue notebook. "My Flossie came to see me." She entered a detailed description of Natalie's outfit—dark wool dress with a green-embroidered white waistcoat, caped coat thrown over the shoulders, a simple felt hat atop the blond head. "With her brisk style, her implacable smile, her tenderness towards me, her instinctively caressing little hands, she looked very young and very happy. I plunged into the renewed contact."[5]

So did Natalie, who felt comfortable enough in the company of her old lover to bring friends along. Liane was thrilled to meet the Duchesse C. T., describing her as "pure Watteau." Lily was equally surprised by the former courtesan. "Where I expected to find no more than a whiff of scent," she confided to Natalie, "I found fresh air."[6]

Bruised and battered by the contemptuous treatment they'd received after their marriage, the Ghikas had kept a low profile ever since, inviting only a tiny circle of trusted friends to their home. When Natalie reappeared in her life, Liane, once seen nightly at the finest restaurants of Paris, hadn't dined out in more than eight years. Encouraged by Natalie, she and Georges risked attending a Friday at rue Jacob.

They needn't have worried. The world had turned upside-down since the war, and Liane was no longer viewed as the scourge of polite society. Her sin against gentility, that of being a whore turned princess, was now viewed as a colorful quirk. Still a great beauty, and surrounded by the aura of Belle Époque glory, she created an absolute sensation. Men who once bought her caresses now bowed and kissed her fingertips, gazing at her with the respectful reverence due a triumphant survivor. The very same aristocratic ladies who had turned their backs in her presence now refused to leave her side. Liane adored the attention, but kept an eye firmly fixed on her Flossie, who looked ravishing "in a white crepe dress and a turquoise blue Spanish shawl embroidered in white, her hair making a turban of gold."[7]

It wasn't long before the old friendship took a surprising new turn.

A few nights after Liane made her salon debut, she and Natalie dined at Lily's rue Raynouard home. Afterward, the servants spread velvet-covered mattresses on the floor of a Chinese-style room and discreetly retired. Liane was persuaded to stretch out. Natalie lay down beside her, and the Duchesse sat close. Nothing was done or said, but a certain intimacy emerged.

On her next visit to the Ghikas', Natalie took Liane into her arms and they lay down amid the scent of flowers. Lunches, teas, and Fridays followed. As in days of old, there were drives in the Bois and trips to the theater. Finally the day came when Liane wrote of seduction. "Nathalie comes to coax and caress me, and murmur 'My first love, and my last.' I see her bending over to enfold me, and it seems that I have never left her arms." Since Liane had promised Georges that everything below her waist belonged only to him, Natalie only "celebrates my body down to the waist."[8]

In August 1922, Natalie and Lily visited the Ghikas' summer residence on the Normandy coast, and the complexity and intensity of all the interrelationships ratcheted upward. Georges, a bit of a voyeur, minded not a whit when Barney climbed into bed beside his wife, who abandoned herself to the "delicious sin" of Natalie's caressing hands. Georges and Lily sat nearby, coolly observing them while discussing literature. The next night Lily joined Natalie and Liane in the bed. While Georges entertained them by reading poetry aloud, the three women exchanged kisses, hugs, and caresses.

Reflecting next day on the experience, Liane decided that it had been charming, though perhaps "a little nerve-wracking." She felt guilty, but decided that what happened wasn't really a big sin, otherwise God wouldn't have sent her "these charming beings . . . so sweetly fond and sensual" to delight "in our true affection for each other."[9] Besides, there was no denying how happy she felt.

This idyllic state evaporated when Liane developed an obsessive crush on the Duchesse. She rhapsodized in her notebook over every aspect of Lily's being: her unclothed body (superb), her style (tremendous), her flute playing (silvery), her clothes (pretty, lovely), her walk (majestic), her nature (loving, joyful, tender). One day in Paris she called upon Lily at home and was overjoyed to find her alone, without Natalie. She ended up in the bedroom, where she spied two pair of slippers under a Louis XVI chest. Convinced that the gray pair belonged to Natalie, she was consumed by jealousy.

Liane doted so thoroughly and so obviously on the Duchesse that Natalie grew sulky and began making countermoves. When she reneged on a promise to bring Lily to Nice, where the Ghikas were spending the winter, Liane wrote directly to Lily and invited her personally. Upon learning of the treacherous invitation, Natalie jotted off a furious letter to Liane. "Nathalie is becoming cantankerous; it must be the change of life,"[10] the princess noted bitchily.

By that summer, the friendship's second blooming had faded drastically. Liane made herself scarce for a while, and eventually the damage was repaired. There would be more shared pleasures and good times, and even a few shocking surprises, between Natalie and Liane.

A CENSORIOUS AMAZON GETS A SMALL COMEUPPANCE

Despite the changes that were churning society, there remained many who disapproved of Natalie and everything she stood for. One surprising example was writer Edith Wharton. It's surprising not only because Wharton's novels show great compassion for and understanding of outsiders, but because the two had much in common. Both were wealthy American women who lived in Paris, held literary salons, and wrote. Maybe, for Wharton, their differences mattered more than their similarities. She was a product of New York society's uppermost reaches, a stratosphere virtually unattainable to upstart midwestern tradesmen like the Barneys and Pikes. Fourteen years older than Natalie and only three years younger than Alice, she came from a different generation. She was a hardworking, serious writer; Barney wasn't. She was heterosexual, and, although she had many male homosexual friends, she disliked lesbians intensely. She particularly disliked Natalie Barney.

There seems no logical reason for this. One of Wharton's biographers hypothesized that her antipathy stemmed from the popularity of Natalie's salon, which "had long been a formidable rival to Mrs. Wharton, and one suspects that it was this, as much as moral disapproval, that aroused Edith's hostility."[11] Another reason might be Wharton's feeling of possessiveness toward Bernard Berenson. Not only was she very fond of the art critic, but she regarded friendship with him as a feather in her cap. His obvious adoration of Natalie, with whom he spent as much time as possible whenever he came to Paris, must have galled her. Whatever the cause, Wharton's feelings about Barney were no secret. She tried to sway others to her point of view.

As for the Amazon, she was quite aware of Wharton's feelings and delighted in making sly little jokes at her expense. For instance, in *Souvenirs indiscrets,* when she mentions the earliest translation of Sappho by Henry Wharton, she adds a parenthetic comment: "No relation to my compatriot, Edith Wharton, who might have shuddered with horror at the idea that there might be any confusion."

Considering all this, it must have been very difficult for Wharton to find herself lunching with Natalie one day in the fall of 1926.[12] The venue was the sumptuous apartment of Wharton's lover, Walter Berry, a wealthy American art and rare book collector who had been close friends with Henry James and Marcel Proust. Sophisticated and intelligent, he surely knew that Edith and Natalie were a volatile mix. That's probably why he invited them.

"The guests at those luncheons were always chosen with great discrimination," recalled Caresse Crosby, who was present that day. "[The luncheons were] a purée of wit, beauty and bitchery, for I think Cousin Walter believed as I do that a woman without a touch of bitchery is like milk without Vitamin D. . . ."[13]

Caresse, who was married to Berry's young cousin Harry, left no record of the day's events. However, it's fair to assume that Barney and Wharton, both well brought up and politically consummate ladies, were able to put aside their bows and quivers and interact with aplomb. Cousin Walter, bright as he was, didn't have a clue about Amazon etiquette.

ENTRY OF THE AMAZONIAN AIDE-DE-CAMP

Natalie's domestic situation had always been unsettled. As charming as she was socially, she could be a martinet in private. This held true not only for friends, but for her hired help. Autocratic, impatient, and demanding, she was difficult to work for. Stories abound of maids reduced to tears, cooks quitting in a huff, and chauffeurs shaking in their boots. Consequently, her staff—consisting in the early 1920s of a majordomo, two maids, a cook, and a chauffeur—was constantly turning over.

But all of that changed in 1927 when a sturdy Burgundian, twenty-three-year-old Berthe Cleyrergue, entered rue Jacob to replace a hastily departed chambermaid. Combining extraordinary competence with patience, thrift, honesty, and what would become a strong lifelong affection for her employer, she quickly became the indispensable key to a smoothly functioning household. Part servant and part friend—but a friend who always knew her place—she stayed until the end of Natalie's life.

She almost quit right at the beginning. Days into her new job, she learned about Miss Barney's proclivities and resolved to leave. On reflection, however, the practical lass couldn't deny that the pay was excellent—nearly twice what she could earn elsewhere. And Miss Barney, when she wasn't in a temper, treated her with remarkable kindness. Also, the job included her own petite but separate lodging across the way, which made for an easy commute. Later, when she ended up marrying a man with a larger apartment in the same building, he was very accepting about her job. "At Miss Barney's it's like anywhere else," he told her.[14]

One of Cleyrergue's most admirable traits was her ability to deal with Natalie's thorny personality. To get along with Natalie in the capacity of housekeeper, one had to live by many unstated rules: *Always* call her Miss Barney. Speak softly. Know when not to speak. Be ready with tea and delicious goodies for callers. Run an orderly establishment despite Natalie's innate disorder (and the fact that she didn't want papers or books to be moved—not ever). Adapt to sudden and sometimes wacky changes in plans. Do not make judgments. Be humorous. Be a good and loyal friend but never forget your place as servant.

Berthe was occasionally pricked by a thorn, of course, that was inevitable. But she found harmless ways to vent. "I would just go down to the kitchen," she explained, "and say, 'In the name of God, what could I have done differently?' And then it would be over."[15]

MOTHER AMAZON

When news broke of Alice's separation from her young husband, the newspapers were pitiless. The attacks commenced in November 1919, when she entertained for the first time without Christian, and never let up. On January 18, 1920, what might be the longest headline in the *Washington Post*'s history announced: "How Mrs. Hemmick Astonished Washington Society: She Sent Out 'At Home' Cards for a Big Reception at her Rhode Island Avenue Residence, and Eliminated Her Husband's Name from the Invitations—Divorce? Oh! No. Just Her Way to Announce Her Estrangement." The accompanying story was subsequently published as far away as California.

The breakup of this May-December union provoked months of coverage, until Alice finally decamped for Paris in June 1920, accepting Natalie's invitation to stay at rue Jacob while weathering the storm. If she'd anticipated the experience in store for her at the home of her eldest daughter, she might have preferred persecution by the press back in Washington.

Natalie's relationship with Alice had always been complicated and had grown more so over the years. As a child, she had loved her mother without condition, viewing her as the epitome of beauty and sweetness. Yet she never felt secure about being loved in return. Alice was not one for hugging and kissing, and young Natalie suffered greatly from her mother's lack of physical affection. Alice's "maternal sense was generally distracted [and] preoccupied with her art," Natalie wrote. "For her, art was what counted the most."[16] All her life Natalie had dreams about her mother in ways that denote insecurity, with Alice lost, taken away, dying, disappearing, or simply overwhelmed by too many projects.

Natalie believed that Alice was incapable of deep feelings for anyone. As she wrote in the late 1940s, her mother "liked nothing more than to shine before a crowd" and "would never be happy shining for a single person."[17] In other words, she "loved everyone and no one."[18] Ellen Pike had concluded the same thing decades before when, learning of her daughter's engagement to Albert Barney, she murmured, "I can't imagine Alice loving anyone. She isn't the kind."

As for her father, Natalie had loved him deeply despite his tragic flaws. She appreciated his generosity and the kindness of which he was capable. She was proud of his dashing good looks, his charm, and his sociability; in fact, all her life she equated her outgoing nature with his. "I'm as social as our father was and like seeing even the people I dislike [who are] few and far between," she once told Laura.[19] But she had also feared and scorned Albert's drinking, his temper, and his rules. Most of all, she disliked the power he had held over her life. "How helpless and awkward was his love," she said, "for I suppose he also loved us under that worldly way of his, bristling with 'though shalt nots.' "[20]

Natalie's love for her parents was made complicated by witnessing Alice's daily submission to a husband who could be tyrannical and abusive. As she began developing her own ideas about the way the world should work for women, the situation grew more confusing, forcing her to juggle deep love with an equally deep anger. All her life she remained angry at Albert for being abusive and at Alice for accepting his abuse. Most of the time, love prevailed, with the anger tucked away on a forgotten burner, simmering way below the boiling point. Every once in a while, though, something new got stirred into the pot and the whole stew bubbled over.

That's what happened when Alice came to visit. Money was the big issue this time, particularly Natalie's pent-up resentment at Alice's lavish spending on her "worthless-boy pederast husband."[21] Among Natalie's complaints: she felt that her inheritance had been diluted and that her gifts and generosity to her mother were unappreciated. Alice responded that Natalie did more for her "many infatuations" than she had ever done for her own mother, and reassured her coldly that, notwithstanding the money spent on Christian, Natalie would inherit a great sum.

Things became so bad between them that Alice stayed in her room, where she worked on a new ballet, *Atlantis*. Hoping to find common ground, Natalie tried writing her own play, *The Lighthouse*. Alice considered it too highbrow and urged Natalie to write for the "middle circles"—the masses. This was an impossible task for the Amazon. Soon conflicts over *The Lighthouse* were added to the simmering stew.

The arguments raged on. Old hurts and resentments bubbled to the surface. Mother and daughter, too irate to converse, began communicating via sharp, hurtful notes. Twenty years had passed since Alice learned that her daughter was a lesbian. She had accepted Natalie's sexuality and even befriended her lovers, but she had never been overjoyed about any of it. Now, she came right out and told Natalie so. "I disapprove of you," she wrote in a note, underlining the words. "My coming to live with you would make it appear otherwise . . . I will no longer conceal my real feelings or pretend to things I believe to be wrong."[22]

Natalie's replies, which no longer exist, apparently made things worse. "Your misrepresentation are unendurable," Alice seethed. "I shall at once [procure rooms elsewhere and] leave your house where I have been insulted. . . . I'll go as <u>soon as possible.</u> . . . I'm enclosing $1000 which will pay for the expenses I've caused you and believe me much obliged for your hospitality. Mother." She noted that "even your father—when drunk—or Christian, have never been more unjust, cruel or insulting."[23]

For a while relations between the two women teetered back and forth between so-so and awful, until finally Alice decided that she had truly had enough. She must remain a few days at Natalie's "because it will be too great an effort for me to pack now and move—but by October 1 I will be gone bag and baggage and I'll never enter your doors again." She signed the letter "Alice Barney."[24] She meticulously added up what she felt Natalie was due for room and board, arriving at a total of 5,950 francs. She deducted 1,600 that Natalie owed her and enclosed a check for the rest.

Alice departed for London in early October, putting up at the Ritz Hotel. Unfortunately, her leave-taking did not return mother and daughter to a peaceful path. When Alice began rewriting Natalie's *The Lighthouse,* her daughter was incensed. Furious letters flew back and forth across the Channel. Alice lectured Natalie on the necessity of writing to please the masses. Natalie responded that her mother's writing was maudlin. Finally Alice threw in the towel, declared herself off the project, and closed her letter on a crisp note: "I'd better not sign lovingly Mother."[25]

However, without informing Natalie, she continued to work on *The Light-house* and eventually entered it in a contest sponsored by the Drama League of America. The cover page showed but a single author's name: Alice Pike Barney. It was an uncharacteristically selfish stunt. The only possible explanation is that, having completely reworked the play, she felt justified in not giving Natalie credit for the script. Natalie might never have known but for the fact that *The Lighthouse* took the Drama League's First Prize. Needless to say, when she found out she was furious.

The bad patch finally ended when Natalie sent Alice a just-published copy of her newest book, *Pensées d'une Amazone.* Alice's response was lovely but also delivered a sting. "How very beautiful," she wrote. "Between heartbreaks, what a wealth you have given."[26]

Returning to Washington in the summer of 1921, Alice's calendar was crowded with activities at Neighborhood House, theater production, playwriting, and painting. She also became a founding member of the National Woman's Party, established to bring women equal rights now that they had won the vote, and continued entertaining at Studio House. Her daughters probably expected her to continue with this familiar routine for the rest of her life, but she still possessed the capacity for surprise. Early in 1923 she took the train to California to visit her sister, Hessie, who was now living there, and fell hard for the green rolling hills, the scent of orange blossoms and roses, the relaxed life, the climate. California had but one drawback, as far as she could see: "the midwest accent one hears."

Alice bought a small, picturesque farmhouse in the Hollywood hills surrounded by avocado and palm trees, and returned East to pack and try to sell Studio House. She hired a second-year college student, William Huntington, to type her scripts and assist her in various other ways. Over time he took on numerous helpful jobs for all three Barney women and came to know them quite well. He would be a confidant to both Natalie and Laura, assisting them with business matters, until their deaths.

By the fall of 1924 Alice had returned to Hollywood and moved into her new home, "Old Garden Cottage." She bought a pretty Persian cat and began throwing theatrical programs similar to those at Studio House. The fledgling movie industry was just getting under way in Hollywood, and she came to know some of its minor and major figures, including Charles Chaplin and Cecil B. DeMille. It wasn't long before Mrs. Barney's was the place to be seen.

THE NOTORIOUS AMAZON SCRIBE

One Friday in 1929, an Englishwoman named Radclyffe Hall was the guest of honor at Natalie's salon. Rue Jacob was packed that afternoon, because John, as Hall preferred to be known, had been the object of great curiosity since the previous summer's publication of her novel *The Well of Loneliness*, which depicted the life of a lesbian.

Hall was accompanied to Natalie's by her lover, Una Troubridge. The two had lived together since 1917, after Una left her husband, a British admiral. Both women enjoyed dressing in well-tailored masculine attire, including vested suits, boiled shirts, and stiff collars. Compton Mackenzie recalled seeing them at the theater in London, where they set off a buzz by topping their skirts with dinner jackets and starched white fronts. Natalie, Romaine, and many of their lesbian friends thought Hall and Troubridge looked ridiculous in such outfits.

Natalie deplored the "scientific" theories, then in vogue, of Richard von Krafft-Ebing, Havelock Ellis, and others. Simply put, these sexologists promulgated the idea that a lesbian was a man trapped in a woman's body, and therefore guaranteed to lead an unhappy, perverted life. To that end, Barney intensely disliked female cross-dressing, unless it came in the guise of an outright costume. She didn't see why women, complete in and of themselves, felt the need to imitate men.

Cross-dressing can be tricky territory, since a fine line exists between masculine and androgynous garb. Romaine Brooks might make fun of Radclyffe Hall's clothing, but she herself had a very "tailored" way of dressing, just masculine enough to telegraph her sexual orientation. As mentioned earlier, when Bernard Berenson met her he immediately abandoned his hopes for a liaison with Natalie. Jean Chalon, introduced to Romaine in the 1960s, thought she resembled nothing so much as a cranky old bachelor. Nonetheless, Romaine, convinced that she resided firmly on the feminine side of that subtle line, showed her scorn for Troubridge's habitual attire by painting a near-caricature of her in 1924. Hair bobbed and dressed in a man's morning suit, she sported earrings and her characteristic monocle while glaring severely from the canvas. A worried Troubridge asked friends: "Am I really like that?"

The Well of Loneliness, the first-ever attempt to ask mainstream society to understand and accept lesbians, was strongly denounced by British newspapers. Its author was accused of advocating "hideous and loathsome vices." One editorialist proclaimed that he'd sooner give someone prussic acid than Hall's book because "poison kills the body, but moral poison kills the soul." Home Office papers, never released until 1997, opined that *The Well of Loneliness* "supports a depraved practice and is gravely detrimental to the public interest."

The Well was almost immediately banned in Britain and ended up being printed in Paris. When copies were sent from Paris to a London bookshop, they were seized by Customs and the bookstore owner was arrested. In the trial that followed, literary luminaries such as E. M. Forster and Virginia Woolf were prepared to attest to *The Well*'s literary merit, but to no avail. Una Troubridge would recall that "the magistrate, having refused to hear any of our fifty-seven witnesses in its favour, had condemned it to death as an obscene book."[27]

With all this fuss, sales skyrocketed throughout Europe and the United States. *The Well* was so popular that American movie impresario Sam Goldwyn, who had no idea what it was about, wanted to make a movie out of it. When told by one of his assistants that he couldn't, he asked "Why not?" "The book's about lesbians!" came the shocked reply. Goldwyn shrugged: "So what?" he said. "We'll make 'em Austrians!"[28]

The Well of Loneliness revolves around a wealthy Englishwoman whose father so desperately yearned for a son that he christened the unborn infant Stephen. Alas, Stephen Gordon was born a girl. Growing up unloved, Stephen tried to please her father by excelling at men's sports like hunting and fencing. This, Hall implies, is why Stephen became an "invert," or homosexual.

Viewing her sexual tastes as an aberration, the tortured Stephen called herself "some awful mistake—God's mistake." She hopes there are no more like her "because it's pure hell." Yet she believes in her right to be let alone, to live as she chooses. The book's last lines are a pitiful plea: "Acknowledge us, oh God, before the whole world. Give us also the right to our existence!"

Nobody ever claimed that *The Well of Loneliness* was a good book. Virginia Woolf, though staunchly defending its right to be published, complained to friends that its indecency lay in its boredom. Edith Wharton considered it "dull twaddle." Romaine Brooks called it ridiculous, superficial, and trite. However, most critics respect the unshrinking bravery it took to write such a book at the time. As Blanche McCrary Boyd pointed out in a 1981 edition, "Hall's courage makes her book matter."[29] Still, even Hall's admirers admit that it's a pretty bad book, hackneyed beyond belief, brimming with self-pity, and crammed with self-loathing. "Today it seems unlikely," an octogenarian Janet Flanner remarked in 1972, "[that] it could ever have created a popular literary social scandal of such proportions."[30]

Despite its faults the book has interesting aspects, particularly the barely disguised portrait of Natalie as Valerie Seymour, a wealthy American living in Paris who presents an optimistic alternative to Stephen's gloomy take on inversion. As Hall's biographer Sally Cline points out, "throughout the narrative, Valerie tries to raise Stephen's low self-esteem. She believes that . . . a good time is coming, recognition is at hand, inverts must merely 'bide their time.' They must be bold and unafraid, must play their trumpets, bang their drums, 'cultivate more pride . . . learn to be proud of their isolation.' "[31]

Like Natalie, Valerie is witty, popular, charming, and good looking. Unlike Stephen Gordon, she's completely comfortable with her sapphism. She is "a kind of pioneer who would probably go down in history . . . her love affairs would fill quite three volumes . . . [and] all intelligent people realized that she was a creature apart."

Hall's description of Natalie/Valerie provides another take on Barney's immense appeal:

> Valerie came forward with a smile of welcome. She was not beautiful nor was she imposing, but her limbs were very perfectly proportioned, which gave her a fictitious look of tallness. She moved well, with the quiet and unconscious grace that sprang from those perfect proportions. Her face was humorous, placid and worldly; her eyes very kind, very blue, very lustrous. She was dressed all in white, and a large white fox skin was clasped round her slender and shapely shoulders. For the rest she had masses of thick fair hair, which was busily ridding itself of its hairpins; one could see at a glance that it hated restraint. . . .

Valerie suddenly smiled at Stephen. . . . She started to talk to her guest quite gravely about [Stephen's] work, about books in general, about life in general; and as she did so Stephen began to understand better the charm that many had found in this woman; a charm that lay less in physical attraction than in a great courtesy and understanding, a great will to please, a great impulse towards beauty in all its forms—yes, therein lay her charm. And as they talked on it dawned upon Stephen that here was no mere libertine in love's garden, but rather a creature born out of her epoch, a pagan chained to an age that was Christian. . . .[32]

Sometime later, attending a reception at Valerie's home, Stephen felt welcomed "by all these clever and interesting people—and clever they were there was no denying; in Valerie's salon the percentage of brains was generally well above the average. . . ." As Stephen looked around, she realized that many of Valerie's guests, though acting perfectly normal, were homosexual "men and women who must carry God's mark on their foreheads." Thanks to Valerie, though, they feel comfortable:

There she was, this charming and cultured woman, a kind of lighthouse in a storm-swept ocean. The waves had lashed round her feet in vain; winds had howled; clouds had spued forth their hail and their lightning; torrents had deluged but had not destroyed her. The storms, gathering force, broke and drifted away, leaving behind them the shipwrecked, the drowning. But when they looked up, the poor spluttering victims, why what should they see but Valerie Seymour! Then a few would strike boldly out for the shore, at the sight of this indestructible creature.[33]

It's easy to poke fun at such purple prose today, but these passages are useful in understanding just how unusual Natalie was in her time, capable of bestowing a sense of pride and self-respect. To Hall, Natalie was the light beckoning tormented beings toward the peaceful shores of acceptance. She transformed Barney, a pagan in her soul and heart, into a near-religious icon—Saint Natalie, Patron of the Outcast.

ADIEU À L'AMAZONE DE JOIE

It took a while, but the slump in Natalie's friendship with Liane, brought about by the latter's attraction to Lily Gramont, recovered. The former grand horizontal once again attended the Fridays, often with her prince in tow, and the occasional lunches, dinners, and get-togethers resumed.

In February 1926, Natalie and Lily were invited to the Ghikas' Mardi Gras costume party. Liane went all out, draping herself in an elaborate Persian costume of rich red cloth embroidered with gold, topped by a gold hat covered with emerald drops. Lily came as Confucius, with a mustache, long queue hanging down her back, narrow spectacles, and a beautiful, elaborately embroidered Chinese robe. As Attila the Hun, Natalie wore a panther skin slung across her body, a "primitive little hat" atop her head, and carried a spear.

It was around this time that Liane developed a crush on a pretty young woodcut artist, Manon Thiébaut, who had "wit, talent, easy manners, charm, wonderful eyes, beautiful tousled hair worn bobbed, a pale skin and an enchanting fragility."[34] Soon Manon was living in the Ghikas' vacation home. Liane nicknamed her Tiny One, and couldn't stop talking about her lovely manners, her intelligence, and her conquest of the entire household.

The conquest was greater than she realized. A month later, in July 1926, Tiny One and Georges ran away together, leaving Liane brokenhearted and humiliated. Natalie came quickly to offer comfort. She held Liane, listened, gave advice, and was generally caring and tender. Her solicitude did not belie the fact that she herself was very much in love. The woman this time was an Italian aristocrat, Mimi Franchetti, then in her early thirties.

Franchetti had played a big role in Compton Mackenzie's *Extraordinary Women* as the beautiful, self-centered, slightly dim heartbreaker, Rosalba Donsante: "Her profile was Greek in the way that Virgil's hexameters are Greek. Every feature was in proportion and every feature was clear cut. Her mouth curved up at the corners like the mouths Leonardo da Vinci loved to paint. . . . Her brown eyes were deep and brilliant beneath . . . [a] rich weight of rippling hair." A simpler description of Mimi's appeal: "To criticize her was to criticize Spring."[35]

The past summer, when Liane had been enamored of Manon, Natalie had confessed her passion for Mimi. It was, she told Liane, a love that outstripped any other love she'd ever had. That was a bit insensitive, considering that de Pougy had been one of those other loves. In fact, the statement so irritated Liane that she responded in a letter by saying, "The best in your life was me! Me! Me!"[36]

One day, a few months after Manon and Georges ran off, Liane was lying in bed, depressed, when Natalie dropped in unexpectedly. She was accompanied by Mimi, whom the princess had never met. Unspoken but understood by all was the fact that Natalie was offering up Franchetti as a sort of temporary gift meant to cheer Liane.

"And in she came," wrote Liane, "tall, slender, white as a magnolia flower, her enchanting gestures so graceful, small, rare, precise, fiery eyes, an almost unreal fineness. She bent over me, over my cruel suffering. Nathalie smiled. It was Nathalie herself who prepared her own fate."[37]

Natalie and Mimi returned the next day, accompanied by a violinist named Pola. While sonatas played discreetly from the next room, Natalie and Mimi climbed into bed with Liane, one on each side. Natalie stroked and caressed her lovingly. Mimi kissed her on the lips. . . .

After a few days of these caretaking visits, the inevitable happened: Liane and Mimi fell in love. Liane claimed that she tried to resist for Natalie's sake, but her passion got the better of her. Finally, she and Mimi, behind Natalie's back, "abandoned ourselves without remorse . . . to the delirium of our love."[38] Natalie, who constantly boasted that she had never known jealousy, was now ravaged by it. She stormed, threatened, and created scenes. When that didn't work, she resorted to childish behavior: when the new lovers made plans to leave for Italy, Natalie hid Mimi's passport. She simply refused to let go of her young lover. Finally Franchetti broke away from her for good and went to stay with Liane.

Out of this experience came one of the most astonishing of Natalie's written works, the unpublished "Amants féminins ou les troisième." Completed in 1926, it is dedicated "pour Mimi Franchetti" and written to "rid myself of desire for her." It shows a Natalie that few believed possible. Far from being the implacable Amazon always invincible in love, she was simply a woman ripped apart by jealousy and heartbreak. It may also be the first literary text in history in which a woman attempts to define her own experience by depicting three women involved in a ménage à trois.

"Amants féminins" tells the whole story in a clear and unvarnished manner. Natalie barely even disguises the characters, using the initials N, L, and M. Like N, M has had more than 100 mistresses and attracts everyone. Unlike N, however, she keeps no one and is suicidal. This attracts N's inborn knight: "If I take her into my life," she reasons, as Natalie once did with Pauline Tarn, "she won't want to die anymore."[39] She promises to be M's refuge and security when others torment her, because "When we love women, don't we take on their pains and abandons?"[40] N feels capable of saving other women because she is "other, more-than-woman. . . ."[41]

When she's not suicidal, M is lighthearted and always singing operatic arias. A tease, she is not afraid to be submissive because she knows that, in the end, she will dominate. She therefore begs to be taken and retaken, to be owned, and even a little humiliated. "Her cry mounted and shook and suffered the joy of her very insides: 'Taaake me! . . . . Taaake me!' . . . Then her body began to dance with love between my arms."[42]

Before M met L, she had been unfaithful to N on numerous occasions. Once she threw herself at a tennis player, and N felt rage and sadness at the sight of them. They were young and beautiful, and when all three were together she felt like their chaperone.

It was to divert L, suffering from her husband's treason, that she brought M along for a visit. L needed to be reminded of tenderness. However, she felt uncomfortable when, upon being introduced, L offered her mouth to M before even giving her hand. With the violinist playing in another room, L, N, and M stretched out together. After murmuring that chastity and insomnia had not been happy companions, L gave herself over to pleasure. N felt powerful, as if she had thousands of hands. M and L became a single mouth. N felt a vast tenderness for all women. It was at such moments, N said, that she gained the power to speak like an apostle who could win over wives, give pleasure to young women, seduce virgins, and console widows.

Later, when the ecstasy subsided, L thanked them for delivering her from pain. Next day she sent them sugared almonds and chocolates with an accompanying note: "Here are two boxes, choose according to your tastes. Here are two mouths, choose according to your tastes. Your happy victim."[43]

Eventually M becomes obsessed with L, and they end up in bed together without N. The next day, appearing happy and momentarily "tranquilized," M returns to N, who intuits her treachery. However, the trio continues meeting as if nothing has changed. One night, drunk on champagne, L declares that "nothing is better in this world than the lips of M on my lips, the hands of N on my body."[44] N and M lie beside L, and the reader is left to imagination.

N grows gradually aware that M and L no longer have need of her. She notices how good M and L look together, a beautiful and modern couple. L has the look of a lost Christian who remembers having been a courtesan; she takes M possessively by the arm, her hand heavy with pearls. N feels that they have become united, that she, a "blonde with messy hair, very petite, a supple smile by her willful nose, and her hard eyes," is somehow accidentally traveling with them in Switzerland. She is supposed to meet her *"l'amie-la-plus-chère"* (Romaine), but puts it off, dreading what will happen when she leaves M and L alone. It's obvious that they are anxious for her departure. When she doesn't leave, they finally board a train and leave *her.* N has never felt more alone.

It is here that Natalie writes one of her most beautiful passages ever, one in which—as in the long-ago *Je me souviens*—she evokes shared memories. But in 1904 Natalie had written for the sole purpose of winning Pauline back; her words were pretty, but they possessed a calculating quality that bespoke a certain insincerity. Twenty-two years later, in "Amants féminins," she has no hopes of winning Mimi back. She has finally learned something that the puerile, inexperienced Pauline knew from the start: there is no such thing as going back. N's liaison with M was over and done; its passions could not and would not be relit. The memories revealed are thus tinged with poignant regret for the loss of something she needed, someone she loved:

> I miss your body with its magnificent joys, with its long vibrations like mine, those certain nights when you murmur: 'If they only knew! If they only knew!' I miss our outings where we encountered unusual people . . . your wide front door where the light streams in and the shadows of the courtyard, your key and its silver serpent chain, the noise of water running when you're washing up, cold suppers and glasses of fresh water before you sleep—which lasts until lunch . . . I miss not having boutonnieres to send you, cigarettes to bring you, pocket change to give you—mouths to fill! . . . I want to die as I lived, between your thighs . . . I miss you, and I miss us.

Georges eventually returned to Liane. Mimi became involved with that ubiquitous former courtesan, Emilienne d'Alençon. But the friendship between Liane and Natalie never recovered. Each kept apprised of the other through mutual friends, particularly Salomon Reinach and Max Jacob. However, Flossie and Nhine would see each other only once more, years later, in a momentary but brutally shocking end to their long, passionate, and legendary union.

The Wilde Amazon

In 1927 Natalie met one of her big loves, Dorothy Ierne Wilde. Known as Dolly, she was the daughter of Oscar's only brother, Willie, a Fleet Street journalist. The Wilde brothers had not only looked alike, but were equally celebrated for wit and brilliance. Both were also self-destructive and met untimely ends. Willie, an alcoholic and drug addict, died shortly after Dolly's birth in 1899, and Oscar was dead soon after. The Wildean wit, intelligence, and charm must have been genetic, because Dolly inherited it in spades—with, unfortunately, an equally generous dollop of the family tendency toward self-destruction.

Most accounts describe Dolly as high-spirited, radiant, indolent, urbane, extremely intelligent, well-read, and—how could she miss?—imbued with stunning wit. Alice Toklas remembered how exciting she was when first appearing on the Parisian scene in 1916; there was, she said, something almost mythical about her. Another word used in relation to Dolly is laughter, for she possessed the gift of making even the most serious-minded dissolve into giggles. Like Natalie, her wit could be cruel and biting. But she was also, again like Natalie, capable of great kindness and thoughtfulness, and was a loyal friend.

Not surprisingly, given the professions of her father and uncle, Dolly was drawn to literature. She was widely read and a good writer (many said a born writer). For some reason—lack of confidence, perhaps, or the inability to concentrate at length—she confined her own considerable talents to letter-writing. If she had pursued the work of writing and been even modestly successful, her life might have turned out differently. As it was, she seemed to have no center, no purpose other than being delightful, amusing, risqué, and sometimes shocking. She possessed only a tiny income, made a bit of money with occasional translations, and was dependent on the generosity of friends to eke by. She often lived in hotel rooms, inexpensive when she paid for them herself, luxurious when treated by another, and made extended visits to the homes of wealthy friends.

Unfortunately for Dolly, her vaunted charms never worked on Romaine Brooks, who considered her a silly, useless drug addict, and a woman of no talent. It bothered her that Natalie seemed genuinely fond of Wilde, who, rather than passing peacefully into friendship like all the others, continued to play a large and passionate role in the Amazon's life. Dolly was even allowed a near-impossible privilege: permission to stay for weeks at a time in the spare bedroom at rue Jacob.

Under her "bright young thing" bravura, Dolly was unhappy, suicidal, and addicted to drugs and alcohol. Stories abound about her public drug use. Berthe Cleyrergue once saw her brandish a syringe during a dinner party and calmly shoot up. In the 1920s she hung out with Jean Cocteau, then a notorious drug user; at one point the association brought Natalie's salon under police surveillance. She lived on an emotional seesaw, often reacting with dramatic, even dangerous, gestures. Once, when Natalie ran off for a fling with the actress Rachel Berendt, Dolly slit her wrists. (Barney eventually lost interest in Berendt, Dolly recovered, and the ugly incident passed.)

The Barney-Wilde relationship illustrates an unusual twist in the Amazon's personality. The daughter of an alcoholic father, Natalie had always been contemptuous of drunks and dopers. Many of her most scathing *pensées* attack the abuse of intoxicants. "One race may assimilate another," she wrote in *Pensées d'une Amazone,* "but no blood is strong enough to absorb the enemy of the human race—alcohol." In *Aventures de l'esprit:* "The consumption of alcohol and the brisk sale of drugs, demonstrate how few are naturally good at living." She herself was so temperate in her use of alcohol that many considered her a teetotaler. She did like an occasional glass of very good wine, but preferred water to all other beverages. It's unlikely that she ever experimented with drugs.

It's therefore curious that she was occasionally drawn to women with serious substance-abuse problems. Pauline Tarn drove herself to an early grave through a combination of alcohol, drugs, and anorexia; Dolly Wilde was a chronic consumer of drink and drugs; Djuna Barnes, a heavy drinker even in her twenties, ended up a hard-core alcoholic.

The question arises: How could Natalie abhor addiction and yet become so closely involved with addicts? Was the attraction due to her knightly predilection for rescue? Did it stem from the childhood familiarity of loving a drunk? Did she enjoy being in control even when another was not? The answer probably has something to do with all those reasons, as well as the fact that she simply loved these women and took the bad along with the good. She did try at times to end their various addictions. Although Natalie remained resolutely free of what is now called codependence, she wasn't above hiding Pauline's chloral bottles, or nagging Dolly and Djuna to change their alcoholic ways. When they didn't, she continued loving them.

THE AMAZON SCRIBE OF GENIUS

Thirty years old when she arrived in Paris from Greenwich Village in 1921, Djuna Barnes slipped easily into the Left Bank scene. Tall and good-looking, with her reddish hair drawn into a careless chignon, she strode with queenly possession through the cobblestoned streets, a floor-length cape thrown insouciantly over her shoulder.

Barnes had already achieved minor success in the States as a writer. Her journalistic pieces—interviews with Diamond Jim Brady, Lillian Russell, D. W. Griffith, Alfred Stieglitz, and other celebrities of the day—had appeared in popular magazines like *Smart Set* and *Vanity Fair*. Her poems and short stories were published in the *Little Review* and the *Dial,* and three of her plays were produced by the Provincetown Players, which also showcased the works of Edna St. Vincent Millay and Eugene O'Neill. Barnes at this point was a good, talented writer with an unusual twist to her outlook, but her early work gave little hint of what was to come.

In Paris, after meeting James Joyce and reading his masterpiece, *Ulysses,* she jokingly announced to friends that she would never write another line. As she put it, "Who has the nerve to after that?" She and Joyce struck a chord, becoming such good friends that he allowed her to call him "Jim." He also presented her with one of the most precious gifts in twentieth-century literature, a bound and annotated copy of proof sheets from *Ulysses* (which, desperate for money, she would sell for a paltry $125 to Harvard's Houghton Library in 1952). Her style, influenced in part by Joyce's writings and their literary conversations, grew steadily edgier.

Around 1924 Barnes was introduced to Natalie by Ford Madox Ford. Natalie admired Barnes's writing, but thought she didn't do enough to promote herself. In "Memoirs of a European American," she described Barnes as "a rough-diamond sort of genius who cut everything to pieces and then blamed the cuts," and in "An Amazon's Notebook" she stated: "Djuna Barnes obstinately denied and derides her brave genius." She also enjoyed Djuna's ribald humor and frank speech, which she likened to the French satirical humanist Rabelais. The two women had a short, intense affair. When the heat wore off, they remained friends, close enough for Barnes to stay in the *pavillon* when Natalie was out of town. Djuna was often at the Fridays, and she was honored with her own day at the Académie des Femmes.

This close association allowed Barnes to become familiar with Natalie's clique and learn fragments of the Amazon's personal history. Her knowledge came in handy when—purely for the sake of amusement, she would later say—she dashed off a small chapbook with a big title: *Ladies Almanack, Showing their Signs and their tides; their Moons and their Changes; the Seasons as it is with them; their Eclipses and Equinoxes; as well as a full Record of diurnal and nocturnal Distempers.* Known simply as *Ladies Almanack,* it is "now recognized as both a brilliant modernist achievement and the boldest of a body of writings produced by and about the lesbian society that flourished in Paris between the turn of the century and the Second World War."[45]

The book's characters are based on Natalie and about a dozen of her female friends. It's easy to imagine how the idea for the endeavor developed. A circle of women with strong personalities and unorthodox, passionate interrelationships practically invited satire, something that Djuna, Natalie, and the more humorous members of the tribe would have appreciated. Exposed as she was to insider stories, laughter about personal foibles, silly nicknames, and the like, Barnes might have been thinking about writing such a book for a long time.

The conception was unique and brilliant, offering up the tale of an audacious modern woman in antique form. The story is told in a calendrical-zodiac fashion that harkens back to medieval times, with twelve chapters representing each month of the year. Djuna, a big Chaucer fan, had long been drawn to old English writing. She might have thus drawn impetus for the design of *Ladies Almanack* by reading such works as Edmund Spenser's 1579 *The Shepheardes Calender,* which consists of an eclogue (pastoral poem) for each month in a year. Each eclogue was preceded by a woodcut, just as each of Barnes's chapters is preceded by one of her pen-and-ink drawings designed to resemble an old woodcut print. The language she uses throughout has been variously described as Elizabethan and Rabelaisian. She certainly borrowed from such archaic sources, but also folded into the mixture her own invented words, bizarre capitalization, and capricious punctuation to arrive at something altogether her own, as can be seen by the opening lines:

> Now this be a Tale of as fine a Wench as ever wet Bed, she who was called Evangeline Musset and who was in her Heart one Grand Red Cross for the Pursuance, the Relief and the Distraction, of such Girls as in their Hinder Parts, and their Fore Poarts, and in whatsoever Parts did suffer them most, lament Cruelly, be it Itch of Palm, or Quarters most horribly burning, which do oft occur in the Spring of the Year, or at those times when they do sit upon warm and cozy Material, such as Fur, or thick and Oriental Rugs.... For such then was Evangeline Musset created, a Dame of lofty Lineage, who, in the early eighties, had discarded her family Tandem, in which her Mother and Father found Pleasure enough, for the distorted Amusement of riding all smack-of-astride.

Musset, of course, is Barney, who had obviously told Barnes about the ruckus created when she rode astride as an adolescent. That particular passage is also a cleverly coded message that young Natalie had abandoned heterosexual partnering, which her parents had enjoyed well enough, to mount a "saddle" of her own choosing.

The book's other real-life counterparts are Romaine Brooks (Cynic Sal), Lily Gramont (Duchesse Clitoressa of Natescourt), Mina Loy (Patience Scalpel), Mimi Franchetti (Senorita Fly-About), Laura Barney (Sister), Radclyffe Hall (Lady Tilly Tweed-in-Blood), Una Troubridge (Lady Buck-and-Balk), Janet Flanner and Solita Solano (Nip and Tuck), Dolly Wilde (Doll Furious), Esther Murphy (Bounding Bess), and Ilse Deslandes (Countess). Of these, all but Mina Loy and Laura Barney were lesbian or bisexual. At least five of the women (Brooks, Gramont, Franchetti, Wilde, and Deslandes) were or had been Barney's lovers.

As the tale continues, Evangeline Musset's parents hoped for a son, but "when therefore, she came forth an Inch or so less than this, she paid no Heed to the Error" and set about seducing every lovely woman possible. (Note that, as opposed to Radclyffe Hall's Stephen Gordon, whose father also wanted a son, Miss Musset is overjoyed to be a woman.) This created scandal and upset Evangeline's father. As Albert once did with Natalie, Evangeline's father takes umbrage with her:

> And she answered him High enough, "Thou, good Governor, wast expecting a Son when you lay atop of your Choosing, why then be so mortal

wounded when you perceive that you have your Wish? Am I not doing after your very Desire, and is it not the more commendable, seeing that I do it without the Tools for the Trade, and yet nothing complain?"

In the days of which I write she had come to be a witty and learned Fifty, and though most short of Stature and nothing handsome, was so much in Demand, and so wide famed for her Genius at bringing up by Hand, and so noted and esteemed for her Slips of the Tongue that it finally brought her into the Hall of Fame, where she stood by a Statue of Venus as calm as you please.[46]

Musset's tongue is almost another character in *Ladies Almanack*. It's mentioned frequently, and when she dies in December at the age of ninety-nine, her corpse is carried through the streets of Paris by forty mourning women. She is cremated, but her tongue remains: "And seeing this, there was a great Commotion . . . [and with the tongue in an urn] they placed it on the Altar in the Temple of Love. There it is said, it flickers to this day."

To the women parodied, the book was a kind of family scrapbook, filled with "in" jokes, buzz words, familiar dialogue, and dead-on characterizations. To outsiders, however, much of the text was difficult if not impossible to decipher. Even scholars are not sure what the underlying messages are. Was Barnes celebrating lesbianism, or exposing it to ridicule? Was she glorifying Barney's powers of seduction, or attacking her lack of fidelity and ceaseless need for conquest? For years, arguments have raged on one side and the other; nothing ever gets resolved.

The confusion probably results from Barnes's own unease about her sexuality. She called herself bisexual, and she had plenty of male lovers, but the most important relationship of her life was with another woman, the artist Thelma Wood, upon whom she based the lead character of *Nightwood*. As she grew older she reportedly felt increasingly uncomfortable about her own lesbianism.

Her torn feelings spilled into the writing of *Ladies Almanack*. She always said it had been written at Natalie's request and as a lighthearted fancy, but there was never really anything lighthearted about Djuna Barnes. True, she could be amusing, but her mind was as complex and winding as a Daedalian labyrinth. Margaret Anderson once said of Djuna that she was "not on speaking terms with her own psyche," and she may not even have realized that her own dark twists and turns became woven into *Ladies Almanack*. Like its author, the book amuses on the surface but possesses multiple levels, each with its own unique intricacy. In Barnes's logic, it makes perfect sense for one level to contradict the existence of another. Sometimes keys are provided, opening doors to unexpected areas. Linkages between levels often start off strong but then disappear. Time and again, short startling phrases are buried deep within endless or seemingly innocuous sentences, as if daring to be found. In sum, this is an easy book with which to be amused. It may, however, be impossible to comprehend.

Barnes originally had no intention of publishing *Ladies Almanack,* but American writer Robert McAlmon talked her into it and paid for the printing as a gift. With the books in hand, Djuna sat on the quay beside the Seine hand-coloring illustrations in fifty numbered copies. Plans for distribution by Edward Titus's Black Manikin fell through, so she and a bevy of young women took to the streets to hawk copies. Plain editions cost the equivalent of $10; hand-colored went for $25; signed and hand-colored brought $50.

The edition of 1,050 sold out quickly and created a small sensation "in literary and lesbian circles."[47] Even though the author's name was given only as "A Lady of Fashion," no one in the American colony of Paris "had any trouble identifying Miss Barnes as the author."[48] Nobody had any trouble determining the real-life counterpart of Evangeline Musset, either.

Natalie loved *Ladies Almanack.* She reread it often over the years, and never stopped thanking Barnes for writing it. She probably did not underwrite any aspect of the book, but in future years willingly provided Djuna with money for emergencies. Later in life she assigned Barnes a monthly stipend, and left her a small sum in her will.

It was a small enough price to pay for immortality. Of all the works Barney inspired, *Ladies Almanack* was the only real masterpiece.

THE PARTY ENDS

The Years of Glory ended abruptly. Ironically, too—at least for the rebellious young Americans who sat around in cafés deriding the folks back home for their "red drug-stores, filling stations, comfort stations, go-to-the-right signs, lurid billboards and automobiles swarming everywhere like vermin . . . and all [that] smug satisfaction."[49] What the rebels never realized (or at least wouldn't admit) was this: it was their parents' very smugness that gave flight to their lives in Paris. When the bubble of American prosperity suddenly burst, wiping out every last vestige of complacency about the future, those pleasant Parisian sojourns evaporated.

Throughout the booming decade of the 1920s, Americans, optimistic about the economy's rosy future, had put billions of dollars in stocks. Investors were rewarded with a market that rose steadily upward, seemingly unstoppable. Many people were so eager to own shares that they mortgaged their homes, yanked life savings from bank accounts, and cashed in safe investments like bonds. Even those with no assets got into the action, purchasing stock on margin. In September 1929, the Dow Jones Industrial Average reached a record high of 381—up from 88 in 1924. Despite the gloomy warnings of a few economic analysts about stock price inflation, people continued to buy into the market.

Everything began to change on October 3, 1929, when, precipitated by a number of controversial factors that economists continue to argue over—and which are far too complex to deal with here—the Dow declined. The next day, $150 million worth of margin loans was called in. Panic spread. By Thursday, October 24, America's long and happy economic rocket ride was in free fall. From that morning's opening bell the market was flooded with sell orders. That afternoon, by pooling resources and buying stock, a coalition of New York City banks managed to stave off a total collapse. Nonetheless, by day's end the Dow closed at 299, with $4 billion lost.

But worse was to come. On Tuesday, October 29—known forever afterward as "Black Tuesday"—the stock market crashed completely. The day's statistics: $14 billion lost; countless people around the nation bankrupt; numerous banks completely failed.

Where there had been so much optimism, fear now reigned. Worried about the future, people stopped buying things. Between October and December 1929, U.S. market production fell a resounding 9 percent. Unemployment rose precipitously. Many factories and businesses were forced to close, increasing the ranks of the unemployed. The downward spiral into the Great Depression had begun.

Shock waves from Black Tuesday spread almost immediately to Europe, where many countries were still recovering economically from the Great War. No one realized just how devastating the result would be: it was only when economic malaise set in that Germany's Nazi Party won mass support and began to grow strong. A decade on, the entire world would suffer the consequences.

On an immediate level, in 1929, the collapse of the U.S. stock market brought an abrupt end to the big crazy party in Paris. "Within less than a year after the stock market tumble began," wrote Virgil Thomson, "virtually all the foreign spenders had gone home. . . ."[50]

A few Americans stayed on, at least for a while. Thomson himself didn't leave until 1933, returning for short stays throughout the rest of the decade. Bob McAlmon and George Antheil remained into the thirties; Djuna Barnes until the war came along. Man Ray would reside in Paris until after the German occupation; then he, too, finally returned to the States.

A number of American women never considered returning to the land of their birth, and would, in fact, remain in Europe until they died. Among them were Gertrude Stein, Alice Toklas, Sylvia Beach, Romaine Brooks—and Natalie, of course, who was destined to outlive them all.

THIRTEEN

The Pause

1930–1938

Creation sleeps! 'Tis as the general pulse
Of life stood still, and Nature made a pause;
An awful pause! prophetic of her end.

—*Edward Young*

What do girls do who haven't any mothers to help them through their troubles?

—*Louisa May Alcott*

*T*HE 1930 SOCIAL SEASON in Paris sparkled with fancy dress balls like never before. There was the White Ball, at which all guests were asked to dress in white; Jean Cocteau, in a white plaster mask and wig, stole the evening. Couturier Jean Patou chose a silver theme for his ball: everything in and around his home, including tree twigs, was wrapped in silver, and huge silver birdcages held faux silver parrots. At another masquerade guests arrived dressed as shepherds and shepherdesses from the time of Louis XIV (one wit came in black pajamas, as a sheep). American hostess Elsa Maxwell's come-as-you-are party featured a man dressed in shaving soap and a towel. The Duchesse de Clermont-Tonnerre held a bal masqué that lasted until five in the morning. Among her guests was Natalie, dressed as a *femme de lettres* in a white scarf stained with ink and carrying a goose feather pen. She was accompanied by Dolly, costumed as her uncle Oscar.

It wasn't just wealthy party givers who seemed unworried about fallout from the stock market debacle; most Parisians were equally unconcerned. So far the Crash had hurt only those dependent on the suddenly absent tourist such as clothing merchants and hotel keepers. According to Janet Flanner, most French people viewed the crisis as strictly an American problem, but were sympathetic. "Only in a few malicious quarters," she noted, "has it been suggested that now certain small American investors can afford to paste Wall Street stocks on their suitcases or toss them to the crowd, as they pasted and tossed five-franc notes here that marvelous summer when the franc fell to fifty."[1]

People were also ignoring the worrisome political scene. In 1934, *Mein Kampf*, a book by Germany's new chancellor, Adolf Hitler, was translated into French. Sales were dismal. That's a pity, because in its pages Hitler made his views and future plans abundantly clear. He assigned a racially inferior position to Jews and Slavs. He declared the Germanic peoples to be a master race that must acquire more land and expand its population, eliminating or enslaving those they conquered. Most important, he announced his intention to take France and avenge the German defeat of World War I. If *Mein Kampf* didn't give notice about Hitler's concept of the future, his stated determination to triple the size of the German army certainly should have. But few paid heed.

Perhaps they just didn't want to. George Antheil spoke for many of his contemporaries when he recalled his 1932 vacation on the French Riviera, a "gorgeous soundproofed paradise, utterly oblivious of the darkness gathering over the rest of Europe. Here a synthetic sun shone on glittering synthetic beaches full of synthetically happy people. I said to myself, 'I don't care. This will be the last fling before I leave Europe forever. In one, two, or five years there will be a war. . . . Here, then, the last orgies before the flood!' "[2]

For most, Paris remained a place of fêtes, bal masqués, and pleasure. The annual Bal des Quat'z Arts, in which art students ran nearly naked through the Left Bank streets, continued. The bals-musette, or public dancing halls, maintained their deliciously bad reputations. Street fairs, with their puppet shows and fortune-tellers, still traveled the city's neighborhoods. The Folies continued to draw crowds, the bar at the Ritz still poured a great cocktail, and Foyot's service remained impeccable.

Everything seemed much as it always had. That, however, was only an illusion. Behind the familiar and comfortable façade, all was in flux. In the immediate past lay the ghost of the glory years; in the immediate future loomed years of pain. Paris—indeed, the entire world—was held breathless between major epochs. Simply put, it was a time of pause.

THE BARNEY WOMEN were mostly untouched by the Crash, although Alice suffered some minor setbacks. Despite this, she was, Natalie believed, squandering hundreds of thousands of dollars on foolish ventures having to do with new theatrical enterprises. Nearly three decades earlier, Natalie had laughed when Albert complained that Alice would drive him to ruin, but now she felt exactly the same way. She intended to do something about her mother's compulsive spending in the first months of 1930, while visiting California.

She and Romaine sailed in early December 1929 for New York, where, through the Christmas holidays, they enjoyed the city's festive spirit, theater offerings, museums, and restaurants. They also spent time with friends, including Esther Murphy, whose father had lost more than $2 million in 1929. Typically, Natalie showed little interest in the effect the massive destruction on Wall Street had wreaked upon the average citizen. When she mentioned the crash at all, it was only in regard to whether and how much it hurt those she knew. After visiting friends in Philadelphia and Washington, Natalie left Romaine to her own endeavors in New York and headed to Los Angeles and a six-week sojourn with her mother.

Alice had bought a theater and started a production company the previous year, intending to stage works by talented but unproduced playwrights (and, of course, herself). Theatre Mart, as it was called, operated on a unique schedule. Each month was ushered in by the five-night run of a new, full-length play. Ensuing weeks were quieter, with the theater lit only once or twice to showcase smaller plays or the kind of grand-scale entertainment Alice loved: tableaux vivants, pantomime, and dance.

The venture received glowing press in California, where Alice and her colorful past had become the darling of feature writers. "Little Alice Pike, who once romped the aisles of Daddy's theater in Cincy," wrote one, "has produced, directed or sponsored more plays in the past two years than have the Shuberts. She pleads guilty to 70 years today and some call her the 'liveliest producer in America.' "[3]

It was the enormous cost of getting Theatre Mart up and running that angered Natalie and, to a lesser extent, Laura. They felt that Alice was lavishing money on an "ill-spirited" theatrical venture to benefit, as Natalie put it, "third-rate playwrighters." Other ideas of Alice's had been equally costly. Studio House, so expensive to maintain, was a white elephant that nobody wanted to buy. Ban-y-Bryn had been Albert's idea to begin with, but Alice's artistic touches had greatly increased the cost of construction. Now, with nobody using the place but renters, she was offering to sell it at a loss, as an advertisement in a 1926 edition of *Country Homes* makes clear: "Sacrifice at Half Cost. Owners Abroad. Large Italian Villa. Ban-y-Bryn, Bar Harbour, Maine. 21 rooms—7 br, 7 servants' br, 5 baths, 2 extra toilets, 5 fireplces, good furnace, very large stable, 3 rooms, bath."

Like anyone who is wealthy and intends to stay that way, the Barney women were supposed to live off income, not principal. Natalie and Laura did so, but Alice had repeatedly nipped away at her foundation over the years in support of her many interests and charities. The result was that her income, as well as money intended for Natalie and Laura, had diminished. The Barneys were still rich, but not as rich as they had been. Reading correspondence between the three women, one is struck by constant talk of economies, disappointments over the reduction in quarterly income, and the like. Natalie began to say that she lived in a state of "demi-luxe," by which she meant that she lived a luxurious life, but that it had limitations.

As William Huntington reported, "Alice spent right up to every penny she had . . . Natalie also spent every penny."[4] He added that Laura was the richest, and that she "was generous with organizations and Natalie was generous with individuals." Jean Chalon agreed with this assessment. "Natalie . . . was not at all concerned with social problems," he said. "She would send money when she heard a troublesome story, but had no desire to resolve the world's problems. She wasn't about to start a foundation."[5] Natalie had always known that she preferred to assist specific people rather than a broad mass. In a letter to Alice written during the Great War, she told of a friend whose philanthropic organization dispensed food to hungry artists. "I can only help individually," Natalie noted. "Anonymous philanthropy not at all my line."[6]

Maybe it's because she did not give money to larger causes that Natalie developed an undeserved reputation for stinginess. She actually was fairly generous, although mostly with friends and acquaintances. She helped many people over monetary hurdles in large and small ways, and she did it quietly. Among the large number of recipients she aided were Djuna Barnes, Mina Loy, Ezra Pound, Ford Madox Ford, Louis Aragon, Marguerite Yourcenar, and Max Jacob. On numerous occasions she helped finance the publication of her friends' books, as she did with Oscar Milosz's *Adramandoni* in 1918 (in which two poems, "H" and "Le Pont," are dedicated to her). During World War II she would be tireless in her efforts to get money to friends suffering badly without it, including Lily Gramont, Lucie Mardrus, Dolly Wilde, Armen Ohanian, and Nadine Hoang. "Natalie," François Chapon told me, "was very, very generous." Renée Lang, who can be harshly critical of Barney, echoed his sentiments: "From the beginning, she was very generous with me."[7]

Still, talk of her tightness persists. Perhaps it's because she was not, as Virgil Thomson once said, "an easy touch." She gave, but didn't gush. She was somewhat cynical about the idea of excessive patronage. "If it were not for money, that wonderful tester of human sentiments," she once wrote, "we should perhaps never know how undear we are to our dear ones." She also felt that concerning herself with someone's career—spending her valuable time and effort on their behalf—was far more important than giving money. As she wrote in *Nouvelles pensées d'une Amazone,* "One becomes a philanthropist from never having encountered anyone." She, having encountered everybody, had no need to be a traditional benefactress.

At any rate, in January 1930, as Natalie left New York, money was the number-one topic on the agenda for discussion with her mother. Second was a long-running, confusing, and volatile controversy over a valuable missing emerald. Third, but by no means least, she still resented the way her name had been removed as coauthor of *The Lighthouse.* As far as she was concerned, the play wouldn't even exist without her initial idea and first draft. Alice might have changed the play all around, but that didn't mean she could ignore her daughter's role in its creation. As her train chugged westward, Natalie steeled herself for the difficult conversations ahead.

However, when she stepped onto the platform in Los Angeles and rested her eyes on Little One for the first time in years, her petty sulks and piques evaporated. For as long as she could remember Alice had looked young—almost like a sister. But now, gazing at that beloved smiling face, she could no longer deny that her indefatigable mother had grown old. Alice was over seventy now, and every single year announced itself. With a cowardice that was completely out of character, Natalie could never bring herself during the visit to openly discuss the topics she considered so important. It was only after her return that she let loose, lashing out in a letter about her coauthorship of *The Lighthouse,* the missing emerald, and Alice's reckless spending.

During the visit Natalie took in Theatre Mart's big monthly production, Alice's *The Scar* (also titled *The Mark of the Beast*). Hanging out in the theater and meeting her mother's cast and crew, she would have learned about earlier performances, including *Legitimate Lovers,* another play that she and Alice had cowritten. Billed as a comedy in three acts, this creaky romantic farce is silly but fun. It's easy to spot Natalie's contributions, since her lines tend to resemble her *pensées*. "Gossip is the petty voice of the unintelligent," announces the Duchesse. "But, alas! The only form of excitement left to divert old age." Turning thoughtful, a character named Horace muses: "I'll tell you the tragedy of a personality like mine. I express more than I can feel." Alice's contributions are evident in the fast pace, broad humor, and countless endearments like "poor boy," "my lamb," and "darling." (During the play's writing Natalie had demanded to know why she insisted on using "all those vulgar 'old chaps,' etc., which make Oscar Wilde's niece and I squirm.") Still, *Legitimate Lovers* was a Theatre Mart hit. "It is a clever little comedy," a reviewer commented. "Alice and Natalie Barney have inserted some crackling lines into the script."[8]

As the time came to leave Los Angeles, Natalie, with a bleak sort of prescience, remembered back to the long-ago day when she'd first learned that mothers could die. One afternoon, notified via cable that her mother had passed away, a visitor to Ban-y-Bryn broke into anguished cries that echoed throughout the cottage. Alone in her room, Natalie quivered. "That mothers should die filled me with a consternation and awe that I never outgrew," she recalled. "And when my own mother, looking into my eyes when I last left her in her Old Garden Cottage, said: 'Isn't it dreadful?,' I trembled, for I guessed what she meant!"[9] Alice must have sensed something, too, for Natalie had scarcely departed when she penned a rare sentimental note: "Dearest, I do miss you very much and every thought is why isn't Natalie here?"[10]

But thoughts of death were only passing. Alice continued writing plays, taking dance lessons, and entertaining. Nothing, not even the heart attack she suffered in late 1930, slowed her down. In letters, Natalie and Laura begged her to start taking it easy. Her reply: she didn't have much time left, and refused to sit home listening to the radio.

Instead, she worked feverishly on a play about her friendship with Whistler, and scored a major coup by getting George Arliss—recipient of the third-ever Academy Award for Best Actor—to sign on as the lead. She lectured about Theatre Mart at art clubs throughout southern California. She read from Natalie's *The One Who Is Legion* to the American Pen Woman's Club. In September 1931 her ballet, *The Shepherd of Shiraz*, played at the Hollywood Bowl.

When the pressure of the Bowl's performance lifted, Alice began looking forward to overlapping springtime visits from her daughters. She wouldn't last that long. On the night of October 12, after a jam-packed day, she attended a concert at the McDowell Town Club. Feeling weak as she entered the performance area, she abruptly sat down. Within minutes she was dead.

"Your dear mother," Aunt Hessie wrote Natalie and Laura a few days later. "You know she would not have a Doctor, and she would not give up and just

rest, but kept on and on to the last." Because Alice had never purchased a burial plot, Hessie said, she had recently offered to share her own back in Dayton.
"She said well Hessie if you feel that way I will. So . . . it was all arranged."[11]
And so it was that Alice came to be buried with her sister rather than Albert,
although his grave was nearby. An inscription she chose for herself was
engraved on the tombstone: "Alice Pike Barney, The Talented One."

Who could deny the truth of that? In Washington, Alice's obituary in the
Evening Star extolled her talents as an artist and humanitarian. "[She enter-
tained] artists, statesmen, the socially select and intellectuals of all classes. . . .
She extended her activities into philanthropy, playwriting and plans for the
beautification of Washington." Her establishment of Neighborhood House to
do "settlement work" and her efforts to create the Sylvan Theater on the
grounds of the Washington Monument were noted, along with her many artistic and theatrical achievements. The writer couldn't help but add that "on several occasions social Washington was thoroughly startled by the escapades of
Mrs. Barney and her daughter, Natalie."[12] There followed yet another retelling
of the nude sculpture scandal.

Nothing would ever replace the deep, complicated love Natalie possessed
for her mother. Alice's prophetic words the last time they said good-bye—
"Isn't it dreadful?"—would haunt her for the rest of her life.

NATALIE'S WORLD CONTINUED to be anchored by the two major loves
of her adult life, Lily Gramont and Romaine Brooks. The situation with Gramont was unusually serene, something that others often remarked upon. In
The Well of Loneliness, Radclyffe Hall says of Valerie Seymour and the
Comtesse de Kerguelen (Natalie and Lily) that "now in the place of that out-
lawed love had come friendship; they were close friends, these one-time
lovers."[13] Lily had long ago made peace with Natalie's infidelities, accepting
her without complaint or pleas to change. She had her own accomplished life
as a writer, a busy social schedule, two daughters whom she adored, and her
own discreet affairs. She and Natalie seemed to come together for the sheer joy
of it, traveling side by side without merging or melding.

The relationship with Romaine was different, and about as close as Natalie
would ever come to coupledom. Their melding was slight, but the mere fact of
its presence in the Amazon's life is significant. By now the two women had settled into a sort of comfortable quasi-marriage in which they watched out for
each other's health, pooled money in a Swiss bank account, and assumed they
would be together for the rest of their lives.

To be sure, Romaine disliked Natalie's infidelity, but had by necessity developed a tolerant attitude. She was even capable of teasing Natalie about a new love—as long as it wasn't serious. If Nat-Nat grew besotted, Romaine simply left Paris, returning after the affair cooled down. Romaine had affairs, too, but of such a perfunctory nature that Natalie had little cause for worry. In fact, if one of Romaine's lovers grew too clingy, she alerted Natalie to send a telegram summoning her away.

The seasons of Natalie's year revolved around her plans to be with Brooks and Gramont. As in the 1920s, she and Romaine enjoyed the Côte d'Azure during the winter and usually traveled to Romaine's home above Florence in the fall. With Lily she ventured to spas in France or Switzerland, and spent time in Normandy. Beginning in 1927, Romaine and Natalie spent late summers at their new vacation home in the south, where Lily was often a guest.

The house was located in Beauvallon, on the tree-laden north shore of the bay at St.-Tropez, then a small fishing village. Both Natalie and Romaine put a lot of thought and planning into the building's design, hoping to develop a dwelling that would allow their independent and often conflicting natures to live together harmoniously. The fact that Romaine preferred being alone and Natalie thrived on socializing presented difficult obstacles, but the final plan shows a good deal of psychological insight. By this point in her life, Natalie knew that, in order to successfully live with someone, she needed plenty of space. For Romaine such space was as necessary as oxygen.

The house succeeded because it was essentially two homes masquerading as one. It was composed of separate wings, one for each, with a connector (the dining room) that could be closed off from either wing. The phrase for "hyphen" in French is *trait d'union,* and so they christened their hyphenated home Villa Trait d'Union. In residence they could be apart or together, as they wished. The idea was probably inspired by other homes Natalie had shared in this way—the two villas on Lesbos with Pauline, and the *pavillon* in Neuilly with a separate accommodation, where Colette had lived for a time after leaving Willy.

Villa Trait d'Union wasn't perfect, but it worked most of the time. Even shut off in her hyphenated share, though, Romaine sometimes resented Natalie's "second-rate" friends. In the summer of 1937, for some reason, she became particularly irate, throwing tantrums and being unpleasant to everybody (Natalie referred to these bursts of temper as "upsets" or "Romaine's bad nerves"). At one point Romaine decided that she and Natalie would be happier visiting each other from their own separate properties; she was serious enough that Natalie discussed with Laura the cost of buying out Romaine's share at

Beauvallon. But then, almost immediately, Romaine hit on another solution: she would build a separate studio on the property, where, free of Natalie's friends, she could work in peace. That project came to nothing, and in the end she stayed on, more or less content, at Beauvallon.

Surrounded by tall coastal pines, the white, flat-roofed buildings of Trait d'Union had a distinctly Mediterranean look. There was a large terrace, where Natalie liked to curl up on a chaise and read. Long dinners were held in the dining room with its huge marble table. On fine clear nights friends were brought up to the roof, and everyone sprawled on cushions to gaze at the stars while eating homemade ice cream. Natalie loved the summer heat, the blissful quiet, the soothing grating of crickets, and driving each day to the nearby coast for the warm sea bathing.

Barney's chauffeur, cook, and two housemaids were always on hand to help with entertaining guests (there were two guest bedrooms). Laura, Lily, and Dolly came every summer, though the latter two usually waited until Romaine returned to Italy. Other visitors included Gertrude Stein, Alice Toklas, Una Troubridge, Radclyffe Hall, Paul Poiret, Sir Francis Rose, Richard Aldington, Mimi Franchetti, Paul Géraldy, and Brooks's close friend Somerset Maugham, who lived not too far away in Cap Ferrat. Colette, whose own summer getaway was nearby, turned up frequently, or Natalie, sometimes with Romaine, would visit her. On one occasion Natalie, Romaine, Colette, and Jean Cocteau spent the day sailing.

Derek Patmore was not yet twenty-five when he visited mutual friends near St.-Tropez in the early 1930s. They thought he should meet Natalie, "and one afternoon we motored along the coast to see her. She received us in a villa surrounded by pines, and even the large living-room where she was waiting for us appeared to be invaded by these dark trees. Still a very handsome woman, she had the natural authority of someone who has been known as beautiful, and her vivid blue eyes were unusually arresting. There was an imperiousness about her blond good looks that explained how she had conquered the intellectual world of Paris and enslaved Remy de Gourmont. . . . Watching Natalie Barney as she acted the charming and gracious hostess, I sensed the ruthlessness beneath the smooth surface of the clever, well-bred wealthy American woman who long ago had decided to conquer Europe."[14]

Richard Aldington's memory of Beauvallon offers a telling glimpse of just how different the mores of that time were from our own. Visiting nearby, he was invited to the villa by Natalie and told to bring his friends along. Among them was a London publisher who, despite Aldington's protests, dressed in casual beach clothes for the visit. When they got to Natalie's, the publisher "was much abashed at finding himself among 'the gentry,' and hid himself under my jacket, which was too large for him. Miss Barney was perfect, saw nothing untoward, and soon discovered they had common friends. . . ." As Aldington remarked about his hostess that day, "like every real aristocrat she had the ability to put everyone at his ease."[15]

One of the great pleasures of Beauvallon was that it enabled Natalie and Romaine to take short jaunts to beautiful nearby villages and towns, stopping to visit friends along the way. One day, on their way to somewhere, they called on Gertrude Stein and Alice Toklas at their vacation home in Bilignin, northwest of Aix-les-Bains.

The four women sat in the garden on brightly striped canvas chairs under a huge umbrella, eating Alice's coconut cake and watching Gertrude's standard poodle, Basket, cavort beneath the trees. As Natalie recalled, "Gertrude sat in the favorite position in which Picasso portrayed her, clothed in rough attire with moccasined feet, knees apart, reminiscent of the gypsy queen under her tent in my old Bar Harbor days. Meanwhile Romaine Brooks contemplated our group and finding it 'paintable,' wished to start a picture of it then and there, before the light should fade. But, I . . . insisted that Romaine and I were due elsewhere. So this picture of us all was left unpainted: mea culpa!"[16]

One day in August 1934 Natalie had the chauffeur take her into Toulon, a pretty seaport not far from St.-Tropez, to do some shopping. As she approached a store, the door opened and out stepped a tall, beautiful, and elegantly dressed woman carrying a small package. It was Liane.

To Natalie's surprise, Liane gasped and recoiled when their eyes met. Then, with nary a word, she turned and ran away. Natalie, stunned, watched her disappear into the old town's maze of narrow, cobbled streets. Liane ran so hard that she became lost. Finally she grabbed a seat at a place she knew, the Café de la Rade. "There I felt safe," she wrote, "lost in the crowd, alone at my table. I was beautiful: white pyjamas, long white crêpe de chine jacket with a navy blue belt. I haven't set eyes on Nathalie for eight years. Will that really turn out to be the last look?"[17]

Indeed it was. That brutal, inexplicable encounter provided the final glimpse Flossie and Annhine had of each other. In 1945, after the death of Prince Georges Ghika, with whom she continued to live after his escapade with "Tiny One," Liane became a Dominican nun and took the name Sister Marie-Madeleine de la Pénitence. Those who knew her well weren't surprised. Her religious faith had been profound since childhood, even during her rule as a courtesan, and had only deepened with age. On some level she was convinced that, if she had lived a purer life, her son would not have been taken from her in the Great War. "I need God, I seek him," she wrote in 1919. "I feel that He has tested me so severely in order to bring me back to Him." When

Liane de Pougy died in 1950, on the day after Christmas, she was buried in the habit of a Dominican nun.

ALTHOUGH NATALIE CONTINUED to want and need the cozy familiarity that came with her two long-term relationships, Lily and Romaine, she refused to give up the thrill of falling in love anew. She never questioned her motivations, since her ends—chase and capture—provided all the reason she needed.

Toward the end of her life, Natalie informally catalogued her longest-lasting relationships, dividing them into three categories in descending order of importance: liaisons, demi-liaisons, and adventures. This list no longer exists, but Natalie showed it to a few people (including Renée Lang, Berthe Cleyrergue, and Jean Chalon), all of whom later revealed a few names to others or in writing. Gathering these various revelations together, it appears that the first category, liaisons, included Eva Palmer, Romaine Brooks, Lily Gramont, Pauline Tarn, Dolly Wilde, and Olive Custance. Colette and Armande de Chabannes were listed as demi-liaisons. Among the adventures were Djuna Barnes, Eyre de Lanux, and Armen Ohanian. Beyond these (and other) long affairs-cum-friendships were, by the estimate of Cleyrergue, hundreds of minor affairs.

Now, as Natalie entered her seventh decade, she seemed just as aggressive in her pursuit of new lovelies as when, at sixteen, she had insistently seduced the "wild rose." For the most part, she was extremely discreet. In her memoirs, Berthe stated that she never once, in all her years at rue Jacob, caught sight of a woman in Natalie's bed. Once in a while, though, she shocked people. Writer Joan Schenkar was told by Clarissa Lada-Grozicka of a 1937 Friday she attended as a young woman. Upon glimpsing sixty-one-year-old Barney "passionately kissing a beautiful, blonde, young American girl whom she called 'Venus,' " said Lada-Grozicka, "I telephoned to my mother & asked her to make some excuse & get me out of there."[18]

More than thirty years after Renée Vivien, Natalie still viewed her flings as necessary but essentially frivolous. If asked, she would have said they had nothing to do with the deep recesses of her heart, where Romaine and Lily resided unchallenged. "One is unfaithful to those one loves in order that their charm does not become mere habit," she stated in *Éparpillements*. However, every now and then a woman came along who came close to those recesses, remaining a passion for years (and, of course, a friend for life). In the 1930s, both Dolly Wilde and Nadine Hoang qualified for that role.

Hoang, of mixed Chinese-Belgian parentage, studied for a legal career and later spent four years in the Chinese army, attaining the rank of colonel. In the early 1930s she moved to Paris to establish a jade importing business. She and Natalie met in 1934, and became involved soon afterward. When the importing endeavor failed, Nadine came to work for Natalie, exchanging part-time secretarial services for room and board. During this period, 1937–1939, it wasn't unusual to see her Chinese friends circulating at the Fridays. Occasionally Nadine slipped into traditional Chinese dress to wow the crowd with a wild saber dance.

Nadine's exotic beauty attracted attention. The journal *À Paris* wrote of a garden party at which an unnamed countess was "chatting with NCB, who was leading around a ravishing Chinese, in a black satin costume, a colonel in the Celestial army."[19] Wearing her military uniform with a masculine haircut, she was often mistaken for a handsome man. André Germain flirted outrageously with her the first time they met and was crushed to learn that she was a woman. In *Nouvelles pensées d'une Amazone,* Natalie's fascination with Hoang is obvious. She writes with attention to detail about the precise yet sensuous way Nadine moved or ate an orange. In her lover's black-coffee eyes, Natalie said, she "learned to decipher every nuance of joy or distress."[20] She was so taken with Nadine, at least for a while, that Dolly Wilde began referring jealously to "the Chinese Situation."

But it was "the Dolly Situation" that brought serious trouble. Romaine, who had resigned herself long ago to Natalie's passing fancies, disliked Dolly intensely. She had been blasé about her in the beginning, but as the years rolled by she was increasingly irked not only by Dolly's continuing presence, but by her role of court favorite. Dolly, who admired Romaine and knew it was politic to be on her good side, tried to endear herself to the fearsome artist. However, no amount of flattery or charm worked. Romaine didn't like Dolly, and that was that.

In 1931, Romaine decided that she'd had enough. After refusing for weeks to visit rue Jacob because of Dolly's constant presence, she departed abruptly for Italy. From there she wrote to Natalie about the "intolerable situation" that had arisen. She never once used Dolly's name; instead, she referred to her demeaningly as a rat. The letter makes clear, however, that Dolly was not the only rat running loose in the *pavillon*. Romaine's long-nurtured animosity toward Natalie's friends, as well as her incipient paranoia, are evident:

> I find myself today faced with the fact that you are weak in all that concerns your personal sanity and that anyone so inclined can play on this even to the point of changing your attitude to an old and trusting friend like

myself. Your life at present Natalie, is infested by rats and one of these rats is gnawing at the very foundation of our friendship. As long as you surrounded yourself by a not unfriendly tribe of second rate young women, though unpleasant, I suffered it to pass; but when I am aware that you have chosen as confidante and friend one inimical to me (my proofs are indisputable) there is no course open to me but to ask you to shake the rat from out of your skirts or to accept my complete retirement.

There follows a long, involved, and nearly incomprehensible discussion about gossiping servants who had meddled in her private affairs. Then came the ultimatum:

So my dear you have rats in your kitchen, rats in your bedroom, and rats in your hall and Laura's rat has even been made "one of the family!" This [is] ludicrous Natalie and unless you as my personal friend can clean up your quarters (friends and servants) I shall not only keep away from your home as has been the case for some time but also break away from you altogether. It has become an impossible situation for me and no compromise is acceptable. So far I have never asked you to change anything in your way of living. I now ask you to change everything otherwise there will be no longer Romaine.[21]

Natalie was devastated. She knew that Romaine was capable of doing just what she said: firmly shutting the door on their years together unless she dumped Dolly for good. Life without Romaine was unthinkable. On the other hand, she did truly love Dolly, and in complex ways. Mixed in with Natalie's romantic and sexual feelings for this woman twenty-three years younger than herself was a hint of big-sisterly or even—though she would have flat-out denied it—motherly protectiveness. In her own way, Natalie never stopped worrying about and looking after Dolly, who was hopelessly inept at life.

Thus, the question of what to do about Romaine's ultimatum was agonizing. For weeks Natalie worried over her reply, writing one draft after another. A few still exist, visible proof of her tortured spirit. One page, first written in ink, has countless words and sentences crossed out in thick pencil. Over this, words are squeezed in between lines and crossed out again and again. The end result is completely unintelligible. In one draft she mildly chastises Romaine for making their relationship "conditional." She particularly takes umbrage at the dramatic statement about rats gnawing at the foundation of their friendship: "This is absurd as far as I'm concerned."

In the end she knuckled under. "And since you affirm that it is 'gnawing at the very foundation of our friendship,' " she wrote, "right or wrong it must be sacrificed to our friendship—which is, as you should know—the most important thing in my life—my love for you is neither changed nor conditional and nothing, no matter what, would alter or corrode the pure metal of it—and I shall always serve under your near or distant banner for all the days or years of my life that remain, Romaine!"[22]

Being sent away broke Dolly's heart. During her subsequent exile, she wrote long letters to Natalie from London, recalling every small moment of their shared happiness. Eventually Romaine would ease the ban and Dolly would be allowed back into Natalie's life. Having wielded power and won the ultimate test, Romaine never again viewed Dolly as a threat, and even came to be fairly tolerant of her foibles. On at least one occasion, hearing of Wilde's dire monetary straits, she sent a generous check. In victory, she had nothing to lose by being gracious.

BY THE MID-1930S, Natalie's Fridays had been in existence for a quarter of a century, regularly hosting the literary stars in France, Europe, and America. By anybody's standards, the Fridays were now an esteemed institution. Attendance was no longer a mere pleasure: it was an honor. There was something queenlike about Natalie now. No longer did she sail from group to group, lightly touching one or whispering to another. These days she observed the goings-on from her armchair. Guests were led to her, one by one, and allowed to sit by her side for a tête-à-tête.

Even now, though, Natalie remained a girlish rebel at heart. One night, walking home by herself, she was accosted by a young hoodlum—an "apache," in the Parisian slang of the day. He tried to take her purse; she resisted, and told him off in no uncertain words. He fled. Ezra Pound was so delighted with this story that he worked it into Canto LXXX.

With the world's economy turned inside out, fewer visitors came to Paris now than at any other time since 1909, but the salon continued to have its exciting moments. In June 1932, the dashing poet Edna St. Vincent Millay drew a large crowd. Another famous visitor in these years was Greta Garbo, brought by her then-lover, Mercedes Acosta.

Gertrude Stein continued coming to the Fridays, especially after she and Alice moved to rue Christine, very close to Natalie's home, in 1937. The proximity brought the two writers closer. They shared an occasional restaurant lunch and fell into the habit of taking long evening walks while talking of literature and food and the people they knew. Although basically wary of one another, they nonetheless developed a gratifying mutual respect. "The night's enchantment," Natalie later recalled, "made our conversations as light, iridescent, and bouncing as soap bubbles—but as easily exploded when touched upon."[23]

From time to time Romaine could be spotted at the Fridays, but she came only to please Natalie. She felt that salon-goers were malicious and always on the attack, and there was some truth to this perspective; Valéry's oft-quoted remark about Natalie's "hazardous Fridays" had been made for a good reason. Companionship, laughter, and wit had characterized these gatherings from the beginning and continued to star, but increasingly, power and factions played important roles. Under the polished manners and polite smiles, the lances were out, with people jousting for ascendancy and recognition. Cliques, gossip, repartée—all could be savage.

Romaine, who was at her best one-on-one or in small groups, tended to be silent in crowds. Various first-person accounts make it clear that she could be amazingly funny when it suited her, but her humor wasn't sharp and clever; she wasn't a wit. She felt doltish and clumsy at Natalie's Fridays, and it was in her nature to blame her bad feelings on the gatherings themselves, as well as on those who attended.

A major crisis erupted early in the decade when Maria, Natalie's cook for many years, died. Berthe took over the job of providing food for the Fridays, but it seemed almost impossible to find a chef for daily meals. In the ensuing two years, more than twenty held the job; some stayed only a few days before hastily departing in the face of Natalie's criticisms. Finally, in 1933, a tiny Chinese man named Ho-man Lau was hired. Nicknamed Van Loo, he excelled at cooking pheasant, game, lobster, and salmon. Naturally enough, he also produced knockout Chinese specialties, which Natalie adored, and could turn out the American dishes she recalled from childhood, including her favorite, Poulet Maryland (better known as southern fried chicken). He stayed until the advent of war.

Natalie liked having guests to dine. Her table seated eight, though more could be squeezed in if need be. She gave frequent lunches, and about twice a month had dinner guests (those late-Friday, post-salon suppers for close friends don't count). The menus on these occasions were fairly elaborate. When she dined alone or with a single friend, she usually requested simple meals.

Perhaps the most unusual dining experiences at rue Jacob were the lunches for the Scorpion Club, composed of friends born on October 31: painter Marie Laurencin, writer Germaine Beaumont, and a bookseller/autograph dealer named Anacréon. They met every year on that date, even if it meant traveling long distances. These lively lunches, which usually ran until late afternoon, lasted for decades. They ended only with the death of Marie Laurencin in 1956.

With all of this excellent eating, Natalie finally gave up her attempts to remain slender. As the decade progressed, her body grew heavier, her face fleshier. She took to wearing flowing outfits designed by Lanvin, Patou, and Schiaparelli (and she wasn't above bickering with top designers for a better price). Her primary wardrobe colors remained true to Romaine's palette: white, black, and gray. She owned a lot of jewelry, much of it quite valuable, but, as in her youth, didn't wear much. The end result was a style entirely Natalie's own, tasteful but with eccentric overtones: mid-calf dresses or elegant suits, long and dramatic capes, high collars, scarves tossed insouciantly across her shoulder. Around the house she wore costumes, or what Berthe referred to as "disguises": kimonos, Arabian djellabas, lavishly embroidered Eastern garments. She was interested in astrology and numerology, and one of her favorite outfits was a long velvet dress emblazoned with astrological signs.

AS IN EACH and every decade of Natalie's adult life, writing continued to play a major role. "From the day I arrived until the end," Berthe recalled, "I always saw her writing."[24] She usually started working after breakfast, which was brought to her around eight in the morning. Her normal fare was tea and toast, though sometimes she enjoyed raisin bread or a brioche; she avoided jams and jellies because they ruined the teeth, and downed butter lavishly. Propped up with a cushion, she might glance through the *New York Herald* or a French literary review while eating. Then, still in bed, she arranged her writing papers and materials on a lap desk and settled in to work. She liked composing with her gray Mont Blanc fountain pen, a present from Romaine.

When involved with a specific project, Natalie often worked straight through to the evening. When writing in the afternoon, she sat at her desk overlooking the garden. Like most early-morning people, she found it impossible to write at night. Her bold handwriting ranged from fairly legible to indecipherable, depending on how rushed or intent she was. When she was on a roll, sheets of paper ended up all over the *pavillon*.

In 1930, Natalie's ninth book and only novel, *The One Who Is Legion, or A.D.'s After-Life*, was privately printed in London. It contained two illustrations by Romaine Brooks. The odd plot revolves around a person who has committed suicide. Brought back to life as a genderless being with no memory of a previous life, she/he is merged with the One. The resultant fusion becomes the narrator, who floats through a semirealistic dreamscape. In a small chapel, he/she discovers a book recounting the love life of someone named A.D., who is presumably itself. Reading the book, A.D. learns that, when alive, she/he had been a slave to physical love. Now in a noncorporeal state, A.D. is able to turn aside from carnality, becoming "legion"—that is, a part of everyone. By moving beyond the bounds of self, A.D. finds eternal life.

The list of dramatis personae is interesting in itself, including A.D., who is described as self-destructive and a lover; the Glow-Woman, "a beauty of the flesh that we have only met in the flesh"; Stella, "a beauty of the spirit that we have met in many ways, and loved and lost, and loved and found again in loving"; A.D.'s horse; and Time, defined as "beyond time."

In explaining the book's intent, Natalie confessed that "for years I have been haunted by the idea that I should orchestrate those inner voices which sometimes speak to us in unison, and so compose a novel, not so much with the people about us, as with those within ourselves, for have we not several selves and cannot a story arise from their conflicts and harmonies?"[25] Perhaps a note she sent to Alice when the book was published was more on point: "It is a weird tale. I hardly realize how I came to write it."[26]

It's interesting that *The One Who Is Legion*, the most modern of all Natalie's books, is also the only one to be written (and published) in English. Did she decide that, in tackling the subjects of death and the afterlife, she was best served by a language of practicality? Or perhaps the fact that she had long ago become a stranger in the land of her birth made her feel freer to expose herself psychologically in her native tongue. One French reviewer hoped that it would be translated, but added that doing so would "yield only half its rhythmic pulse."[27]

ANOTHER BOOK PUBLISHED that year added itself to the list of works inspired by Natalie. *L'ange et les pervers* (The Angel and the Perverts), by Lucie Delarue-Mardrus, was a roman à clef with Miss Barney in the starring role. Any doubts on the matter were eradicated a few years later when Lucie acknowledged that the book had "analyzed and described at length Natalie and the life into which she initiated me."[28]

Lucie presents a detached, mostly accurate, and absolutely merciless portrait of Natalie. It's a curious book, as eccentric in its way as *The One Who Is Legion*. In fact, the two books have a startling similarity: a hermaphroditic central character. In *L'ange et les pervers*, this character, who alternates between being a man named Mario and a woman named Marion, attracts both sexes but is interested in neither. Mario/Marion, the title's Angel, is an unhappy writer who thinks most people are self-centered and cynical. The only person he/she really likes is a woman named Laurette Taylor (Natalie). Despite Laurette's many faults, she has good qualities. For this reason, M/M is usually willing to assist with her schemes, which invariably center around the conquest of a new love.

The main plot involves Laurette's desire to win back an old love, Aimée de

Lagres, who appears to be a combination of Renée Vivien and Lucie. Laurette had won Aimée from her husband (as Natalie had once won Lucie from hers). The couple divorced and four months later the heartless Laurette broke off the relationship. But now Aimée has found solace in the arms of a jealous countess (as Renée once did with Hélène), a fact that drives Laurette to distraction.

"It seems she is consoling herself with the old Countess Talliard," Laurette complains to M/M, "and that I cannot bear. She must be torn free from the clutches of that banal giraffe. She dishonors me. I cannot accept such a successor."

"But what if she's happy?"

"Happiness is of no consequence. I prefer to take her back."

"It will mean certain heartache for her!"

"Marion, she is worthy of being made to suffer."[29]

Thus Lucie strips bare Natalie/Laurette's need to triumph in love no matter the consequences to anyone else. Laurette is "sure of her success in advance as always . . . despite both her experience and her skepticism" because she has "in her blood the prodigious American optimism."[30]

Others have hinted at how drama-prone Natalie could be in the throes of love, and she herself has made it clear that she enjoyed love's "suffering." For her, such suffering almost always came at the beginning of a relationship, before she had firmly won the love of a potential quarry. As long as things were in doubt, her emotions were heightened with excitement, longing, and lust. When the objective was attained—that is, when the woman was finally and unequivocally hers—she stopped suffering, her emotions leveled out, and she began to lose interest.

In L'ange et les pervers, things don't go well in Laurette's attempt to win back Aimée, and her "temper became more and more unbearable. This was her way of expressing unhappiness. Every second day she took to her bed. Seeing Aimée de Lagres again became an almost dangerous obsession. Muffed up in her ermine counterpane, steely-eyed, she performed quite a ritual of romantic mourning around this sorrow, which she had invented out of thin air and in which she ended up believing to the point of giving herself an attack of neurasthenia. Her choir of favorites suffered a thousand snubs and indignities; to the servants, she was a tyrant."[31]

Aimée has a child by another man, gives it away, and returns to her husband. Laurette's innate kindness is revealed when she cares enough about the abandoned baby to find it a foster home. M/M finally finds happiness by adopting and raising the child.

Natalie must have had a few difficult moments reading this book, and it's interesting that she never mentioned it in her long portrait of les Mardrus in

Souvenirs indiscrets (or anywhere else, for that matter). Typically, whatever pain and embarrassment the portrayal caused her, she never allowed it to affect her friendship with Lucie.

NATALIE ONCE REMARKED that she traveled as well as a basket of raspberries; in other words, not very well. She had always insisted on creature comforts—firm mattresses, quiet rooms, excellent cuisine—but at this point in her life she was becoming a trifle obsessive.

In 1935, in the kind of "roast" introduction so popular in those days, Germaine Lefrancq described to an audience Natalie's "irritability of a tiger, cruelties of a grand Inquisitor . . . [and] extravagant demands of a Mikado." Most of her examples were culled firsthand from travels they had taken together, as when she described the routine Natalie went through in choosing a hotel room. Quaking beneath Barney's intimidating gaze, a desk clerk showed her one room after another, with Natalie rejecting each. The first room, in the middle of a long hallway, was prey to excessive foot traffic; the second was too close to the office; the third, to the elevator; the fourth, to the dining room. "I don't want to hear the breakfast noise," she said. One room was rejected because it had black curtains, which made her think of death. Another met all her qualifications, except that it didn't face southwest. "I want the southwest," she said, in no uncertain terms.

Lefrancq also told of going to stay on her own at a country auberge that she had visited the year before with Natalie. The first day, sitting at lunch, she was approached by the owner, who regarded her sternly.

"She's not with you?" he asked. "The blond woman who was here last year?"

"No," Lefrancq said.

"Good," he replied crisply. "Because I would have refused to serve you."[32]

Natalie tended to stay in the same hotels year after year, simply because she knew they would please her. When she took the water in Brides-les-Bains, she stayed at the Hôtel des Thermes. In London, she liked the Royal Court Hotel on Sloane Square. In Nice, the Hôtel d'Angleterre. She wrote letters on stationery from these and a few other hotels—the Lausanne Palace in Switzerland, the Hôtel de la Prairie in Yverdon—for decades, until she became too infirm to travel.

In sum, when it came to voyaging, she preferred the tried and true. By this point in her life she had a comfortable routine of places to visit throughout the year. Aside from the Beauvallon/Normandy/Italy axis, she took other, shorter respites during the year. Although she often complained about London, she didn't mind quick hops across the Channel. Give her a good enough reason and she would happily travel to other parts of Europe, as when she and Romaine visited Frankfurt in 1930 to attend the premiere of George Antheil's new opera.

Natalie did occasionally try something new, though. Toward decade's end she traveled with Romaine to Morocco and Tunisia. She was fascinated by Fez, an ancient city dating back to A.D. 800, and with Tunisian souks, where coffee sellers squatted atop mountains of coffee beans and essence of roses could be bought by the drop. She enjoyed the local cuisine, particularly couscous, and grew to love mint tea. This would be the last "adventure" trip of Natalie's life. The war would soon intervene; when it ended, she would be seventy. After that, she traveled only to places she knew well.

Natalie also visited the United States twice in this decade, in 1934 and 1938. One of the main reasons for the first trip was to finalize matters involving Alice's estate. Laura, as executor, had taken on most of the burden, ably assisted by William Huntington. She had been unable to find a buyer for Studio House, whose many eccentricities made it unsuitable as a home, so Natalie proposed the idea of turning it into a small museum for Alice's paintings. Laura seemed agreeable until, one day in Washington, Romaine committed a major gaffe.

According to William Huntington, who was present, the unforgivable words were said over lunch: "Suddenly Romaine said, 'Laura, you talk entirely too much about your mother. She was not a great painter. She was a very agreeable person and painted academically well.' Silence, and I pushed the silver to the floor and the maid came in. Always push the silver to the floor when things get hot and heavy. Laura always had a little too much excitement about her mother. Spoke about her constantly, about her beautiful work. It was a little bit beyond." He added: "Laura never forgave [Romaine]."[33] Laura was so angry over the perceived insult to Alice's talent that the idea of using Studio House as a museum fell to pieces, at least for the short term. It would be resurrected and realized in the 1950s.

Back in New York, Natalie connected for a day with Gertrude Stein and Alice Toklas. Stein's *Autobiography of Alice B. Toklas* had been published the previous year (1933), and, to the surprise of everyone, the buying public adored it. As a happy Gertrude admitted, the book was "a conspicuous *succès d'estime* and commercial as well."[34] Filled with highly readable anecdotes and tales about friends like Pablo Picasso, Ernest Hemingway, Georges Braque, Henri Matisse, and many others (including Natalie), the book turned Stein into a kind of Dada-esque folk heroine. Arriving in New York for a nationwide lecture tour—her first visit home in thirty years—she was greeted by a moving tickertape headline atop the New York Times building: "Gerty Gerty Stein is Back Home Home Back." For Stein and Toklas, the trip that followed turned into a whirlwind of crowded lecture halls, interviews with journalists, and posing for magazine and newspaper photographers. It was, as Natalie said, Gertrude's "lionized winter."

As Natalie prepared to sail back to France, she summed up her feelings about her native land in a letter to Laura. "America is efficient but soulless," she said, "except for cranks and religious fanatics."[35]

Nonetheless, she returned in 1938 to visit Romaine, who had been living there a good deal since purchasing a high-ceilinged suite of rooms at Carnegie Hall in 1935. During the visit she dropped in on Mina Loy, who had fallen on hard times since relocating to New York in 1936. Natalie found her depressed and living in near-poverty, and was shocked to see that the much younger woman's hair had turned completely white. Upset by the fact that Loy could not afford an icebox, she bought one and had it delivered to her apartment.

Natalie also renewed her friendship with Eva Palmer-Sikelianos, who was visiting New York. Eva professed herself pleased to see that time had made them far more similar than they had ever been in the past. "I came away feeling that absence and years really don't make a difference," she wrote later.[36]

ONE EVENING TOWARD the decade's end, Derek Patmore was invited to a dinner party at the home of Lily Gramont. Early in the evening, cocktails were served on the terrace by hushed servants, and Patmore remembered that Paris seemed "magically enveloped in that misty blue light which has given its name to a famous perfume, L'Heure Bleu."[37] As it grew darker, soft lights came on around the garden and the group moved inside to dine.

Patmore discreetly took stock of his companions, who were polite and charming in "that distant French way." The conversation was learned and mostly literary. People drank champagne and spoke of Proust, whom they had known, identifying the real-life people behind his characters. Patmore noticed a beautiful blond couple, and was fascinated when they turned out to be siblings Jean and Isabelle Bourguin, the models for Jean Cocteau's *Les enfants terribles*.

Talk of Proust and poetry, of Cubism and the Comédie-Française, of Picasso and the Ballet Russe. Nobody mentioned politics or spoke of the future, perhaps deliberately so. By that night the signs of coming turmoil were obvious. Lily's guests, in full accord with human nature, were clinging to life in a golden bubble and pretending it wouldn't pop.

It would, though, and on some level everyone present that night knew it. From mid-decade onward, Germany had been rattling its sabers, and not metaphorically. Adolf Hitler had grown steadily more aggressive toward weaker neighboring states, bullying them into making territorial concessions. Realists across the globe understood that these early, easy conquests were only the start of a much grander Hitlerian scheme. And all the while, whispers of persecution and punishing laws—directed at Jews, homosexuals, Gypsies, and anyone else the Führer didn't like—were spreading.

Around the time of Lily's party, Germany, without warning, annexed Austria and threatened to take the western border of Czechoslovakia. Spurred to action, British prime minister Neville Chamberlain initiated talks that led to the Munich Pact, which essentially caved in to Hitler's aggressive tactics. Czechoslovakia, encouraged to do so by Britain and France, gave up its western portion to Germany. In return for this, Hitler promised to make no more territorial demands. Britain and France chose to believe him. Chamberlain even spoke confidently to his countrymen of "peace in our time." Less than two years later, the Munich Pact would be seen as a useless act of appeasement, and Chamberlain, his reputation sullied, would resign. Well before that, however, even the most optimistic souls could see the grim visage of war looming on the horizon.

But nobody was thinking about such things on the night of Lily Gramont's party. "Fête-galante!" wrote Patmore. "Spectres of Marcel Proust! A doomed playground! It was Paris on a warm, moonlit summer evening before the Second World War, with the fascinating but imperturbable Duchesse de Clermont-Tonnerre as hostess—a woman who in her own memoirs already realized that an era was passing and . . . would never come again."

FOURTEEN

War Redux

1939–1945

A pattern called a war.
Christl! What are patterns for?

—*Amy Lowell*

We have been called the Amazon, but surely our great adventure is
with life, not death.

—*Natalie Barney*

*I*N MARCH 1939, Germany abruptly seized all of Czechoslovakia,
thereby breaking the Munich Pact. As fears rose that Poland might be
taken next, Britain promised to aid that country if need be (France
already had a mutual defense treaty with the Poles). Unconcerned, Hitler
began to gather allies of his own, signing a mutual support pledge with Italy in
May and a secret nonaggression pact with Russia in August. Europe held its
collective breath, waiting to see what would happen next.

The wait wasn't long. On September 1, Germany invaded and easily
defeated Poland in a blitzkrieg—a "lightning war." On September 3, after
Hitler refused British and French demands to withdraw, those countries
declared war on Germany. Within days, Canada, Australia, New Zealand, the
Union of South Africa, and India backed the British Commonwealth. Hitler

ordered his generals to prepare for an early October attack on Belgium, Luxembourg, the Netherlands, and France. However, the German high command, skeptical of their ability to take France, requested more preparation time. Various events—including unusually bad weather and a plane crash that delivered German battle plans to the Belgians—helped delay the attack for seven months. This long period of relative inactivity, following on the heels of a formal declaration of war, was dubbed "the phony war" by American newspapers. Germans called it the *Sitzkrieg*, or "sitting war," since they had every intention of getting up and marching forward. It was just a question of when.

"In the first eight months nothing happened," Man Ray recalled. "Aside from . . . small air raids when all the traffic had to stop, nothing much changed, the restaurants were full at lunchtime, at night people sat and ate behind blacked-out windows taped against concussion. They went to cinemas and the theater, got home as best they could, mostly on foot."[1]

Meanwhile, the British and French laid defensive plans. Britain transferred four military divisions to the continent and, hoping to create starvation and confusion, instituted a Royal Navy blockade of Germany. France shored up its Maginot Line, an eighty-seven-mile barrier with Germany consisting of barbed wire, tank traps, big gun emplacements, and underground forts. These defensive measures accomplished little. With Germany amply supplied from the east by the Russians, the British naval blockade had little effect. And by placing so much emphasis on the Maginot Line, France not only ignored other easily breached parts of the country, but revealed its naïveté about the mobility of Germany's modern army.

On May 10, 1940, Germany began its fateful westward push. The phony war was over.

AT THE YEAR'S START Natalie was preoccupied with the publication of her tenth book, *Nouvelles pensées de l'Amazone*. Published as Europe worried increasingly about war, the book garnered little attention. That is probably just as well because, despite its small gifts, the book is marred by Natalie's conservative political views and anti-Semitic statements.

Trying to comprehend Natalie Barney's anti-Semitic writing is a frustrating exercise, because it makes no sense. She was partly Jewish, and wrote proudly at times of her Jewish heritage. "That drop of Jewish blood," said Jean Chalon. "She was very proud of it."[2] Her sister married the Jewish Hippolyte Dreyfus. She had countless numbers of Jewish friends, most or even all of whom would be flabbergasted to hear her described as an anti-Semite. "I had never, never, ever felt any anti-Semitism," Renée Lang stated emphatically. "I would have. I am sensitive to it. And [I never sensed it] among the people I met in her salon. That would have been a very shocking thing for me, if I had noticed that she was anti-Semitic." She added that Natalie "often used to say there was no anti-Semitism on *her* side."[3]

So how does one explain *Nouvelles pensées de l'Amazone?* "Profiles of Jews turned toward all horizons," she wrote, ". . . a people always nomadic, a race ever on the march . . ." Or, "the vendors of the Temple, sent back by Jesus, are now settled in New York."

Actually, Natalie's unsavory writings neither began nor ended with *Nouvelles pensées.* In 1904, aboard the *Deutschland* with her mother, she came on deck to find "many energetic undersized people, mostly of the Jewish form of countenance madly promenading—one especially little man with a huge nose carrying ostentatiously as though to disguise his origins, a volume largely lettered 'Buddha.' Finds he his God therein when so obviously featured otherwise?"[4] Occasional epigrams in her earliest books show similar attitudes. "What nation will love the Jews so well that they may stop being Jewish?" she wrote in *Éparpillements.* Remarks emerged over the years regarding straightened Jewish noses, the Jews' burden of guilt for the death of Christ, the need for assimilation.

For those who admire the personal courage and bold spirit that Barney exhibited so often throughout her life, it is difficult to deal with this unpalatable aspect of her character. But Natalie's writings are a part of who she was. Her failings cannot be ignored.

Back in 1935, Natalie was introduced to a literary group by her friend Germaine Lefrancq, who warned the audience that she would tell them not only of Natalie's heroic qualities, but of her eccentricities and failures. "I admire Miss Barney," she said, "and I do not want to be one of those cowardly admirers who, for justifying the person they admire, deny their defects [and] camouflage their peculiarities, reducing them to nothing."[5] In that spirit, let's closely examine the ugly wart that sits atop Natalie's legacy, trying to understand how a woman heroic in so many ways came to write such repellent words.

The most logical place to start is with the zeitgeist of her times, which supported intolerance toward Jews. A careless anti-Semitism—careless in the sense that otherwise kind and thoughtful people took it as a matter of course—had long been ingrained in Western culture. In the late nineteenth and early twentieth centuries few, even among the most enlightened, questioned it.

Anti-Semitism was particularly rife in Europe, but there was no lack of it in the United States, where many hotels, civic associations, men's clubs, and other organizations barred Jews. One turn-of-the-century college fraternity explained its exclusionary policy by announcing: "We do not like the Jews as a class. There are some well behaved people among them, but . . ."[6] Many respected Americans, including Henry Ford and Charles Lindbergh, were brutally frank about their anti-Semitic attitudes (Hitler, pleased by Ford's enthusiastic dissemination of anti-Semitic literature in the United States, hung the automaker's photograph in his office). An essay by Calvin Coolidge on race pollution once appeared in *Good Housekeeping,* and debates rage even today over the anti-Semitism in T. S. Eliot's poetry. Mary Cassatt, known for her gentle depictions of motherly love, wrote to her sister from Paris of how the Stein family had bought up Matisse's pictures cheaply when he was still an unknown. She added that they were "not Jews for nothing."[7]

Natalie's own family had been victimized by anti-Semitism. Alice never made a secret of the fact that her father was one-half Jewish, but she considered herself an Episcopalian like her husband. The Barneys funded a pew in Washington's St. John's Church, Albert sat on the cathedral building committee, and both daughters were baptized there. Nonetheless, Alice was sometimes the focus of anti-Semitic remarks, and around 1900, as Washington society prepared itself for entry into its first official Social Register, the remarks became nasty. She was mildly upset by this, but far from devastated. Albert, however, was apoplectic.

Such an experience should have made Natalie more sensitive to the subject of anti-Semitism, but that's not what happened. Instead, she decided, probably in an unconscious fashion, to both distance herself from, and celebrate herself for, her Jewish background. She was quick to claim what she viewed as the positives of her heritage, once suggesting that her mother's many talents had descended from King Solomon himself. She also felt that her one-eighth measure of Jewish blood was just enough to lend her a dash of exoticism. Those who knew her agreed. "In Miss Barney were combined the trenchant grace of the American woman . . . and Palestinian nonchalance," Lily Gramont said.[8] Simultaneous to honoring what she liked about her ancestry, Natalie also rejected everything she viewed as a stereotyped negative. In one sense, her anti-Semitic epigrams were a way of saying "My heritage adds a few delicious fillips to my nature, but I'm really no different from you."

In her early Paris years, Natalie would have known about the Dreyfus affair, which split the country into violent factions. Alfred Dreyfus, a Jew, had been an anonymous French army captain when, in 1894, his name was suddenly on the tongue of every citizen. Papers had been discovered that led French authorities to believe that a military officer was providing secret information to the German government. Dreyfus became a suspect. Although he protested his innocence, he was found guilty of treason in a secret military court-martial that denied him the right to examine the evidence against him. Stripped of his rank, he was imprisoned in the dreaded Devil's Island penal colony.

Two years after the trial, a renowned anti-Semite, Lieutenant Colonel Georges Picquart, was appointed chief of army intelligence. To the surprise of everyone, Picquart, after reexamining the evidence against Dreyfus, concluded that he was innocent. He named another officer, a Major Esterhazy, as the traitor. But the army, which cared more about preserving its image than calling itself to account for punishing the wrong man, transferred Picquart to Tunisia to prevent him from reopening the Dreyfus case. A subsequent military court ignored Esterhazy's guilt and acquitted him.

In 1899, following Émile Zola's famed denunciation of the army's treachery and the discovery of forged documents designed to frame Dreyfus, the army conducted another court-martial. Once again, against all evidence to the contrary, they found Dreyfus guilty. Later that year he was pardoned by the president of France. It wasn't until 1906 that the stoic Dreyfus, who had never given up hope, was fully exonerated. He was returned to the army, promoted to the rank of major, and awarded the Legion of Honor. In 1995, a full century after the event, the French army finally admitted that it had been wrong all along.

During the many years it raged, the Dreyfus affair intensified bitter divisions within French politics and society, and placed the country's strong anti-Semitic sentiment on full display. No one at any level of society was immune. Waiting impatiently at the opera for her carriage, the Jewish Baroness de Rothschild was approached by a well-dressed stranger who snarled: "When someone like you, Madame, has been hoping for your Messiah for two thousand years, you certainly can wait five minutes for your carriage." Asked her profession, the Comtesse de Martel responded without hesitation: "Anti-Semite!"[9] Many salons became firmly anti- or pro-Dreyfus, excluding anyone with an opposite point of view. Salons open to all comers frequently burst into the kind of violent quarrels that progressed to a duel.

In those years a person could be revered for possessing genius while being simultaneously reviled for being Jewish—even partly Jewish. Sarah Bernhardt may have been the world's most famous actress, but the fact that she was half-Jewish subjected her to vicious remarks all her life. She was once caricatured in *Puck* with an exaggerated hooked nose under the caption "The Jewish Danae." The failure of logic behind bigotry can be seen in the fact that Bernhardt's son, himself one-quarter Jewish, was rabidly anti-Semitic. At the height of the Dreyfus matter, mother and son, who stood on opposite sides of the question, stopped speaking to each other for more than a year.

The few references Natalie ever makes to Dreyfus in her writings are dismissive and impertinent, but the affair undoubtedly influenced her attitudes. She would have known both pro- and anti-Dreyfusards, and she would have heard the arguments boiling over everywhere. With her vaunted lack of opinion, she would have responded to anything she heard by making a quip, simultaneously provoking laughter and cooling tempers. Many of these quips made it into her writings.

The decades passed. Natalie may have been a radical in her personal life, but politically she had always been a conservative. As she grew older, she became even more so. She couldn't care less about the political (or other) persuasions of those she knew, so they were a varied lot. Among her friends were socialists, right-wingers, and everything in between. Romaine Brooks was an archconservative. The Duchesse de Clermont-Tonnerre, who for years considered herself a Communist, once marched through the streets of Paris with her fist raised high.

In the mid- to late-1930s, as the situation in Europe heated up, Natalie's personal views began to be swayed by her more conservative friends. She was far from politically astute, as those who knew her have been quick to point out. "She was completely out of it politically," Jean Chalon said. Renée Lang declared emphatically: "Natalie was absolutely apolitical! And better it was that she was apolitical, because she was stupid in politics!"[10] Even Barney's housekeeper, Berthe, weighed in on this one, admitting that Natalie "wasn't very well informed politically."[11]

As war loomed and as rumors circulated of Hitler's attitude toward Jews, Natalie stopped discussing her Jewish heritage. In her essay "The Trouble with Heroines," Anna Livia suggests that Barney's writings around this time provided her with a way to prove, if necessary, that she was Christian, not Jewish. It's a plausible theory. Natalie's Jewish background was widely known. Anyone in France who possessed the slightest measure of Jewish blood worried about the Nazis' anti-Jewish rhetoric—with good reason, as it turned out. Of the 333,000 Jews living in France in 1940, about 76,000 were deported to Nazi concentration camps; of this number, only 2,500 survived. Foreigners were not immune to the slaughter, either; they were routinely rounded up and shipped off.

And Natalie Barney, despite her anti-Semitic epigrams, would not escape harassment by the Nazis, who would eventually pursue rumors of her Jewish ancestry. If she had stayed in Paris, she might have ended up in a camp, like some of her friends.

EZRA POUND WAS ONE of those whose political views influenced Natalie in the late 1930s. Oddly enough, a gift from Natalie kicked off the circum-

stances that ultimately branded him a traitor and landed him in a mental institution for twelve years.

In the fall of 1939, at the start of the phony war, Natalie and Romaine
motored east from Nice to Brooks's new villa in the hills above Florence. In the
Italian coastal town of Rapallo they stopped to lunch with Ezra and Dorothy
Pound, whose apartment on the top floor of an old hotel had a beautiful view
of the Tigullian Gulf.

Pound had been interested in politics and economics for decades, but had
grown increasingly fascist in his views throughout the 1930s. Living in Italy, he
came to admire Mussolini for his social and monetary reforms. Like the fascists, he believed that the looming war resulted from rivalry between international capitalists. He was particularly contemptuous of American capitalism,
heaping scorn on bankers and industrialists, whom he felt were under the
power of "the Jews." Pound's anti-Semitism had become so virulent, his political beliefs so extreme, that old friends dropped him.

Not Natalie. It wasn't in her nature to drop friends to begin with, but she
also agreed with much of what he said. Or at least she thought she did. By the
time of her Rapallo visit, Pound often made no sense, and he *always* sounded
angry. His daughter later said that he had become like a man fighting a wasp
nest in his brain.

Natalie probably extracted what she could from his rants—capitalists were
bad, Mussolini good, the Jews responsible for all the current troubles—and
ignored the parts she didn't understand. To Natalie, Ezra would always be her
self-assured, brilliant American brother; the literary mover and shaker of the
1920s; the influential powerhouse who guided men like T. S. Eliot and Ernest
Hemingway into major writing careers; a genius who could write both music
and epic poems, read Chinese and Latin, edit journals, fight with his fists, and
snarl back at critics. He had already begun to lose touch with reality, but to
Natalie he still had the look and manner of an invincible lion. Perpetually at
sea on political issues, she implicitly trusted his judgments. If Ezra said that the
coming war was caused by Churchill and the Jews, he knew what he was talking about.

During the visit Pound remarked that he didn't own a wireless radio, and
didn't want one, either. No, no, Natalie protested, "you'll not be able to live
without one." Before leaving town she bought him a small wireless and had it
delivered. Writing to a friend in his characteristic abbreviated manner, Ezra
said: "Blasted friends left a goddam radio here yester. Gift. God damn destructive and dispersive devil of an invention."[12]

However, he took to the device immediately. He particularly liked listening
to a man Natalie recommended, William Joyce, who broadcast as "Lord Haw-

Haw." An American who grew up in Britain, Joyce had traveled to Berlin during the phony war to volunteer his services to Joseph Goebbels in the Nazi propaganda ministry. With a strong English accent, he delivered his profascist, anti-Semitic words while snickering, which earned his nickname. In 1945 he would be arrested by the Allies, tried for treason, and hanged.

Pound began broadcasting his own views over Rome Radio in a program called *The American Hour*. In these rambling, nearly incomprehensible talks he attacked America and Great Britain and expounded upon other topics. He would make more than three hundred such broadcasts throughout the war. Here's an excerpt from a typical address, delivered in April 1943:

> I think it is time more American Masons developed a curiosity about the possible relations of their order to Jewry as such, and to at least a sect or portion or selection of ORGANIZED Jews as a possible enemy of mankind, and of the American people, the British people in particular. I think it might be a good thing to hang Roosevelt and a few hundred yidds IF you can do it by due legal process, NOT otherwise. Law must be preserved. I know this may sound tame, but so is it. It is sometimes hard to think so. Hard to think that the 35 ex-army subalterns or whatever who wanted to bump off all the kike congressmen weren't just a bit crude and *simpliste*. Sometimes one feels that it would be better to get the job done somehow, ANY how, than to delay execution. . . .

Natalie often listened to Ezra and sincerely believed that his unique idiom and forceful manner were sure to win over even the most stubborn of his listeners. Everybody else Pound knew thought he'd lost his mind. Hemingway voiced the opinions of many when he said, toward war's end, that Pound belonged in a "loony bin."[13] He certainly ended up in one.

AFTER A BRIEF stay in Italy, Natalie and Romaine returned to France and nestled into Beauvallon for the winter. They stayed through Christmas, worrying about the looming war.

By the time the German push began in early May, Natalie was back in rue Jacob and Romaine had returned to Florence. Laura, worried about being persecuted by the Germans for being the widow of a Jewish man, was intent on returning to the States immediately. She pushed Natalie to accompany her. Loath to go but worried about the ramifications of staying behind, Natalie couldn't decide what to do. Even if she stayed, where? Being partly Jewish could be dangerous in Paris—or anywhere in France if the Germans took over. Should she try neutral Portugal or Switzerland? Italy? Delaying her decision, she opted to remain in Paris for the moment while doing everything possible to get Laura off.

At Cook's, while Laura booked passage, Natalie suddenly decided to join Romaine in Florence and take shelter under what they considered to be Italy's neutrality. The fates were smiling. Despite the mass exodus from Paris, a train ticket on the May 17 *Rome-Express* became suddenly available and Natalie snapped it up. Prudently, she also booked a cabin aboard a ship leaving the next month for the States (she later gave it to a young Jewish couple anxious to leave Europe).

Laura continued pleading with Natalie to accompany her home until the train pulled away from the station. Crying and waving good-bye, each must have wondered: "Will I ever see her again?" Once in Washington, Laura immediately set to work, doing whatever she could to aid the war effort. Among other endeavors, she served as vice chairwoman of the Commission of Women's International Organizations for the Control and Reduction of Armaments, represented the National Council of Women of the U.S. on the Coordinating Committee for Better Racial Understanding, and served as honorary chair of the Barney Neighborhood House board of trustees. She also organized exhibits of her mother's paintings. First Lady Eleanor Roosevelt attended a 1941 showing.

After Laura's departure, Natalie arranged for Dolly's safe return to London. Try as she might, she couldn't get her a reservation until May 28, more than ten days after her own departure for Italy. Thus it was that Dolly remained behind in Paris after Natalie's train had chugged slowly out of sight.

Natalie packed hurriedly, cramming two small suitcases with her most precious papers and toiletries, and filling a large trunk with clothes, shoes, and hats. Berthe and Dolly saw her off. Berthe remembered her stepping onto the train and offering a simple "Good-bye," as if leaving for an afternoon's frolic. The train pulled out, with all three waving, and something in Dolly's smile clutched at Natalie's heart. It would be six long years before she laid eyes on Berthe. She would never see Dolly again.

Whatever sadness Natalie felt as the train pulled away disappeared when she struck up a conversation with a much younger woman. One thing led to another. "I followed her into her compartment," Natalie recalled, "and when I left her at my Pisa junction for Florence, I felt that several years of casual acquaintance could not have revealed so much. I am not a good traveler at best and torn now between such a departure and [such an] arrival, this diversion had been propitious."[14]

Three days after Natalie's departure a German panzer group seized Abbeville at the mouth of the Somme and commenced a northward push. By the twenty-sixth the French and their British allies had retreated to a narrow beachhead near Dunkirk. More than three hundred thousand soldiers were rescued in a massive sealift of navy and civilian craft, everything from huge destroyers to tiny fishing boats.

The Germans commenced their drive into France, unstoppable. On June 17, the country's new premier, former World War I hero Marshal Henri Philippe Pétain, who had halted the Germans at Verdun in the last war, capitulated. An armistice agreement was signed, giving Germany control of northern France and the Atlantic coast. Pétain established the new French capital in Vichy, an area unoccupied by the Germans, where his fascist regime began its collaboration with the Nazis. After the war, convicted of treason, Pétain would be sentenced to death (General Charles de Gaulle commuted the sentence to life imprisonment).

Meanwhile, Germany's early success inspired Mussolini to openly ally himself with Hitler. On June 10, Italy—no longer neutral—declared war on Britain and France. Italian forces occupied British Somaliland and began a pincerlike movement on the British in Egypt.

At Romaine's villa, Natalie thought of her friends so far away, and penned "Poem Written in Florence, 1940":

> Our dearest now are scattered
> As thou it no wise mattered
> My old love's in south-western France
> With spy and refugees
> My sister's on the sea
> My Dolly ill in London town
> Lives horror through a trance?
> Where air-raid bombs were thundered down;
> My faithful maid in Paris stayed
> to welcome Germany
> And others, where? If still they be?
> Here I remain
> Beside Romaine

Natalie's immediate worry was for friends living in France under German rule. "It's a subtle torture to have everything one needs," she wrote Laura, "money, food, warm clothes and coal, and yet shiver to think that perhaps those we are fondest of may lack some, or all, of these vital necessities."[15] Throughout the war she would be forever shuffling funds between accounts in Switzerland, London, France, and the United States, transferring large sums to friends, including Dolly, Lily, and Lucie. She also sent money to Nadine Hoang until she was incarcerated in Ravensbrück, the only concentration camp specifically for women (Nadine survived). Through Berthe, who owned a farm near Paris with her husband, she was able to get fresh meat, produce, and even those famous salon pastries to friends in and around Paris.

In the fall of 1940 foreigners still in Italy were advised to return to their native countries. Natalie and Romaine debated whether to return to the United States, to France, or to simply stay put. In the end, as travel permits became nearly impossible to obtain, the decision was made for them. Whether they liked it or not, they were in Italy for the duration. "We are being caught in a net!" Natalie complained.[16]

AND SO THEY SETTLED in. All things considered, there were worse places to endure the war than in Romaine's Villa Sant' Agnese on the Via San Leonardo. This picturesque street, which twists and winds into the hills above Florence, is lined with ancient stone walls and massive wooden gates concealing homes that date back to the fourteenth century. A high gate bearing the crest of the once-powerful Guidetti family welcomed visitors onto the property. Inside was a very old two-story, white stucco villa, topped by a red tile roof and fronting a cobblestoned courtyard. Beyond this was a big expanse of lawn bordered by box hedges, huge sprays of flowers, and small orange trees in terra-cotta pots, all backdropped by a captivating view of rising hills dotted with olive and cypress trees. A short distance away was the adjoining "farm," big enough to graze three cows and support fruit and olive trees, grapevines, peas, beans, carrots, radishes, lettuces, melons, celery, potatoes, cabbage, and cauliflower. The entire enterprise was managed by Romaine's longtime helper, Antonio, who also did most of the cooking. Additional staff cared for the farm, the gardens, and the house.

One of the best things about being in Florence, at least for Natalie, was that friends lived nearby. A short hop away in Settignano, Bernard and Mary Berenson resided in the fabulous I Tatti, with its formal terraced gardens, ancient statuary, and rooms filled with paintings by Renaissance masters such as Giotto, Martini, Sassetta, and Landi. "The Ritz," the Berensons' two-room guest suite, had silk-covered walls, overlooked the gardens, and was furnished with fine eighteenth-century Italian furniture and priceless art. A frequent I Tatti visitor in these years, Natalie deepened her long friendship with Bernard and came to know his wife, Mary, much better.

Closer to home were the immediate neighbors. A lively cast of characters, they included Antonio's sour-faced wife, an invalid with an enormous appetite; a fiercely antifascist Frenchwoman married to a rabidly fascist Italian professor; a charming American-born countess who somehow always had the latest news of mutual friends in Paris; a poverty-stricken baroness who was terrified of Communists; thieving peasant brothers who threatened the locals and constantly brandished big knives; and a lively musical family who liked to gather neighbors around their piano to sing the evening away. A local teenager named Marie-Christine, who may have been an orphan, developed a unique bond with Natalie, whom she viewed as a sort of mother figure. The Amazon responded with gifts of hard-to-obtain items such as talcum powder, dental paste, a pen, ink, and paper.

On a day-to-day level, things were not always easy between Romaine and Natalie. They had traditionally spent far more time apart than together, and had even built a hyphenated vacation home allowing for daily separation. Now, trapped together in a walled enclosure, they took great pains to give each other space. Natalie spent a lot of time in her room writing, and Romaine was often in her studio. They met best, Natalie thought, in the garden. As at Beauvallon, they enjoyed relaxing outside, reading side by side on chaise longues. With lots of time to fill up, Natalie took to reading Will and Ariel Durant's multibook series on the history of civilization.

Natalie's wartime writing consisted of letters, poetry, and a few literary projects. Most European mail service had continued despite the war, though delivery was a hit-or-miss proposition; letters and telegrams to/from the United States and Britain went through Lloyd's Bank in neutral Switzerland. Once, writing to Laura, Natalie joked that if worse came to worst they could communicate via mental telepathy, as in childhood.

Most of Natalie's letters throughout the war were upbeat and chatty. She constantly sought news of friends, passed on what she had heard, invoked shared memories, and talked of the increasing hardships in Florence. She generally avoided discussions of politics and the war, which may have had something to do with postal censors. Once she taped a flower onto the writing paper of a letter to Lily.

The prolific correspondence of these years was vital to Natalie, since it was the only way she had of being with those she loved. Each letter she received held the promise of a future meeting with its sender and went far in sustaining her positive outlook despite the long confinement. In June 1944, as liberation drew near, she reread all of Lily's wartime letters, "these dear packets of paper in all colors: soft green, red, midnight blue and sea blue, sun-yellow, white, beige, gray . . . all of it dressed and ennobled by your precious writing."[17] If the letters could take such a voyage, she wondered, why not they?

Whenever possible, Laura sent care packages via American Express in Switzerland. Hands down, the item Natalie and Romaine requested most was coffee. Sometimes entire letters are devoted to nothing but java: where Laura might obtain it, how to package it, how much could be shipped at one time (twenty pounds, Natalie thought), and so on. In espresso-loving Italy, the beans must have been one of the first items to disappear from the shelves. As early as November 1940—just a few months after her arrival—Natalie noted that coffee's scarcity was becoming such a big problem that they were making a pot last for three days by extending it with water.

Natalie's literary endeavors in Florence included completion of the unpublished "Memoirs of a European American." This document rambles incessantly. It jumps from one unrelated topic to the next, loosely wrapping everything within the context of war. The lack of focus is probably an outgrowth of the inconsistent way Barney worked on the manuscript. For five years, from 1940 to 1945, she picked it up when she had an idea or felt like getting something off her chest. Mission accomplished, she put it down and forgot about it for a while.

"Memoirs of a European American" covers wide ground, including glimpses of Barney's childhood, thoughts about Albert ("My worldly father, whose mind reproached him the little use he put it to . . ."), colorful anecdotes about the travels of Laura and Hippo, and recollections of the World War I pacifist meetings held at the Temple of Friendship. It also contains many rants about the then-current state of American culture. Natalie, at least in these pages, considered the average American to be crass and crude. She felt that the moral fiber of her native land was falling apart, and that people were turning to drink and drugs because there was nothing going on in their heads. She looked to the past, when America was founded on solid principles, when character counted for something, and when people like her grandfathers ran things. Occasionally she makes a comment so unrealistic that one can't help but burst out laughing. For instance, discussing the fact that American soldiers drink too much, she suggests: "Our boys must learn to drink mint tea instead and accustom their jaded palates to this more delicate and spiritual intoxication."[18]

Natalie's political views make an appearance, looking heavily influenced by Pound: "The Roosevelts—he and she—always had a red lining to their coats . . . Red was becoming the exclusive color of the white house and American imperialism [was] getting to be a very red affair indeed."[19] She pens odious epigrammatic phrases about Jews, such as: "If Benjamin Franklin could foresee that if we let the Jews in, we would risk being subjugated by them, why cannot we at least see this most real of the Semitic perils developing under our very eyes?"[20]

While Natalie busied herself with letters and manuscripts, Romaine tried to paint. She met with little success, which wasn't surprising: she had scarcely turned out any works since the previous decade, blaming her artistic block on her failing eyesight. Rather than mope around, she decided to write her memoirs. She labored mightily over the story of her life for years, writing and rewriting, and finally bestowed upon it the unhappy title *No Pleasant Memories*. She also kept a wartime diary, "On the Hills of Florence During the War." From time to time the latter manuscript offers up waspish observations about Natalie, no doubt written after one of their tiffs. "Natalie's hostility to maids forms part of our daily life here," she groused in a typical passage. "Nag she must and all the time."[21] Another good example: "Natalie's brain must always be concocting complicated situations, and these she directs usually with success though at times with fatal results. Then again she may abandon a plan half way through, leaving to those near her the task of unraveling the tangle that ensues."[22]

BACK IN FRANCE, Berthe was doing everything she could to safeguard the *pavillon* and fulfill Natalie's ceaseless demands. Letters arrived from Italy on the average of three times a week, each containing requests nearly impossible to carry out under wartime austerity and restrictions. The Paris marketplace no longer existed, at least for noncollaborationists like Berthe and her husband, who was active in the Resistance. When Natalie asked for half a dozen hairnets, it took Berthe months to find a single one. Rather than appreciate her efforts, Natalie complained.

In her memoirs Berthe expressed resentment at Natalie's seeming disconnect with the cold, hard reality of war. Parisian residents were suffering mightily, she said, while her employer, comfortably ensconced in Italy, had everything she needed. But, loyal and loving, Berthe continued doing everything she could for Miss Barney—including, at least twice, running interference with the Nazis.

The first time followed the sad aftermath of Dolly Wilde's death from cancer in April 1941. Through Lloyd's Bank, Natalie received a telegram from a mutual friend informing her that Dolly had died peacefully in her sleep. The news laid Natalie flat, and for a couple of weeks she couldn't even write a letter. When she finally penned a note to her sister, she apologized for the long silence and thanked her for having always tried to appreciate Dolly's many good qualities.

Dolly had always been broke, and Natalie often helped her out financially. That was why Dolly had written a one-page will back in 1932, naming Natalie as her sole heir, with Laura as a witness. When Dolly died, Natalie asked Berthe to search for the will. After months of investigating every nook and cranny of the *pavillon*, the only place left to look was in Natalie's safe deposit box at Crédit Lyonnais. Opening it required German permission. Berthe asked Natalie's friend Gaston Bergery, a member of the Vichy cabinet, to intercede, but he was reluctant to do so. At his wife's insistence, he found a lawyer able to obtain the necessary permissions for an exorbitant fee.

Scrutinized by a party of German soldiers, Berthe opened the box with Natalie's secret combination: 7–7–7. The box was so stuffed with belongings that, when the lid lifted, twenty or thirty gold coins burst from the container and rolled onto the floor. They were quickly "disappeared" by the soldiers. While they scrambled after the coins, Berthe removed the will as well as Natalie's valuable jewelry, including the gold hairpins given to her decades before by Lord Alfred Douglas. She later hid the jewelry in the *pavillon*, where it remained safely until Natalie's return.

Berthe's next brush with the Nazis came in 1942, when they became interested in rue Jacob. They first went after the Bertheims, Natalie's Jewish landlords, seizing all their possessions. Then they informed Berthe that, because Natalie was Jewish, her property would be taken. Berthe said that they were mistaken; if Natalie was Jewish, why would she have sought shelter in Mussolini's Italy? When the Germans insisted that they had heard talk of Natalie's Jewish blood, Berthe suggested that they had confused Natalie with her sister, Laura, the widow of a Jewish lawyer. If so, there was little they could do, since Mrs. Dreyfus-Barney now lived in America. The Germans left. For the moment, any difficulties they presented were in abeyance.

Natalie's Jewish heritage had pursued her to Florence, as well. In 1941 Italian authorities came to the villa to investigate whether she was truly a Protestant, as she stated on all official documentation. Learning of this via cable from Natalie, Laura contacted the Rector of Washington's St. John's Church to ask for a notarized statement attesting to Natalie's confirmation there on March 27, 1892. After Natalie exhibited the resultant proof of her Protestantism, the Italians left her alone.

Dolly wasn't the only friend of Natalie's to die while she was in Florence. One of the most wrenching deaths, because of its circumstances, was that of Max Jacob. His 1915 conversion to Catholicism and subsequent passionate faith hadn't prevented his arrest by the Nazis, in February 1944, for the crime of being born Jewish. He was brought to Drancy, a deportation camp outside Paris, where he died the next month of bronchial pneumonia.

Natalie had known Max Jacob since the 1920s, and in all the years since he had attended the salon. They were frequent correspondents, they knew dozens of people in common, and she had dedicated a short chapter to him in *Aventures de l'esprit*. One can't help but wonder what she thought when hearing of his death in a Nazi camp. Was she angry that a friend died under harsh circumstances because he possessed Jewish blood? Did she think about her own Jewish blood and breathe, "There but for fortune . . . ?" Surely, with her grand intelligence and quick grasp of the unobvious, she pondered the despicable circumstances surrounding Jacob's demise. Alas, she left no record of her thoughts on the subject.

Another difficult death to endure was that of Lucie Delarue-Mardrus on April 21, 1945. The last years of Lucie's life had been difficult. The young woman who had once cantered along the Seine in cowboy gear, riding fearlessly toward taunting boys, had ended up wracked by a painful form of arthritis. Her money gone, she had been reduced to living on the generosity of friends, including Natalie, and a tiny stipend from a French writers' organization.

Others who died during the war included Oscar Milosz, Emma Calvé, Radclyffe Hall, Olive Custance, Paul Poiret, Paul Valéry, and Lord Alfred Douglas. Stuck in Florence, Natalie sometimes learned of their deaths months after the fact. But whether she learned quick or late, the result was always the same. One more connection to the past had broken.

Death was on everyone's mind. In 1945 Gertrude Stein's *Wars I Have Seen* was published. A day-to-day overview of life in occupied France, it contained a passage about Natalie that illustrates just how tentative existence seemed:

> One dreams funny dreams these days. I dreamed one about Nathalie Barney. I dreamed that she always left the plants of her Paris apartment at a florist's to have them watered over the summer and returned in the winter and now would she have them back again, would she, would the florist would there be a florist, would there be an apartment, would there be she. I do not know whether she did do this ordinarily with her plants or whether she had plants but all the same I did dream it.[23]

Indeed. When it was all over, would Natalie have the flowers back again? Would there be an apartment? Would there even be a she?

IN ITALY, naturally enough, wartime propaganda had a decidedly Fascist slant. Axis victories and might were trumpeted; Allied victories were ignored or downplayed. The newspapers and radio constantly broadcast the government's point of view, which boiled down to two simple beliefs: first, that Hitler and Mussolini had always wanted peace; second, that they had been pushed to fight because the allies loved and needed war. This viewpoint was parroted by everybody who wanted to stay alive, from the truest believer to the most extreme antifascists and pacifists.

Day in and day out, Natalie and Romaine heard the message—and they believed what they heard. They had no other input. Fear of gossips and spies kept local lips buttoned up, and the dreaded censors guaranteed that letters contained no contrary political views. About the strongest comment Natalie wrote in four years of correspondence was "What a wretched mess man has made of this world," a sentiment with which few, including Nazis and Fascists, would have disagreed.

"Memoirs of a European American" reflects this one-sided input for about two-thirds of its length, with Natalie recording events as she would have heard them reported by the governing Fascists. Reading Hitler's "Last Appeal to Reason" in the newspapers, she believes it's a legitimate appeal for peace. She seems to think that only the Brits are bombing towns populated by civilians. As the war progresses, and as Italy's weakness becomes increasingly revealed in the newspapers and talked about in drawing rooms, her attitudes change, and she begins entertaining thoughts of an eventual Axis defeat. By mid-1943, Italy had lost most of its army. When Mussolini was deposed and thrown in jail, crowds of antifascists came out of hiding to drag statues of him through the streets. Right around this time Natalie, like everyone else she knew, began to view the Allies as liberators. Food was scarce. There was no electricity, no gas, and only limited water. Everyone wanted the war to end.

In the summer of 1944, as the Allies drew near to Florence, the Germans were on the run. On August 3 a party of retreating German soldiers took up residence in Villa Sant'Agnese, installing a cannon in the courtyard. They were civil enough, but Natalie and Romaine slept that night in the cellar of a friend's home, sharing the space with several neighbors. The next day, briefly returning home, they were dismayed to find the cannon firing skyward in short intervals, while soldiers lay about in the courtyard, sunning themselves or writing letters. Inside, more soldiers were playing disks on Romaine's gramophone. After a quick meal, the two women returned to their neighbor's cellar. In a symbolic portent, as they left their villa Romaine unknowingly stepped on several German postage stamps bearing Hitler's head. They adhered to her shoes until coming off on the neighbor's doormat.

That night the group camping out in the neighbor's cellar were asked upstairs, where they mingled uncomfortably in the music room with an occupying German general and several of his men. At one point they were entertained by a young, flute-playing German officer whom Natalie thought resembled a "better edition" of the actor Leslie Howard. He was accompanied on piano by the neighbor's daughter. They ran through Gluck's *Orfeo*—including the song Emma Calvé had once sung beneath Renée Vivien's balcony while Natalie collected coins—and a few sonatas by Liszt. At one point the general and his men retreated behind closed doors for a meeting. Eavesdropping, one of the neighbor women heard plans to blow up Florence's bridges.

The explosions came in the middle of night as the Germans departed. In morning's light, Natalie and Romaine walked down the hill in the eerie quiet. "The sight of the ruins completely benumbed me," Romaine wrote.[24] Gone were the ancient buildings with their balconies, statues, loggias, arches. The only bridge still standing was the Ponte Vecchio. Yet, "splendid signs of the Renaissance still towered above, [including] the Duomo with its campanile . . . British troops [were] spreading over and taking possession of the southern bank of the river where a patient and long-suffering population awaited their liberators!"[25]

THE EUROPEAN WAR was over, but it wouldn't be until 1946 that Natalie would see Paris again. As an American living in Italy who wanted to relocate to France, she had to deal with the bureaucracy and paperwork of three national governments and Florence's occupying army. For the agencies involved, besieged with problems of every kind, Natalie's visa problems were not top priority.

Soon after the Germans fled, Natalie and Romaine went into town to seek help from the occupation army in dealing with two neighborhood ruffians. Entering the Palazzo Vecchio, Natalie caught sight of a familiar-looking young blond woman dressed in an American khaki uniform and wearing a military reporter's badge. As Romaine described her, she "was an American woman of the super-efficient variety and what is more she was very good looking."[26]

"Why, Natalie!" the woman exclaimed, and reminded her that they had last met at Sylvia Beach's bookshop in Paris on the night that Ernest Hemingway and T. S. Eliot read aloud. "And afterwards," the blond said, "you went off with Eliot."

Natalie remembered the woman but couldn't quite place her. No matter: she seemed like she knew how to get things done, and that's what they needed. Whisking Natalie and Romaine off to the proper offices, the woman turned them over to someone able to fix their problems. She then said that, as she was leaving Florence immediately, they must say good-bye. Natalie asked when she would return.

"We never can say!" came the reply. "My husband is at present in Normandy, and I don't even know when or where we shall again meet."

Natalie remarked that she didn't remember her having a husband, and at any rate she looked too young. "She flashed a delighted smile on me," Natalie said, "and as I asked for her address she tore a page out of her notebook and wrote in her clear, backhand writing: Martha Hemingway, c/o D.A.D.—P.R.8th Army & c/o American Embassy London. Then, without waiting to see the effect, she kissed me and waved a farewell from her car as she was driven away."[27]

The woman who rescued Natalie and Romaine was writer and famed World War II reporter Martha Gellhorn, who married Ernest Hemingway in 1940.

Eventually, after a year of effort, Natalie amassed all the required papers, visas, stamps, and a valid new passport. Irreverent as ever, she penned a ditty on the back of an extra passport photo:

> Been through two wars
> Most mountain passes—
> And met the world's
> Most famous asses!
> NCB/45

She was sixty-nine, and after the long years of war she was ready to go home. "Natalie has departed for Paris," Romaine confided to her journal a few days after she left. "I miss her very much."[28]

FIFTEEN

The Amazon in Winter

1946–1960

She is a most triumphant lady . . .
Age cannot wither her, nor custom stale
Her infinite variety.

—*William Shakespeare*

Deck yourself, dance, laugh. I could never throw Love out the window.

—*Arthur Rimbaud*

ATALIE WAS SIXTY-NINE YEARS OLD when she returned to Paris on May 24, 1946. As she stepped from the train, her eyes landed on the smiling Berthe. "Bonjour!" she said lightly, as if she'd been off on a pleasant jaunt.

The Paris Barney returned to would be slow to recover from war's devastation. Stanley Karnow, who came to the city around this time as a young reporter, recalled the daily hardships: "Such essentials as milk, bread, butter, cheese and eggs were rationed, and even foreigners like me had to queue up [for food coupons]. . . . Neglected for years, public and private buildings needed repainting and other repairs."[1]

Rue Jacob, too, was in abysmal condition. The garden's majestic centerpiece, the huge chestnut tree, had fallen. The *pavillon*'s roof leaked badly, windows needed replacement, there was no coal to heat the furnace, and everything was in a sad state of disrepair. Living at Beauvallon was impossible, since it had been virtually destroyed, first looted by the Germans and later bombed. Neither Natalie nor Romaine had the desire to rebuild, marking a definite end to their hyphenated existence. Natalie moved into Laura's rue Raynouard home, remaining until the *pavillon* became habitable in the spring of 1949.

Since Romaine's apartment was immediately above Laura's, the daily intimacy of Florence might have continued. However, Romaine, grown tired of the hectic Parisian pace, now preferred the Mediterranean's slower tempo and warmer climate. Renting out her top-floor rue Raynouard residence, she took a two-room apartment in Nice. She would continue to spend part of each year in Italy, eventually exchanging the Villa Sant'Agnese for a smaller place in the hills of nearby Fiesole. She would never live in Paris again.

IN THE FALL OF 1947, Natalie and Romaine visited the United States. Most of their time was spent in Washington with Laura, trying to decide what to do about Studio House and Alice's paintings. Laura had become interested in the Smithsonian Institution and its associated National Collection of American Art (later the National Museum of American Art, or NMAA, it was renamed the Smithsonian Museum of American Art in 2001), and in 1951 they established a memorial fund at the NMAA in their mother's name. Over the ensuing two decades they donated hundreds of artworks to the organization, including many of Alice's paintings and pastels. Among them are portraits of Natalie, including *Natalie in Fur Cape, Natalie with Mandolin, Natalie with Flowing Hair, The Writer,* and—a title sure to delight her detractors—*Lucifer.* Reviewing Alice's paintings, Natalie was amused at the poses and costumes of long ago. As she told Laura: "We were evidently very unconsciously ridiculous in our youth!"[2]

Hearing that Natalie was in Washington, Eva Palmer, now living in New York City, contacted her. "I would like to sit with you quietly, and perhaps talk a little," Eva wrote. "I am glad you're alive."[3] Natalie ran up to New York, and the visit between the two old friends—Natalie now seventy-one, Eva two years older—was a happy one. Eva felt that something vital from their past had been restored, and she admired the way Natalie continued to make the difficult seem easy. "I think you are nicer than ever," she wrote, "which is a great deal to say after more than 50 years of friendship."[4]

Around this same time a significant part of their shared past, Bar Harbor, was struck by a disaster of epic proportions. Maine had experienced an unusually dry summer that year. In late October, when a fire broke out on Mount Desert Island, the forests were tinder-dry and water supplies were dangerously low. By the time the fires were completely extinguished weeks later, the disaster had claimed three lives and demolished almost 20,000 acres. Of the 237 homes destroyed, 67 were on Millionaires' Row, with its lavish nineteenth-century cottages. Among them was Ban-y-Bryn.

WHEN THE FRIDAYS BEGAN again in 1949, one change was immediately apparent. Before the war, people had enjoyed the food but never looked upon it as a necessity. Now, with Paris still suffering postwar deprivation, many of Natalie's guests were truly hungry, devouring anything placed on the table. The continued rationing made it difficult for Berthe to find enough food in the markets, but somehow she managed to set out a buffet each week.

There was another, more symbolic change at rue Jacob. The floor supports of the Temple had completely given out, making it dangerous for anyone to enter. As if forever closing off access to its sprightly past, the Temple's ancient door now remained firmly shut. Soon the entrance would be barred by a rope on which a suspended sign declared "Danger!"

However, much about the salon remained the same. Invitations still came in Natalie's hand. The familiar regulars, those who had survived the war, returned to enjoy "the same magical petit fours and the same jewels of the spirit that had enchanted us in our youth."[5] The conversation still centered on literature, with a dose of spicy gossip thrown in. And the *pavillon,* though a little dustier, continued to look as Paul Morand had defined it back in 1909: "very Fiesole 1895." As journalist Denise Bourdet described it around this time, "one enters groping, or rather, one dives in. The garden's immense shade is also in the house, the trees pressing against the windows, and it's in this underwater light that the firm hand of Miss Barney guides the swimmer among the hazards of the living room. Across the blue-green light filtering through the leaves, she discerns little by little a great amount of furniture, paintings, photographs, books, stuffed cushions."[6]

New faces continued to appear. Although the Amazon and her salon were showing unmistakable signs of age, she still possessed clout. Visiting writers sought invitations or were brought by a mutual friend, and Natalie didn't hesitate to ask those she had heard about or whose books she liked.

One of the earliest newcomers was also one of the youngest: Truman Capote. His first book—*Other Voices, Other Rooms*—had been published in

1948 when he was only twenty-three. The book's upfront discussion of homo-sexuality, as well as the jacket cover of Capote stretched seductive and pouting on a couch, had elicited a good deal of talk. Arriving in Paris on the first wings of his fame, he met NCB through his agent, Jenny Bradley.

Natalie took a shine to the young man. It's easy to see why, as many pas-sages in *Other Voices, Other Rooms* expressed her most cherished beliefs. Con-sider this sentence: "Any love is natural and beautiful that lies within a person's nature; only hypocrites would hold a man responsible for what he loves, emo-tional illiterates and those of righteous envy, who, in their agitated concern, mistake so frequently the arrow pointing to heaven for the one that leads to hell." Natalie would be disappointed in Capote's later works, however. She dis-liked 1951's *The Grass Harp* so much that she spoke against it in half a dozen letters to friends. "I'm afraid he's a one-book boy,"[7] she advised Romaine.

Capote was fascinated by Natalie's dichotomy, saying that she looked "like a refined lady from Shaker Heights. But of course she wasn't that at all."[8] He found her so compelling that, in 1975—more than twenty-five years after they met—he described her in his unfinished novel, *Answered Prayers*, as the "pre-mier American expatriate" in Paris, an independent-minded heiress who pos-sessed her own set of morals. He recalled the day she took him to Romaine Brooks's studio, "a sort of unkempt shrine-museum . . . There were perhaps seventy [paintings], all portraits of a flat and ultra realism; the subjects were women. . . . You know how you know when you're not going to forget some-thing? I wasn't going to forget this moment, this room, this array of butch-babes, all of whom, to judge from their coifs and cosmetics, were painted between 1917 and 1930."[9]

While writing *Answered Prayers*, Capote was interviewed by George Plimp-ton for the spring 1975 issue of the *Paris Review*, which featured a long, multi-person tribute to Natalie Barney. Capote described the salon's decor in the years after the war ("totally turn-of-the-century"), food ("marvelous things—delicious kinds of strawberry and raspberry tarts in the dead of winter; and always champagne"), and atmosphere ("very proper"), and once again told of his trip to Romaine's studio.

"The paintings were wonderful, they really were," Capote said. "And of course [there was one of] Miss Barney herself . . . that's what made the whole thing so eerie. Because it had so little to do with the Miss Barney I was standing with, this cozy little Agatha Christie–Miss Marple lady."[10]

Renée Lang met Natalie sometime in 1952, and for a few years became the Amazon's handpicked biographer, although in the end the project came to naught. Born in Switzerland and schooled in Geneva, Berlin, Rome, and Cam-bridge, Lang had attained an American Ph.D. in comparative literature at

Columbia University in 1946. Her first book, about Natalie's old friend André Gide, was published to scholarly acclaim in 1949, after which she turned her attention to the German poet Rainer Maria Rilke. "I came to Paris," she said, "because it is where Rilke spent 1926, the last year of his life. I wanted to meet the people he had known."[11]

When she heard that André Germain had known Rilke well in the 1920s, she asked for an interview. He responded immediately, saying that the first person she must see was "the Amazon, the most intelligent woman in Paris," who possessed several letters written by Rilke. Lang was taken aback at the word "Amazon." She thought immediately of Remy de Gourmont's letters, which had so enthralled her as a girl. She remembered that the Amazon to whom he wrote had also been the inspiration of Renée Vivien's poetry. But surely Germain was referring to some more recent, self-styled Amazon, she thought. After all, Gourmont had died in 1915.

As she soon found out, Gourmont's Amazon lived on. The astonished Lang sent a note outlining her Rilke project to Natalie, who telephoned immediately. In an authoritative, slightly hoarse voice she arranged for Lang to drop by rue Jacob a few days later.

"Renée Vivien's poetry gave me the image of a young woman with beauty like that of a fairy, and hair the color of moonlight," Lang said. "I saw instead a small, elderly woman of 75 who stood very straight and was absolutely imposing." What really grabbed Lang's notice was Natalie's eyes, of a "beautiful icy blue, with a direct, penetrating and absolutely pitiless gaze."[12] The conversation went well, and Natalie invited Lang to the next Friday.

The petite, attractive, and much younger Lang quickly drew Natalie's deep interest, but not for the reasons we've come to expect. It was Lang's highly praised book about Gide that excited Natalie; she wanted a biography written about her life, and in Renée Lang she felt that she had found the perfect person for the job. "Natalie saw immediately in me her wish to be immortalized," Lang admits.[13]

When Lang expressed interest, Natalie allowed her unlimited access to personal books, letters, and manuscripts. Even when Barney was away from Paris, Lang had the privilege of coming and going as she pleased, taking whatever papers she needed. Natalie willingly answered her questions, and asked her friends to do the same. Desiring easy access to her Boswell, Natalie arranged for Lang to live nearby in a separate apartment within the magnificent eighteenth-century house of her friend Marcelle Fouchette-Delavigne.

With this largesse came a downside. Barney grew possessive, constantly referring to Lang as "my biographer" in her conversation and letters. "Natalie was eager to see the book and to control it," Lang said. "She was used to controlling everything . . . and that brought a lot of tension between us. One day I told her, truly, I said, I would like to write a book which is *not* controlled by you."

Natalie had complaints of her own. She felt that Lang was too easily distracted from the biography by more scholarly projects, or allowed such nonsense as a broken heart to bring work to a standstill. At one point, believing that a confidence had been broken, Natalie demanded that Lang sign a legal paper agreeing to never again reveal personal information. Natalie also wanted the right to review the manuscript, removing anything she considered to be objectionable. Lang, a freethinking scholar, wasn't about to agree to such restrictions. The project fell apart, but the two women maintained a wary friendship into the 1960s.

Another new friend was French writer Marguerite Yourcenar, whom Natalie met in 1951 at the home of Marie Laurencin. Known best for her fictionalized historical reconstructions, most notably *Memoirs of Hadrian,* in 1980 Yourcenar would become the first woman ever admitted to the Académie Française.

A surprising entry into Natalie's life was the U.S. ambassador to France, David K. E. Bruce. A founding member of the Office of Strategic Services (OSS) during World War II, he was the first American ever appointed ambassador to all top three world capitals: Paris, Berlin, and London. Another of his claims to fame is that he shared, with Ernest Hemingway, the first jeep to enter and "liberate" Paris on August 25, 1944. As the German army fled the city, Hemingway and Bruce steered the jeep through the ecstatic crowds, intent on reaching the Ritz, where they retired straightaway to the bar and ordered martinis.

On July 3, 1951, Bruce and his wife, Evangeline, attended a reception at Natalie's home. It's not clear how they came to be invited. Bruce had a literary bent, so perhaps his appearance had something to do with the writing prize being awarded to Germaine Beaumont that night.

At some point Bruce and Natalie began discussing their ancestors and were shocked to discover that his great-grandmother, Louise Miller Este, and her grandmother, Ellen Miller Pike, were sisters! Thus, David was a distant cousin to Natalie and Laura. Though much younger than Cousin Natalie, he had also developed his lifelong love of France from Louise.*

Both the Barney sisters were delighted by David and Evangeline (Natalie described them to Laura as "these most official and yet most charming and human-y cousins"). According to Bruce's biographer, the affection was returned: "It gave the ambassador a sweet sensation of kinship with Paris to discover that this left bank icon, and such a notorious one, was a relative."[14]

---

*Louise Este was the eccentric French-speaking great-aunt who had so impressed Natalie as a child.

Françoise Sagan was one of the more unusual guests in these years, if only by virtue of her extreme youth. She was only nineteen when her first novel, *Bonjour tristesse,* was published in 1954. The book, which offered a spare, chilling look at a sophisticated and disillusioned segment of French society, made her instantly famous in Europe and the United States and became a popular movie. How strange it must have been for Sagan, poised at the very threshold of life, to sip tea and eat cucumber sandwiches with a group of ancient icons straight from the Belle Époque. Intimidating, too. Someone who was there that day observed that she sat quietly in a corner and issued nary a peep. She never returned.

Sometime in the mid-1950s Natalie and a young man named François Chapon, who was pursuing a scholarly interest in the deceased Oscar Milosz, were introduced by a mutual friend. They hit it off tremendously, and from then on he was almost always to be found at the Fridays. "The Salon was at the end of its 'glorious' period then," he recalled. "There would usually be 20–30 people there, Florent Schmitt, Vildrac, Germaine Beaumont, André Rouveyre."[15] The friendship would prove to be propitious, as Chapon would someday be responsible for Natalie's papers coming to the Bibliothèque Jacques Doucet, which he headed from 1960 until 1993.

ALL THE CHARMING NEW FACES in the world couldn't deny a brutal reality: more and more of the familiar old faces were disappearing.

One of the first to go was Gertrude Stein, whose death from cancer in early 1946 took everyone by surprise. She had always been so immutable, so stolid, so very *there.* And then she wasn't.

Returning to Paris after the war, Stein had plunged into her latest work, an opera based on the life of Susan B. Anthony. Suddenly, with no warning, she developed what Alice later referred to as "physical problems." A doctor advised Stein to see a specialist, but she ignored him and continued on as usual—until, on an outing to the countryside, she became extremely ill. An ambulance awaited their train's arrival in Paris to whisk Gertrude, with Alice at her side, to the American Hospital. After an examination, Stein was scheduled for an immediate operation. Just before leaving for the operating table, she gazed at Toklas. "What is the answer?" she asked. The distraught Alice remained silent. "In that case," murmured the Mama of Dada, "what is the question?" She died in the operating room.[16]

The last time Natalie saw Gertrude they had lunched at Prunier's. The restaurant was famous for its seafood, and all through the war they had each fantasized about returning someday for a meal. When they finally made it, everything they asked for was unavailable (thanks to postwar restrictions and red tape, it was still difficult to get fish and shellfish from the coast). Gertrude was so disappointed that she'd dropped her head into her hands and moved it back and forth like a dejected child. She and Natalie made do with Prunier's meager offerings. Later, strolling along the rue de Rivoli, they stopped at their favorite pâtisserie, Rumpelmeyer's. Once they walked through the door and into the sweet-smelling room, with its gorgeous cakes and beautiful tarts on lavish display, Gertrude perked up noticeably.

After Stein's death Natalie proved a steadfast friend to Alice, who now became a regular visitor to the salon. Natalie called upon her often, took her to lunch, offered advice, and included her in outings with close friends. Alice appreciated the attention. In *Staying on Alone,* a collection of letters she wrote after Gertrude's death, Natalie's name is liberally sprinkled about: "The other day at Natalie Barney's . . . Natalie Barney has gone to Italy . . . Natalie and I went to Raymond Duncan's birthday party . . . Natalie and Romaine Brooks and the Duchesse had tea with me yesterday." In her delightful *Alice B. Toklas Cook Book,* she included the recipe for one of Natalie's favorite dishes, Stuffed Eggplant with Sugar.

A few years after Stein's death, Yale University Press began bringing out her unpublished works on a yearly basis. The series would eventually consist of eight volumes, each with a foreword by one of Gertrude's friends. Alice asked Natalie to write the foreword for *As Fine as Melanctha,* the fourth volume, to be published in 1954. Another possible choice had been Janet Flanner, but Alice ultimately decided against her. "Natalie on the whole would do a better piece than Janet," she told Carl Van Vechten. "First she would stick to all of the facts she possessed—second she knew Baby better—3rd she is genuinely witty."[17]

Natalie's initial reaction to this honor was one of dismay. "I had never read her," she said. "I was a friend of her's, but her books hadn't attracted me. Moreover, I wasn't about to read further to write this preface. I therefore wrote one à coté de ses livres. Voila tout!"[18]

Natalie was exaggerating about never having read Stein. She had browsed Gertrude's books for years, picking out passages that interested her for closer scrutiny. Once, for an Académie des Femmes meeting dedicated to Stein, she translated a few pages of *Making of Americans* into French. In a 1938 letter to Romaine she mentioned that she'd been reading and enjoying Stein's *Everybody's Almanach* [*sic*], which she considered "naked and unashamed."[19] Still, her bottom-line feeling was that much of Gertrude's writing was "bluster."

Natalie's foreword to *As Fine as Melanctha* was warm and nostalgic, recalling such things as their mutual enjoyment of Rumpelmeyer's, their visits in the south of France, and being in New York during Gertrude's triumphant 1934–1935 visit to promote *The Autobiography of Alice B. Toklas.*

She spoke frankly about her inability to read Stein at length. "Being a writer of pensées," she said, "I like to find a thought as in a nut or sea-shell, and while I make for a point, Gertrude seems to proceed by avoiding it . . . getting at a subject by going not for but around it, in snowball fashion, gathering up everything she meets on her rounds." Her attempts to write like Stein ("Did I like it? Did I like liking it? Or did I dislike liking it or did I dislike it or dislike disliking it? Or did I dislike liking to dislike it? Or did I like disliking to like it?") convinced her that "it's hard to get something to mean nothing and nothing to mean something."

Toklas liked Natalie's piece a good deal, considering it "very witty." Natalie was pleased with it, too, and in 1963 translated it into French for inclusion in her last book, *Traits et portraits.*

Stein's was the first of many postwar deaths. J. C. Mardrus, grown senile, died in 1949; Liane died in a Swiss convent in 1950; André Gide in 1951; Bernard Berenson in 1959 at age ninety-four.

Eva Palmer-Sikelianos, "the mother of my desires, the initiator of my first joys,"[20] died on the island of Delphi in early June 1952, while watching a performance of *Prometheus Bound.* Her obituary in the *New York Times* credited her with having inspired the modern-day rebirth of the Delphic Festival and doing "much to revive the ancient culture of Greece . . . she created something of a sensation by arriving in New York by ship in ancient Greek costume. She announced that she had renounced modern dress. A crowd followed her, causing her to eschew appearances in public wherever possible."[21] Eva was buried on Delphi, the island she loved so much. Natalie devoted a Friday to her on June 24, 1952.

Colette, after living for years with painful rheumatoid arthritis, passed away in 1954. Writing to Laura, Natalie said that she felt less sad than one would expect since now Colette's sufferings had ended. She took comfort in the fact that the rest of her, her writing, would survive. Still, "since the precious, life-giving habit of going to see Colette had been taken from me, with what could I replace it?"[22]

Marie Laurencin's death in 1957 came as a shock. Just over seventy, she appeared to be in perfect health. One morning she woke up, didn't feel well, and called the doctor, who told her to stay in bed. The next morning she felt worse and asked a friend to call the priest. The day after that she was dead. Natalie blamed her passing on the stress caused by the three lawsuits Laurencin had waged to win back the apartment she'd lost during the war.

By far the greatest blow to Natalie came with the death of the Duchesse de Clermont-Tonnerre in 1954. Lily had been in declining health since her daughter's death in 1950; she had suffered a heart attack the day of the funeral, and a few since. "She will never recover from [her daughter's death]," Alice Toklas wrote a friend. "She is now only a memory of what she was—but a very tender poignant one . . . a portrait beyond all painting."[23] Natalie's letters to Laura often mention Lily's increasingly frail body, her failing strength. Her death, like those of Laurencin and Stein, came so suddenly that it caught those who loved her by surprise. One afternoon Lily came to Natalie's for tea and left in the early evening. Returning home, she went straight to bed, and by two o'clock that morning she was dead.

Natalie came to the Duchesse's home as soon as she got the news. She stood at the bedroom door, never crossing the entry, gazing at Lily's body stretched peacefully on the bed. She shook with sobs, ashamed at how unworthy such tremors were of her calm, dignified friend. She felt caught in a hellish limbo, able neither to resuscitate Lily, whose hands were surely still warm, nor to join her in a peaceful death. Without entering the room, she turned, walked outside, and allowed the chauffeur to help her into the backseat of the automobile. She asked to be taken to the florist, where she waited for a basket of white lilacs and calla lilies to be arranged, and then returned to Lily's. She remained in the car while her chauffeur placed the flower basket beside Lily. When he returned a few minutes later, he told her that, as he leaned to place the flowers down, tears had fallen from the Duchesse's closed eyes.

Renée Lang dined at rue Jacob a few nights later. After dinner, Natalie began to talk about the Duchesse, recalling her vibrant personality, her kindness, and her wit. Feeling Natalie's immense grief, Lang wondered aloud how she could bear to talk about Gramont so soon. "Is it not painful?" she asked.

Natalie nodded slowly, staring into her with that cold blue gaze. "It's necessary to use suffering," she said. "Otherwise, one is used by it."[24]

ROMAINE, COMPLAINING that she had been completely forgotten as an artist, grew increasingly depressed and listless, withdrew into long periods of silence, and became fanatically concerned about her health. Once briskly efficient, she began to find even small tasks difficult to complete. She worried incessantly about her eyes, often secreting herself for entire days in darkened rooms. Meryle Secrest believed that Brooks's eye problems may have been subconsciously exaggerated (thus providing an excuse for the creative block that kept her from painting). Berthe, too, once remarked that Romaine was "blind when she wanted to be."

Natalie's boundless energy, on the other hand, showed few signs of slowing down. She reacted to Romaine's problems like a knight in battle, marshaling forces on her lover's behalf. No mission was too grand, no task too small for the Amazon's attention. When Romaine grew disheartened because her memoirs couldn't find a publisher, Natalie trotted them around to all her connections (to no avail).* She spent months working on a booklet of Romaine's oeuvres, choosing the paintings, arranging with printers, writing a preface, deciding on a cover, approving distribution methods. With Romaine tucked firmly away in Nice, she took an official inventory of the paintings at the rue Raynouard studio. She made Romaine's purchases, from government bonds to pillowcases to anti-moth products. Romaine needed a new refrigerator in Nice? No problem! Natalie bought one in Paris and had it trucked down. For Romaine's neglected Steinway she found an expert piano cleaner, had it tuned, and negotiated its sale to a Belgian antiques dealer. When Romaine came for a rare Paris visit and insisted on staying at a hotel, Natalie inspected the place first to make sure it would be good enough for "My Angel." For Romaine's constipation problems, she mailed off a helpful four-page booklet and recommended a harmless child's laxative, Sirop de Figues.

And all the while, she juggled dozens of other projects. For instance, in 1948 she reestablished and endowed the Prix Renée Vivien. The original prize had been established after Pauline's death by Baronne Hélène de Zuylen (one of its awards had gone to Lucie Delarue-Mardrus). Natalie's reestablished award, intended to honor women poets writing in French, was placed under the aegis of the Société des Gens de Lettres. In future years, Germaine Beaumont, Marguerite Yourcenar, Yanette Delétang-Tardif, Ann-Marie Kegels, and Lucienne Desnoues would be the winners. Some years ago the prize was transferred to the stewardship of the Société des Poètes Français, who continue its administration.

In 1951, Natalie funded the private publication of three books that honored two deeply loved friends. *In Memory of Dorothy Ierne Wilde*, published in an edition of two hundred, appeared in the spring. It included Natalie's poems about Dolly, Wilde's own letters, which showcased her sparkling wit, and affectionate remembrances from friends. When all copies sold, Natalie brought out a second edition the following year.

The second book, *Choix de poèmes*, was a compilation of published and unpublished poetry by Lucie Delarue-Mardrus, as well as some of her poetic translations from English (including works by Edna St. Vincent Millay and Anna Wickham). The book was brought out by Lemerre in a small edition.

---

*An amusing response came from Max White, who said: "Admittedly, it is sometimes unwise to give names in biographies, but I feel Mrs. Brooks has been too discreet—calling Stalin 'S,' for instance."

Third was *Nos secretes amours,* the extremely passionate love poems written to Natalie by Lucie in the century's early years. Natalie discreetly kept Lucie's name off the forty-six-page book, which was printed in an edition of 710. Writing to Romaine after its appearance, she asked hopefully: "I don't suppose you want a copy of such a past? Of mine? All in passionate verse."[25]

Natalie's own contributions to literature were honored by a group of friends on the afternoon of December 3, 1952. The program, entitled "The Thoughts and Poems of Miss Barney," was held at Le Pullman on rue des Petits Champs. The afternoon opened with selections from the work of the composer Florent Schmitt. Natalie was presented to the audience, and then a series of friends—Fanny Robin, Guy Squares, Jeanne Sully, and André Picot— recited from her works. Among the readings were "Sonnet to Renée Vivien" and a selection from *Pensées d'une Amazone.*

On the writing front, Natalie completed a play and began work on another book of memoirs. Tentatively titled "Diversité," it would be published in 1960 as *Souvenirs indiscrets.* She had already picked out an epigraph: "I want to be at once the bow, the arrow, and the target." For some reason, she didn't use it in the final manuscript.

She continued to travel. Her winters were still spent in Nice with Romaine, but she made frequent trips with others: Évian and Aix-les-Bains with Lily, London with Laura, Beaulieu-sur-Mer, Fontainebleau, Geneva, Monaco.

In Paris she was always on the go. She bought a new car, a Citröen. When Gertrude Stein's *Four Saints in Three Acts* booked into the Théâtre des Champs-Elysées, she immediately bought tickets. She and Laura enjoyed meeting for lamb couscous in the small restaurant of the mosque near the Jardin des Plantes. She read (Camus, Waugh, Robert Louis Stevenson). She enjoyed movies *(Come Back Little Sheba,* which won a Best Actress Oscar for Shirley Booth; *Five Fingers,* a spy thriller starring James Mason and Danielle Darrieux; and a 1952 Japanese film she doesn't name). In spring she walked in the Bois, where the smell of lavender inspired a feeling of déjà vu for her youth.

And then, in mid-decade, a most unexpected and startling event occurred. Natalie Barney fell in love.

NATALIE'S EARLIEST MEMORIES of the area around Nice dated from 1887, just before entering Les Ruches. Fond of the southern sun's warmth, sea bathing, and the pervasive smell of lavender and honey, she had returned ever since. After Romaine moved there sometime around 1950, Natalie began staying on her own at the Hôtel d'Angleterre. She spent her mornings alone, peacefully writing letters, reading, or simply gazing seaward from the balcony.

Afternoons, beginning with lunch, were reserved for Romaine. If they were getting along well, they might take a nap after lunch or go see a movie. If at odds, Natalie went off on her own, either back to her hotel or out with others. With friends living nearby, and others constantly visiting the coast, she could be social or not, just as she pleased. One of her favorite afternoon activities was to stroll along the Promenade des Anglais. This broad avenue, which runs for miles beside the Matisse-blue Bay of Angels, passes by Roman ruins, ancient alleyways, flower-filled gardens, and ritzy hotels.

Walking one afternoon during her 1955–1956 winter visit, Natalie suddenly felt tired and stopped in a flower-filled park to rest. When an attractive woman in her early fifties sat beside her, a conversation ensued. On the surface the women had little in common. Janine Lahovary was married to a retired Romanian ambassador. She and her husband lived most of the year in Grandson, a small town on Switzerland's Lake Neuchâtel. She had never been sexually attracted to another woman and would later profess that she had no idea such a thing was even possible. Nonetheless, a friendship grew from this chance encounter and developed in short order into a passionate, loving relationship.

Natalie was unusually discreet about her new amour, and many friends were slow to learn that she had a new love. Renée Lang was one of the few people Natalie confided in. "I have known about that liaison from the beginning," she recalled. "I will never forget. Natalie had been away, every winter she spent some time in Nice." Calling at rue Jacob the day Natalie returned, Lang found her walking slowly in the garden, lost in thought. "Straight," she recalled, referring to Barney's posture, which refused to bend to old age. "She was still straight, she was walking in meditation."

The two women hugged and chatted a moment. "Then Natalie looked at me and said 'I have to tell you a story. Can you imagine that I met a woman who loves me and who wants me? What should I do?' . . . And I laughed, and said 'Well, Natalie, it's a new pearl in your crown.' And she took it without laughing or joking. She said, 'What should I do? She really wants me!' I said, 'How do *you* feel?' She said, 'Well, that's what I'm asking you. I don't *know* how I feel. As you know, I considered that part of my life as finished. But she is *passionately* in love with me.' And finally she said, 'Well, you'll see. You'll meet her soon.' "[26]

When Lang finally met Janine, she wasn't impressed. Her opinion, that Lahovary "lacked class," was shared by many of Natalie's friends and even her housekeeper. "For me," Berthe sniped, "she was nothing more than a typist become an ambassador's wife."[27] Yet others who knew Janine considered her to be intelligent, kind, and thoughtful.

The difference in opinion had much to do with an atmosphere of jealousy that had come to define Natalie's inner circle. Explaining the group dynamics that existed when he met Barney in 1963, Jean Chalon said, "Natalie was the sun, and everyone revolved around her. There was a great deal of jealousy. She believed in the tête-à-tête, so if there were three, one was left out."[28]

The rivalrous atmosphere wasn't much different in the mid-1950s, when Janine arrived on the scene. For years a feeling of complacency had reigned in which everyone was confident of his or her exact place in Natalie's affections. Lahovary's sudden appearance, and particularly the way she was doted on and adored by Natalie, was a major threat to the status quo. Anti-Janine forces quickly developed. To them, nothing about the interloper would ever be good enough; nothing she ever did would be valued.

Jean Chalon, when introduced into these circles, accepted the "anti" point of view without question. This was obvious in his merciless depiction of "Gisèle" (Janine) in *Chère Natalie Barney*,* his 1976 portrait of Natalie. However, he developed objectivity with the passing years, and when a new edition of the book appeared in 1992 he offered a generous apologia "for the black portrait I painted of Natalie's last love, Gisèle." He had been punished with terrible remorse, he said, for not having understood "how much Gisèle had surrounded Natalie with constant and daily tenderness. Natalie loved Gisèle and Gisèle loved Natalie. That says all and everything. I should never have had anything but respect and reverence for the Amazon's last love."[29]

The anti-Janine forces among Natalie's friends were relentless in their criticisms. They said her clothes were wrong, too fussy, frilly, and showy. Her witticisms weren't cutting or funny enough. She wore too much jewelry and perfume. She put on airs. Some of these complaints probably had a valid basis. George Wickes, who met her briefly both before and after Natalie's death, felt that there was something a bit too "grand dame" about her. Even Chalon couldn't help but hazard in his apologia: "Gisèle did have certain irritating aspects, but nobody's perfect."[30]

The only important thing is this: in each other, Natalie and Janine found someone to love. To Natalie, Janine was an intelligent being, conversant with philosophy, psychology, and religion. She was also sensitive, unusually tactful, a good listener, and, as even her detractors admitted, a very pretty woman. Not least, the fact that she was unhappy in some ways allowed Natalie to play, one last time, the role of rescuing knight. Among other things, she urged Janine to take more control of her life. A poem Natalie wrote to her new lover asked: "Must you live like a slave? Have you need of the customs of another time?"

*Published in the United States as *Portrait of a Seductress*.

Janine later told friends that Natalie gave her a sense of self and a feeling of confidence that she had never before possessed.

From her home in Switzerland, Janine peppered Natalie with phone calls, letters, and plans for upcoming visits. She came to Paris as often as possible, even if only for a couple of days. To keep up appearances, she left her baggage at a nearby hotel where her family and friends could leave messages, returning only to bathe, change, or pack an overnight case for rue Jacob. If she happened to be in Paris for one of the Fridays, she attended the get-together briefly and then returned to her hotel.

Janine's visits were never frequent or long enough to please Natalie. She reacted furiously to broken plans, was jealous of the time Janine spent with her husband, and complained when too long a time elapsed between visits. But she was visibly rejuvenated by the affair. In June 1956, Alice Toklas, who as yet knew nothing about Janine, raved about Natalie's "lovely new blossoming—she looks wonderfully flourishing—she's the one bright spot in a fairly cheerless world."[31] A few months later she reported to another friend that "Natalie Barney has they say a new love affair isn't it a miracle?"[32]

At least two credible sources say that Nicholas Lahovary eventually learned the truth about his wife's affair from a spiteful André Germain, who was repaying Natalie for a past insult, and that his resultant anguish caused Janine to think about ending the affair. If these reports are true, the trio must have worked out their difficulties, because Natalie's weeks-long summer visits to the ocher-colored stone house in Grandson continued. The beautiful lakeside town now became one of the four major points on her compass, along with Paris, Nice, and Fiesole.

AND WHAT OF ROMAINE through all this? For fifteen years, since the start of the last war, she had had Nat-Nat to herself (except, of course, for those pesky "second-rate" friends). Given their ages, she assumed that they would remain together until their deaths. Now, just as in their youth, she found herself forced to share. No matter how much Natalie insisted that Romaine alone was her life's major love, the only one who really and truly mattered, it still hurt. She was angry and unhappy, and there were times she didn't hesitate to make her feelings clear.

However, at the beginning Romaine did not really view Janine as much of a threat. For one thing, the woman had a full life of her own in Switzerland. For another, she didn't think Janine possessed the kind of aristocratic cachet that tended to keep Natalie interested and respectful.

She was also partially assuaged by Janine's attempts to win her friendship.

Natalie's health, well-being, and happiness were important to Janine, and she knew that Romaine was vital in that equation. No matter what her own feelings about Brooks may have been, she went out of her way to be pleasant. She invited Romaine to stay at her home in Switzerland whenever Natalie was there. She hung a painting of Romaine's, a portrait of writer Anna de Noailles, in her living room. She sent letters, telephoned, extended numerous courtesies.

In return, Romaine tried to be agreeable. "I am glad you have found a nice friend," she told Natalie late in 1956, referring to Janine.[33] Half a year later she continued to sound a convivial note: "Darling . . . Of course you must have your many friends and above all your special one whom I think you are very lucky to have found as you are both des femmes du monde."[34] And the pleasantries continued: "No doubt you are now at your friend's lovely quiet home," "Affectionate greetings to Janine," "Hope Nat-Nat is careful and follows Janine's good advice." When Natalie began experiencing heart problems, Romaine cautioned: "A love affair can cause trouble at our age. So do be careful!"[35]

In many ways Natalie and Romaine continued as before. The love and affection between them is certainly undiluted in their letters. "I find myself longing for Angel," Natalie scribbled in one typical passage, "and the soft and sore spot I bear for you in my heart! Ever my all loving Angel's Nat-Nat."[36] Or from Romaine: "As usual I miss Nat-Nat very much. At the station in her dark comfortable car I was sad and kept thinking about our long friendship which on my part is as great as ever."[37]

They also continued to spend months together in Nice and Italy, often venturing out for chauffeured side trips. One summer day in 1956 or 1957 they motored into the mountains above Cannes to see Renée Lang, who was spending time at a writers' colony. She tells a revealing story about their visit.

She took her two callers for a walk around the colony's sumptuous grounds, with its many excellent sculptures scattered about. "Was it a Rodin?" Lang mused. "I don't remember. But I took them around, and showed them this very beautiful sculpture. Romaine, with much authority, said: 'Ça, c'est beau!' And after a while, Natalie, in a very sweet voice like a child, asked 'Pourquoi c'est beau?' And Romaine, like a queen, said: 'Parce que c'est beau!'* That was the answer, and Natalie asked no more. . . . Romaine was the one exception, the only person Natalie ever really respected—not only respected, but when I saw them together it was another Natalie, a Natalie who would lis-

*"Now that, that's beautiful!" "Why is it beautiful?" "Because it's beautiful!"

ten to every word as if Romaine were a sainted spirit. She recognized Romaine as *the* friend she had chosen for her life."[38]

Or, as Natalie wrote to Romaine around the same time, "Nothing and no one is—or ever will be—as dear to me."[39] She meant it, too. The great tragedy of her life was that Romaine did not believe her.

SIXTEEN

Slowly Comes the Night

1960–1972

That's all there is, there isn't any more.
—*Ethel Barrymore*

HE YEAR 1960 was kicked off by the surprising appearance of a new book by Natalie Clifford Barney, the first in twenty-one years. *Souvenirs indiscrets* is her recollection of friends and lovers from the early years in Paris: Renée Vivien, Remy de Gourmont, the Duchesse de Clermont-Tonnerre, les Mardrus, Oscar Milosz, and Colette.

Natalie had always wanted to write a memoir of Pauline but, overwhelmed by the confused feelings she continued to feel about this early love, had never been able to do so. Instead, throughout the decades she wrote of Pauline in smaller ways, via poems, analyses of her work, and the like. But the publisher of *Souvenirs indiscrets* insisted on a full narrative about Renée Vivien. He added that, if Natalie didn't write about their relationship, someone else would—probably vulgarizing it in the process. Propelled by this unpleasant truth, she got to work.

All these many decades Natalie had carried around a kit bag initialed "P.T." and stuffed to the clasp with guilt, remorse, love, anger, joy, hurt, and "if onlys." Now, turning the bag upside down, she emptied the contents and tried to make sense of the past.

Much of what she says is on target, even when it forces her to portray herself as brutal, cold, and self-centered. She admits that her lack of fidelity created many problems. She is honest about her inability and complete lack of desire to change for the sake of love. She's at least partly right in saying that Pauline deified her, refusing to accept her as simply another flawed human being—and thereby created her own suffering.

However, Natalie sometimes seems intent on settling scores in *Souvenirs indiscrets,* as in her vengeful portrait of "la Brioche," Baronne Hélène de Zuylen. With nobody remaining who was capable of disputing her point of view, she was also able to have the final word on Pauline. In the seventy-two-page chapter entitled "Renée Vivien," Natalie shaped a view of the poet that has since been universally adopted: that of a sad woman-child who, forever wounded from her failed love for the Amazon, drifted toward death. This tragic and only partly accurate take has added luster to Natalie's legend, literally transforming her into a lady-killer.

Souvenirs indiscrets was a critical success and garnered good reviews, but sales were disappointing. According to Berthe, the publisher had expected a kiss-and-tell memoir brimming with bedroom secrets. Contrary to the book's title, however, Natalie revealed no indiscreet memories. Marguerite Yourcenar admired the book's tact and subtle humor, and the fact that Natalie did not resort to psychological jargon to explain herself. "One is especially grateful that you have remained so jauntily yourself," she wrote, "without ever letting the vogues that have successively arisen between 1900 and our time rub their colors off on you."[1]

Eighty-three when *Souvenirs indiscrets* was published, Natalie still wasn't finished as a writer. Three years later, her last book, *Traits et portraits,* was published by Mercure de France. It contained two prefaces, each a portrait of the author. One was by Natalie's friend of many years, Magdeleine Wauthier. The other is by Natalie herself:

> Attentive to others, it's only in solitude that she takes back her power and recharges her batteries. . . . She doesn't follow fashion, nor does fashion follow her. . . . A feeble but tenacious heart. A hardness no one suspects. Nerves of steel. Sociable, but impossible to live with. Courteous toward strangers, frank with friends. A good enough opinion of herself to have no need of flattery. An absence of humility and a taste for fame which laziness prevents her from pursuing. She holds few beings or things sacred. . . . Without conviction, her viewpoint changes according to what she finds. She appreciates virtue less for itself than as a rule of the game. Supple and sophisticated, she loathes justice as much as those who make a profession by it. Her judgment is a sign of vengeance. It pleases her to dominate, but

she quickly tires of what is dominated. Predatory by nature, but seeks no profit thereby . . . Some consider her needy, but others find her shrewd.[2]

The remainder of *Traits et portraits* consists of essays and literary sketches (of Bernard Berenson, Gertrude Stein, Harold Acton, Gabriele d'Annunzio, Rabindranath Tagore, Max Jacob, Edmond Jaloux, André Gide, Jean Cocteau, and others).

The essay "Breasts" was originally written in the 1920s as a response to the Spanish avant-garde writer Ramón Gómez de la Serna. Known simply as Ramón, he invented the *greguería*, a sort of surrealist metaphor-epigram, and wrote more than eighty books. Unfortunately for Ramón, one of his books managed to demean women's breasts in a way that infuriated the Amazon and many of her friends. After reading his offensive words, Liane noted crisply that "breasts—my own and almost all those I have known—the little points of breasts live a life of the most intense passion. What an idiot . . . The man must be a brute."[3] Natalie was so upset by his comments that she wrote a forceful response. "Those peaks, difficult of ascent," she proclaimed, "reserved for the elect, determine the quality and breeding of a lover so much better than any fun and games below!"[4] Ramón later published a semihumorous apology, "The Irritated Amazon."

The essays were clever, but most readers of *Traits et portraits* were more interested in Natalie's impressionistic profiles of famous literary figures. Reviewing the book in *Le Phare,* Franz Hellens noted that "literary portraiture has produced some works of art. Saint-Simon, Dudeffand and Proust are but several of many gifted author-artists. Among these, also, is Natalie Barney. . . . The portraits which she presents in her *Traits et portraits* are strikingly vivacious and the creation of a sorceress in every sense of the word." Natalie's piece on Cocteau, he felt, was both tellingly true and excessively unjust, a dichotomy that could be reconciled only by cruelty, one of her "strongest and most genuine characteristics." Another review, by Yves Florence, discussed "this superb frankness, this proud innocence, the stuff of her diverse writings . . ."[5]

ALTHOUGH HER LAST two books achieved moderate success, by now Natalie had become almost completely forgotten in the larger world of literature. An occasional mention of Gourmont's Amazon appeared in the press or in someone's memoirs, but few young people had any idea who she was—or, for that matter, who Gourmont was. The few who had heard of Barney figured that she, like the Belle Époque, had long since disappeared.

Natalie was at peace with having lived past the time for plaudits and honors. She rejoiced in having many friends, two major loves, a raft of ongoing projects, and, despite two minor heart attacks and other physical vicissitudes of old age, relatively good health. Most of all, she took comfort in the fact that she had lived fully; as she put it, she had extracted from life even more than it contained.

"She's kept her pride, her power, her dignity, and her vast and lively intelligence," Magdeleine Wauthier wrote. "She sees everything with that icy blue gaze, which sees through yours and into your thoughts before you've even expressed them. . . . She has now a relaxation, a repose that I never perceived before. It's the end of the day, for her as for me. The air is peaceable, the pillows deep, the tea golden, and two friends evoke their common memories. . . . It's the peace of night. It's no longer the hour of love, but the hour of the meditation on love."[6]

Now, in that peace of night, Natalie was largely content. "I strongly feel that to live is more difficult than to die," she wrote. "In order to die, all you have to do is to let go. It's very simple."[7] Looking ahead, she saw herself gradually letting go, disappearing slowly but peacefully into the folds of time.

But that, of course, was not the way it played out. As impossible as it seemed, an entirely unexpected chain of events would combine to resuscitate the Amazon's legend. Brought to the attention of a new generation, Miss Barney was to be bathed in glory one last time.

AROUND THE TIME that *Traits et portraits* appeared, a respected literary journal, *Adam International Review,* devoted an entire issue to Natalie. Begun in 1935, this bilingual French-English publication struggled financially but attracted a devoted coterie of readers. *Adam*'s eclectic list of authors ranged from Jean-Paul Sartre to Winston Churchill, from T. S. Eliot to Jacques Prévert. Occasionally an issue featured a single subject, such as "Italian Theater and Cinema" or George Bernard Shaw.

Adam's editor, Miron Grindea, first approached Natalie in the summer of 1960, asking her to be the sole subject of the coming winter issue. Not sure if she wanted to devote time and money to such an undertaking—it was understood that she would help subsidize the effort—she put him off with excuses. He returned a few times, and finally she agreed to cooperate.

Before long Natalie was complaining to Laura about being "in the throes of Adam," by which she meant not only the magazine, but its editor. She felt that Grindea ceaselessly bothered her with demands for information about her family background, requests for never-published aphorisms, and, always, pleas for more money. Her impatience began to wear thin a few months into their collaboration. To friends she referred to Grindea as *"un espece de demi-fou"* and a poor organizer who "goes wool gathering unless brought to order." In January 1963, she informed Laura that her total outlay so far was more than £1,000 (about $3,000 in 1963 dollars). But, she added, the issue was finally under way.

Publicly, Natalie was blasé about the upcoming edition of *Adam*. If anything, she claimed to fear success, saying that it had a tendency to shatter one's life. As one of her *pensées* in *Adam* put it, "Success leads to a dispersion of self and of one's private life." Such talk was merely bravura. At heart, she was happy and excited by the prospect of an entire issue of an elite magazine devoted to herself.

And it was worth the wait. *Adam's* issue No. 299, "The Amazon of Letters: A World Tribute to Natalie Clifford Barney," is now a prized collector's item. In his editorial, Grindea paid tribute to Natalie as "one of the most astonishing victims of neglect in modern literature: modern because, although she was born eighty-five years ago in Ohio, USA, the two main activities of her life—her own writing and the influence of her magnetic intelligence and wit upon other artists—continue as strongly today at her villa at 20 Rue Jacob in Paris as they have throughout more than sixty creative years."

Selections from Barney's work, including aphorisms, essays, portraits, playlets, and poetry, took up almost one hundred pages. Another sixty pages was devoted to dozens of friends and acquaintances singing Natalie's praise through revealing anecdotes or affectionate poetry.

"She is the child of a patrician America that no longer exists," Paul Morand observed, "and from this aristocracy she retains two treasures: daring and manners."

Said Georges Cattaui: "Miss Barney enjoys that rare privilege of being of interest to her contemporaries at once as a poet, an inspiration, a Maecenas [patron] and a witness of an epoch . . . this very refined 'egoist' always thinks of others before thinking of herself and always takes pleasure in someone else's joy. . . . Natalie, while effacing herself before her friends, gave me, however, the impression that she dominated them all. She appeared to me exactly as Gourmont had described her—delicate, proud, enigmatic—I should be inclined to add faustian. Yet, what was most striking in her was that spontaneity, that simplicity and that 'quelque chose de fier et même un peu farouche'* which Racine attributes to the son of the Amazon."

"The Amazon is a unique and formidable person," wrote Edmond Jaloux, "one of the few I know who is capable of tenderness and yet stripped of illusions."

Over and again, friends speak of Natalie's generosity and kindness. They

---

* "something proud and even a little ferocious"

talk of how she wrote and sent poems at pivotal moments, gave encouragement, surprised them with flowers. Renée Lang recalled the time she admired a small eighteenth-century marquetry box on Natalie's desk. "Remy de Gourmont gave it to me," Natalie said. "He kept it on his secretary to hold stamps." The next day, Berthe brought a little package to Lang's lodgings. Inside was the box: "I have so often thought," Natalie wrote in the accompanying note, "that things frequently end up with the wrong owners; only those who really care for them should possess them."

"How pleasant to read a special number about a celebrity who is still alive," Cyril Connolly wrote in London's *Sunday Times* about the *Adam* issue. "Death is the more illustrious, but being alive makes an even greater appeal, especially when one is dealing with a mistress of life."[8]

In the fall of 1963, a twenty-eight-year-old journalist at *Le Figaro Littéraire,* Jean Chalon, received a review copy of *Traits et portraits* in the mail. Puzzled at the appearance of a new book by Remy de Gourmont's Amazon— he was certain that she had died years ago—he called the publisher to ascertain if it was a posthumous release. He was surprised to learn that not only was Miss Barney alive, but she just might be willing to sit for an interview. One afternoon soon after, Chalon walked into 20, rue Jacob for the first time. When he left a few hours later, completely seduced by the charismatic octogenarian, he had become Natalie's last great conquest.

Young Chalon was Natalie's closest male friend in her remaining years, filling the void left by André Rouveyre's death in 1962. For Chalon the relationship was equally rewarding. For years he arrived at the *pavillon* each Wednesday afternoon at four o'clock—the same hour at which Natalie and Gourmont used to meet—for his own personal tête-à-tête with the Amazon, a few hours in which they spoke of anything and laughed at everything. To this day he feels that his chaste friendship with Barney constituted one of the greatest loves of his life.

On November 3, Chalon's article, "Natalie Barney Reveals the Secrets of an Amazon," appeared in *Le Figaro Littéraire.* The great, historical names blazed from the page: Marcel Proust, André Gide, Gourmont, Elizabeth Gramont, Lucie Delarue-Mardrus, Gertrude Stein, Colette, Apollinaire, Renée Vivien, Anatole France. The article made it clear that the Amazon, though old, was still capable of cocking her bow and letting fly with a well-aimed arrow. She had, in fact, pierced Chalon once or twice during their conversation with her bold questions and unnerving insight. Wrote he: "I felt like Napoleon scrutinized by twenty centuries of pyramids."

From this, helped along by *Adam,* came the deluge: the *New York Times.* The London *Sunday Times. La Revue de Paris. Elle Magazine.* The *Observer. Réalités.* The *International Herald Tribune.* The *New York Times Book Review.** A television film crew arrived from the BBC, followed by another from Germany. Even Dayton, Ohio, got into the act with a five-part article in the *Journal Herald* that proudly gushed over its native-born Amazon. From then on, Natalie's yearly birthday initiated a new spate of articles worldwide. "Natalie Barney, 88, Reviews Paris Life," a headline informed *New York Times* readers in 1964. "Miss Natalie Barney Joyfully Turns 90," Mary Blume enthused two years later in Europe's English-language newspaper, the *International Herald Tribune.*

Nostalgia for 1920s Paris was beginning to blossom, especially in America, which only added to people's fascination with Natalie. A few early books in that line had already discussed her: George Antheil's *Bad Boy of Music* (1945), *The Autobiography of William Carlos Williams* (1951), Caresse Crosby's *The Passionate Years* (1953), and Sylvia Beach's *Shakespeare and Company* (1959). In the 1960s, when Lost Generation members began hitting their sixties and seventies, memoirs of the "crazy years" really took off. Ernest Hemingway's *A Moveable Feast* (1964) devoted a malicious chapter to Natalie, Ezra, and Bel Esprit. Matthew Josephson's *Life Among the Surrealists* (1962) took a more positive look at "Miss Barney," rue Jacob, and the salon. In *What Is Remembered* (1963), Alice Toklas spoke warmly of the friendship between Natalie and Gertrude. Other books that discuss Natalie include *Virgil Thomson* (1966) by Virgil Thomson, Robert McAlmon's *Being Geniuses Together* (1938), Janet Flanner's *Paris Was Yesterday* (1972), Morrill Cody's *Women of Montparnasse* (1984), and Samuel Putnam's *Paris Was Our Mistress* (1947).

In short, Natalie Clifford Barney was in the news again. As she wrote to Romaine on Bastille Day, 1966, "Here I am being interviewed and televisionized sans fin."[9] Although pretending to indifference, she was delighted by the attention to the point of exchanging giddy notes with Laura on the subject of her sudden fame.

Along with the renewed celebrity came something even more surprising. Natalie, once the scourge of decency, was now something of a heroine. Young women in particular seemed to view her as a daring foremother, sending her fan letters and arriving breathlessly at the *pavillon's* door. On one memorable occasion, a woman in her twenties pushed rudely past Berthe and fell to her knees before Natalie, spouting words of adoration. She was quickly escorted out. "Don't ever let another of these little fools in!" Natalie snapped at Cleyrergue.

It may have been this revitalized interest in the Amazon that brought

*Unusual for the *Review,* this long 1969 article discussed not books, but Natalie's life.

Natalie's home to the attention of French movie director Louis Malle, because in 1963 he filmed a portion of his latest movie on the grounds. *Le feu follet** revolves around Alain (Maurice Ronet), a suicidally depressed alcoholic. Released from a private hospital in Versailles, he makes his way to Paris, where he visits old friends. One of them, Eva (Jeanne Moreau), is ostensibly living in Natalie's *pavillon*. Only the grounds were filmed, resulting in a few quick glimpses of the courtyard, garden, and temple. Natalie met some members of the crew (including Moreau, who was reportedly fascinated by her), but remained upstairs while the filming went on. When the project wrapped, Malle presented Moreau with a watch from Cartier engraved: "To friendship, in memory of the Temple à l'Amitié which we visited together at Natalie Barney's home."†

THE SALON SOLDIERED ON. Most Fridays consisted of an ever-smaller group of regulars. François Chapon remembered seeing an average of thirty guests in the mid-1950s, but by now the numbers were rapidly dwindling until, by the late 1960s, only six or seven people showed up on a given Friday.

Younger writers continued to appear, brought by agents, publishers, or friends. Many who came felt that they'd stepped into a sort of time warp connected to fin de siècle Paris. Natalie herself sometimes seemed caught in the warp. Mention a current event and without hesitation she could relate it to something that happened in the previous century. Once, hearing about a fire raging in the Left Bank, she launched into a tale about the 1897 conflagration at the Bazar.

But Natalie's mind remained sharp, her intelligence demanding, her humor firmly intact. "I do love Cousin Natalie," David Bruce wrote in his 1962 diary. "At 85, she is much more amusing than most of my contemporaries. Nor is she idle as a poetess, and is a pundit on rhyming and life."[10] Natalie was plucky as ever, and even now did everything possible to ensure that her guests were entertained. She even continued to focus occasional Fridays on a particular person. In June 1965 she honored Philippe Jullian when his book *Robert de Montesquiou, un prince 1900* was published. One day that November the star turn belonged to American writer Mary McCarthy, whose *The Group* had caused a major stir two years before.

On October 31, 1964, Natalie's eighty-eighth birthday celebration became the last large party to be held at rue Jacob. Soon after, photographer Michele

---

*The film has two English titles: *The Fire Within* and *A Time to Live and a Time to Die*.

†Jeanne Moreau told this story to Jean Chalon at a 1978 cocktail party. It's included in his 1963–1983 *Journal de Paris* (page 212).

Brabo visited the *pavillon* with her friend Jean Chalon, who wanted a photograph taken of himself with Natalie. "She really didn't want to be photographed," Brabo recalled. "After all, she was eighty-eight years old. She wasn't what she had been. She wouldn't agree to be lit, so I couldn't use a flash. She wouldn't pose for long, and I had to take the shot quickly, nearly in the dark. The whole *pavillon* was dark, for that matter." It was a Friday, and when Brabo peeked into the salon, "it was populated with people even older than Natalie! One woman had to be about one hundred years old. I was astonished."[11]

When I interviewed Brabo in her splendid, high-ceilinged rue de Rivoli apartment, she brought out the proofs and a magnifying glass, allowing me a glimpse at one of Natalie's last salons. Half a dozen people, men and women, sat in a dark room lit by only one or two dim lamps. Ancient survivors of another time, they were well dressed and engaged in subdued conversation. One woman in a hat may have been Alice Toklas. "She wore incredible hats," recalled François Chapon. "She was so tiny that she would be lost deep in an armchair. You wouldn't even notice she was there and suddenly this voice would come from within the armchair."[12]

Two of the most interesting events at the salon during the 1960s revolved around Marguerite Yourcenar and Ezra Pound.

On May 3, 1968, a young man named Daniel Cohn-Bendit led a demonstration at the Sorbonne that ended with a student occupation. When the police charged onto campus, arresting five hundred and injuring many more, a riot ensued and the university closed its doors for the first time in its seven-hundred-year history. The situation escalated, and for weeks the streets of the Latin Quarter were nearly impassable as rioters were held behind barricades.

These circumstances did not prevent Natalie from holding her Friday, as planned, on May 17, to celebrate publication of Yourcenar's *L'oeuvre au noir.* Informed that taxis were avoiding the area, Natalie remained unruffled. Her guests, she said, would come on foot. And they did, arriving in various states of exhaustion and terror. Sipping champagne and eating Berthe's cucumber sandwiches, they could hear loud explosions a few blocks away. But the day, all agreed, was a great success.

As for Ezra, things had not gone well for him. His pro-Mussolini broadcasts had brought an indictment for treason while the war still raged, but he continued with his rants until the bitter end. Arrested in May 1945, he was held in an American army prison camp near Pisa. While awaiting transfer to the United States for trial, he penned the majority of *The Pisan Cantos,* considered to be his most personal and perhaps finest poems. Eventually indicted on nineteen counts of treason, he was found mentally incompetent to stand trial and placed in St. Elizabeth's, a Washington, D.C., mental hospital.

In 1949, *The Pisan Cantos* won the first-ever Bollingen Prize for achievement in American poetry. This prize, which today is one of the most prestigious poetry awards in the world, had been established the previous year by the Library of Congress. Thus, in an irony that would have delighted the younger Pound, he was simultaneously incarcerated and celebrated by the U.S. government.

News of Pound's award created a furor. "Pound, in Mental Clinic, Wins Prize for Poetry Penned in Treason Cell," announced the *New York Times*. Bitter infighting broke out among literary intellectuals. Pulitzer Prize–winning poet Robert Hillyer hinted in the *Saturday Review* that the award represented a conspiracy against the American way of life and its literature. William Carlos Williams was accused of contempt for American ideals because he defended Ezra, his friend for decades. Congress got involved, and soon the Library of Congress was asked to disassociate itself from the award. Yale University Library took over the prize in 1950.

Pound remained at St. Elizabeth's for twelve long years. He continued to work on his *Cantos*, wrote letters to friends (including Natalie), and translated a wide range of works. Over time he became something of a cause célèbre, particularly with writers, many of whom worked for his release. Freed in 1958, he ultimately settled in Venice, where he spent most of his time reading and writing. He rarely spoke, even to his wife, and lived most of his days in silence. On the few occasions he felt moved to say something, he was both succinct and observant. Asked what he thought of the "beatnik poet sensation," Allen Ginsberg, Ezra replied: "He's vigorous."

In the fall of 1965 Pound traveled to Paris, where he made his last visit to Natalie's salon. Many old friends dropped in that day to see him. He sat beside Barney, listening happily to the conversation around him, but spoke not a word. He was interviewed that day or the next for BBC television and, once again, Natalie sat companionably by his side. "I did all the talking," she told an American journalist. "Ezra wouldn't—or couldn't—say a word. He only occasionally nodded or shook his head."[13] Later she confided to Romaine that she was glad she would never see the result (the interview was televised only in Britain). "A near view of me in flash-lights can hardly prove becoming!"[14]

Natalie never saw Ezra again after this visit, though she continued to watch over him from afar. He had little money, and she helped subsidize his income. In 1966 she paid for Pound and Olga Rudge, his now-elderly mistress, to vacation in Greece. Pound was to die in November 1972, a few months after Natalie.

SINCE THE DEATH of their father, Laura had handled money and legal matters for herself and Natalie. She doled out money to her sister as needed or wanted, gave her documents to sign, dealt with various banks and money managers, and kept the estate running smoothly. Both women were happy with the situation. They had their points of contention, but arguments about money were rare.

Laura's management of family matters took a different turn around 1960, when she began making preparations for their deaths. From then on, much of their correspondence was devoted to discussions of property dispersal—who should get what, and whether they should get it before or after the sisters died. They took a practical approach, often discussing tax considerations and almost never resorting to sentiment. They both seemed to approach the inevitability of death with calm acceptance.

One of the great decisions facing them was what to do with Studio House, which had been rented out since Alice's death. The history and architecture of the place made it into something of a treasure, they thought, and apparently the Smithsonian Institution agreed. In 1960, they gave Studio House to the Smithsonian, under whose aegis it would serve a variety of functions—including art exhibits and performances—for decades.

Other items were easier to dispose of. In early 1960 they shipped the family silver to a niece in Massachusetts. They discussed the idea of giving copies of Natalie's books to Yale University and the Library of Congress, especially *Quelques portraits-sonnets de femmes,* "as they are rare and illustrated by our little one."[15] Natalie authorized David Bruce to remove (and keep) a child's diamond necklace from her safe deposit at Rigg's Bank in Washington, D.C. With Laura taking the lead, they planned the disposition of the bulk of their money to charitable and artistic organizations. One of Natalie's bequests, to the Philadelphia Yearly Meeting (Quakers), was specifically targeted at birth control. Since 1976, income from this bequest has helped support CHOICE, an organization offering counseling on birth control, sexuality, and reproductive health.

Natalie also devoted a lot of time to promoting Romaine's artistic legacy and helping decide where her paintings should go. Partly through her own and Laura's contacts, the Smithsonian's National Museum of American Art grew interested in receiving Brooks's works. In 1966, with Laura assisting in the legal details, Brooks arranged to donate five paintings, including the 1923 *Romaine Brooks (A Self-Portrait).**

The Barney sisters also began planning their burials, although this may

---

*In 2000, a major retrospective of Brooks's work was held at the National Museum of Women in the Arts in Washington, D.C., and then traveled to the UC Berkeley Art Museum in Berkeley, California. The exhibit included fifty-four works from the Smithsonian's NMAA, and fifty other works from public and private collections in the United States and abroad.

have been done at Laura's insistence. "Don't let yourself be influenced by the *lugubre* Laura," Romaine advised Natalie. "Tombs, burying grounds and now perhaps the collection of nails for the coffins. Be aware, to be sure, but not be a victim of hefty funereal thoughts."[16]

In the mid-1950s Natalie's friend Paul Boncour gave her a plot in the ancient and picturesque Passy cemetery just off the Place du Trocadéro. In a July 1955 letter to the cemetery's caretaker, she made a formal request for two people to be buried in the plot, saying that either her sister, Madame Laura D. Barney, or her "friend, Madame Romaine Brooks," would be interred with her.

Over the years, the Barney sisters had occasionally discussed being buried together. They had a precedent right in their own family, since Alice and her sister Hessie shared a grave. Once, a few years before, Natalie had cut a photo from a newspaper that showed the side-by-side gravestones of Vincent and Theodore van Gogh, each stone displaying only a name, a date, and the words *"Ici Repose."* She mailed the clip off to Laura with a note: "Keep this in case & let's not put 'Ici Repose.'" Everyone who knew Natalie remarked on how much she hated platitudes, and she had no intention of reposing in a cliché-laden grave.

In the mid-1950s she had not yet decided with whom to be buried, her sister or her closest love. One can't help but wonder how she intended to resolve such a dilemma. Ultimately, and not for the best reasons, the decision would be made for her.

THE DEATH OF NICHOLAS Lahovary in the summer of 1963 left Janine free to spend more time with Natalie. No longer did she steal visits to Paris, discreetly arriving at rue Jacob from her hotel with an overnight case. Now she stayed for weeks and even months at a time, right in the *pavillon.*

Janine's presence was becoming a necessity. Natalie, eighty-six when Nicholas Lahovary died, was weakening. She had experienced two heart attacks, and she often felt tired. In the many thousands of letters written in her younger years, she almost never mentioned illness or fatigue. Now every communication began to bear witness to the debilitating signs of age. In matter-of-fact sentences, and with never a hint of self-pity, her physical ills present themselves one after the other. Her eyes are inflamed and bloodshot, forcing her to wear dark blue glasses for a week. Her "heart doctor" orders a few days of bed rest and prescribes digitaline. A strained calf muscle makes walking difficult. She has pain in her left hip, problems with a knee, an ulcer on her leg that refuses to heal. . . .

Even more telling was the fact that Natalie—once described by Lucie

Delarue-Mardrus as having dozens of appointments at the same time—began clinging to rue Jacob, refusing all but the rare invitation. "Florence Gould is again having her literary lunches at Hotel Meurice," she informed Romaine, "but I shall no longer find my way there. . . . My future excuse to all invitations: 'I no longer go anywhere.' "[17]

Around 1965, Natalie began truly needing the constant care of an able-bodied companion, someone to help her dress and bathe, ensure that she took her medication, be there in the middle of the night when problems arose. While Berthe cared beautifully for Natalie, as well as for her home, finances, and other matters, she had a husband she loved to whom she returned each night. It was thus Janine who watched over Natalie's physical needs.

When her husband died, Janine was in her early sixties—still relatively young. She could easily have opted for a carefree widowhood filled with travel, interesting people, and worldly pleasures. Instead, she embraced the responsibility of caring for Natalie. Whatever her faults may have been, she remained true and loving. In a letter written after Natalie's death, David Bruce remarked that he had found Janine's care of Natalie "quite extraordinary."

Romaine, too, was failing. While some complaints resulted from her life-long hypochondria, others—including digestive problems and rheumatism—were serious. The woman who had spent her adult life in a constant series of departures for exotic shores began to find travel difficult. When Natalie tried to arrange a get-together in late 1966, Romaine turned her down flat. "Don't bother making plans that I can't carry through," she wrote. "Romaine has lost her independence and must face the fact; no going to hotels good or bad. As you know I've fallen down three times in my garden and put it down to shoes etc., but it is really weakness in either leg (cause: old age)."[18] In another letter a few months later she penned a long list of physical problems and added this sad conclusion: "Find a brilliant aphorism for my state, darling, and then let's not talk about it anymore."[19]

According to Meryle Secrest, Romaine began to grow extremely paranoid and somewhat irrational around the mid-1960s. She covered the door of her Nice apartment with locks and bolts, grew "wary of newcomers, who might steal from you," and suspected that Gino, her "devoted chauffeur, valet, and companion of her final years . . . [who was] incapable of a dishonest act,"[20] was stealing her valuables and planning to poison her because she had left him money in her will.

Other old friends fell under the spotlight of Romaine's wrath, too, with sometimes near-comical results. Over the decades Natalie had developed the tradition of celebrating Thanksgiving at rue Jacob, inviting Laura and various friends for turkey, corn muffins, and a pumpkin tart. Late one November in the mid-1960s, Romaine happened to be Paris. For some reason she was angry at Laura, and also at William Huntington, who was visiting from the States, and refused to sit at the same table with them on Thanksgiving Day. Natalie's solution: she hauled the gang off to dine at the luxurious Hôtel Meurice, where they divided into two separate tables. At the first sat Natalie, Laura, and Huntington. At the second were Romaine and Berthe, who was invited along to keep Romaine company. "It was funny," Berthe wryly recalled. "I still laugh about it."[21]

Nobody was subjected to Romaine's wrath more than her Nat-Nat. The complaints were familiar: Natalie's second-rate friends, her infidelities, Janine. Jean Chalon met Romaine sometime in early 1964. At that point he had known Natalie for only half a year and looked forward to meeting the woman who played such a big role in her life. To his dismay, he found Romaine's "gruff amiability" chilling. Even worse, he, like Lahovary and others, thought that Natalie was frightened by her. No matter how hard Natalie tried to placate her beloved "angel," she was met with anger and recrimination.

For decades Natalie had handled Romaine's moods and complaints with a funny quip, logical reasoning, or by simply leaving her alone for a few hours to mellow out. Now, in the Amazon's weakened state, every cruel word from Romaine cut deeply. Their meetings grew increasingly stressful for Natalie, who became tearful, pale, and dizzy. Janine worried that she would have another heart attack. As Romaine grew more demanding and difficult, the detente between her and Janine shattered.

When she wasn't acting badly, Romaine could be wonderful company, and had always possessed the gift of making Nat-Nat laugh. To be sure, Romaine wasn't everybody's cup of tea. But Natalie loved her, pure and simple, and was usually happy and content in her presence. She felt as much that way now, near the end of their lives, as she had at the beginning, when they were young and seemingly invincible.

Romaine had never been a mean-spirited or cruel person; she was simply the unhappy result of a tragic upbringing. She lacked the kind of innate, triumphant spirit that might have provided rescue from her demons, and she was born far too early to reap the benefit of self-help books and childhood abuse counselors. Stuck forever with her formidable childhood pain and the twisted psyche she developed to deal with it, she did the best she could. She never stopped trying to be better than she was, and in many ways achieved her own kind of greatness. Natalie always understood the immensity of Romaine's struggle. She loved her for trying so hard, and she always—always!—made a point of celebrating her greatness.

That spring of 1968 Natalie and Romaine, both now over ninety, traveled back to Paris together. Romaine stayed at rue Jacob in the spare room that had been used over the years by many others, including Alice, Dolly, and Djuna Barnes. One day in June, shortly after Brooks returned to Nice, Natalie stretched out on the bed in the spare room. "My angel's voice [came] to me as I lie in your bed," she wrote Romaine, "the windows open to the second day of summer with the chirp of birds and the cuddling sound of doves—and my thoughts of you! . . . [I] love and look forward to my angel with the love of her Nat-Nat."[22]

But by now the unhappy Romaine looked forward to nothing. Later that summer Natalie was told by a friend in Nice that Romaine no longer left her apartment and spent entire days sitting alone in a darkened room. The news "came as a shock to me," Natalie replied. "Shocks are often due to a lack of foresight? But the idea of Romaine's spending the whole summer alone in the dark of her flat at Nice is more than my weak heart and great love of her can stand!"[23]

That coming winter of 1969 marked the last visit between Natalie and Romaine, and their time together was difficult. Romaine, sinking each day deeper into a depressive state, refused to see the doctors Natalie sent, and sometimes refused to see Natalie herself. At one point, writing from the Hôtel d'Angleterre, Natalie begged pathetically for a meeting: "My Angel, and cruel love—after half a century of being our nearest and dearest, do you treat me at present like an unwelcome stranger? That you 'wished to see no one'—not even your doctor last night . . . Why can't I come now or tomorrow Monday just to be near you—and reassure us that all is well as possible—Do, please, I beg of you, and our everlasting friendship, reassure me or let me go to you: just for a moment: to put your head on my shoulder and carry out whatever wish you may express to your ever loving and faithful friend Natalie."[24]

Flying back to Paris on May 3, ninety-two-year-old Natalie clung to the belief that everything was basically fine between her and her lover of nearly six decades. However, for reasons of her own, Romaine had decided to descend forevermore into a sanctum of silence, firmly shutting the doors behind her. As the weeks passed without replies to her letters or phone calls, Natalie grew increasingly worried.

MEANWHILE CAME ANOTHER brutal blow: the loss of rue Jacob.

Natalie had always rented the *pavillon*. When she took up residence in 1909, it probably never occurred to her that she would still be living there sixty years later. She was only thirty-two then, brimming with life and plans and people. With her innate dislike of possessions, the idea of being tied to a house through ownership simply didn't appeal. Renting, on the other hand, kept her options open.

There had been times over the years when she could have moved. In 1914 the landlords put her on notice that she might have to depart. "The decision about my house Rue Jacob still pending," she informed Alice. "I'm enjoying it now at any rate and shall hate giving it up if I must!"[25] The crisis passed. Ten years later, Alice discovered a fixer-upper in a good Parisian neighborhood, and offered to buy it as Natalie's permanent home. But, happy in the *pavillon*, Natalie delayed making a decision and the house was purchased by someone else. When Romaine bought an apartment in the rue Raynouard building where Laura lived, Natalie mentioned that she might join them there someday "when this place drives me away."[26] It never did.

So in the end Natalie remained the renter, but not the owner, of rue Jacob. In her later years she occasionally equated her union with the *pavillon* to a marriage that had lasted more than half a century, but in truth she lacked the legal benefits that "marriage"—in this case ownership—would have conferred. The ugly truth was that, when it came to rue Jacob, Natalie was merely a commonlaw wife whose tenancy rights were not protected by the length of her cohabitation. She discovered that with a sickening jolt when, in 1966, her property was purchased by Michel Debré, the former minister of justice under Charles de Gaulle. He immediately and with no warning served legal notice that she would have to move in 1970 (the minimum time required for "expulsion" notice was four years).

The news that Natalie Clifford Barney was being kicked out of rue Jacob caused a media sensation, helped along by her adept touch at public relations. "My salon is a monument to contemporary literature," she informed a reporter from *France-Soir*. "No one has the right to alter it. I have sworn to defend to my last breath this house where the mind has ruled."[27] Letters arrived from all over France and abroad, protesting the news. President Georges Pompidou himself intervened. After he asked Debré to end the scandal, the new owner eventually withdrew the order of expulsion.

However, M. Debré sought other ways to hasten his tenant's departure. The kitchen and other rooms were condemned as unsafe, which necessitated shoring up the building's supporting beams—a major job of reconstruction. Natalie could remain if she wished, but her life would be miserable. Her influential friends, including David Bruce, tried to intercede, but to no avail. The reconstruction proceeded.

For two years Natalie lived with the *pavillon* sheathed in building materials. Access was often difficult and sometimes downright impossible. At one point, coming for his weekly visit, Jean Chalon had to jump up and climb in through a window. Still, Natalie clung like a barnacle to her home. At her age, with so much of her life invested in rue Jacob, the thought of going anywhere else was simply impossible. And so, as things grew worse, she continued to tough it out.

Finally, in late 1969—or, at the latest, early January 1970—Natalie moved across the Seine and into a suite at the four-star Hôtel Meurice, with a view over the Tuileries Gardens.[28] The chief reason for the move was that life at rue Jacob, with the constant construction, had become intolerable. With her usual positive attitude, Natalie believed that the move was only temporary; she fully expected to return home in the spring. The *pavillon* was still in her possession, after all, and Berthe continued to care for it as if Natalie were in residence. A few prized effects were arranged about the hotel rooms: the Carolus-Duran painting of ten-year-old Natalie; her favorite photograph of Romaine; a reproduction of the Levy-Dhurmer painting of Renée Vivien; a photograph of Liane de Pougy.

In the hotel, Natalie grew increasingly distraught over the situation with Romaine, and in February Berthe, without telling her, flew to Nice to try to set things right. Romaine received Berthe, whom she had always liked, pleasantly. However, whenever the subject came around to Natalie, she declared emphatically that she could no longer live as part of a threesome, that she didn't want to continue sharing Nat-Nat with Janine. She and Natalie should have lived their last years together, she said, and they would have if the Villa Trait d'Union hadn't been destroyed. She complained at length about Janine, adding nastily that it was a good thing for Natalie to have her own live-in nurse (Janine). For three afternoons Berthe sat holding Romaine's hand while the older woman reminisced about the past. In each conversation her love for Natalie was just as obvious as her determination to be done with her completely and forever.

Back in Paris, Berthe told Natalie about the visit. Distraught and disheartened, Natalie nonetheless continued sending letters to Romaine, with never a reply. They are heartbreaking to read, these last few missives, written in a quavering, barely legible hand. One by one they become shorter, until the final few contain but a single sentence. Most are undated, and so it's difficult to know which was the last. Perhaps it was this:

> From NatNat's weak heart full of love for her angel.
> NatNat[29]

The break with Romaine was the single most painful event of Natalie's life. She found it almost impossible to accept that this time Romaine's tantrums wouldn't fade away into a distant memory; that this time the two of them would not return to a state of loving harmony; that this time was the last time. Nearly sixty years after their first meeting, it was finally over.

Romaine's silence would continue until her death on December 7, 1970. Natalie accepted the news stoically, but sometime later the lifelong pagan made an odd remark. If what the believers said was true, she told a friend, then she and Romaine would meet again.

BY THE TIME OF Romaine's death, it had become obvious—if not to Natalie, at least to those who cared about her—that she would not be returning to rue Jacob. The final straw had come in mid-1970, when Berthe suffered an attack of peritonitis and was laid up indefinitely. No one could run the residence in her stead; the idea was unthinkable. With no Berthe, Natalie announced, there could be no rue Jacob—*c'est tout!* But, ever the optimist, she continued to believe that the situation was temporary. After Berthe's recovery and when things returned to normal, she would go home.

Years before, Natalie had written about Colette's final days, when she was confined to her apartment. "The time of diminishment arrives," she said. "One first renounces the large horizon for a smaller landscape; then the landscape for a garden; then, one is reduced to the house; and, finally, confined to bed—where each day leaves you with a little less strength, a little less courage."[30]

Now began Natalie's own days of diminishment. Before her final departure from rue Jacob, she had still managed to get out occasionally, meeting Florence Gould for lunch, dining with her sister at Laperouse, attending a reception at the home of an old friend. But since being stripped of her home—her life!—she had become increasingly disoriented. "She completely lost the notion of time," Chalon said. "She faded away, slowly, over time. She no longer read the newspapers. The outside world simply ceased to exist."[31] She lived increasingly in the past, telling and retelling stories about her old loves, the scandals she'd created, the famous people she had known.

Journalist Derek Patmore, an old friend, came to visit her at the Meurice in 1970. He found her lying on the couch in a mauve-colored velvet robe. Her hair was snow white but her eyes, he said, were as beautiful as he'd remembered from the early 1930s. He noted that Natalie didn't seem to like discussing the present, but preferred talking about the past, particularly her love life.

American writer George Wickes, after jumping through a few hoops of approval held by François Chapon and Janine Lahovary, was allowed to meet Natalie in 1971. "There she was," he wrote later, "this small, fragile, incredibly aged person, wrapped in a pale-blue dressing gown to match her pale-blue eyes and very fine white hair. She looked like a carefully wrapped doll in that expensive hotel drawing room with its vases of tall expensive flowers . . . but there was still a spark of animation behind the vague look in her eyes." He found her to be "a very frank and forthright old lady," whose wits were sharp "when they were not rambling."[32] Thirty years later, looking back on that day, Wickes was struck most by the sentiment Natalie repeated over and over: "Why didn't you come sooner?" It was clear, he said, that she wanted to be remembered.[33]

Some visitors to the Meurice were disturbed by Natalie's late tendency to harp on her remembered sensual joys. Marguerite Yourcenar later recalled with regret that "in the last years of her life, passionate love and the pleasures of passion had become for [Natalie] the kind of obsessive, legendary, and, dare I say, somewhat excessively dwelled-upon themes that they also can be for certain elderly gentlemen. . . . There is a time for everything, as Ecclesiastes says, and once that time has passed, certain importunities become disturbing."[34]

Sometimes Natalie talked about death. "She had no fear of death at all," Chalon recalled. "She didn't believe in god. She was serene about it all. 'My life will be finished,' she would say. 'I've had an incredible life. That's how it goes.' "[35]

Some of the worst stories about Janine were born at this time. There was talk of her outrageous pretension, of her superior air. She was said to be surrounded by a coterie of leechlike friends who hung on her every word. Some have said that she began receiving guests on Fridays as if she were the Amazon, that she left Natalie on her own to go off with her own friends, that she spent Natalie's money and accepted the gift of Natalie's valuable jewels.

It seems only fair to give Janine the benefit of the doubt insofar as Natalie's last months. She was there because she loved and respected Natalie. She was by Natalie's side most of every day, and each and every night. She doled out the medicines. She undressed, and washed, and then dressed again that frail and helpless body. She listened patiently to the stories of all the past loves. She fielded the phone calls, ushered the respectful visitors in and out. She herself was not a well woman, and knew it; she was destined to die only a year after Natalie.

However plush, a hotel room is not a home, but everyone did what they could to make it seem so for Natalie. When Berthe recovered from her operation, she came every day, bringing flowers and Maryland chicken, cinnamon cake, fresh fruit, and chocolates. Jean Chalon carried on the years-long ritual of calling on Natalie each Wednesday at four o'clock. Other friends came by to visit or telephoned for long-distance tête-à-têtes.

The weeks and the months passed. As Natalie had written in *Adam*, she was now "retired into that no-man's land of old age: that age of shawls and chills and increasing ills, where with resignation, if not anticipation, one awaits that unavoidable last visitor."[36]

ON JANUARY 20, 1972, *Le Figaro* wrote about a new petition intended to stop construction on the *pavillon* and temple in order to preserve them as they were. Addressed to the minister of cultural affairs, it was signed by three hundred major personalities, including Louis Aragon, Paul Morand, Philippe Soupault, Nadia Boulanger, and *"beaucoup d'autres aussi éminents."* The petition stated that "the temple of friendship represents one of the unique curiosities of the 6th arrondissement, and is one of the rare surviving witnesses to the end of the 18th century; in addition, the mysterious edifice has been rendered celebrated through the world by the salon of Miss Nathalie Clifford Barney, who has contributed to the great currents of French literature."

Beautiful words—but, unfortunately, they came much too late.

On February 1, after a light supper, Natalie retired early. Waking around 9:30, she complained of chest pains. Janine called for the doctor, who examined Natalie and determined that the pains weren't serious. He left. Natalie fell back asleep, but awakened again before midnight. This time the pain was much worse. The doctor was called again and came at once. After giving Natalie an injection to relieve her discomfort, he massaged her heart. Even as he did, she slipped into a coma. Cradled in Janine's arms, Natalie Clifford Barney died at 2:30 in the morning on February 2. She was ninety-five years old. The official cause of her death: heart failure. Her body was taken to the American church on avenue George V, where she lay in state dressed in a pretty white satin nightgown and a white flannel dressing gown. Romaine's photo was tucked close to her breast.

On February 4, twenty-three friends—including Germaine Beaumont, Bettina Bergery, Miron Grindea, François Chapon, Jean Chalon, Carlos de Angulo, Jean Denoël, Dr. Marthe Lamy, Philippe Jullian, Edouard MacAvoy, Betsy Gautrat, Berthe Cleyrergue, and Janine Lahovary—met at the American Cathedral to accompany Natalie's coffin to the Passy cemetery. Not present was Laura Barney, who, at ninety-two, was too ill to leave her apartment.

At four o'clock in the afternoon on that cold, crisp, and brilliantly sunny day, not far from the tomb of Pauline Tarn, Natalie Clifford Barney was lowered into the winter ground. In accordance with her wishes, no prayers were said. Instead, a shocked stillness reigned, the kind that had always followed her best remarks.

For a while the group milled about, not wanting to leave. Jean Chalon, shaking with sobs, moved away to be alone with his grief. François Chapon joined him to offer a few words of comfort. Journalists from *Réalités* and the London *Times* talked of reviving Natalie's works. A young stranger whose name was recorded as "Mlle X, an admirer of Miss B," stood around looking awkward. There was talk of gathering for tea at the Meurice, or, even better, at rue Jacob.

Eventually someone made the first move, and the group began walking away, reluctantly leaving Natalie in the past. As they slowly trickled past the ancient tombs and headed down the cracked cement stairway that led to the busy street, someone remarked on the sheer beauty of the day and noted that it was a Friday.

It was, as everyone understood, the Amazon's last Friday.

*T*he Amazon in winter.
(Michelle Brabo)

Afterword

MANY YEARS BEFORE her death Natalie had been dismayed to encounter a newspaper photograph of the Van Gogh brothers' side-by-side gravestones, each bearing the identical banal sentiment, "Ici Repose." To ensure that she didn't spend eternity stretched beneath a cliché, she put together her own epitaph. She chose to be remembered as a writer and as the Amazon of Rémy de Gourmont, but what made her epitaph truly inimitable was a phrase she composed, "Je suis cet être légendaire où je revis."

This lofty phrase uses an ancient, obscure form that has often been misinterpreted, even by native-born French speakers (a common mistaken interpretation is "I follow this legendary being [Rémy de Gourmont] in whom I will live again.") Much of the trouble, according to Françoise Chapon, revolves around Natalie's obscure utilization of the adverb *où*, derived from the language's grand stylistic tradition (from research, he determined that the phrase is exactly the kind to be found in the work of Racine, Molière, or Mme. de Sevígné). But as Natalie told Chapon directly, the phrase meant: I am this legendary being [the Amazon] in which I will live again (i.e., have a second life as a legend or myth).

Despite her planning, Natalie almost ended up with a banal inscription anyway. After Natalie's burial Laura told William Huntington that the stone should simply read: "American poet and writer." Dismayed, he enlisted Jean Chalon's help in convincing Laura to stick with Natalie's wishes. The two men called on Laura, expecting a difficult conversation; to their surprise, after hearing them out she agreed without demur to the phrasing Natalie had wanted. Perhaps she feared Amazonian retribution from beyond the grave: as she confided in all seriousness to Chalon, "I don't want her getting angry over something written on that tomb."[*]

In August 1974 Natalie's grave was opened once again, this time to receive the coffin of Laura Barney. Today, backdropped by the Eiffel Tower, the sisters lie at peace with one another.

NATALIE CLIFFORD BARNEY

ECRIVAIN

1876 • 1972

ELLE FUT L'AMAZONE DE REMY DE GOURMONT

JE SUIS CET ETRE LÉGENDAIRE

OÙ JE REVIS N.C.B.

ET SA SOEUR

LAURA CLIFFORD BARNEY

OFFICIER DE LA LÉGION D'HONNEUR

1879 • 1974

VEUVE D'HIPPOLYTE DREYFUS

MEMBRE

DE

LA COMMUNAUTÉ BAHA'IE

[*]Author's interview with Jean Chalon

Acknowledgments

IN EVERY STAGE of researching and writing this book I experienced generosity of spirit from almost everyone with whom I came in contact. The listing below cannot even begin to express my sincere gratitude.

For archival research: François Chapon and Paul Cougnard of the Bibliothèque Littéraire Jacques Doucet in Paris; Jill Rosenshield and Birute Ciplijauskaite, Memorial Library, University of Wisconsin at Madison; Lori Curtis, McFarlin Library, University of Tulsa; William Cox, David Burgevin, and Josephine Jamison at the Smithsonian Institution Archives (and especially Bruce Kirby, now with the Library of Congress). Also thanks to Charles Amirkhanian, Other Minds Foundation; Valerie Komor, Archives of American Art; and the helpful staffs at many major libraries, particularly the University of California at Berkeley, Davis, and Los Angeles, and the Library of Congress.

Among the many who directly provided useful information are: William Barney of the Barney Family Historical Association; Deborah Dyer, Bar Harbor Historical Society; Joyce Rose, Rapides Parish Library, Alexandria, Louisiana; Nancy Horlacher, Dayton/Montgomery County Public Library, Dayton; Anne Cavanagh, Montgomery County Records Center and Archives, Dayton; Maurice Herron, Jefferson County (N.Y.) Genealogical Society; Alexandra Karafinas of the Long Beach (N.Y.) Historical Society.

The help of François Chapon, Jean Chalon, and Renée Lang extended far beyond interviews: time and again, each responded—not only willingly, but gladly—to questions that arose as I wrote. Other people who contributed in various ways include: Gina Sikelianos, Christine Clark, Betsy O'Brien, George Wickes, Imogen Bright, Richard Schaubeck, Nelson Lankford, Mauro Piccinini, Chelsea Ray, Lore Lawrence, Francesco Rappazzini, and Michele Brabo. Scott Stinson, the owner of Alice Barney's Studio House until early 2002, generously allowed me the run of the place for three days and nights. The Debré family allowed me a tour of Natalie's former *pavillon* and garden, and the Temple of Friendship.

I also want to express profound gratitude to my agent, Richard Abate of ICM, for his unswerving belief in this project; to my publisher, Dan Halpern, for wanting the book the moment he read the proposal; and to my editor, Julia Serebrinsky, for her insight, grace, and enthusiastic embrace of *Wild Heart.*

The very deepest thanks to Meg Lundstrom, who has critiqued my work and helped me over writerly hurdles since we sat side by side in Stanford University's graduate journalism program more than twenty years ago; Dennis Allison, who long shared and helped further my interest in Natalie; Pauline Baggio and Patrick Huerre, who always make Paris feel like a second hometown; Janice Matthews, my best pal for thirty years, who among many delightful habits enjoys rescuing me from geekdom at the end of research trips (especially in Paris); all my siblings for leading admirable lives; my father, who is a prince; and most of all to my mother, who survived three mean-spirited cancers and fought the fourth to the very end with courage and a never-ending sense of humor.

Notes

Authors with a single title in the Bibliography are cited only by last name. An author with two or more bibliographic titles is cited by both name and an abbreviated title. When more than one author has the same last name, the first name is given as an initial or in full.

Archives containing letters, manuscripts, and other documents are denoted by the abbreviations shown below. No date is indicated by "n.d." Unless otherwise indicated, translations of archival and bibliographic material are my own.

AAA   Archives of American Art (Smithsonian Institution), Washington, D.C.

JD   Bibliothèque Littéraire Jacques Doucet, Paris

McF   Special Collections and Archives, McFarlin Library, University of Tulsa, Tulsa, Oklahoma

ML   Special Collections, Memorial Library, University of Wisconsin at Madison, Madison, Wisconsin

OMF   Other Minds Foundation (George Antheil Archive), San Francisco, California

SIA   Smithsonian Institution Archives, Washington, D.C.

Names are abbreviated as follows:

ACB   Albert Clifford Barney

APB   Alice Pike Barney

EP   Eva Palmer

LCB   Laura Clifford Barney

LDM   Lucie Delarue-Mardrus

LDP   Liane de Pougy

LG   Lily Gramont

NCB Natalie Clifford Barney
PT Pauline Tarn
RB Romaine Brooks

ONE: BEAUTY IN THE BLOOD . . .

1. Stafford, p. 331.
2. Ibid., p. 333.
3. *Louisiana Historical Review:* "Featuring Rapides Parish," p. 8. Relevant excerpts from this undated pamphlet were provided by Joyce Rose of the Rapides Parish Library in Alexandria, Louisiana.
4. Barney, Alice: *Stanley's Lady Alice,* p. 21 (SIA: Record Unit 7473, Box 1).
5. Stafford, p. 341.
6. *Louisiana Historical Quarterly,* Volume 24, p. 733.
7. Miller's January 13, 1804, commission from Laussat, the French colonial prefect, authorizes him to "receive the command" of the Post of Rapides from Ennemond Meuillion on behalf of France. Then, "you will enter into occupation in the name of the United States, and hold it entirely at the disposal of your government."
8. Barney: *Aventures,* p. 25.
9. From William Claiborne's May 3, 1805, letter appointing Miller judge; reprinted in "Sketch of My Grandfather's Connection with the Louisiana Purchase," published by Alice Barney, p. 21 (SIA: Accession 96–153, Box 4).
10. Wittington, p. 103.
11. Dickens, p. 131.
12. Barney, Alice: *Stanley's Lady Alice,* p. 8.
13. Howe, p. 849.
14. *Adam International Review* #299 (1963), p. 158.
15. Joseph Holliday: "Notes on Samuel N. Pike and His Opera Houses," *Bulletin of the Cincinnati Historical Society,* July 1967, p. 183.
16. Barney, Alice: *Stanley's Lady Alice,* p. 21.
17. McAllister, p. 132.
18. *Cincinnati Commercial,* 6/7/1860.
19. Barney, Alice: *Stanley's Lady Alice,* p. 35.
20. *The New Yorker,* 6/25/1960.
21. William C. Barney, president of the Barney Family Historical Association, provided this information.
22. Conover, p. 15.
23. Trustees' Minutes, Book B, Union College, 7/26/1831, pp. 156–157. Collection of Schaffer Library, Union College, Schenectady, N.Y.
24. Conover, pp. 15–16.
25. Cited in "Cooper Female Academy," *Dayton Daily News,* 8/31/1996.
26. Latrobe.
27. Edgar.
28. Conover, p. 18.
29. Estabrook, p. 94.

30. Barney, Alice: *Stanley's Lady Alice*, p. 23.

31. Ibid., p. 21.

32. Ibid., p. 141.

33. Cited in Bierman, p. 153.

34. Barney, Alice: *Stanley's Lady Alice*, p. 7.

35. Ibid., p. 54.

36. Ibid., p. 75.

37. Ibid., p. 250.

38. Clipping from unattributed Dayton newspaper, December 1902 (SIA).

39. Barney, Alice: *Stanley's Lady Alice*, p. 261.

40. Ibid., p. 262.

41. Ibid., p. 263.

42. Ibid.

43. Ibid., p. 292.

44. Ibid., p. 296.

45. Ibid., p. 292.

TWO: CHILD OF WITCHES AND SAINTS

1. Interview with William Huntington by Smithsonian Institution staff member, 10/24/1979 (SIA: Accession 96–153, Box 6).

2. Barney: *Mémoires secrets*, p. 1 (JD).

3. Barney, Alice: *Stanley's Lady Alice* (SIA: Record Unit 7473, Box 1).

4. *New York Times*, 11/4/1877.

5. Cited in Bierman, p. 213.

6. Cited in Hall, Richard, p. 95.

7. Cited in Bierman, p. 213.

8. Cited in Kling, p. 72.

9. *Chicago Journal*, 5/2/1911.

10. Unattributed Dayton newspaper clipping, December 1902 (SIA).

11. Barney: *European American* (JD). Natalie copied the letter into the manuscript.

12. Barney: *Souvenirs*, p. 28.

13. Barney: *Mémoires secrets*, p. 27 (JD).

14. Barney: *Souvenirs*, p. 28.

15. Barney: "N.C.B. sur sa mère Alice Barney," address delivered at Alice's memorial service (SIA).

16. *Dayton Journal Herald*, 12/31/1965.

17. Barney: "N.C.B. sur sa mère Alice Barney."

18. Barney, Alice: *Stanley's Lady Alice*.

19. All descriptions of the Long Beach Hotel: *Harper's Weekly*, 8/14/1880.

20. Barney: *Aventures*, p. 31.

21. All remaining quotations and dialogue regarding the Oscar Wilde encounter from Barney, Alice: *Stanley's Lady Alice*, pp. 300–314.

22. NCB to ACB, n.d. (JD).

23. Wickes, p. 267.

24. Lankford, p. 15.

25. David K. E. Bruce to NCB, 6/27/1960 (SIA: Accession 96–153, Box 5).

26. Barney: *Mémoires secrets,* p. 20 (JD).

27. Ibid., pp. 4–5.

28. Kling, p. 86.

29. Barney: *Mémoires secrets,* p. 8 (JD).

30. Cited in Cook, p. 105.

31. Roosevelt, p. 30.

32. Natalie lists her grades for the term in a 4/15/1888 letter to her parents (JD).

33. NCB to her parents, 6/28/1888 (JD).

34. NCB to ACB, 3/21/1888 (JD).

35. Burke, Mary Alice, p. 93.

36. Crespelle, p. 22.

37. Ban-y-Bryn's original architectural blueprints are stored at the Smithsonian archives.

38. Unattributed newspaper clipping in Alice's scrapbook (SIA: Accession 96–153, Box 4).

39. From "The Birth of a World Class Resort," Bar Harbor Chamber of Commerce guide, 1997.

40. Unattributed newspaper clipping, c. 1889 (SIA).

41. Unattributed newspaper clipping (SIA).

42. Barney: *Memoires secrets,* p. 26 (JD).

43. Ibid., p. 27.

44. Barney, Alice: *Stanley's Lady Alice,* p. 235.

THREE: ADOLESCENT AND DEBUTANTE

1. Barney: *Mémoires secrets,* p. 12 (JD).

2. Ibid., p. 21.

3. Ibid., p. 14.

4. Ibid., p. 21.

5. Ibid., p. 22.

6. All quotes regarding the house party from Barney: *Mémoires secrets,* p. 23 (JD).

7. LCB to APB, 8/5/no year (SIA: Accession 96–153, Box 7).

8. Barney: *Mémoires secrets,* p. 29 (JD).

9. Ibid., p. 28.

10. Author's interview with Gina Sikelianos.

11. Barney: *Souvenirs,* pp. 64–65.

12. Barney: *Mémoires secrets,* p. 29 (JD).

13. Pougy: *Idylle saphique,* p. 215.

14. Barney: *Mémoires secrets,* p. 31 (JD).

15. Ibid., pp. 33–34.

16. *Washington Capital,* 9/12/1898.

17. Barney, Alice: *Stanley's Lady Alice* (SIA: Record Unit 7473, Box 1).

18. NCB to APB, 12/22/1894 (SIA: Accession 96–153, Box 6).

19. Barney: *Mémoires secrets,* p. 51 (JD).

20. ACB to NCB, ca. 1898–1899 (SIA: Accession 96–153, Box 6).

21. Barney: *Mémoires secrets,* p. 46 (JD).

22. Dwight, p. 24.

23. Luhan: Vol. 1, p. 276.

24. Palmer-Sikelianos, pp. 26–27.

25. Barney: *Mémoires secrets,* p. 41 (JD).

26. Ibid., p. 40.

27. Alice and Natalie Barney: *The Color of His Soul* (SIA: Record Unit 7473, Box 2).

28. NCB to LCB, 4/7/1894 (JD).

29. All quotes involving the Wild Rose: Barney: *Mémoires secrets,* pp. 46–48.

30. NCB to EP, n.d. (ca. 1908) (JD).

31. Barney: *Mémoires secrets,* p. 52 (JD).

32. Ibid., p. 56.

33. NCB Diary & Souvenir Book (JD).

34. NCB to LCB, 6/22/1894 (JD).

35. Ibid.

36. Davis, pp. 69–70. The chapter on Paris was written by Sarcey.

37. Thurman, p. 137.

38. NCB to LCB, 10/5/1894 (JD).

39. NCB to APB, 10/9/1894 (JD).

40. NCB to APB, 2/26/1895 (JD).

41. Barney: *Mémoires secrets,* p. 43 (JD).

42. Ibid.

43. NCB to APB, 4/21/1895 (JD).

44. *Bar Harbor Record,* 7/20/1895.

45. All quotations regarding Natalie's debut: newspaper clips in Alice's scrapbook (SIA: Accession 96–153, Box 4).

46. Natalie absentmindedly thrust this undated letter into the diary/scrapbook she kept while on her Grand Tour with Miss Ely, and that's where I found it many, many years later, in the Bibliothèque Jacques Doucet.

47. *Washington Post,* 6/12/1897.

48. Unattributed newspaper clipping, n.d. (SIA: Accession 96–153, Box 6).

49. Delarue-Mardrus: *Mes mémoires,* p. 144.

50. Barney: *Mémoires secrets,* p. 63 (JD).

51. Ibid., p. 66.

52. Ibid., p. 63.

53. Smith, pp. 57–60.

54. Skinner, p. 23.

55. Ibid., p. 56.

56. *New York Times,* 5/5/1897.

57. Unattributed newspaper clipping, ca. 1898 (SIA).

58. Barney: *Mémoires secrets*, p. 75 (JD).

59. Ibid., p. 76.

60. Pougy: *Idylle saphique*, p. 55. This quote is taken from a chapter Natalie contributed to the book.

61. Mathews, pp. 154–155.

62. Barney: *Mémoires secrets*, pp. 108–109 (JD).

FOUR: NATALIE AND THE COURTESAN

1. Gramont: *Pomp*, p. 219.

2. Pougy: *Blue*, p. 134.

3. Ibid., p. 14.

4. Barney: "Jews/Poets and Poets" (JD). This remark appears not in the notebook itself, but in papers stuck between the pages.

5. Barney: *Mémoires secrets*, p. 71 (JD).

6. Wickes, p. 144.

7. In the 10/26/1901 *La Vie Parisienne*, de Pougy notes that *Idylle saphique* is in its sixty-ninth edition.

8. Pougy: *Blue*, p. 253.

9. Ibid., p. 51.

10. Chalon: *Portrait*, p. 30.

11. Barney: *Mémoires secrets*, p. 100 (JD).

12. Ibid., p. 96.

13. Ibid., p. 103.

14. Ibid., p. 116.

15. Pougy: *Blue*, p. 44.

16. Barney: *Mémoires secrets*, p. 127 (JD).

17. Ibid., p. 132.

18. Ibid.

19. Cited in Goujon: *Tes blessures*, p. 114.

20. Pougy: *Blue*, 44.

21. Barney: *Mémoires secrets*, p. 142 (JD).

22. The same story, with slight variations, is told in *Mémoires secrets*, p. 145, and "Lettres à une connue," p. 59 (JD). Dialogue is as recorded by Natalie.

FIVE: NATALIE AND THE VIRGIN

1. Barney: *Souvenirs*, p. 40.

2. Vivien, p. 2.

3. Goujon: *Tes blessures*, p. 34.

4. Luhan: Vol. 1, p. 272.

5. Pringué, p. 78.

6. Barney: *Mémoires secrets*, p. 158 (JD).

7. Ibid.

8. Ibid., p. 164.

9. Cited in Goujon: *Tes blessures*, p. 165.

10. Author's interview with Renée Lang.

11. Introduction to Vivien, p. viii.

12. Cited in Goujon: *Tes blessures*, p. 129.

13. *La Vie Parisienne*, 6/1/1901.

14. Cited in Goujon: *Tes blessures*, p. 200.

15. Jay, p. 119.

16. Wickes, pp. 45–46.

17. Benstock, p. 282.

18. Barney: *Mémoires secrets*, p. 159 (JD).

19. Vivien, p. 33.

20. Barney: *Souvenirs*, p. 65.

21. Cited in Goujon: *Tes blessures*, p. 141.

22. Palmer-Sikelianos, p. 24.

23. Barney: *Mémoires secrets*, p. 168 (JD).

24. NCB to EP, 8/10/1905 (JD).

25. EP to NCB, 3/7/1902 (JD).

26. EP to NCB, n.d. (JD).

27. NCB to EP, 12/21/1900 (JD).

28. Unattributed clipping in Alice's scrapbook (SIA: Accession 96–153, Box 4).

29. Ibid.

30. *Washington Mirror*, 3/9/1901.

31. *Dispatch-News* (Parkersburg, West Virginia), 9/17/1911.

32. Brooks: *No Pleasant Memories*, p. 277 (AAA).

33. Cited in Lewis, R. W. B., p. 444.

34. Barney: *Souvenirs*, p. 190.

35. *Washington Post*, 2/12/1974.

36. APB to NCB, 1/25/1901 (JD).

37. APB to NCB, n.d. (JD).

38. All quotes in this anecdote: Barney: "N.C.B. sur sa mère Alice Barney," address delivered at Alice's memorial service (SIA).

39. NCB to EP, 12/21/1900 (JD).

40. Barney: *Souvenirs*, p. 60.

41. Cited in Goujon: *Tes blessures*, p. 165.

SIX: UNE JEUNE FILLE DE LA SOCIÉTÉ FUTURE

1. Goncourt and Goncourt, p. 365.

2. Author's interview with Renée Lang.

3. *Fanfare* (James Camner), July/August 1997 (Vol. 20, No. 6).

4. Delarue-Mardrus: *Mes mémoires*, p. 141.

5. Goujon: *Croisées,* p. 24.

6. Cited in Chapon et al., p. 49.

7. PL to NCB, June 1901; cited in Goujon: *Croisées,* p. 48.

8. Benstock, p. 283.

9. NCB to PL, summer 1901; cited in Goujon: *Croisées,* pp. 52–53.

10. PT to APB, 6/18/1901 (JD).

11. Cited in Goujon: *Tes blessures,* p. 175.

12. PT to NCB, various letters written in early August 1901 (JD).

13. PT to NCB, 8/29/1901 (JD).

14. Barney: *Souvenirs,* p. 75.

15. PT to NCB, 7/18/1902; cited in Goujon: *Croisées,* p. 106.

16. PT to NCB, 8/28/1901 (JD).

17. Barney: *Mémoires secrets,* p. 82 (JD).

18. Delarue-Mardrus: *Mes mémoires,* p. 144.

19. Barney: *Cinq petits,* p. 17.

20. NCB to LCB, late 1901 (JD).

21. Cited in Chapon et al., p. 27.

22. *Adam International Review* #299 (1963), p. 108.

23. NCB to APB, ca. autumn 1902 (SIA).

24. Ibid.

25. NCB to LCB, n.d. (JD).

26. Ibid.

27. Pougy: *Blue,* p. 253.

28. NCB to LCB, 1901 (JD).

29. Barney: *Souvenirs,* p. 71.

30. Magdeleine Wauthier: Preface to Barney: *Traits,* p. 12.

31. Barney: *Souvenirs,* p. 71.

32. Lacheny to NCB, 5/8/1903 (JD).

33. Lacheny to NCB, 3/25/1903 (JD).

34. NCB to LCB, n.d. (JD).

35. PT to NCB, 7/18/1902; cited in Goujon: *Croisées,* p. 107.

36. Ibid.

37. Barney: *Mémoires secrets,* p. 183 (JD).

38. Magdeleine Wauthier: Preface to Barney: *Traits,* p. 23.

39. Germain: *La bourgeoisie,* p. 291.

40. Delarue-Mardrus: *Mes mémoires,* p. 144.

41. Ibid.

42. Ibid.

43. Ibid.

44. ACB to NCB, summer 1902 (SIA).

45. Barney: *Mémoires secrets,* p. 187 (JD).

46. *Adam International Review* #299 (1963), p. 108.

47. Barney: *Mémoires secrets,* p. 187 (JD).

48. NCB to LCB, June 1904 (JD).

SEVEN: THE HEIRESS

1. Barney: *Souvenirs,* p. 91.

2. NCB to APB, n.d. (JD).

3. Jaloux, p. 100.

4. Colette: *My Apprenticeships,* p. 128.

5. Palmer-Sikelianos, p. 43.

6. *La Vie Parisienne,* June 1905.

7. Germain: *Les fous,* p. 211.

8. Delarue-Mardrus: *Mes mémoires,* p. 145.

9. LDM to NCB, n.d. (JD).

10. Germain: *La bourgeoisie,* p. 99.

11. Barney: *Souvenirs,* p. 167.

12. Ibid., p. 157.

13. LDM to NCB, n.d. (JD).

14. NCB to EP, 9/25/1905 (JD).

15. Delarue-Mardrus: *The Angel and the Perverts,* p. 140.

16. Germain: *Les fous,* p. 216.

17. Palmer-Sikelianos, p. 44.

18. Ibid.

19. Author's interview with Renée Lang.

20. Barney: *Mémoires secrets,* p. 192 (JD).

21. Cited in Wickes, p. 254.

22. Interview with Laura Barney by Delight Hall, 11/8/1961 (SIA: Accession 96–153, Box 7).

23. *Town & Country,* 1/30/1904.

24. Unattributed newspaper clipping (SIA: Accession 96–153, Box 4).

25. Barney, Alice: *Stanley's Lady Alice,* p. 332 (SIA: Record Unit 7473, Box 1).

26. Delarue-Mardrus: *The Angel and the Perverts,* p. 82.

27. Cited in Goujon: *Tes blessures,* p. 292.

28. Barney: *Mémoires secrets,* p. 189 (JD).

29. Cited in Chalon: *Portrait,* p. 81.

30. Barney: *Mémoires secrets,* p. 210 (JD).

31. NCB to EP, July 1906 (JD).

32. EP to NCB, ca. 1907 (JD).

33. EP to NCB, 8/21/1907 (JD).

34. EP to NCB, ca. 1907 (JD).

35. EP to NCB, 4/27/1930 (ML).

36. *Dayton Journal,* 11/14/1909.

37. Jaloux, p. 102.

38. NCB to EP, ca. October 1908 (JD).

EIGHT: THE SALONIST

1. *Adam International Review* #299 (1963), p. 68.
2. *New York American,* November 1909.
3. NCB to EP, n.d. (JD).
4. Leonard Tancock, in the introduction to La Rochefoucauld's *Maxims* (Penguin, 1959), p. 10.
5. Gramont: *Pomp,* p. 32.
6. *New York Times Book Review,* 9/28/1969.
7. *Adam International Review* #299 (1963), p. 15.
8. Aldington, p. 315.
9. Germain: *La bourgeoisie,* p. 96.
10. Cited in Wickes, p. 252.
11. Germain: *La bourgeoisie,* p. 5.
12. Jaloux, p. 101.
13. Delarue-Mardrus: *The Angel and the Perverts,* p. 81.
14. *Adam International Review* #299 (1963), p. 54.
15. Ibid., p. 113.
16. McAllister, p. 255.
17. Author's interviews with Chapon and Chalon.
18. Interview with William Huntington by Smithsonian Institution staff member, 10/24/1979 (SIA: Accession 96–153, Box 6).
19. Jaloux, p. 102.
20. Benstock, p. 11.
21. Hall, Radclyffe, p. 352.
22. Kling, p. 215.
23. *Post-Telegram* (Camden, New Jersey), 3/14/1911.
24. NCB to EP, October 1908 (JD).
25. Colette: *Pure and Impure,* p. 95.
26. Brooks: *No Pleasant Memories,* p. 238 (AAA).
27. *Mercure de France,* December 1953.
28. Cited in Goujon: *Tes blessures,* p. 40.
29. Barney: *La poète Renée Vivien: Evolution d'une mystique* (ML).
30. *Adam International Review* #299 (1963), p. 106.

NINE: THE AMAZON

1. Cargill, p. 222.
2. Germain: *La bourgeoisie,* p. 101.
3. Gourmont: *Lettres intimes,* p. 177.
4. Gramont: *Years of Plenty,* p. 306.
5. Cited in Wickes, p. 260.
6. Gard, p. 211.
7. Cargill, p. 222.

8. Chalon: *Portrait*, p. 107.

9. Gourmont: *Lettres intimes*, p. 200.

10. Germain: *La bourgeoisie*, p. 102.

11. Gourmont: *Lettres intimes*, p. 250.

12. Pringué, p. 128.

13. Flanner, p. 43.

14. Ibid.

15. Antheil, p. 182.

16. Delarue-Mardrus: *Mes mémoires*, p. 132.

17. Pringué, p. 128.

18. Gramont: *Pomp*, p. 217.

19. Cited in Cleyrergue, p. 223.

20. Chapon et al., p. 22.

21. Pringué, p. 131.

22. Renée Lang Notes (ML).

23. NCB to LG, n.d. (JD).

24. Hall, Radclyffe, p. 351.

25. Barney: *Souvenirs*, p. 114.

26. Gramont: *Years of Plenty*, p. 307.

27. Gourmont: *Lettres intimes*, p. 338.

28. Jaloux, p. 100.

29. Bourdet, p. 239.

30. Cited in Léautaud, p. 57.

31. Barney: "Accident" (JD).

32. NCB to LCB, postmarked 1912 (JD).

33. Barney: "Accident" (JD).

34. *Adam International Review* #299 (1963), p. 56.

35. Ibid., p. 49.

36. Barney: *Mémoires secrets*, p. 197 (JD).

37. Author's interview with Renée Lang.

38. Pringué, p. 55.

39. *Paris Herald*, 6/26/1910.

40. *Tatler*, 6/15/1910.

41. Palmer-Sikelianos, p. 39.

42. *New York Herald*, October 1910.

43. *Press*, October 10, 1910.

44. *New York Herald*, n.d. clipping (SIA).

45. Unattributed newspaper clipping, October 11 (no year) (SIA).

46. *Bar Harbor Record*, 10/19/1910.

47. Unattributed newspaper clipping (SIA).

48. National Museum of American Art, Sculpture Inventory 1968.159.383, Call Number: 08580067.

49. NCB to Renée Lang, 1/30/1961 (ML).

50. *Boston American,* 3/26/1911.

51. *Chicago Journal,* 5/2/1911.

52. *Club Fellow and Washington Mirror,* 11/15/1913.

53. Pougy: *Blue,* p. 77.

54. *La Vie Parisienne,* 6/18/1910.

55. Ibid., 9/24/1910.

56. Rouveyre, p. 6.

TEN: THE GREAT WAR

1. London *Times,* 6/29/1914.

2. Gramont: *Years of Plenty,* p. 363.

3. Ibid.

4. Draper, p. 196.

5. Ibid., p. 237.

6. NCB to LCB, n.d. (JD).

7. NCB to LCB, n.d. (JD).

8. NCB to APB, 12/9/1915 (JD).

9. Adam, p. 37.

10. Elizabeth Nourse: "Extracts from the Diary of an American Artist in Paris [in] August and September, 1914," *Art & Progress* 6, No. 2 (December 1914), pp. 41–48.

11. Adam, p. 46.

12. Pringué, p. 123.

13. Barney: *European American,* p. 66 (JD).

14. Pougy: *Blue,* p. 28.

15. Magdeleine Wauthier: Preface to Barney: *Traits,* p. 14.

16. Pringué, p. 54.

17. Barney: *European American* (JD).

18. NCB to APB, 1/1/1916 (JD).

19. Barney: *European American,* p. 71 (JD).

20. Ibid., pp. 72–79.

21. Ibid., p. 66.

22. Secrest, p. 10.

23. NCB to RB, n.d. (McF).

24. *International Studio,* February 1926.

25. Gramont: *Years of Plenty,* p. 338.

26. Brooks: *No Pleasant Memories,* p. 239 (AAA).

27. Ibid., p. 238.

28. Mackenzie, Compton: *My Life and Times,* p. 158.

29. Mackenzie, Compton: *Extraordinary Women,* p. 234.

30. Mackenzie, Faith: *More Than I Should,* p. 24.

31. Cleyrergue, p. 94.

32. RB to NCB, n.d. (McF).

33. *Adam International Review* #299 (1963), p. 56.

34. Gramont: *Years of Plenty,* p. 338.

35. NCB to APB, 1917 (JD).

36. Claudel, Vol. 1, p. 307.

37. Pougy: *Blue,* p. 141.

38. Magdeleine Wauthier: Preface to Barney: *Traits,* pp. 16–17.

39. Barney: *Souvenirs,* p. 116.

40. Ibid.

41. Delarue-Mardrus: *Mes mémoires,* p. 125.

42. Cited in Chapon et al., p. 50.

43. Gramont: *Years of Plenty,* p. 289.

44. *Adam International Review* #299 (1963), p. 42.

45. *Le Figaro,* 10/16/1917.

46. *San Francisco Examiner,* 10/16/1917.

47. *Dayton Journal Herald,* 12/29/1965.

48. Pougy: *Blue,* p. 99.

49. Flanner, p. 126.

50. Adam, p. 221.

51. NCB to APB, 1917 (JD).

52. *Club Fellow and Washington Mirror,* 7/21/1915.

ELEVEN: YEARS OF GLORY: THE SALON

1. *La Vie Parisienne,* 8/15/1925.

2. Pougy: *Blue,* p. 37.

3. Coco Chanel writing in *Vogue,* 11/1/1925.

4. Pougy: *Blue,* pp. 82–91.

5. Morand, p. 277.

6. *La Vie Parisienne,* 6/27/1925.

7. Jacob and Reinach, p. 222.

8. Germain: *Les fous,* p. 164.

9. Brooks: *No Pleasant Memories,* p. 278 (AAA).

10. The photograph belongs to the Smithsonian Archives (SIA: Accession 96–153).

11. Barney: *Aventures,* p. 125.

12. Cited in Savigneau, p. 233.

13. *Ere Nouvelle,* 6/12/1920.

14. Putnam, p. 74.

15. *Dayton Journal Herald,* 12/31/1965.

16. Barney: "Le Livre d'Heures de l'Année" (JD). A special thanks to Chelsea Ray for bring-
    ing this material to my attention.

17. Cited in Chalon: *Portrait,* p. 164.

18. Wilson, p. 203.

19. Aldington, p. 315.

20. Hall, Radclyffe, p. 380.

21. Ibid., p. 382.

22. Bourdet, p. 244.

23. Cody, p. 135.

24. Author's interview with Chapon.

25. Barney: *European American* (JD).

26. *Chicago Tribune* Paris edition, 1/19/1924.

27. Mauro Piccinini in a 5/28/2001 letter to the author.

28. *Criterion,* October 1926.

29. Antheil, p. 173.

30. George Antheil Archive (OMF).

31. Antheil, p. 173.

32. Colette: *Pure and Impure,* p. 131.

33. Josephson, p. 324.

34. Cleyrergue, p. 114.

35. NCB to APB, n.d. (JD).

36. Wickes, p. 159.

37. Pougy: *Blue,* p. 97.

38. Gramont: *Years of Plenty,* p. 309.

39. APB to NCB, 1921 (SIA: Accession 96–153, Box 7).

40. *Realités,* February 1966.

41. Unless otherwise noted, all critical comments about *Pensées d'une Amazone* are taken from "What the Men Think," a booklet privately printed by Natalie Barney in 1920.

42. All definitions from the *American Heritage Dictionary of the English Language,* Third Edition.

43. NCB to APB, 8/25/1928 (JD).

44. EP to NCB, 4/27/1930 (ML).

TWELVE: YEARS OF GLORY: THE AMAZON'S TRIBE

1. Toklas: *What Is Remembered,* p. 115.

2. Cited in Wickes, p. 242.

3. Ibid., p. 247.

4. Author's interview with Chapon.

5. Pougy: *Blue,* p. 125.

6. Ibid., p. 138.

7. Ibid., p. 140.

8. Ibid., p. 149.

9. Ibid., pp. 154–155.

10. Ibid., p. 162.

11. Lewis, R. W. B., p. 444.

12. This lunch was cited in Lewis, R. W. B., p. 444.

13. Crosby, Caresse, p. 119.
14. Cleyrergue, p. 79.
15. Ibid., p. 87.
16. Barney: *Mémoires secrets,* p. 44 (JD).
17. Ibid., pp. 27, 45.
18. "The Amazon's Notebook" (JD).
19. NCB to ACB, 8/4/1937 (JD).
20. NCB: *European American* (JD).
21. NCB to APB, n.d. (JD).
22. APB to NCB, ca. September 1920 (JD).
23. Ibid.
24. APB to NCB, ca. late September 1920 (JD).
25. APB to NCB, 11/28/1921 (JD).
26. APB to NCB, n.d. (SIA: Accession 96–153, Box 7).
27. Troubridge, p. 94.
28. London *Sunday Times,* 8/3/1994.
29. From the afterword to the 1981 Avon edition of *The Well of Loneliness.*
30. Flanner, p. 48.
31. Cline, p. 228.
32. Hall, Radclyffe, p. 244.
33. Ibid., pp. 351–352.
34. Pougy: *Blue,* p. 191.
35. Mackenzie, Compton: *Extraordinary Women,* pp. 41, 135.
36. Pougy: *Blue,* p. 202.
37. Ibid., p. 203.
38. Ibid., p. 205.
39. Barney: "Amants fèminins ou les troisième," p. 18 (JD).
40. Ibid., p. 24.
41. Ibid.
42. Ibid., p. 20.
43. Ibid., p. 42.
44. Ibid., p. 50.
45. Susan Lanser: Introduction to the 1972 republication of Barnes: *Ladies Almanack.*
46. Barnes: *Ladies Almanack,* p. 9.
47. Glassco, p. 40.
48. Ford: *Published,* p. 131.
49. Crosby, Harry, p. 116.
50. Thomson, pp. 155–156.

THIRTEEN: THE PAUSE

1. Flanner, p. 62.
2. Antheil, p. 265.

3. *Quill,* May 1931.

4. Interview with William Huntington by Smithsonian Institution staff member, 10/24/1979 (SIA: Accession 96–153, Box 6).

5. Author's interview with Chalon.

6. NCB to APB, 12/9/1915 (JD).

7. Author's interviews with Chapon, Lang.

8. Unattributed newspaper clipping, ca. 1929 (SIA).

9. *Adam International Review* #299 (1963), p. 104.

10. APB to NCB, 3/21/1930 (JD).

11. Aunt Hessie to NCB/LCB, 10/27/1931 (SIA: Accession 96–153, Box 7).

12. *Washington Star,* 10/13/1931.

13. Hall, Radclyffe, p. 351.

14. Derek Patmore: "Passionate Friends," *Observer,* September 1971.

15. *Adam International Review* #299 (1963), p. 26.

16. Barney: Preface to Gertrude Stein's *As Fine as Melanctha, 1914–1930* (New Haven, Conn.: Yale University Press), 1956.

17. Pougy: *Blue,* p. 258.

18. Schenkar, p. 141.

19. *À Paris,* 6/8/1934.

20. Barney: *Nouvelles pensées,* p. 36.

21. RB to NCB, 2/18/1931 (McF).

22. NCB to RB, n.d. (McF).

23. *Adam International Review* #299 (1963), p. 92.

24. Cleyrergue, p. 167.

25. *Adam International Review* #299 (1963), p. 76.

26. NCB to APB, 6/24/1930 (JD).

27. Renée de Brimont writing in *Le Manuscrit Autographe;* cited in Chalon, p. 155.

28. Delarue-Mardrus: *Mes mémoires,* p. 144.

29. Delarue-Mardrus: *L'Ange,* p. 122.

30. Ibid., p. 128.

31. Ibid., p. 139.

32. Speech entitled "Miss Barney presentée par Madame Germaine Lefrancq," December 1935 (ML).

33. Interview with William Huntington by Smithsonian Institution staff member, 10/24/1979 (SIA: Accession 96–153, Box 6).

34. Gertrude Stein writing in *Wings,* September 1933, p. 9. *Wings* was the monthly publication of the Literary Guild, for which *The Autobiography of Alice B. Toklas* was the September selection.

35. NCB to LCB, 4/4/1935 (JD).

36. EP to NCB, 5/8/1939 (JD).

37. All quotes in this section: Patmore, pp. 191–194.

FOURTEEN: WAR REDUX

1. Ray, p. 295.
2. Author's interview with Chalon.
3. Author's interview with Lang.
4. NCB to LCB, June 1904 (JD).
5. Ms. for a talk, "Miss Barney présentée par Mme. Germaine Lefrancq," c. 1935 (ML).
6. Cited in Birmingham, p. 165.
7. Cited in Mathews, p. 283.
8. Gramont: *Years of Plenty*, p. 309.
9. Rothschild and Martel anecdotes: Skinner, p. 18.
10. Author's interviews with Chalon and Lang.
11. Cleyrergue, p. 121.
12. Cited in Tytell, p. 259.
13. Ibid., p. 275.
14. Barney: *European American* (JD).
15. NCB to LCB, 9/12/1940 (JD).
16. Brooks: "Hills of Florence," p. 13 (AAA).
17. NCB to LG, June 1944 (JD).
18. Barney: *European American*, p. 158 (JD).
19. Ibid., p. 106.
20. Ibid., p. 112.
21. Brooks: "Hills of Florence," p. 34 (AAA).
22. Ibid., p. 31.
23. Stein: *Wars I Have Seen*, p. 127.
24. Brooks: "Hills of Florence," p. 113 (AAA).
25. Barney: *European American*, p. 250 (JD)
26. Brooks: "Hills of Florence," p. 113 (AAA).
27. Barney: *European American*, p. 273 (JD).
28. Brooks: "Hills of Florence," p. 147 (AAA).

FIFTEEN: THE AMAZON IN WINTER

1. Karnow, p. 5.
2. NCB to LCB, 4/18/1962 (JD).
3. EP to NCB, 11/28/1947 (JD).
4. EP to NCB, 1/1948 (JD).
5. Germain: *Les fous*, p. 11.
6. Bourdet, p. 242.
7. NCB to RB, 4/25/1952 (McF).
8. *Paris Review*, Spring 1975, p. 118.
9. *Esquire*, May 1976, pp. 64–65.
10. *Paris Review*, Spring 1975, p. 121.

11. Author's interview with Lang.

12. Ibid.

13. Ibid.

14. Lankford, p. 231.

15. Author's interview with Chapon.

16. Toklas: *What Is Remembered,* pp. 171–173.

17. Toklas: *Staying on Alone,* p. 290.

18. Renée Lang Notes (ML).

19. NCB to RB, 1/18/1938 (McF).

20. Pougy: *Idylle saphique,* p. 215.

21. *New York Times,* 6/5/1952.

22. Barney: *Souvenirs,* p. 206.

23. Toklas: *Staying on Alone,* p. 218.

24. Author's interview with Lang.

25. NCB to RB, 1/3/1952 (McF).

26. Author's interview with Lang.

27. Cleyrergue, p. 175.

28. Author's interview with Chalon.

29. Chalon: *Chère Natalie Barney* (revised 1992 edition), p. 333.

30. Ibid.

31. Cited in Toklas: *Staying on Alone,* p. 338.

32. Alice Toklas to Brion Gysin, 6/11/1957 (McF).

33. RB to NCB, 10/13/56 (McF).

34. RB to NCB, 5/20/1957 (McF).

35. RB to NCB, 9/6/1963 (McF).

36. NCB to RB, 3/13/1958 (McF).

37. RB to NCB, 5/10/1962 (McF).

38. Author's interview with Lang.

39. NCB to RB, 5/15/1957 (McF).

SIXTEEN: SLOWLY COMES THE NIGHT

1. Cited in Savigneau, p. 269.

2. Barney: *Traits,* pp. 33–34. The preface originally appeared in the April/May/June 1932 issue of *Le Manuscrit Autographe.*

3. Pougy: *Blue,* p. 163.

4. Barney: *Traits,* p. 181.

5. *Le Phare,* 12/22/1963. Yves Florence: unattributed clipping (ML).

6. Barney: *Traits,* pp. 26–27.

7. Barney: "Salle des pas perdus" (JD).

8. London *Sunday Times,* 3/10/1963.

9. NCB to RB, 7/14/1966 (McF).

10. Diaries of David K. E. Bruce (9/24/1962), Archives of the Virginia Historical Society.

11. Author's interview with Brabo.

12. Author's interview with Chapon.

13. *Dayton Journal Herald,* 12/31/1965.

14. NCB to RB, 7/19/1965 (McF).

15. NCB to LCB, 11/16/1961 (JD).

16. RB to NCB, 10/31/1960 (McF).

17. NCB to RB, 10/4/1965 (McF).

18. RB to NCB, 10/9/1966 (McF).

19. RB to NCB, 7/9/1967 (McF).

20. Secrest, p. 376.

21. Cleyrergue, p. 160.

22. NCB to RB, 6/22/1967 (McF).

23. NCB to Helen (no last name), 6/24/1968 (McF).

24. NCB to RB, n.d. (McF).

25. NCB to APB, 1/12/1914 (JD).

26. NCB to APB, n.d. (JD).

27. *France-Soir,* 10/12/1966.

28. In *Portrait of a Seductress,* Jean Chalon gave a later date for Natalie's move from rue Jacob. He asked me to correct the error here. My sincere thanks to him for setting the record straight.

29. NCB to RB, n.d. (McF).

30. Barney: *Souvenirs,* p. 208.

31. Author's interview with Chalon.

32. Wickes, p. 212.

33. Author's conversation with George Wickes, November 2001.

34. Cited in Savigneau, p. 338.

35. Author's interview with Chalon.

36. *Adam International Review* #299 (1963), p. 113.

Bibliography

WORKS BY NATALIE CLIFFORD BARNEY

Published Works

Actes et entr'actes. Paris: Sansot, 1910.

Aventures de l'esprit. Paris, 1929; rpt. New York: Arno, 1975; rpt. New York: New York University Press, 1992.

Cinq petits dialogues grecs (antitheses et paralleles). [Tryphé.] Paris: Plume, 1902.

Éparpillements. Paris: Sansot, 1910; rpt. Paris: Persona, 1982.

Je me souviens. . . . Paris: Sansot, 1910.

Nouvelles pensées de l'Amazone. Paris: Mercure de France, 1939; rpt. Paris: IVREA, 1996.

The One Who Is Legion, or A.D.'s After-Life. London: Partridge, 1930; rpt. Orono, Maine: National Poetry Foundation, 1987.

Pensées d'une Amazone. Paris: Émile-Paul, 1920

Poems & poèmes: autres alliances. Paris: Émile-Paul; New York: Doran, 1920.

Quelques portraits-sonnets de femmes. Paris: Société d'Éditions Littéraires, 1900.

Souvenirs indiscrets. Paris: Flammarion, 1960.

Traits et portraits. Paris, 1963; rpt. New York: Arno, 1975.

Literary Works/Translations in Periodicals

"Au temps de la décadence grecque." (Extract from *Cinq petits dialogues grecs.*) *La Plume,* December 1, 1902.

"Poèmes: À la mémoire de Renée Vivien." *Mercure de France,* May 1, 1910.

"D'une Amazone Americaine." (Poem.) *New York Herald,* April 26, 1917.

"An Evening with M. Teste." (Trans. of short story by Paul Valéry.) *Dial,* February 1922.

"Les pensées d'une Amazone: Réponse à André Germain." *Les Écrits Nouveaux,* No. 6 (1922).

"Two Poems." *Transatlantic Review,* October 1924.

"Excerpts from Pensées d'une Amazone." *This Quarter,* 1929.

"On Writing and Writers." *This Quarter,* October–November–December 1929.

"The One Who Is Legion" (Chapter XII), "Eleven Poèmes," and "Two Chapters from an Unpublished Novel." *Le Manuscrit Autographe,* April–May–June 1932.

"Attentes et habitudes." (Selected epigrams extracted from *Nouvelles pensées d'une Amazone). Revue de Paris,* March 15, 1939.

[Various Topics]. *Adam International Review,* No. 299 (1963).

"A Few Last and Stray Thoughts." *Adam International Review,* No. 300 (1965).

"Les êtres doubles." (Excerpts from a three-act play.) *Les Cahiers des Saisons,* Summer 1966.

SELECTED SECONDARY SOURCES

Adam, H. Pearl. *Paris Sees It Through.* London: Hodder & Stoughton, 1919.

Aldington, Richard. *Life for Life's Sake: A Book of Reminiscences.* New York: Viking Press, 1941.

Antheil, George. *Bad Boy of Music.* Garden City, N.Y.: Doubleday, 1945.

Barnes, Djuna. *Ladies Almanack.* New York: Harper & Row, 1972.

Beach, Sylvia. *Shakespeare and Company.* New York: Harcourt, Brace, 1959.

Benstock, Shari. *Women of the Left Bank: Paris, 1900–1940.* Austin: University of Texas Press, 1986.

Bierman, John. *Dark Safari: The Life Behind the Legend of Henry Morton Stanley.* New York: Knopf, 1990.

Birmingham, Stephen. *Our Crowd.* New York: Harper & Row, 1967.

Bourdet, Denise. *Pris sur le vif.* Paris: Librairie Plon, 1957.

Bryher. *The Heart to Artemis.* New York: Harcourt, Brace, 1962.

Burke, Carolyn. *Becoming Modern: The Life of Mina Loy.* New York: Farrar, Straus and Giroux, 1996.

Burke, Mary Alice. *Elizabeth Nourse: A Salon Career.* Washington, D.C.: Smithsonian Institution Press, 1983.

Cargill, Oscar. *Intellectual America: Ideas on the March.* New York: Macmillan, 1941.

Chalon, Jean. *Journal de Paris: 1963–1983.* Paris: Plon, 1999.

———. *Liane de Pougy: Courtisane, princesse et saint.* Paris: Flammarion, 1994.

———. *Portrait of a Seductress.* Trans. Carol Barko. New York: Crown, 1979.

Chapon, François, Nicole Prévot, and Richard Sieburth (eds.). *Autour de Natalie Clifford Barney.* Paris: Bibliothèque Littéraire Jacques Doucet, 1976.

Claudel, Paul. *Journal.* Paris: Gallimard, 1968.

Cleyrergue, Berthe. *Berthe ou un demi-siècle auprès de l'Amazone.* Paris: Éditions Tierce, 1980.

Cline, Sally. *A Woman Called John.* New York: Overlook Press, 1997.

Cody, Morrill (with Hugh Ford). *The Women of Montparnasse.* New York: Cornwall Books, 1984.

Colette, Sidonie Gabrielle. *Claudine and Annie (Claudine s'en va).* Trans. Antonia White. London: Secker and Warburg, 1962.

———. *My Apprenticeships and Music-Hall Sidelights.* Trans Helen Beauclerk. London: Secker and Warburg, 1957.

———. *The Pure and the Impure.* Trans. Herma Briffault. New York: Farrar, Straus and Giroux, 1966.

Conover, Charlotte Reeve. *Some Dayton Saints and Prophets.* Dayton, Ohio: United Brethren Publishing House, 1907.

Cook, Blanche Wiesen. *Eleanor Roosevelt, Volume 1: 1884–1933.* New York: Viking, 1992.

Crespelle, Jean-Paul. *The Fauves.* Greenwich, Conn.: New York Graphic Society, 1962.

Cronin, Vincent. *Paris on the Eve: 1900–1914.* New York: St. Martin's Press, 1991.

Crosby, Caresse. *The Passionate Years.* New York: Dial Press, 1953.

Crosby, Harry. *Shadows of the Sun: The Diaries of Harry Crosby.* Santa Barbara, Calif.: Black Sparrow Press, 1977.

Davis, Richard Harding. *The Great Streets of the World.* London: Osgood, McIlvaine & Co., 1892.

Delarue-Mardrus, Lucie. *Mes mémoires.* Paris: Gallimard, 1938.

———. *The Angel and the Perverts.* Trans. Anna Livia. New York: New York University Press, 1995.

Dickens, Charles. *On America and the Americans.* Ed. Michael Slater. Austin: University of Texas Press, 1978.

Draper, Muriel. *Music at Midnight.* New York/London: Harper & Brothers, 1929.

Dwight, Eleanor. *Edith Wharton: An Extraordinary Life.* New York: Harry Abrams, 1994.

Edgar, John F. *Pioneer Life in Dayton and Vicinity.* Dayton, Ohio: U.B. Publishing House, 1896.

Estabrook, H. M. *A History of the Barney & Smith Car Company of Dayton, Ohio.* Dayton, Ohio: Privately printed, 1911.

Field, Andrew. *Djuna: The Life and Times of Djuna Barnes.* New York: G. P. Putnam's Sons, 1983.

Flanner, Janet. *Paris Was Yesterday.* New York: Viking Press, 1972.

Ford, Hugh (ed.). *The Left Bank Revisited: Selections from the* Paris Tribune, *1917–1934.* University Park: Pennsylvania State University Press, 1972.

———. *Published in Paris: American and British Writers, Printers, and Publishers in Paris, 1920–1939.* Yonkers, N.Y.: Pushcart Press, 1980.

Gard, Maurice Martin du. *Les mémorables.* Paris: Flammarion, 1957.

Germain, André. *La bourgeoisie qui brûle: Propos d'un témoin: 1890–1940.* Paris: Éditions Sun, 1951.

———. *Les cles de Proust.* Paris: Éditions Sun, 1953.

———. *Les fous de 1900.* Paris: La Patatine, 1954.

Glassco, John. *Memoirs of Montparnasse.* New York: Viking Press, 1970.

Goncourt, Jules de, and Edmond de Goncourt. *Pages from the Goncourt Journals.* Trans. Robert Baldick. London: Folio Society, 1962.

Goujon, Jean-Paul. *Album secret: Renée Vivien, Natalie Barney, Eva Palmer.* Muizon: Éditions À l'Écart, 1984.

———. *Correspondances croisées.* Muizon: À l'Écart, 1983.

———. *Renée Vivien à Mytilène.* Reims: À l'Écart, 1978.

———. *Tes blessures sont plus douces que leurs caresses: Vie de Renée Vivien.* Paris: R. Deforges, 1986.

Gourmont, Remy de. *Letters to the Amazon.* Trans. Richard Aldington. London: Chatto & Windus, 1931.

———. *Letters à l'Amazone suivi de Lettres intimes à l'Amazone.* Paris: Mercure de France, 1988.

Gramont, Elizabeth de (Duchesse de Clermont-Tonnerre). *Pomp and Circumstance.* Trans. Brian Downs. New York: Jonathan Cape, 1929.

———. *Years of Plenty.* Trans. Florence Llona and Victor Llona. London: Jonathan Cape, 1931.

Hall, Radclyffe. *The Well of Loneliness.* New York: Avon Books, 1981.

Hall, Richard Seymour. *Stanley: An Adventure Explored.* Boston: Houghton Mifflin, 1975.

Hemingway, Ernest. *A Moveable Feast.* New York: Charles Scribner's Sons, 1964.

Herring, Phillip. *Djuna: The Life and Work of Djuna Barnes.* New York: Viking Press, 1995.

Howe, Henry (ed.). *Historical Collection of Ohio in Two Volumes: The Ohio Centennial Edition, Volume I.* State of Ohio, 1908.

Jacob, Max, and Salomon Reinach. *Lettres à Liane de Pougy.* Paris: Plon, 1980.

Jaloux, Edmond. *Les saisons littéraires (1904–1914).* Paris: Librairie Plon, 1950.

Jans, Adrien. *De Montmartre à Montparnasse.* Paris: Sodi, 1968.

Jay, Karla. *The Amazon and the Page.* Bloomington: Indiana University Press, 1988.

Josephson, Matthew. *Life Among the Surrealists: A Memoir.* New York: Holt, Rinehart and Winston, 1962.

Karnow, Stanley. *Paris in the Fifties.* New York: Random House, 1997.

Kling, Jean L. *Alice Pike Barney: Her Life and Art.* Washington, D.C.: NMAA and Smithsonian Institution Press, 1994.

Lankford, Nelson D. *The Last American Aristocrat.* New York: Little, Brown, 1996.

Latrobe, John. *The Baltimore and Ohio Railroad: Personal Recollections.* Baltimore: Privately printed, 1868.

Léautaud, Paul. *Journal littéraire (Vol. 5).* Paris: Mercure de France, 1958.

Lewis, Lloyd, and Henry Smith. *Oscar Wilde Discovers America.* New York: Harcourt, Brace, 1936.

Lewis, R. W. B. *Edith Wharton: A Biography.* New York: Harper & Row, 1975.

Livia, Anna (ed.). *A Perilous Advantage: The Best of Natalie Clifford Barney.* Norwich, Vt.: New Victoria, 1992.

Lorenz, Paul. *Sapho 1900: Renée Vivien.* Paris: Julliard, 1977.

Loüys, Pierre. *Collected Works of Pierre Loüys.* New York: Shakespeare House, 1951.

Luhan, Mabel Dodge. *Intimate Memories (Vol. 1): Background.* London: Martin Secker, 1933.

Mackenzie, Faith Compton. *More Than I Should.* London: Collins, 1940.

Mackenzie, Sir Compton. *Extraordinary Women.* London: Martin Secker, 1929.

———. *My Life and Times.* London: Chatto & Windus, 1956.

Mathews, Nancy. *Mary Cassatt: A Life.* New York: Villard Books, 1994.

McAllister, Ward. *Society as I Have Found It.* New York: Cassell, 1890.

Morand, Paul. *Journal d'un attaché d'ambassade: 1916–1917.* Paris: Gallimard, 1963.

Nevill, Ralph. *Days and Nights in Montmartre.* New York: George H. Doran, 1927.

Ohanian, Armen. *The Dancer of Shamahka.* Trans. Rose Wilder Lane. New York: E. P. Dutton, 1923.

O'Neal, Hank. *Life Is Painful, Nasty & Short: Djuna Barnes, 1978–1981.* New York: Paragon House, 1990.

Painter, George D. *Marcel Proust: A Biography.* New York: Random House, 1959.

Palmer-Sikelianos, Eva. *Upward Panic: The Autobiography of Eva Palmer-Sikelianos.* Ed. John P. Anton. Philadelphia: Harwood Academic Publishers, 1993.

Patmore, Derek. *Private History: An Autobiography.* London: Jonathan Cape, 1960.

Plat, Hélène. *Lucie Delarue-Mardrus: Une femme de lettres des années folles.* Paris: Bernard Grasset, 1994.

Pougy, Liane de. *Idylle saphique.* Paris: Edition des Femmes, 1987.

———. *My Blue Notebooks.* Trans. Diana Athill. New York: Harper & Row, 1979.

Pringué, Gabriel-Louis. *Trente ans de diners en ville.* Paris: Édition Revue Adam, 1948.

Putnam, Samuel. *Paris Was Our Mistress.* London: Plantin Publishers, 1987.

Ray, Man. *Self Portrait.* Boston: Little, Brown, 1963.

Roosevelt, Eleanor. *The Autobiography of Eleanor Roosevelt.* New York: Harper & Brothers, 1958.

Rouveyre, André. *Souvenirs de mon commerce.* Paris: Les Éditions G. Crès, 1921.

Savigneau, Josyane. *Marguerite Yourcenar: Inventing a Life.* Chicago: University of Chicago Press, 1993.

Saxon, A. H. *P. T. Barnum: The Legend and the Man.* New York: Columbia University Press, 1989.

Schenkar, Joan. *Truly Wilde.* New York: Basic Books, 2000.

Secrest, Meryle. *Between Me and Life: A Biography of Romaine Brooks.* Garden City, N.Y.: Doubleday, 1974.

Shattuck, Roger. *The Banquet Years.* New York: Random House, 1968.

Sherard, Robert. *Twenty Years in Paris.* Philadelphia: Jacobs & Co., 1905.

Skinner, Cornelia Otis. *Elegant Wits and Grand Horizontals.* London: Michael Joseph, 1963.

Smith, F. Berkeley. *The Real Latin Quarter.* New York: Funk & Wagnalls, 1901.

Souhami, Diana. *The Trials of Radclyffe Hall.* London: Weidenfeld & Nicolson, 1998.

Stafford, Dr. N. G. *The Wells Family of Louisiana and Allied Families.* Alexandria, La.: Privately printed, 1942.

Steele, Robert W., and Mary Davies. *Early Dayton.* Dayton, Ohio: W. J. Shuey, 1896.

Stein, Gertrude. *Paris France.* New York: Liveright, 1940.

———. *The Autobiography of Alice B. Toklas.* New York: Harcourt, Brace, 1933.

———. *Wars I Have Seen.* London: Brilliance Books, 1984.

Thomson, Virgil. *Virgil Thomson.* New York: Alfred A. Knopf, 1966.

Thurman, Judith. *Secrets of the Flesh: A Life of Colette.* New York: Alfred A. Knopf, 1999.

Tocqueville, Alexis de. *Journals.* Ed. J. P. Mayer. New Haven, Conn.: Yale University Press, 1960.

Toklas, Alice B. *Staying on Alone: Letters of Alice B. Toklas.* New York: Liveright, 1973.

———. *The Alice B. Toklas Cook Book.* New York: Harper & Brothers, 1954.

———. *What Is Remembered.* New York: Holt, Rinehart and Winston, 1963.

Trostel, Scott D. *Barney & Smith Car Company.* Fletcher, Ohio: Cam-Tech, 1993.

Troubridge, Lady Una. *The Life of Radclyffe Hall.* New York: Arno Press, 1975.

Tytell, John. *Ezra Pound, the Solitary Volcano.* New York: Doubleday, 1987.

Vivien, Renée. *A Woman Appeared to Me.* Trans. Jeannette H. Foster. Tallahassee, Fla.: Naiad Press, 1982.

Weiss, Andrea. *Paris Was a Woman: Portraits from the Left Bank.* San Francisco: Harper, 1995.

Wheeler, Kenneth, and Virginia Lee Lussier (eds.). *Women, the Arts, and the 1920s in Paris and New York.* New Brunswick, N.J.: Transaction Books, 1982.

Whittington, George. *Rapides Parish, Louisiana: A History.* Baton Rouge: Louisiana Historical Quarterly, n.d.

Wickes, George. *The Amazon of Letters.* New York: G. P. Putnam's Sons, 1976.

Williams, Elizabeth Otis. *Sojourning, Shopping & Studying in Paris: A Handbook Particularly for Women.* Chicago: A. C. McClurg, 1907.

Williams, William Carlos. *The Autobiography of William Carlos Williams.* London: MacGibbon & Kee, 1968.

Wilson, Robert Forrest. *Paris on Parade.* New York: Bobbs-Merrill, 1924.

Wuerpel, E. H. *American Art Association of Paris.* Philadelphia: Times Publishing House, 1894.

Index